BERLIT

DISCOVER
GERMANY

Edited and designed by
D & N Publishing,
Lambourn, Berkshire.

Cartography by
Hardlines, Charlbury, Oxfordshire.

Although we have made every effort to ensure the accuracy of all the information in this book, changes do occur. We cannot therefore take responsibility for facts, addresses and circumstances in general that are constantly subject to alteration.

If you have any new information, suggestions or corrections to contribute to this guide, we would like to hear from you. Please write to Berlitz Publishing at the above address.

Photographic Acknowledgements

© Berlitz Publishing Co. Ltd. 6, 16, 18, 24, 28, 33, 35, 40, 42, 44, 45, 48, 49, 51, 52, 55, 60, 65, 66, 73, 82, 100, 104, 116, 118, 120, 121, 123, 124, 130, 134/5, 136, 144, 150, 153, 157, 168, 173, 176, 177, 184/5, 187, 188/9, 192, 194, 196, 198, 203, 204, 208/9, 210, 215, 218, 220, 222, 224/5, 229, 232, 236, 240, 242, 248, 253, 255, 257, 258, 264, 269, 272, 274, 276, 281, 283, 285, 287, 289, 291, 294/5, 301, 303, 305, 306, 312, 316, 318, 322/3, 325, 327, 328, 330, 333, 335, 341, 346, 348, 351, 352, 353; Colorific! 1, 10, 32, 107, 112, 138/9, 180, 182, 234, 252, 263, 284, 298/9, 315; Cinémathèques suisse 308, 309, 310, 311; Natural Image 9, 15, 142 (Bob Gibbons); Steve Neville 20, 26; Telegraph Colour Library 146, 212, 337, 343.

Front cover photograph: Tübingen (DominiqueMichellod/ BerlitzPublishing)
Back cover photograph: Zugspitze (Berlitz Publishing)

Photograph previous page: Royal Castle, Neuschwanstein, Bavaria.

 The Berlitz tick is used to indicate places or events of particular interest.

Phototypeset, originated and printed by
C.S. Graphics, Singapore.

BERLITZ®

DISCOVER
GERMANY

Jack Altman

Contents

MAPS: Germany 4, 8; Bavaria 102; The South-West 170; The Centre 206–7; The North-West 250; Eastern Germany 314. Town Plans: Berlin 278–9; Bonn 214; Cologne 207; Dresden 320; Frankfurt 239; Hamburg 251; Leipzig 320; Munich 103; Stuttgart 190.

Planning for a
Successful Journey

Germany may be one again, but that doesn't make for uniformity. On the contrary, there's even more variety than before, not least among the people. A world of difference separates the snow-capped Alps from the sand dunes of the Baltic Coast, and the toytown villages of the south-west from the baroque splendours of restored Dresden. And you can hardly ignore Berlin or Munich. Excellent trains and roads allow you to cover a lot of ground, but we don't suggest using up your days in rushing between one region and another. You'll have to make some compromises. A lot will depend on the time – and the money – you are prepared to spend.

Choosing among Germany's varied destinations has always been difficult, the more so since unification. History has spread the cultural attractions evenly, and the choice among the beauties of its countryside is just as tough. The people have always attached equal importance to nourishing body and soul. We will help you to do the same.

It is worth planning a trip that takes in more than one region. You will quickly dispel the myth of a stereotype to be labelled simply "the German", though it

Share the fairy-tale fantasies of Ludwig of Bavaria with a stroll around the grounds of his dream castle at Linderhof.

may take several visits to appreciate all the differences between Bavarians, Northerners, Rhinelanders and Berliners. ON THE SHORTLIST (see page 80) lists the most important attractions, the "musts" in each area. In LEISURE ROUTES AND THEMES (see page 83), you will find suggested itineraries that concentrate on special tastes or interests—historic, cultural, sporting or gastronomic.

Our six regional chapters follow a certain geographical rather than political logic. Anybody with a systematic turn of mind—and enough time—could in this way *do* Germany in a circuit, chapter by chapter, without doubling back. We begin in **Bavaria**, in cheerful Munich, with tours of the Alps to the south, and the Romantic Route, Bamberg and Nuremberg to the north. The **South-west** region takes in

GERMANY

DENMARK

Baltic Sea

North Sea

N

ROSTOCK

LÜBECK

A7

A1

KIEL

HAMBURG

A24

POLAND

E74

NETHERLANDS

BREMEN

Weser

A7

HANNOVER

A2

BERLIN

A1

A30

Elbe

E8

MAGDEBURG

E6

E8

E15

MUNSTER

A3

A2

A7

E22

ESSEN

DORTMUND

A44

HALLE

E15

A2

DÜSSELDORF

KASSEL

LEIPZIG

DRESDEN

KÖLN

A4

E63

CHEMNITZ

E63

A44

BONN

A45

A48

E6

E62

BELGIUM

A3

A5

A48

FRANKFURT-AM-MAIN

A61

Mosel

WÜRZBURG

A7

A9

CZECH REPUBLIC

A3

LUXEMBOURG

A1

A6

A81

HEIDELBERG

NÜRNBERG

A6

A5

A6

REGENSBURG

STUTTGART

Donau

A90

A3

FRANCE

A8

AUGSBURG

A9

ULM

MÜNCHEN

AUSTRIA

A81

Rhine

A7

A95

A8

Land above 500m (1,640ft)

0   100km

0   60 miles

SWITZERLAND

PIPES TO PORSCHES

The Germans' range of interests is illustrated by the scores of museums. Beyond the usual arts, archaeology and folklore, you will find museums for bread, brooms, doorknobs, typewriters, cigars and hairdressing. In recent years, open-air museums have sprung up all over the country, usually devoted to regional folklore. Typical old houses, even whole villages, have been rebuilt, lock, stock and barrel in pleasant natural surroundings, to maintain links with a past that might otherwise have disappeared in the rubble of World War II. Others are part of the many nature parks established to preserve the countryside against the onslaught of industry and urban construction.

mountains and the Ruhr. Our chapter on **Berlin** without the Wall shows the unified city in its proper perspective. The section on **Eastern Germany** tours the historic centres of Potsdam, Leipzig, Dresden and Weimar, the Thuringian Forest and the Baltic coast. *Gute Reise* or, as they say in English, Bon voyage!

When to Go

The best time of year to visit Germany stretches a comfortable six months from May to October. Spring comes relatively late, but the forests are splendid. Out in the country people are in a good mood, happy

Heidelberg and Baden-Württemberg, the Black Forest and Lake Constance. The **Centre** covers the Rhine and Moselle valleys, Frankfurt and Hesse, and the Palatinate. We then move to the **Northwest** to visit Hamburg, the North Sea Islands, Schleswig-Holstein, the Harz

*J*oin the outdoor-loving Germans in one of their favourite pastimes, walking in the countryside amid wild flowers, and breathing the fresh air.

Stiltmen have processed through Munich since the Middle Ages. In those days, they had to avoid getting stuck in the mud: the modern equivalent is the tram tracks.

to get their walking shoes back on. Summer is drowsy along the rivers, often sweltering in the cities. It is also the season of the great arts festivals—Wagner at Bayreuth, avant-garde art at Kassel—and spectacular fireworks at Heidelberg.

The sunniest regions are to be found, naturally enough, in the south—Baden-Württemberg and Bavaria—but also up in the north-east around Kiel and Lübeck, and along the Baltic coast. Germans, who take their health very seriously indeed , have long prized the invigorating interaction of sun and sea air along both North Sea and Baltic coasts for their beneficial influence on respiratory, skin and metabolic disorders.

In autumn the countryside is alive with wine harvests and fruit picking while the cities start up their new music and theatre seasons; Munich has its Oktoberfest and Frankfurt its Book Fair.

Away from mountain ski resorts, where facilities and comforts are first class (most notably Garmisch-Partenkirchen), winter is often penetratingly cold and damp. Even then, life warms up at countrywide old-fashioned Christmas fairs, the February international film festival in Berlin and the crazy Fasching (Mardi Gras) carnivals in the Rhineland and Bavaria. One word of warning: many hotels outside the major cities close down for the whole winter season.

Pack clothing appropriate to the season—a heavy coat in winter, and a raincoat for the unexpected showers in any season. Lightweight clothes are fine for summer, but don't forget a sweater or

AVERAGE TEMPERATURES FOR VARIOUS REGIONS

Degrees Fahrenheit:

		J	F	M	A	M	J	J	A	S	O	N	D
Berlin	max.	35	37	46	56	66	72	75	74	68	56	45	38
	min.	26	26	31	39	47	53	57	56	50	42	36	29
Frankfurt	max.	38	41	51	60	69	74	77	76	69	58	47	39
	min.	29	30	35	42	49	55	58	57	52	44	38	32
Freiburg	max.	39	41	51	59	67	72	76	75	69	58	47	40
	min.	29	28	34	41	48	53	57	56	51	43	36	31
Hamburg	max.	36	37	44	55	64	69	73	72	66	55	45	39
	min.	28	28	31	38	45	51	55	54	49	43	37	31
Munich	max.	35	38	48	56	64	70	74	73	67	56	44	36
	min.	23	23	30	38	45	51	55	54	48	40	33	26

Degrees Celsius (Centigrade):

		J	F	M	A	M	J	J	A	S	O	N	D
Berlin	max.	2	3	8	13	19	22	25	23	20	13	7	3
	min.	−3	0	−3	4	8	12	14	13	10	6	2	−1
Frankfurt	max.	3	5	11	16	21	23	25	24	21	14	8	4
	min.	−2	−1	2	6	9	13	14	14	11	7	3	0
Freiburg	max.	4	5	11	15	19	22	24	24	21	14	8	4
	min.	−2	−2	1	5	9	12	14	13	11	6	2	−1
Hamburg	max.	2	3	7	13	18	21	23	22	19	13	7	4
	min.	−2	−2	−1	3	7	11	13	12	9	6	3	−1
Munich	max.	2	3	9	13	18	21	23	23	19	13	7	2
	min.	−5	−5	−1	3	7	11	13	12	9	4	1	-4

* Minimum temperatures are measured just before sunrise, maximum temperatures in the afternoon.

jacket, especially if visiting the Alps. Dress is fairly casual, though in high-standard hotels and restaurants more formal attire is expected. In business circles, conservative colours and patterns are the rule.

If you intend to go swimming, take a bathing cap as these are compulsory in all pools (they can also be hired on the spot). At the coast and on some lakes, nude bathing beaches are clearly indicated, often with the rather coy German sign: FKK. It stands for *Freikörperkultur*, approximately "cult of freedom for the body", dating back to the 19th-century fad for mass physical exercise.

Time Differences

Germany follows Central European Time (GMT + 1), and in summer the clocks are put forward one hour.

Here is a summer time chart:

Los Angeles	3 a.m.
Chicago	5 a.m.
New York	6 a.m.
London	11 a.m.
Berlin	noon
Johannesburg	noon
Tokyo	7 p.m.
Sydney	8 p.m.
Auckland	10 p.m.

Getting to Germany

By Air

Frankfurt is the main gateway to the western parts of Germany for flights from overseas, with good onward connections. Hamburg, Munich, Berlin and other points are linked either directly or with connecting flights to major cities within Europe and the Middle East. The cheapest tickets for scheduled flights are generally APEX, but they must be bought and paid for in advance (three to four weeks), there are minimum and maximum lengths of stay, and you cannot change your flights once they are booked.

Many packages are available from Britain, Ireland and North America, some geared to themes such as Munich's Oktoberfest, wine-tastings or river cruises. These inclusive tours cover transport, hotel accommodation, transfers, baggage handling, taxes, meals, sightseeing and the services of an English-speaking guide. Less comprehensive packages on offer include long weekend breaks with concert tickets, and fly-drive arrangements with car hire included.

Airports (*Flughafen*)

Terminals are modern and efficient, with restaurants, snack bars, news- and souvenir-stands, hotel reservation desks, banks, post offices, duty-free shops, and so on. Information offices are normally open from 6 a.m. to 10 p.m. Taxis are always available, but there are also buses, and most airports have a rail link too. Among the major international airports:
Berlin: Tegel Airport is 8km (5 miles) from the city centre. Buses go every 15 minutes to the city centre (Zoo station). Others serve northern Berlin (terminus at Wilhelmsruh). Schönefeld (eastern Berlin) is 19km (12 miles) from the centre, with S-Bahn or bus service (to S-Bahn Grünau station). There is a half-hourly airport-transfer bus between Schönefeld and Tegel, crossing the city centre.
Bonn and **Cologne** share the Köln-Bonn Airport at Wahn on the right bank of the Rhine, 28km (18 miles) from Bonn, 18km (12 miles) from Cologne. Airport bus links to Bonn run every 30 minutes, and to Cologne main railway station and Köln-Deutz station every 20–30 minutes.
Düsseldorf's Lohausen Airport is 8km (5 miles) from the city centre. Rail services by S-Bahn from the main railway station take about 15 minutes. Tickets must be bought from vending machines before you board the train. InterCity trains connect frequently to Frankfurt airport.
Frankfurt: Rhein-Main Airport is one of the world's busiest. It lies 10km (6 miles) from the city centre, with an S-Bahn service from the main railway station (a 15-minute ride). You must buy a ticket before boarding. Frequent InterCity trains to Cologne, Düsseldorf and Dortmund, to Stuttgart and to Würzburg and Munich also stop at the airport station. (Some trains to Düsseldorf and Stuttgart have seats specially reserved for Lufthansa passengers making connections.)
Hamburg's Fuhlsbüttel Airport is 12km (8 miles) from the city centre. Buses go to the main railway station (a 35-minute trip). It's cheaper to get the Airport Express bus to Ohlsdorf station and take the S-Bahn or U-Bahn to the city.
Hanover Airport is 11km (7 miles) from the city centre, with a bus service to the terminal behind the main railway station. The trip takes 25 minutes.
Leipzig: Schkeuditz Airport is 23km (14 miles) from the city centre and an airport bus connects the two.

Munich's new airport is 29km (18 miles) north-east of the city. There is a rail link by S-Bahn as well as a bus service to the main station.

Stuttgart Airport is 14km (9 miles) from the city centre with frequent connections by S-Bahn or bus to the main station and Airport Express bus to the city terminal. InterCity trains link the Stuttgart and Frankfurt Airports.

By Road

(*See also* DRIVING, page 15)

Now that the East has opened up, Germany can be entered from all sides. From Britain, there is a direct ferry link every other day between Harwich and Hamburg; the journey takes 21 hours. Otherwise the Netherlands' ferry ports are the best for visiting the north of Germany; choose a Belgian port if you intend to visit the centre or south. Motorway links from the French ports are longer.

Regular coach services operate from major European cities; the Europabus network is operated jointly by several European railway systems through areas of special touristic interest. In Germany the carrier is:

Deutsche Touring-Gesellschaft: Am Römerhof 17,
60486 Frankfurt am Main
Tel. (069) 7 90 31.

If you are arriving by car, you should carry the car registration papers, a national driving licence (international licence for those coming from the USA, Australia and South Africa), a red warning triangle in case of breakdown, a first-aid kit and a spare set of light bulbs. The car needs a national identity sticker.

Third-party insurance is compulsory, and full cover strongly recommended. Unless they are from another EC country and their insurance extends to Germany, visitors should have an international insurance certificate (Green Card). Otherwise they must take out insurance at the German border. Seat belts are obligatory, and that includes back-seat passengers if the car has them. If you don't wear your seat belt, insurance companies reduce the amount of compensation paid in the event of an accident.

By Rail

There are plenty of train routes to Germany from London and other cities in the UK, using various ferry connections. Direct trains go from Paris, Brussels, Amsterdam, Basel, Vienna and Copenhagen. Look into the various possibilities for reduced-price tickets and rail/road combinations—travel agents can advise you. Seat reservations are recommended. London to Munich, via Dover and Ostend, takes 17 hours, via Harwich and Hook of Holland 20 hours. When you reach Germany, the trains are an excellent way to get around (*see* page 17).

Customs and Entry Regulations

For a stay of up to three months, a valid passport is sufficient for citizens of Australia, Canada, New Zealand, South Africa and the USA. Visitors from the UK and the Republic of Ireland technically need only an identity card, but most will still carry a passport. (At Germany's land frontiers with other EC countries, you may not even have to stop: it is assumed that the prescribed controls have been exercised at your first point of entry to the EC.)

The chart overleaf shows what you can take into Germany duty free and, when

DUTY-FREE ALLOWANCES INTO AND FROM GERMANY

	Cigarettes		Cigars		Tobacco	Spirits		Wine
Germany*	200	or	50	or	250 g	1 litre	and	4 litres
Canada	200	and	50	and	900 g	1.1 litres	or	1 litre
Eire*	200	or	50	or	250 g	1 litre	and	2 litres
UK*	200	or	50	or	250 g	1 litre	and	2 litres
USA	200	and	100	and	**	1 quart	or	1 quart

* Visitors entering from EC countries with goods bought tax free, or from non-EC countries.
Note: Visitors entering from EC countries with *tax-paid* goods may bring any reasonable quantities, provided they are for their personal use.
** A reasonable quantity.

returning home, into your own country (as these allowances tend to change, ask at customs when you leave home for the leaflet listing current allowances).

Currency Restrictions

There are no restrictions on the import or export of Deutsche Marks or any other currencies.

Money Matters

Germany's monetary unit is the Deutsche Mark (DM), referred to on the spot simply as the Mark. It is divided into 100 Pfennig (Pf).

Coins in use are for 1, 2, 5, 10 and 50 Pfennig and DM 1, 2 and 5. Banknotes come in denominations of DM 5, 10, 20, 50, 100, 500 and 1,000.

Foreign currency can be changed in ordinary banks (*Bank*) and savings banks (*Sparkasse*), where the exchange rates are better than in hotels, travel agencies or currency exchange shops. If you need to change money outside banking hours, the main railway stations in larger towns have exchange offices (*Wechselstube*) open from early till late, and at weekends.

Traveller's cheques are welcome almost anywhere, and most major hotels and many restaurants and shops accept major credit cards. If you find the appropriate bank, you can get a cash advance on a major credit card. Eurocheques are in common use.

Getting Around

Travel facilities in Western Germany are excellent, while major investment is going into improving the neglected roads and railways of the East. The network of autobahns—super highways—built since 1945 places every major destination within easy reach, and autobahns are still toll-free, although charges are being discussed. Those in less of a hurry will find the secondary roads also in very good condition. One of the pleasanter attractions of these secondary roads is the signposting of itineraries of special interest. The most famous is the Romantic Route (*Romantische Strasse*), linking the picturesque medieval towns from Füssen to Würzburg. Others follow the vineyards of Rhine or Moselle, areas of exceptional wild game, baroque churches and castles, sites of old fairy tales or quite simply panoramic routes through the Alps or Black Forest.

The InterCityExpress and InterCity trains are fast and efficient. More romantic are the little old steam trains that you can take from nowhere to nowhere outside some of the major towns.

Car Hire (*Autovermietung*)

Rentals can be arranged at the airports and railway stations or through your hotel receptionist. You can also book a car through your travel agent at home—it saves a lot of hassle and might work out cheaper this way. Firms offer a full range of German cars, and chauffeur-driven vehicles are also widely available. You must have held a valid driving licence for at least six months; the minimum age is 18. Unless you have one of the major credit cards, a large deposit will be charged.

Special weekend and weekly unlimited mileage rates are available, and it is possible to have the car delivered to your hotel. Major firms allow you to turn the vehicle in at another point within Germany with no extra charge. If you want to travel outside the country, confirm that the contract allows this and that the insurance coverage is complete.

Many airlines arrange fly/drive holidays, and German Rail operates a car hire service, Rail & Road, available at most stations and at a special discount with a train ticket.

Driving

Traffic jams, parking woes and general frenzy can make big-city driving a harassing experience. Use public transport instead, reserving your car for excursions into the countryside. Traffic in Germany

*G**erman roads are among the world's best, but they don't look as empty as this in the hectic morning and evening rush-hours.*

follows the basic rules that apply in most countries, though some may differ.

Drive on the right, pass on the left. Where there's a green arrow, you are allowed to turn right on a red light—take great care.

On the autobahns, passing another vehicle on the right is prohibited. Cars with caravans (trailers) are not allowed to overtake on certain stretches (watch for signs). Should police or emergency vehicles need to pass through a traffic jam, the cars in the right lane must move over to the right and those in the left lane to the left, thereby opening up a passageway down the middle.

At intersections without traffic lights or signs to stop or yield right of way, vehicles coming from the right have priority, unless otherwise indicated.

At roundabouts (traffic circles), approaching cars must give way to traffic already engaged, unless otherwise indicated.

Trams must be passed on the right and never at a stop, unless there is a traffic island.

At dusk, and in cases of poor visibility, headlights or dipped headlights must be used: driving with parking lights (side lights) only is forbidden, even in built-up areas.

The speed limit is 100kph (62mph) on all open roads except motorways and dual carriageways (divided highways). On these roads there is no limit unless indicated (the suggested maximum speed is 130kph, or 81mph). In towns, the limit is

---

TWO SURVIVAL TIPS

To keep your driving in Germany a pleasure, there are a couple of important things to avoid. First, the monstrous traffic snarls at the approaches to the big towns. From 7–9 a.m. and 5–7 p.m., especially on Friday evenings, it can be murder in the Cologne-Düsseldorf area and around Munich, Frankfurt and Hamburg. If you cannot follow German-language radio, the news broadcasts of British or American Forces Network give regular bulletins on traffic conditions.

Do not be tempted to join in autobahn races with the locals. Many Germans are excellent drivers with superb cars and are happy to demonstrate this fact as often as possible. Out on the open road, their fierce BMWs and Mercedes seem to hunt in small packs of three and four, zooming past the sprightly but more modest Volkswagens at unverifiable speeds. Watch your rear-view mirrors and move aside when you see them approaching, lights flashing imperiously. This is a private race and it would be impolite for you to intervene.

A colourful and jolly road sign to keep you on the right track on your travels around Germany.

ROAD SIGNS

Most road signs employed in Germany are international pictographs, but here are some written ones you might come across:

Einbahnstrasse	*One-way street*
Einordnen	*Get into lane (Merge)*
Fussgänger	*Pedestrians*
Kurzparkzone	*Short-term parking*
Links fahren	*Keep left*
Parken verboten	*No parking*
Schlechte Fahrbahn	*Poor road surface*
Strassenarbeiten	*Road works*
Umleitung	*Diversion (Detour)*
Vorsicht	*Caution*

50kph (31mph). Cars towing caravans may not exceed 80kph (50mph). Be careful to respect speed limits; heavy fines are imposed on offenders.

Traffic police may confiscate the car keys of persons they consider unfit to drive. Drinking and driving is a very serious offence. The permissible level of alcohol in the blood is very low; the equivalent of a small glass of beer or wine.

If you break down on the autobahn and other important roads, use one of the emergency telephones located every second kilometre (the nearest one is indicated by a small arrow on the reflector poles at the roadside). Ask for the *Strassenwacht*, a service run jointly by the German automobile clubs ADAC (Allgemeiner Deutscher Automobil Club) and AvD (Automobilclub von Deutschland). Assistance is free; towing and spare parts will have to be paid for. In Eastern Germany, emergency telephones are less frequent. Some may be located on the central reservation.

You will find service stations everywhere, many of them self-service. It is customary to tip attendants for any extra attention. Lead-free *(bleifrei)*, high octane fuel and diesel are widely available.

Air

Germany has a well-developed air network with frequent services to all parts of the country. Early-morning flights provide direct links between many German cities, but later in the day a change of plane is often involved. Advance reservation is recommended. Except for long distances such as Munich–Hamburg, many people prefer to travel by rail within the country itself.

Rail

Until fairly recently, the reputation of the German train service and its efficiency was often better than the reality. Now the federal railway's determination to match France's super-expresses is improving all-round quality. At peak holiday periods, it is advisable to make advance seat-reservations. To avoid the long queues at the station, you can book by phone or pay a small nominal charge and use a travel agency.

The Deutsche Bundesbahn (DB) trains are comfortable, fast, punctual and highly recommended. They are classified as follows.

ICE (InterCityExpress): Superfast trains cruising at up to 250kph (156mph), linking the big German cities in an ever-expanding network.
EC (EuroCity): International trains linking major cities across Europe.
IC (InterCity): Operating between major cities within Germany.
IR: Inter-regional trains; supplement on trips of less than 50km (30 miles).
RSB and **RB**: Regional trains.
S-Bahn and **CB** (City Bahn): Local, city and suburban trains.

Boasting high-speed and special facilities such as public phones, the ICE and IC trains are popular with business travellers as well as tourists wanting to cover a lot of ground in a short time. Dining service ranging from adequate to excellent is offered on most trains, with sleeping-car accommodation on certain long runs. Booking in advance is a good idea— and essential at peak periods. First class costs 50 per cent more than second. A number of reduced-price rail-passes and bargain tickets are available, such as the Germanrail tourist card. If you are travelling through other European countries, consider investing in a Eurailpass which gives excellent value. Both these passes are only for those who live outside the Eurailpass area, to be purchased before leaving home. For more details, ask at your local travel agency, who may also be able to supply you with brochures. German Rail has its own offices at Victoria Station, London and at the German National Tourist Office in New York (*see* page 20). They can give you information on special-rate tickets, cheaper passes for the young or the elderly, and so on. Passes like Eurailpass and Inter-Rail cards are also valid for federal bus routes like the special *Romantische Strasse* excursion bus, some Rhine cruises and other river or lake boats, even some ferries to the North Sea islands.

The Eastern German rail network, Deutsche Reichsbahn (DR) still functions separately. It is being rapidly upgraded to DB standards with a view to integrating the systems.

A service of car rental and parking operates in main train stations, offering free parking for travellers with train tickets covering more than 100km. Rent-a-car service combined with rail tickets is handled by interRent; their counters are normally open from 7.30 a.m. to 6 p.m.

Public Transport

In many cities, an efficient network of bus, tram and underground railway (subway) operates as an integrated system, with easy transfers and interchangeable tickets. Single or multiple tickets are available, as well as day or month passes; you can buy them from vending machines and ticket kiosks. The underground trains, U-Bahn, serve the inner city, while the S-Bahn lines are those running out from the centre to

*T*he rail system is just as well organized, clean and punctual as you would expect of the public services in Germany.

the suburbs. Maps showing the various routes and stations are displayed outside every station. Information explaining the transport system can also be found at the tourist office. Public transport generally runs from 5 a.m. to 1 a.m.

Rural areas are served by buses operated by the railways and the Federal Post Office (*Bundespost*), as well as by local companies. Bus terminals are invariably close to a railway station, and there you'll find information about routes and fares.

River Cruises

Daily scheduled services on the Rhine and Mosel operate from April to the end of October, with the best choice of boats and trips during the high season (July–August). The Köln–Düsseldorf line (KD Rhine Line) offers excursions on motorboats, paddle-steamers and hydrofoils. The most popular tour, between Cologne and Mainz, has about 35 stops. Boats are usually well equipped, with restaurants and sometimes cabins for overnight journeys.

Regular services also operate on other rivers, including the Main, Danube and Elbe, and on Lake Constance and the Ammersee and Chiemsee in Bavaria.

Take advantage of boat services to explore harbours such as Hamburg's, or the Kiel fjord.

Taxis

Other than telephoning for one directly, you can catch a taxi at a rank (taxi stand), or hail one on the street (more difficult at rush hour). Taxis, often beige-coloured new-looking Mercedes, are fairly expensive, and all have meters. Tip the driver by rounding up the fare by a modest amount (not more than 10–15 per cent). If you need a receipt, ask for a *Quittung*.

Bicycle Hire (*Fahrradverleih*)

Discovering the beauty of the German countryside by bicycle is a delightful experience. Train and S-Bahn stations in small outlying towns and villages in Western Germany provide a year-round bicycle hire service, *Fahrrad am Bahnhof*. A list of 250 participating stations is available at ticket counters and tourist offices. (It is generally possible to hire a bicycle at one station and then return it to another.) Suggested itineraries are indicated on notice boards at the stations. Railway passengers hiring bikes pay half price.

Hiking

The German countryside has a great deal to offer the hiker and nature lover.

The following organization can give you information about the possibilities:

Verband Deutscher Gebirgs- und
 Wandervereine
Hospitalstrasse 21 B
70174 Stuttgart
Tel. 29 53 36

or, for young people:

Deutsche Wanderjugend
Herbergstrasse 11
70439 Stuttgart
Tel. 46 60 05.

Hitch-hiking

There is nothing to discourage hitch-hiking, but little to encourage it either: you will be lucky if anyone stops for you. On the autobahns and access roads hitch-hiking is illegal. Student associations can often arrange intercity lifts (*Mitfahrgelegenheit*). There are centres (*Mitfahrer-Zentrale*) in most German cities which arrange lifts to numerous destinations. A fixed contribution towards petrol costs is established by the centre.

Bonn: Tel. 69 30 81
Cologne: Tel. 21 99 91
Düsseldorf: Tel. 36 05 15
Frankfurt: Tel. 49 06 53

Guides and Tours

Local tourist offices can put you in touch with qualified official guides and interpreters if you want a personally conducted tour or linguistic assistance. Ask at the same place for details of city sightseeing tours by bus or excursions to outlying sights.

Tourist Information Offices

The German National Tourist Board has offices in many countries:

A tourist information office housed in a windmill at Kappeln in Schleswig-Holstein.

Australia
Lufthansa House
143 Macquarie Street
12th floor
Sydney 2000
Tel. (02) 367 3890

Canada
175 Bloor Street East
North Tower
6th Floor
Toronto
Ontario M4W 3R8
Tel. (416) 968 1570

Japan
7-5-56 Akasaka
Minato-ku
Tokyo 107
Tel. (03) 3586 0380

South Africa
Lufthansa Airlines
22 Girton Road
Parktown
Johannesburg 2000
Tel. (011) 643 1650

United Kingdom
65 Curzon Street
London WIY 7PE
Tel. (071) 495 0081

USA
747 Third Ave
33rd floor
New York

NY 10017
Tel. (212) 308 3300

Broadway Plaza
Suite 2230
444 South Flower Street
Los Angeles
CA 90071
Tel. (213) 688 7332.

In Germany, the tourist board, Deutsche Zentrale für Tourismus e.V. (DZT), can provide you with free maps, brochures, price lists and general information. Headquarters for all of Germany is at:

Beethovenstrasse 69
60325 Frankfurt am Main
Tel. (069) 75 720.

Local offices (*Verkehrsamt*) can be found at airports, main railway stations, and in the centres of big cities, for example at the following addresses:

Berlin. Europa Center
Tel. 262 60 31
Cologne (Köln). Am Dom
Tel. 221 33 40
Dresden. Pragerstrasse 10
Tel. 495 50 25
Düsseldorf. Konrad-Adenauer-Platz
Tel. 35 05 05
Frankfurt. Römer
Tel. 21 23 87 08
Hamburg. Bieberhaus. Tel. 30 05 12 45
Heidelberg. Hauptbahnhof (main station)
Tel. 213 41
Leipzig. Sachsenplatz 1
Tel. 795 90
Munich. Pettenbeckstrasse 3
Tel. 239 12 72
Upper Bavaria. Sonnenstrasse 10/III
Tel. 59 73 47/48.

Maps

You can get excellent free maps from the German National Tourist Office in your home country, or, in Germany, at local tourist offices, hotels and car-hire firms. For the hiker, there is a series called *Kompass Wanderkarten*, on sale in most book-stores, to keep you on the right track.

Children

The nation which produced some of the world's great spinners of fairy stories and best toymakers is well able to keep children entertained. Puppet theatre is a continuing tradition in several cities; you'll keep coming across travelling circuses and fairs; and the toyshops and toy departments of stores are magical. The countless museums include many with "hands-on" exhibits to do with science and engineering, as well as museums of folklore, childhood, mechanical toys and dolls.

Health and Medical Care

Ask your insurance company before leaving home if medical treatment in Germany is covered. If your insurance does not reimburse medical bills abroad, you can take out a short-term holiday policy. Citizens of EC countries may use the German Health Services for free medical treatment. UK citizens should ask for the leaflet SA 28 and the CM 1 application form at their local Health and Social Security Office.

Bring personal medication along with a explanatory letter from your doctor if you suffer from a particular ailment—especially if you must carry drugs or hypodermic needles through customs.

In the event of accident or serious illness, call the Red Cross (Rotes Kreuz), or the medical emergency service, *Ärztlicher Notdienst* (telephone number in the local directory), which will give you doctors' addresses. In a real medical emergency dial 115 for an ambulance.

Pharmacies are open during normal shopping hours. At night and on Sundays and holidays, you'll find the addresses of duty pharmacies listed in the newspaper or displayed on all pharmacy windows.

Embassies and Consulates (*Konsulat*)

Pending the eventual move to Berlin, embassies are in Bonn. Many countries have consulates in Berlin and some in other big cities too. Get in touch with your consulate if you're in trouble—for example, if you lose your passport, have problems with the police, or have a major accident. Consuls can issue emergency passports, give advice on obtaining money from home, and provide a list of lawyers, interpreters and doctors. They cannot pay your bills, lend you money, find you a job or obtain a work permit for you.

Canada
Consulate:
Europa-Center
10789 Berlin
Tel. (030) 261 11 61
Embassy:
Godesberger Allee 119
53175 Bonn
Tel. (0228) 23 01 61
or
Maximiliansplatz 9
80333 Munich
Tel. (089) 55 85 31

Eire
Consulate:
Ernst-Reuter-Platz 10
10587 Berlin
Tel. (030) 348 08 22
Embassy:
Godesberger Allee 119
53175 Bonn
Tel. (0228) 37 69 37

South Africa
Consulate:
Rankestrasse 34
10789 Berlin
Tel. (030) 82 50 11
Embassy:
Sendlinger-Tor-Platz 5
80336 Munich
Tel. (089) 260 50 81

United Kingdom
Consulate:
Unter den Linden 32–34
10117 Berlin
Tel. (030) 220 24 31
Chancellery:
Friedrich-Ebert-Allee 77
53113 Bonn
Tel. (0228) 23 40 61
Consulate-general:
Yorckstrasse 19
40476 Düsseldorf
Tel. (0211) 944 80

Bockenheimer Landstrasse 51–53
60325 Frankfurt am Main
Tel. (069) 72 04 06

Amalienstrasse 62
80799 Munich
Tel. (089) 39 40 15

USA
US Services:

Tempelhofer Damm 1–7 (Tempelhof Airport)
12101 Berlin
Tel. (030) 819 74 65
Consulate:
Neustädtische Kirchstrasse 4–5
10117 Berlin
Tel. (030) 220 27 41
Embassy:
Deichmanns Aue 29
53179 Bonn
Tel. (0228) 339 26 67

Siesmayerstrasse 21
60323 Frankfurt am Main
Tel. (069) 753 50

Königinstrasse 5
80539 Munich
Tel. (089) 288 81

Accommodation

The range of Western German hotels is wide, the standard of service and cleanliness among the best in Europe. At the top of the scale are classic, luxuriously appointed hotels, marvellously comfortable but sometimes a shade formal; and international style Sheratons, Hiltons and Inter-Continentals, making up in efficiency what they might lack in character. Even at the most modest level, boarding houses (*Gasthof*) or simply private houses offering rooms to rent, you usually get a clean bed, hot bath and good breakfast.

In the middle, and very comfortable, range are hotels often converted from historical buildings—post houses, breweries, customs toll-houses, medieval or Renaissance mansions, Gothic castles, farmhouses or baroque hunting lodges. To add to the charm, you will occasionally be informed that Martin Luther, Johann Wolfgang von Goethe or Otto von Bismarck slept there.

In Eastern Germany there is still a shortage of hotels in all categories, so try to book rooms ahead through your travel agent or direct, and stick to your programme. Many formerly state-owned hotels have been sold off, some to Western groups; names have changed in the process. It will take some time for the tourist infrastructure here to meet the standards and variety of the West.

Choosing a Place to Stay

In **hotels**, most rooms have private bathroom with shower, direct-dialling telephones, colour TV and minibar. Breakfast is usually a copious affair, with cereals and many kinds of bread, cold meats, liver sausage, boiled eggs, cheese, yoghurt, fruit juice and, if you're lucky, fresh fruit, cake and gingerbread. Although there is no official star system, high-quality hotels with business facilities (such as conference rooms, telex, fax and photocopying services), health clubs and elegant restaurants often award themselves five stars in their brochures.

A **Hotel garni** offers accommodation, breakfast, beverages and snacks but no full meals, while a **Pension** or the simpler **Fremdenheim** serves meals only to house guests. A **Gasthof** is an inn providing accommodation, food and drink.

Local tourist offices publish annual lists of accommodation with full details of amenities and prices. The German Hotel Guide (*Deutscher Hotelführer*), distributed by the German National Tourist Office (*see* page 20) includes a wide selection of hotels all over Germany. Prices quoted include service, taxes and usually breakfast as well.

23

hr. Herr unser Seefahrt stets bewar.

Allen zu gefallen

Different and original accommodation can be found in **castles** and **mansions**. For information write to the association, Gast im Schloss:

Vor der Burg 10
34388 Trendelburg.

Self-catering Accommodation

Renting a bungalow or flat (*Ferienwohnung, Ferienapartment*) is very reasonable. Details are available from the local and regional tourist offices, or from the German Automobile Association, ADAC. The German Tourist Board (DZT) booklet, *Self-Catering in Germany,* lists ski chalets, apartments on Baltic islands and other holiday possibilities.

Farms

The German Agricultural Association (DLG) issues a brochure listing inspected, graded farms offering accommodation:

DLG Reisedienst
Agratour
Zimmerweg 16
60325 Frankfurt/Main.

Bed and Breakfast

Look out for private homes advertising *Zimmer frei* (rooms to let). *Besetzt* means there are no vacancies. The German Tourist Board (DZT) puts out a *Bed and Breakfast in Germany* booklet giving addresses for the local booking service in 500 towns and villages.

*F*rom the bold innovations of the Bauhaus movement to this painted stone pillar, art in Germany caters to everyone's tastes.

Reservations

During the summer months, at weekends and especially during trade fairs and conventions (when prices go up), you should book ahead to be sure of getting a room (at least a year in advance for the Frankfurt Book Fair and Munich's Oktoberfest). The Allgemeine Deutsche Zimmerreservierung (ADZ) operates a computer reservation service at:

Corneliusstrasse 34
60325 Frankfurt/Main
Tel. (069) 74 07 67.

Large towns have booking services at the airports and railway stations; they sometimes charge a small fee.

Youth Hostels (*Jugendherberge*)

Germany's 600 youth hostels are open to members of associations affiliated to the International Youth Hostels Federation. Cards are available from your national association. For a list of German youth hostels, write to the:

Deutsches Jugendherbergswerk (DJH)
Bismarckstrasse 8
32756 Detmold.

There is no age limit except in Bavaria, where you have to be under 27.

Camping

Camping is highly developed in Western Germany. Sites are usually open from May to September, and rates are sometimes reduced for members of the International Camping Association. For full information about sites and facilities, consult the guide published by the German Automobile Club (ADAC):

Am Westpark
81373 München

or the annual list of the German Camping Club (DCC):

Mandlstrasse 28
80802 München.

If you camp off the beaten track, be sure to obtain the permission of the proprietor or the police. Camping in the rest areas off motorways is not permitted.

Communications

The postal and telecommunications services of the Bundespost are highly reliable for both domestic and international use.

Post Offices (*Postamt*)

These handle mail, long-distance phone calls and telegrams, and sometimes have public telex or telefax facilities. Opening hours are generally 8 a.m. to 6 p.m., Monday to Friday, and 8 a.m. to noon Saturdays. Late-night and weekend service is available at main railway stations and airports, and in most cities the main post office is open 24 hours a day.

Mail boxes are yellow with a black post horn. Stamps can be bought from yellow vending machines near mailboxes, and also at some tobacconists and stationers.

NEW POST CODES

New five-figure post codes have been introduced for the whole of Germany: the old four-figure codes also still operate, but because there was duplication in East and West Germany, you should put an O- (for *Ost*) before the old Eastern codes to avoid ambiguity.

Poste Restante (General Delivery)

This service is handled by the central post office of each town. Have your mail addressed to you c/o Hauptpostlagernd. You will have to show your passport or identity card when you collect your mail.

Telegrams

Go in person to a post office or phone in messages from your hotel or any private telephone (Tel. 1131). Night letters at a reduced rate for a minimum of 22 words can only be sent overseas.

Telephone

In most of Germany the telephone network is fully automatic; you can dial direct to most foreign countries. Some places in the Eastern area await modernization. A call to the information (*Auskunft*) number given in the front of the telephone directory will put you in touch

A friendly, four-footed native welcomes you to rural Germany. Take a break from the art and architecture to visit some of the local countryside.

with an English-speaking operator who can assist in case of difficulty or emergency.

Communications within Germany and to neighbouring countries are cheaper from 6 p.m. to 8 a.m. weekdays and all day Saturday and Sunday. Reduced rates to Canada and the USA apply from midnight to noon.

Phone calls from your hotel room generally carry a surcharge that can double the cost.

To call other cities in Germany, you have to dial an area code (*Vorwahlnummer*), which you will find listed in a special telephone book known as *Avon*, or next to the town name in the general phone directory.

Some useful numbers valid in most towns:

Fire/First aid (nationwide)	112
Ambulance	115
Information (inland)	1188
Information (international)	00118
Operator (inland)	010
Operator (international)	0010
Police (emergencies)	110
Telegrams	1131
Weather	1164

To make an international direct dial call, first dial 00, followed by the country code (1 for the US and Canada, 44 for the UK, 61 for Australia, 64 for New Zealand and 27 for South Africa).

Radio and TV (*Radio; Fernsehen*)

You can easily pick up the BBC World Service, American Forces Network (AFN) or the Voice of America anywhere in Germany. Shortwave reception is excellent, especially at night.

As for television, there are two national channels—ARD (Channel One) and ZDF (Channel Two)—plus a regional station called *Drittes Programm*. English and American films are sometimes shown in the original version. Many hotels have CNN and various British channels among an array of satellite programmes.

Newspapers and Magazines (*Zeitung; Zeitschrift*)

Major British and continental newspapers and US news magazines are on sale at railway stations, airports, news-stands and leading hotels. The *International Herald Tribune,* edited in Paris, the *Wall Street Journal* and *Financial Times* are printed in Europe and efficiently circulated. The larger cities publish entertainment guides in English of the type *This Week in . . .*

Principal German dailies include *Die Welt* (Bonn), *Frankfurter Allgemeine* (Frankfurt), *Süddeutsche Zeitung* (Munich) and *Stuttgarter Zeitung* (Stuttgart).

Photography and Video

Some of the world's best cameras come from Germany but if you dream of owing a Leica, you'll need a fat bank balance. All makes of film are easily found and developed overnight if need be. Some shops provide a one-hour service for colour prints. Airport security machines use X-rays which won't affect normal film, used or unused. If you have extra fast film (over 400 ASA), ask for it to be handchecked.

All kinds of videotape are available, but note that equipment operates on a different system from North America, and pre-recorded tapes are incompatible.

Eating Out

There is a new German cuisine. Prosperity and constant travel to the rest of Europe and further afield to the old civilizations of Asia have created a demand for greater culinary refinement. Good old German dishes are not being replaced but, increasingly, they are cooked with a new delicacy and imagination. One thing has not changed: generous portions for robust appetites. You will not starve.

The ecological movement and new national pride have revived interest in traditional recipes using natural products prepared in a simple, hearty and savoury manner.

In a country with almost 5 million foreign residents, a great variety of Balkan and Mediterranean restaurants have sprung up. Italian restaurants may be the best outside Italy, particularly in Munich and Berlin. Compare Turkish and Greek cuisine and decide who does the same dishes better. Thai, Vietnamese and other oriental restaurants are multiplying fast.

Meal Times

Lunch *(Mittagessen)* is usually served from 11.30 a.m. to 2 p.m., dinner *(Abendessen,* or in some places *Abendbrot)* from 6.30 p.m. to 9.30 p.m. (later in large establishments). Most Germans like to eat their main meal in the middle of the day.

Where to Eat

The range is from high-class *Restaurant* and bourgeois *Gaststätte* via the chic and

The varieties of bread, ham and sausage are practically endless, and perfect for a fortifying lunch, though the locals might regard them merely as a snack.

sometimes arty *Bistro* to the popular *Kneipe*, originally student slang for a bar or tavern where you can have a drink and a snack heavy enough to call a meal. More and more places spill out onto the streets and squares for open-air meals as soon as

28

the weather is warm enough. This is as true of restaurants in Berlin's Charlottenburg or Hamburg's Pöseldorf in the north as of Frankfurt's Fressgass or Munich's Schwabing in the south.

Call them *Bräuhaus* (literally brewery) or *Bierkeller*, the old beer-halls are still going strong, becoming *Biergarten* in the parks—brass oom-pah-pah bands and all. In vineyard country the cosy *Weinstube* serves open wine by the glass. Almost every town hall has its *Ratskeller*, often a handsome setting for a lusty meal in vaulted cellars with wood panelling and old barrels.

The *Konditorei* is in a category of its own. Some are just pastry shops, but in many of these bourgeois fairylands, you can stuff yourself with pastry, ice cream, coffee, tea, hot chocolate and fruit juices, even a good selection of wines. Some also offer egg dishes, light snacks and salads. The clientele varies in age but everybody looks 55. A more youthful outgrowth in the big cities is the *Frühstückskneipe*, a café specializing in breakfast, sometimes starting as early as 3 a.m. and going on all day long.

Vegetarians are well catered for; there are *Vegetarische Restaurants* in almost every town. Health foods are sold in shops known as *Bioladen*.

Breakfast (*Frühstück*)

Germans start the day with a meal that is somewhat more substantial than the typical continental breakfast. The distinctive touch is the selection of cold meats—ham, salami and liver sausage *(Leberwurst)*—and cheese served with the bread. Not just one kind of bread, but white with sesame or poppy seeds, brown rye with caraway seeds, rich black *Pumpernickel* or crisp wafer-thin *Knäckebrot*. If you like boiled

---

TABLE MANNERS

On one or two of the long tables in the beer halls or other big restaurants, you will occasionally see a sign proclaiming *Stammtisch*—table for regulars. The custom dates back to the medieval craft guilds, and today the tables are kept for firms, social clubs or big families. It is otherwise customary for strangers to sit together, usually after a polite query as to whether one of the empty places is *"frei"*. As they sit down they wish each other *"Mahlzeit"* or *"Guten Appetit"*.

It may come as a surprise that each bread roll (*Brötchen* or *Semmel*) is charged separately; you are expected to keep a count of how many you have eaten.

---

eggs, try *Eier im Glas*, two four-minute eggs served whole, already shelled, in a glass dish. Gone the problem of whether to crack or guillotine the top. And with all that, tea, hot chocolate or coffee that is stronger than the Anglo-American brew, but weaker than French or Italian.

Most restaurants display a menu (*Speisekarte*) outside. Besides the à la carte menu, they usually offer one or more set menus (*Menü* or *Gedeck*). Value-added tax (MWST) and the service charge (*Bedienung*) are usually included. Appetizers (or starters) are listed on the menu under *Vorspeisen, Kleine Gerichte* or *Kalte Platten*. Soups (*Suppen*) and stews (*Eintopfgerichte*) can be very hearty and sometimes enough for a whole meal. Fish and seafood come under *Fisch und Meeresfrüchte*, meat is *Fleisch*. Vegetables (*Gemüse*) served with the main dish are referred to as the *Beilage*, which can be simply potatoes, or sometimes rice or pasta, or several green vegetables. Cheese is *Käse*, fruit *Obst*, and dessert is *Nachtisch, Nachspeinsen* or *Süsspeisen*.

Note that the word *Art* means "style", so *Griesspudding nach Grossmutters Art* is semolina pudding the way Granny made it. We have listed in the language guide on pages 356–361 a few basic terms to help you understand the menu, but remember that in German words are often strung together and you will have to do some detective work—for example, *Kalbsbrust* means breast of veal, *Erdbeereis* strawberry ice-cream.

Regional Specialities

Put together from all those kingdoms and duchies, the country always had scores of regional variations on the national themes—soups, stews and roasts, sausages and sauerkraut, herring, carp and eel—with a few constants. For instance, Germans like to mingle sweet and sour. Meat or fish are often combined with fruit and vegetables on the same plate. Each region is rediscovering its specialities. As you travel around the country, try some of the following:

Bavaria: A sacred midday dish is the pork and veal *Weisswürste*, white sausages flavoured with pepper, parsley and onions and eaten neatly skinned, with sweet mustard. Munich gourmets insist they must never be served after noon as they are no longer fresh enough for the discerning, that is, the Bavarian palate. Just as revered are the Nuremberg *Blaue Zipfel*, little finger-size sausages poached with onion rings in vinegar, sugar, salt and bay leaves, or *Bratwürste*, grilled chipolatas. A favourite soup is *Leberknödelsuppe*, liver dumplings in beef bouillon. Or start with an *Ochsenmaulsalat*—ox-muzzle salad with onions.

Main dishes include *Kalbsvögerl*, veal rolls stuffed with onion, morel mushrooms, bone marrow, garlic and sour cream; hot or cold *Schweinebraten in Milch*, roast pork cooked in milk and herbs; and Franconia's famous *'Pichelsteiner*, a four-meat stew of mutton, veal, beef and pork with potatoes, turnips, celery, onions, savoy cabbage and parsley. At the Oktoberfest, one imperative for the *Brathendl*, barbecued chicken, or *Schweinshaxe*, pig's knuckle: insist on crackling crispy skin.

Classic desserts include *Schmarren*, oven-baked pancake chopped up with apples and raisins, and *Zwetschgendatschi*, yeast-dough pastry with plums, cinnamon and sugar.

Baden-Württemberg: The old duchy of Baden with its sunny vineyards around the Black Forest has long had a gourmet reputation. First, a couple of savoury starters: onion and bacon pie (*Zwieweldinne*) or potato soup (*Kartoffelsuppe*) with celery, leeks, turnips, garlic, diced bacon and a boiled sausage. Black Forest sausage, ham and juniper-cured bacon are highly prized, as are the dark pine honey and wild cherries. But best of all is its wild game: venison with chanterelle mushrooms (*Rehrücken mit Pfifferlingen*), wild duck in sour cream (*Wildente mit saurem Rahm*) or wild pig with pears (*Wildschwein mit Birnen*). Try, too, the local trout (*Forelle*) or pike (*Hecht*) in almonds. *Gaisburger Marsch* is not a brass-band favourite, but a great hotpot of beef braised with potatoes, onions, turnips, celery, parsley, chives and little curly noodles known as *Spätzle*. Browned potato-flour *Schupfnudeln* are Baden's delicious answer to gnocchi.

At Lake Constance, the *Felchen* of the salmon family is superb. Look, too, for small sour kidneys (*saure Nierchen*) and egg pancakes with veal (*Eierhaber mit Kalbschnitzel*).

The Allgäu produces Germany's best-known cheese. Martin Luther said of it: "Not with a hundred eyes like Argus, but full of big holes, not as old as Methuselah, but full of tears like Mary Magdalen, no soup like the one Habbakuk cooked, but still a little smelly like Lazarus; this cheese is good." The cheese noodles here, *Käsespätzle*, are a national treasure.

Swabia is reputed for its soups and potato salad. *Flädlesuppe* has thin ribbons of pancake in a bouillon flavoured with wine and muscat. *Maultaschen* are a kind of sturdy ravioli stuffed with spinach or sausage-meat, served in soup or sautéed brown. Stuttgart is the place to try the potato salad (*Kartoffelsalat*), which becomes high art with the proud title of *Der klassische Schwäbische* (Swabian Classic) prepared with caraway seeds, tomatoes, cucumbers, apple slices and diced bacon.

Rhineland: The Catholic stronghold offers *Himmel und Erde* (heaven and earth), which sits a spicy black blood sausage on a bed of stewed apples and boiled potatoes. A popular Cologne joke is a local dish named *Kölsche Kaviar*—blood sausage and slices of raw onion. But the sweet and sour beef (*Sauerbraten*) cooked in red wine with currants, onions, juniper berries and pepper and served with potato dumplings (*Kartoffelklösse*), has become a serious national dish.

Hesse is a strong contender for the national lentil soup championship with its *Hessische Linsensuppe*—a subtle, savoury concoction with celery, leeks and turnips, diced bacon and sausage. In Frankfurt's cider-taverns, it is a sacred duty to try at least once the *Handkäs mit Musik*, a pungent round cheese, for which the "musical" accompaniment is chopped onions, oil and vinegar, served with black bread.

The North: Seafood is most often prepared here without fuss—good shrimps and mussels, smoked eel (*Räucheraal*), steamed turbot (*Butt*), besides the staple herring and cod. But Hamburg has a surprise: *Labskaus*, a concoction of sweet beetroot and potato mashed with minced beef and chopped herring and served with a poached egg and gherkin (dill-pickle). The equally famous *Aalsuppe* (eel soup) has as many variations as there are retired sailors in the kitchens around the harbour. Typically, the eel is cooked in white wine and vinegar with a ham and ox-bone flavouring, celery, turnips and parsley roots plus peas, leeks, pears, apples and mixed dried fruit.

Lübeck does a fine haddock soufflé (*Schellfisch-Auflauf*) and its buckling soup (*Bücklingsuppe*) was immortalized in Thomas Mann's *Buddenbrooks*. For a heart-warming pork and turnip stew, try the *Lübecker National*. The local favourite dessert is baked apples (*Bratäpfel*) stuffed with raisins and rum. Bremen completes the Hanseatic hat-trick with its *Braunkohl mit Pinkel*, green cabbage cooked brown with sausage, bacon and groats, a hearty dish that demands an accompaniment of beer *and* Schnaps.

After the Schleswig *Gersteneintopf*, barley and cauliflower cream soup, try Holstein cottage ham. Gourmets get ecstatic about the *Kückenragout*, a ragout of young chicken with asparagus and mushrooms. The Frisian Islands have all appropriated the Heligoland fish stew (*Helgoländer Fischertopf*) and each claims the birthright of the plum pie (*Plumtortjes*).

Berlin: Berliners smirk at Hesse's claims to the lentil-soup title. Plain and with no frills except a superior chopped sausage is how their well-seasoned *Linsensuppe* is

ICH BIN EIN BERLINER

The once and future capital is eager to set the record straight on a few culinary originals. A doughnut should be known not as a *Krapfen*, but quite simply as a *Berliner*. The smoked pork chops dubbed *Kasseler Rippen* came not from Kassel but from a Berlin butcher named Herr Kassel. Berlin also claims two world-famous sausages: the giant *Bockwurst*, so named since a local butcher advertised it suspended between the mouths of two goats *(Bock)*. Even the Viennese sausage or *Wiener* was invented, they say, in Berlin.

Fish comes fresh from the Havel: *Havelaal grün*, eel boiled in a dill sauce, or *Havelzander*, pike-perch served simply with boiled potatoes. Potatoes are a Berlin obsession—you can still find potato shops selling nothing but eight or more different varieties.

The supreme Berlin delicacy is *Eisbein mit Sauerkraut und Erbsenpüree*—pig's knuckle with a purée of peas and sauerkraut prepared in white wine with juniper berries, caraway seeds and cloves.
Saxony: In future, the Cold War may

served. Other typical starters include *Hackepeter*, a steak tartar, and *Soleier*, eggs pickled in brine, then peeled, halved and seasoned with salt, pepper, paprika, vinegar and oil, and downed with a dab of Berlin mustard—*Mostrich*.

*P*icture-book villages and vineyards line the gently winding valley of the Mosel, and produce plenty of delicately fruity white wine.

continue to be waged over potato salad. Saxons challenge Swabians with a *Kartoffelsalat* that adds fish and green vegetables to its artillery. Carp can be murderously dull, but quite delicious Saxon style (*Karpfen Sächsisch*), sautéed and then braised and served with a potato dumpling. A great vegetable dish is the Leipzig hotchpotch (*Leipziger Allerlei*) of tenderly cooked peas, carrots, morel mushrooms, asparagus and cauliflower. Sweet-toothed Dresden is famous for its plum cake (*Pflaumenkuchen*) and Christmas fruit loaf (*Weihnachtsstollen*). **Mecklenburg**: This tradition-minded farming country still serves two time-honoured peasant dishes—duck stew (*Enteneintopf*), with cauliflower, leeks, celery and turnips, and breast of veal with gooseberries (*Kalbsbrust mit Stachelbeeren*).

Wine

German wines are concentrated in the west of the country south of Bonn (except for a few vineyards around Meissen in Saxony). The red wines cannot compare in quality to the famous whites of the Rhine and Mosel valleys, but the whole family of German wines is very respectable indeed.

The most highly reputed wines are those of the **Rheingau**, where the river bends west towards Rüdesheim so that the vineyard slopes all face due south to the sun. The late-harvested Riesling grape constitutes 80 per cent of the crop, producing a fine, fruity, mellow wine. Among the top labels are *Schloss Johannisberger, Hattenheimer, Kloster Eberbacher, Steinberger* and *Rüdesheimer*. Some very creditable sparkling wine (*Sekt*) is produced in Eltville and Hochheim. The latter's

1983er
Bernkasteler Badstube
Riesling - Auslese

READING THE LABEL

Since 1971, the Germans have divided their wines into three categories of ascending quality: *Deutscher Tafelwein*, ordinary table wine; *Qualitätswein bestimmter Anbaugebiete*, a wine certified to be from a specific region; and *Qualitätswein mit Prädikat*, a quality wine. The label also distinguishes the stages at which the wine's grapes were picked. *Kabinett*, wine produced from the earliest picked grapes is the lightest and driest of the crop. *Spätlese*, from grapes picked later, makes for a riper, more full-bodied and often sweeter wine. *Auslese* wine is richer than the *Spätlese*, coming from a selection of the very ripest grapes picked while others remain on the vine. *Beerenauslese*, from grapes picked one by one in an overripe state, goes a stage further in honeyed richness. And the ultimate is *Trockenbeerenauslese*, comparable to the best Sauternes.

vineyard provides the origin of the word "hock", the English gentleman's all-purpose name for German white wines in honour of the Hochheimer Königin-Viktoria-Berg. The best of the reds are produced nearby at Assmannshausen and Ingelheim.

Besides the popular *Liebfraumilch*, the **Rheinhessen** region on the left bank south of Mainz boasts the great *Niersteiner Domtal* and *Oppenheimer*. More than honourable are the wines of the **Rhein-pfalz** (Rhineland Palatinate) further south along the *Deutsche Weinstrasse*, especially the *Wachenheimer* and *Deidesheimer*. The **Mittelrhein** vineyards north of Rüdesheim to Koblenz—Bingen, Bacharach, Boppard and Oberwesel—have nothing to be ashamed of.

The **Mosel** wines, bottled in green glass to distinguish them from the brown Rhine bottles, enjoy their own delicate reputation, the most celebrated being the *Bernkasteler, Piesporter, Graacher* and *Zeltinger*.

The **Baden** wines, again mostly whites with a few light reds, range from full-bodied *Rulander* to the light and aromatic *Gutedel* and fiery *Kaiserstuhl*, revealing something of its volcanic origin. New sweet *Sauser* wine is delicious with onion pie. **Württemberg** produces some of the better German reds from the *Trollinger* grape and the popular *Schillerwein*, a light red from black and white grapes.

In the famous round-bellied *Bocksbeutel* bottle, **Franconia's** whites are a delightful picnic wine, but they also travel well for presents back home.

Beer and Schnaps

The acknowledged high temple of beer is not Munich but Dortmund, where beers of refined taste are sipped appreciatively, like good wine. Every region, however,

has its admirers. It is served *vom Fass*, on tap, or bottled in several varieties: *Export*, light and smooth; *Pils*, light and strong; and *Bock*, dark and rich (very good with the sausage of the same name).

Bavarian beer is generally lighter than other German brews. It can be ordered on tap by the half-litre in restaurants, but in the serious beer-hall it is most often served in a one-litre tankard known as the *Masskrug* or simply *Mass* (measure). Brunswick's dark *Mumme* is so strong— 50 per cent malt content—that it is usually mixed with lighter ales. As a refreshing surprise in summer, try the *Berliner Weisse*, a foaming draught beer served in a huge bowl-like glass with a shot of raspberry syrup or liqueur—or green woodruff syrup (*Waldmeister*).

Schnaps is the name applied to any hard, clear alcohol made from either potato, corn, barley, juniper or any other grain or berry that will distil into something to warm the cockles of your heart. If they are too austere for you, try the Black Forest's fruit Schnaps that is distilled from raspberry (*Himbeergeist*), cherry (*Kirschwasser*) or plum (*Zwetschgenwasser*). *Prost!*

Opening Times

Banks are normally open weekdays from 8.30 a.m. to 1 p.m. and 2.30–4 p.m. (5.30 p.m. on Thursdays).

The Germans like to see a good head of foam on their beer. The moustache it leaves after the first sip is like an impudent little kiss.

Museum hours vary, but are usually from 9 a.m. to 4 p.m. Most museums close on Mondays. For exact timetables, enquire at the tourist office.

Shops are generally open from 8.30 or 9 a.m. to 6.30 p.m., Monday to Friday, till 2 p.m. on Saturdays (and till 4 p.m. or 6 p.m. on the first Saturday of the month). Shops outside city centres usually close from 1 to 3 p.m. Railway stations in big cities have good shopping centres that stay open outside normal hours.

Public Holidays

The chart below shows the public holidays celebrated in Germany, when banks, official services and many restaurants are closed. If a holiday falls on a Thursday, many people take Friday off, too.

1 January *Neujahr* (New Year's Day)
6 January *Heilige Drei Könige**
  (Epiphany)
1 May *Tag der Arbeit* (Labour Day)
15 August *Maria Himmelfahrt***
  *(*Assumption)
3 October *Tag der Deutschen Einheit*
  (Day of Unity)
31 October *Reformationsfest****
  (Reformation Day)
1 November *Allerheiligen*****
  (All Saints' Day)
25 December *Weihnachten*
  (Christmas Day)
26 December *Zweiter
  Weihnachtsfeiertag* (Boxing Day)

Movable dates:
Karfreitag Good Friday
Ostermontag Easter Monday
Himmelfahrt Ascension Day
Pfingstmontag Whit Monday

*Fronleichnam****** Corpus Christi
Buss-und Bettag Day of Prayer and
  Repentance (3rd Wed. in Nov.)

* in Baden-Württemberg and Bavaria
** in Bavaria and Saar
*** in the Eastern states
**** in Western states and Catholic areas
  of Thuringia
***** in south-western states

On 24 December (Christmas Eve), theatres and cinemas, concert halls, shops, restaurants and coffee houses close at midday.

Daily Life

Hairdressers (*Friseur*)
Most establishments close on Saturday afternoons and all day Monday. Prices are usually displayed in the window. It's best to phone in advance for an appointment. You should tip 10–15 per cent.

Laundry and Dry Cleaning
Having your laundry washed or cleaned by your hotel is the quickest and most convenient method, but prices are correspondingly high. It is worth seeking out a laundromat (*Waschsalon*) or neighbourhood dry-cleaners (*Reinigung*). Dry-cleaning usually takes two days, unless there is a special rapid service available (*Schnellreinigung*), which takes a minimum of two hours.

Electric Current
Germany has 220–250-volt, 50-cycle AC. Plugs are the standard continental type, for which British and North American appliances need an adaptor.

Water

Tap water is perfectly safe to drink; only rarely will you see the warning *Kein Trinkwasser* (not suitable for drinking).

Religious Services

In big cities, some services are held in English—ask for details at the local tourist office. Otherwise, you'll be welcome at the cathedral, church, temple, synagogue or mosque.

Social Customs

When you enter a shop, or approach a hotel front desk, it is polite to open with a *Guten Morgen* ("Good morning"), *Guten Abend* ("Good evening") or *Gute Nacht* ("Good night"). *Bitte* ("Please") and *Danke* ("Thank you") will smooth your way, and a cheerful *Auf Wiedersehen!* at the end will leave a good impression.

Germans shake hands when they meet, as well as when they take leave. People address each other as Herr X, Frau Y, Fräulein Z—and Herr Doktor X or Frau Doktor Y when appropriate. Don't use first names until invited to do so. Punctuality is the norm for business and social occasions.

Invitations into German homes are a special privilege; meals involve a few rigid rules. Always wait for your hosts to wish you *"Guten Appetit"* before you tuck in. Bread rolls should be broken with your fingers, and potatoes cut with the side of your fork. In some homes, you will be invited to help yourself to the food spread out on a large wooden wheel rotating in the middle of the table. Wine and beer are served with evening meals, which are topped off with coffee and brandy, or perhaps German champagne (*Sekt*). The host will raise a toast with *"Prost"*, or *"Prosit"*, to which you should

reply. Smoking between courses is not appreciated, and at the end of the meal you should wait until all others have finished eating before lighting up. Be careful about smoking cigars and pipes—always ask first. When introduced, greet women first, but don't reach for their hand unless it is extended. A man should bring flowers (but not red roses), to be unwrapped and discreetly offered to the hostess upon arrival. It is polite to send a thank-you note to the host within a few days of your visit.

Tipping (*Trinkgeld*)

Since a service charge is normally included in all hotel and restaurant bills, tipping is not obligatory. However, it is appropriate to give something extra to bellboys, hat-check attendants and so on, for their services.

Toilets

Public toilets are easily found: most museums, all restaurants, bars, cafés, large stores, airports and railway stations provide such facilities. If an attendant is present, you should leave a small tip. Always ensure you have several 10-Pfennig coins for a pay toilet.

Toilets may be labelled with symbols of a man or woman, or the initials WC. Otherwise *Herren* (men) and *Damen* (women) or a double zero (00) are indicated.

Lost Property

General lost property offices are listed in the *Yellow Pages* under *Fundbüro*. Tracing your belongings depends on where they went astray—if it was in a post office or telephone box, enquire at the main post office; if on a train, call at the central railway station.

Complaints

If something goes wrong that you cannot take care of yourself, report the matter to the local tourist office. In hotels and restaurants, discuss any problems with the proprietor or manager. Department stores have a special counter (*Kundendienst*) to deal with customers' complaints.

Crime and Theft

The crime rate is quite low in Germany, although you might feel a bit uneasy walking round the red-light districts in the cities, especially alone at night. Take normal, common-sense precautions—keep an eye on your luggage, watch out for pickpockets in crowded places, and put your wallet in an inside pocket. Leave money and valuables in your hotel safe, not in your car or hotel room, and avoid carrying large sums of money. Always lock your car: you can be fined otherwise and car theft has reached alarming levels. (Most of the stolen vehicles—Mercedes and BMWs are the favourites—are spirited away across the borders to Eastern Europe and beyond.)

If you are robbed, report the incident to the hotel receptionist and the nearest police station. The police will provide you with a certificate to present to your insurance company, or to your consulate if your passport has been stolen.

It is a good idea to keep photocopies of the important pages of your passport. If it does ever go missing, embassies will accept photocopies as proof that you do possess a passport, and within a few days they will issue a replacement document. Also keep a list of all your credit card numbers, separate from your cards, and photocopies of your plane tickets.

Police (*Polizei*)

Germany's police, in green uniforms, ride around on white motorcycles or patrol the streets in green and white cars. Parking in towns is supervised by police in dark blue uniforms. If they fine you for a parking offence, you may be obliged to pay on the spot.

Emergencies

See also EMBASSIES AND CONSULATES, DRIVING, HEALTH AND MEDICAL CARE according to the type of emergency. The national number for police is 110, for fire 112 and ambulance 115.

Festivities

Given the Germans' attachment to their folklore and the performing arts, there is some kind of festival or market going on all year round. Historic monuments such as Heidelberg Castle and Potsdam's Sanssouci Palace or the grandiose backdrop of the Rhine Valley itself provide a spectacular setting for open-air theatre, operas, concerts and pageants.

January Kamenz (Saxony): Gotthold Lessing theatre festival. Naumburg (Saxony-Anhalt): pigeon market.

February Berlin: international film festival. Aachen, Cologne, Düsseldorf, Mainz, Munich: carnival.

March Eisenach, Erfurt: Thuringian Bach festival. Hamburg: "Dom" folk festival.

April Berlin: *Kunsttage* art exhibitions and "happenings". Wittenberg: pottery market. Weimar: Shakespeare festival. Stralsund: spring market. Lake Constance: blossom festivals.

May Leipzig: 4-yearly Bach festival. Hamburg: German Open Tennis. Nuremberg: Jazz from East and West. Munich: *Biennale* avant-garde music and opera. Erfurt: *Krämerbrückenfest* arts and crafts.
May–June Dresden: music festival.
June Potsdam: music and theatre in Sanssouci. Hanover: Herrenhausen music, ballet and theatre. Bad Doberan (Mecklenburg): *Kamp* concerts. Wetzlar: ballet and theatre (and July). Heidelberg: fireworks in castle. Freiburg: jazz, rock, pop, classical music, ballet and cabaret. Göttingen: Händel music festival. Schwäbisch Hall: theatre (also July and August). Augsburg: children's festival (conjuring, ballet, music and theatre). Munich: international film festival; chamber music at Schloss Nymphenburg. Würzburg: Mozart festival.
July Nuremberg: International Organ Week. Munich: opera festival. Lake Constance (Friedrichshafen, Konstanz): music, ballet and theatre. Koblenz: floating operetta festival on the Rhine. Bayreuth: Richard Wagner festival (and August). Travemünde: regatta.
August Heidelberg: music and opera in castle. Koblenz to Braubach: "The Rhine in Flames"—fireworks on the river. Baden-Baden: Iffezheim horse racing. Berlin: Pankow folk festival. Weimar: Goethe's birthday commemoration (28

THE MOST MOVABLE FEAST OF THEM ALL

Bavarians and Rhinelanders love an old-fashioned party, and what could be more old-fashioned than the Carnival, going way back to the Romans, long before the Christian rituals that it is supposed to honour? The maddest, longest-lasting party in Germany is known as *Fasching* in Bavaria and *Fastnacht* in the Rhineland. It is at its craziest in Munich, Aachen, Mainz, Cologne, Bonn and Düsseldorf.

With a few regional variations, this is how it goes: the festivities are announced at a meeting of all the town's various carnival clubs at 11 minutes past 11 on the 11th day of November, the 11th month—11 being the madman's lucky number. After this preliminary party, a mild warm-up so to speak, the revellers break up till the New Year when the round of balls and banquets and masked processions begins in not-too-much earnest. They serve to brighten up the long winter nights with party-goers wandering the streets in harlequin costumes and other inspired paraphernalia derived from the great Venetian revels of the 18th century.

Every trade and profession worthy of the name—cobblers and doctors, carpenters and lawyers, tailors, commodity traders and computer salesmen—vie to put on the most ingenious and outrageous ball possible. The climax is the last long weekend leading to Shrove Tuesday (Mardi Gras), before all good Catholics settle down to a more sober Lenten existence of abstinence and seemly behaviour.

The tone is set on the Thursday with *Weiberfastnacht* (Women's Night) when wives lord it over their husbands and their friends' and enemies' husbands, dancing and dallying with whom they choose. Nobody knows or worries who beneath the masks and costumes is married to whom. Friday and Saturday, chic dinner parties turn into uproarious revels, spilling out into the streets and onto railway platforms to drag late-comers off the trains.

Sunday it is the kids' turn to parade. On *Rosenmontag* (Rose Monday) comes the climactic procession, with scores of elaborate floats displaying giant papier-mâché masks of popular and unpopular political figures.

On Tuesday, hung-over, everybody goes back to work. Or Wednesday.

August). Mainz: wine market (and September). Frankfurt: *Mainfest* (by the River Main.
September Berlin: *Festwochen*—concerts, ballet, theatre. Dürkheim: Würstmarkt wine festival. Meissen: wine festival. Munich: Oktoberfest (late September–early October). Leipzig: music festival. Stuttgart: Cannstadt folk festival.
October Bavaria and North Germany: shooting festivals. Frankfurt: book fair. Neustadt (Palatinate): wine festival. Bremen: folk festival. Halle: music festival.
November Berlin: jazz. Stuttgart: avantgarde symphony and chamber music.

Hamburg: folk festival. Brunswick: modern chamber music.
December Munich, Nuremberg, Stuttgart, Augsburg, Freiburg, Cologne, Mainz and many other German cities and towns throughout the country: *Christkindlmarkt* (Christmas Market).

Students' street theatre entertains children in Munich's Schwabing district.

Distance Chart (kilometres)

	Aachen	Berlin	Bonn	Bremen	Cologne	Constance	Dresden	Erfurt	Frankfurt	Freiburg	Hamburg	Hanover	Kassel	Leipzig	Lübeck	Munich	Nuremberg	Regensburg	Rostock	Stuttgart
Stuttgart	441	626	356	692	373	191	542	425	206	204	704	555	373	479	767	242	188	293	809	
Rostock	762	236	739	413	710	1161	474	542	545	742	994	447	622	420	117	786	621	779		809
Regensburg	584	543	510	707	504	527	460	318	326	570	736	570	404	336	803	120	105		779	293
Nuremberg	481	438	409	606	403	379	354	273	221	380	635	469	299	291	698	165		105	621	188
Munich	647	584	561	779	575	407	519	438	390	421	808	642	472	456	871		165	120	786	242
Lübeck	545	339	510	190	485	928	576	648	557	827	63	229	399	524		871	698	803	117	767
Leipzig	599	185	536	383	579	670	88	146	412	661	430	276	334		524	456	291	336	420	479
Kassel	315	387	260	307	248	566	397	188	199	460	336	170		334	399	472	299	404	622	405
Hanover	355	286	319	137	294	716	379	358	349	625	166		170	276	229	642	469	570	447	555
Hamburg	488	290	452	127	427	865	632	524	498	779		166	336	430	63	808	635	736	994	704
Freiburg	501	804	419	752	436	142	724	543	277		779	625	460	661	827	421	380	570	742	204
Frankfurt	268	555	199	486	189	367	475	266		277	498	349	199	412	557	390	221	326	545	206
Erfurt	454	309	402	428	434	616	210		266	543	524	358	188	146	648	438	273	318	542	425
Dresden	663	237	615	486	644	733		210	475	724	632	379	397	88	576	519	354	460	474	542
Constance	606	925	525	843	542		733	616	367	142	865	716	566	670	928	407	379	527	1161	191
Cologne	70	571	27	321		542	644	434	189	436	427	294	248	579	485	575	403	504	710	373
Bremen	379	408	346		321	843	486	428	486	752	127	137	307	383	190	779	606	707	413	692
Bonn	91	603		346	27	525	615	402	199	419	452	319	260	536	510	561	409	510	739	356
Berlin	636		603	408	571	925	237	309	555	804	290	286	387	185	339	584	438	543	236	626
Aachen		636	91	379	70	606	663	454	268	501	488	355	315	599	545	647	481	584	762	441

A Land of Workers and Dreamers at the Heart of Europe

Once they got the chance, they put it all back together before you could say "Bismarck". The Germans do nothing by halves. Collapse in 1945, unification in 1990; they made a thorough job of both. Visitors can once more compare the baroque of Dresden and Munich, trace Goethe's life in Frankfurt and Weimar, or hike through the Harz mountains without an electrified fence to stop them. Berlin is one vast buzzing metropolis. A great civilization is whole again.

In some ways, this was always a divided country, torn between fairy tale and hard reality. Earnest businessmen drive off in their Mercedes to relax among gingerbread houses and rococo cherubs. People bring equal enthusiasm to the gregarious joys of romantic Rhine river cruises or raucous Bavarian beer gardens, and the solitary pleasures of exploring the cool depths of the Black Forest or the sand dunes of the Baltic coast.

Having a good time in Germany can be a raucous affair, but festive costume—like this Bavarian's from Lindau on Lake Constance—is meticulously prepared.

Thoroughness, *Gründlichkeit,* is the supreme German virtue and vice, in things great and small, glorious and infamous. Remember how thorough East Germany was with its swimmers when trying to win the world's respect with Olympic medals? Thoroughness is the first quality cited in the success story of German business and manufacturing, in management, production and after-sales service, giving the time-honoured phrase *deutsche Wertarbeit* a more profound meaning than merely "German workmanship". Beethoven working inexorably towards his Ninth Symphony left little for his followers to add to the form. To give fullest expression to his genius, Goethe tried *every* literary form: poetry, novel, drama, philosophical and scientific essays. To Karl Marx's all-embracing theories, Lenin could append

43

*B*lacksmiths put a rim on a cartwheel. Traditional craftsmanship is highly respected, and standards are diligently preserved.

only an operating manual (if it did not work, Marx would say, that was not his fault). After World War II, the people applied equal thoroughness to making the western part of divided Germany into Europe's most prosperous democracy. Even in the context of the more fragile Eastern bloc, East Germany had always been the Soviet Union's most solid ally, in the end more thorough in its Communist orthodoxy than the Soviet Union itself.

Geography

Three main regions go to make up Germany. The northern lowlands are a continuation of the north European plain sweeping from the Russian Urals across Poland and on through the Netherlands and Belgium to France. They embrace most of Eastern Germany, Schleswig-Holstein, Lower Saxony and the northern Rhineland. The area is mainly agricultural, devoted to pastures for cattle and pig breeding, sugar beet, and that most German of vegetables, the potato.

A central plateau stretches from the Erzgebirge range on the Czech border across Thuringia to Hesse and the industrial Ruhr, then down the wine-growing Mosel and Rhine valleys to the Palatinate around Heidelberg.

*T*ypically complementing the landscape, a little parish church nestles amid Danube valley farmland at the eastern edge of the Swabian mountains.

The southern region becomes more mountainous as Baden-Württemberg's Black Forest climbs towards the Swiss Alps, with the Swabian and Bavarian Alps to the east. This is grand hiking, climbing and skiing country though none of the mountains rises above 3,000m (10,000ft)—Germany's highest peak being the Zugspitze, at 2,963m (9,719ft).

The great rivers link the country to its western and eastern neighbours, the Rhine to France, the Danube to Austria and Hungary, the Elbe flowing from the Czech lands through Dresden to Hamburg, while the Oder and Neisse define the frontier with Poland redrawn by the Allies at Yalta in 1945 (finally accepted by Germany in 1990).

A Love Affair with Nature

Nowhere is the Germans' predilection for the romantic world of the fairy tale more evident than in their forests. Pollution has left them less vast and dense than they used to be, but beech, oak, chestnut and, above all, pine woods remain the country's pride. From the Harz mountains across to the Hunsrück, the Taunus north of Frankfurt, the Black Forest, the Swabian Odenwald and the great forests of Bavaria and Thuringia, the Germans continue on the tracks of Hänsel and Gretel or Red Riding Hood. If West Berliners were able to keep their sanity during 45 years of isolation, it may be in large part due to the great expanse of woodland inside the city's borders, in which to stroll and forget their Cold War worries.

Rambling through dense woods, in search of mushrooms or just a moment of secluded peace, remains a great German passion. For many, it is a pleasure that has an exquisite tinge of melancholy, for which the Romantic German poets of the 19th century coined an almost untranslatable word, *Waldeinsamkeit,* literally "the loneliness of the forest". Indeed, it was to preserve this pleasure against the ravages of acid rain and traffic fumes that West Germany first developed Europe's most powerful ecological party, the Greens. The quiet revolution that undermined Communism in East Germany began with the famous Monday meetings of ecological reformists in Leipzig, worried, among other things, about the dying evergreens of Thuringia.

When they're not hiking, they're biking. No country in Europe seems to have catered more thoroughly to the needs of the cyclists. In almost every town, specially paved bicycle lanes run between cars and pedestrians, and they are *sacred.* Woe betide you if, accustomed to watching out only for passing cars, you wander without a second look into the bicycle lane. Crossing Rommel's path in the desert may have been more dangerous, but the look he would have given you could scarcely have been more withering.

The fabled discipline of the Germans is dying fast, but it is still on show at traffic lights. Take a walk at three o'clock in the morning and you will see, with not a car in sight, a lone night-owl waiting patiently at a pedestrian crossing for the light to turn from red to green before making a move. By and large, times have changed since 1918 when Berlin revolutionaries bought platform tickets before invading a railway station. Today's ecological or political rebels are less polite, and German football hooligans match any the British or Dutch can offer. More positively, people are generally more relaxed and easy-going.

Holiday contacts with the Mediterranean countries have nurtured a taste for more outdoor cafés, and a more public city life.

Prosperity has also made the Germans more discerning and demanding in their culinary tastes. The ecological movement has had its impact on a renewed interest in authentic traditional food. After years of unimaginative cooking, regional cuisine has been resurrected with pride. The result is robust and savoury, bringing refined innovations that are not *nouvelle cuisine* but *neue deutsche Küche*.

A Country of Many Capitals

For better and for worse, Germany has never known the kind of national unity which gave to both Britain and France a strong, dominant, even overwhelming capital. Important as it has remained in modern German social and cultural life, Berlin was the political capital of a united Germany only from 1871 to 1945. Instead, several large, thriving cities, each with a vibrant character of its own, continued into the modern era. Some were originally the capital of an ancient duchy, principality or kingdom, like Frankfurt, Munich, Heidelberg, Dresden and Leipzig; some powerful city states in their own right, like the Hanseatic trading towns of Hamburg, Lübeck and Bremen; and others the centres of veritable ecclesiastical empires such as Cologne and Mainz.

This historical fragmentation has spread the cultural riches more evenly around the country. You will find great art collections not only in Berlin, but also in Munich, Dresden, Frankfurt and Cologne. Some of Europe's finest modern art is to be found in the industrial Ruhr district—

Dortmund, Essen and Düsseldorf. Many of these cities have internationally renowned opera and ballet companies and symphony orchestras, just like Stuttgart, Leipzig, Bamberg and Hamburg. Most of them are also the home of first-rate theatre—classical and avant-garde. In this league, West Germany's political capital Bonn was always, for all its charm, something of a joke, which its fine university and the house where Beethoven was born never quite overcame.

Whatever harm Hitler's war did to the world around him, it cannot be forgotten just how much of a catastrophe it was for Germany itself. A vital part of the "miracle" of reconstruction after 1945 is to be seen in the rescue and restoration of the country's historic monuments. Much was irretrievable, but wonders were worked with the cathedrals of Bamberg, Cologne and Mainz, the Renaissance houses of Nuremberg, Frankfurt's patrician Römerberg, and Dresden's Zwinger palace and opera house. And the work is not yet completed. In some places bombed-out shells remain as solemn reminders, like Berlin's Gedächtniskirche or Dresden's Frauenkirche. Will they also one day take on the romantic aura of the Rhine valley's medieval castles, victims of earlier wars?

Germans and Germans

Despite the many migrations, notably of refugees from the eastern territories that Germany lost after World War II, the people have retained much of their regional character. The most marked distinction can still be drawn between tough, jovial Bavarians and the more sober, diligent Prussians. Political rivalry is less

A street musician entertains shoppers and strollers on Berlin's Ku'damm.

pronounced than in the past, but culturally and socially it is as strong as ever. Until recently, a happy colony of Berliners—artists, writers and film makers who fled Cold War constraints—had settled in Munich, retaining the particular sharp ironic wit of their home town in face of the more banana-skin humour of the locals. Many have now gone back home. And the story is told of the Bavarian peasant girl who confesses in church that she is pregnant with the child of a Yugoslav immigrant worker. "Praise the Lord," says the priest, "I was afraid the father might be a Prussian."

The Bavarians' Swabian neighbours are more serious—"the northerners of the south," according to one wag. A beggar knocking at a housewife's door in Augsburg to announce he had not eaten for three days was told: "You really must force yourself."

Rhinelanders, no doubt aided by their splendid wines, are renowned for their party spirit and political satire, particularly at Carnival time in Düsseldorf, Cologne and Mainz.

In the north, the people of the venerable Hanseatic towns of Hamburg, Lübeck and Bremen are cool, elegant and dignified, worthy descendants of the characters in Thomas Mann's celebrated novel *Buddenbrooks*. Retrieving its traditional hinterland through the opening of the East German border, Lübeck hopes to return to its old prosperity, while the other two towns continue to thrive on their great port traffic.

A leader in world trade since the medieval Hanseatic League, Hamburg remains Germany's great gateway to the Seven Seas.

DATA BOX

Geography: Germany's northern borders are bounded by the North Sea, Denmark and the Baltic. To the west, beyond the Rhine river, are the Benelux countries and France, while the Black Forest, Lake Constance and the Bavarian Alps trace the frontier with Switzerland and Austria. South of the Erzgebirge (Ore Mountains) is the Czech Republic. To the east, the Oder and Neisse rivers mark the frontier with Poland. Other major rivers include the Danube starting high in the Black Forest on its way to the Balkans, the Elbe flowing north via Dresden to the sea at Hamburg, and the Weser from Westphalia north to Bremen. The country covers an area of 357,039km^2 (137,852 square miles). Highest mountain: Zugspitze 2,963m (9,719ft).
Population: 79,000,000 of whom about 5,000,000 are resident foreigners. Berlin 3,450,000; Hamburg 1,572,000, Munich 1,275,000, Cologne 915,000, Essen 616,000, Frankfurt 593,000, Leipzig 552,000, Dresden 519,000.
Government: A parliamentary democracy was formed in 1990 from the unification of the Federal Republic of Germany and the German Democratic Republic, founded as separate countries in 1949. The new federal republic comprises 16 *Länder* (states): West Germany's Schleswig-Holstein, Lower Saxony, North Rhine-Westphalia, Hesse, Rhineland-Palatinate, Saarland, Baden-Württemberg, Bavaria, and East Germany's Brandenburg, Mecklenburg, Thuringia, Saxony and Saxony-Anhalt, with three city-states—Bremen, Hamburg and Berlin. The *Bundestag* (federal assembly), popularly elected for a 4-year term, passes legislation over which a *Bundesrat* (federal council), appointed by the *Länder*, has limited veto power. Head of state is a president with largely symbolic status but considerable moral influence.
Religion: The southern and western *Länder* are predominantly Catholic, the northern and eastern mainly Protestant. There are small minorities of other Christian sects, Muslims, Buddhists, Jews, atheists and a growing number of people with no declared religious belief.

The people of Saxony have long been the butt of gibes about their shrill accent, but their stock has risen in the recent past. Those who have chosen to stay in Dresden, Leipzig and Weimar rather than seek an easier life in the West are defending a grand cultural tradition.

If Berlin never knew for more than a brief moment the pre-eminence of a Paris or London, its citizens have remained a breed apart. The good humour and deep, warm emotions displayed on that November night in 1989 when the Wall was opened laid to rest forever that foreign image of a cold and austere people, which the Germans themselves and anyone who spent time in Berlin always knew to be a false cliché. The intense creativity and intelligence of the 1920s were halted by Hitler and largely driven into exile, but since 1945 they have revived. Reunited, the city is once again resuming the country's spiritual and political leadership. These are exciting and challenging times for Germany, well worth a closer look.

History

Until modern times, Germany has been easier to define by its language and culture than as a political reality. The ideal of a unified German empire or nation was as inspiring for its people as it was formidable for their Slavonic and Latin neighbours. Today, with the people's creative energies and great cultural tradition placed in a broader European context, unity has become a fact. The new Germany is a stimulating challenge for its own people.

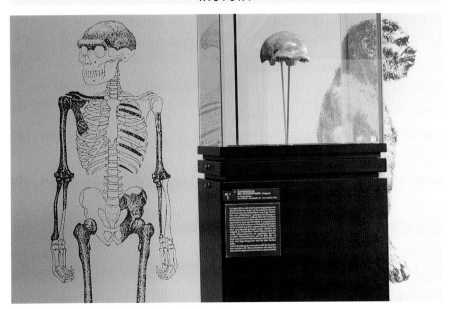

*T*he many bones of a
*50,000-year-old Neanderthal man
in the anthropology section of the
Rheinisches Landesmuseum,
Bonn.*

Even for its new allies and old enemies, it may not be such a bad idea after all.

The earliest known German, *Homo erectus heidelbergensis*, is also our first tangible European. The evidence of fossils and his jawbone suggest he lived about 600,000 years ago and hunted mammoth, rhinoceros and elk in the Rhine and Neckar valleys. More recent, a mere 50,000 years old, is the celebrated Neanderthal man dug up by railway workers in 1856 in a cave near Düsseldorf. This *Homo sapiens* is generally considered to be a branch off the main genealogy of modern man, an uncle rather than a father.

Like the rest of Europe, the German region evolved through the Stone, Bronze and Iron Ages from hunting to agriculture with the aid of wheeled wagons, the plough and other farming techniques imported from Asia. Also from the east came a mixture of nomadic peoples: the Celts stopped off on their way west and south, Illyrians passed through eastern Germany towards the Balkans, but it was the Germanic tribes occupying central Europe who left their name on the land.

The nomadic life nurtured a competitive spirit and aptitude with weapons against wild beasts and rival bands. The battleaxe is prominent in prehistoric tombs uncovered in Saxony, Thuringia and Bavaria.

Inside and Outside
the Roman Empire

By the time of the Romans, as described by historian Tacitus, the Germans were bold and pugnacious in time of war, but otherwise inclined to laziness. They enjoyed their leisure, lengthy banquets and siestas, leaving the farm work to conquered serfs. For exercise, they trained with weapons and galloped their horses. Julius Caesar decided they were nothing but trouble. Constant raids on his fledgling colony in Gaul persuaded him to make the Rhine the empire's frontier from about 58 BC. Garrisons on the Rhine and Moselle rivers, notably at Cologne (*Colonia*), Koblenz, Mainz and Trier, became outposts of Roman civilization, recruiting Germanic mercenaries for their armies.

Forgetting Caesar's misgivings, Drusus pushed north to the estuaries of the Weser and Elbe, and Tiberius sought an alliance with the Germanic Cheruscans to establish Roman administration—and taxes—east of the Rhine. A Cheruscan noble, granted Roman citizenship and the name of Gaius Julius Arminius, balked at paying taxes. In AD 9 he led his Cheruscans and other Germanic tribes to a great victory over 20,000 Roman troops in the Teutoburger Wald in Westphalia. The commander Varus fell on his sword rather than face a defeat which shattered Roman confidence and halted the conquest of Germany. In the nationalistic fervour of the 19th century, the victor, now known as Hermann, was commemorated with a gigantic monument (near Detmold in the Teutoburger Wald) to Germany's first hero of national freedom and unity.

Emperor Vespasian effected a more modest settlement of the right and left banks of the Rhine with a mixture of Germanic and Roman communities—the Franks. Taking in the Black Forest and part of the Swabian mountains, this melting of the two cultures formed a link between antiquity and the Middle Ages.

Germanic tribes, notably the Saxons, Franks, Alemanni and Burgundians, hacked away at the dwindling Roman empire and then themselves came under attack from Attila's Huns pouring in from the east. The Huns' defeat of the

*M*unich's grand public buildings include the Maximilianeum, the impressive seat of the Bavarian parliament at the end of Maximilianstrasse.

Burgundians at Worms in 436 gave rise to the Nibelungen saga that inspired Richard Wagner's opera cycle.

Roman civilization survived principally through the Christian Church, the first German bishopric having been founded at Trier in 314. Christianization, led by an energetic bunch of Irish and Anglo-Saxon monks, served to diminish the Germanic threat to Rome, but the German princes quickly took over from the Pope the appointment of bishops and the lucrative administration of Church lands. The princes' independent attitude was to remain a constant of German history right up to modern times.

The Empire of Charlemagne

It was Charlemagne (Karl der Grosse) who conducted the first serious effort to unite German lands under one ruler. By the end of his reign (768–814), the Frankish empire he inherited from his father King Pippin stretched from the Pyrenees to the Elbe. He achieved this through military conquest and forced Christian conversion, but also by cunningly arranged marriages and alternately mild-mannered and arm-twisting diplomacy. In 794, he established Aachen as his imperial residence and intellectual capital under the guidance of his friend Alcuin, an Anglo-Saxon scholar from Northumbria. The scientific and cultural academy at Aachen, and church schools set up throughout the empire, were vital in preserving classical literature through the Middle Ages. Latin was the written and spoken language at court, but German was nurtured at the episcopal school of Fulda, where legends, historical deeds, songs and scientific names were compiled in German, along with a German translation of the Bible.

In exchange for protection against the troublesome Roman nobility, Pope Leo III gave Charlemagne the crown of the Holy Roman Empire. In Rome on Christmas Day, 800, he was proclaimed: "Charles, the pious and gentle Augustus, crowned by God, the great and peace-bringing Emperor of the Romans." To the Byzantine emperor in Constantinople, furious to discover this new upstart rival, Charlemagne sent envoys with gifts and letters calling him "Brother", which only made him more furious.

The political and cultural unity of the empire gave western Europe an enduring distinctive identity, but under Charlemagne's son Louis, the empire was battered by dynastic rivalries. France split off from Germany, and the German empire broke down into duchies, principalities and kingdoms. Germany's vulnerability became apparent in 845 when the Normans sailed into Hamburg and destroyed it, later moving through Belgium to burn Aachen, Cologne, Bonn and Trier.

Typically, in 911, when Duke Conrad of Franconia sought recognition as king, he was resisted by the powerful duchies of Saxony, Bavaria and Swabia. His successor Henry of Saxony was more self-assertive in proclaiming the German kingdom, *Regnum Teutonicorum*, but even then, Bavaria held out. He was able to impose his choice of son Otto as his heir, but only by giving the dukes a paramount role in the king-making ceremony.

Power Struggles in the Middle Ages

The crowning in Aachen of Otto I in 936 can be regarded as the true beginning of Germany's history as a nation. The ceremony illustrated the distribution of powers throughout the realm. The Archbishop

53

of Mainz performed the coronation, thus assuring Otto the support of the greatest Church dominion outside Italy. The Dukes of Bavaria, Franconia, Swabia and Lorraine brought their Saxon peer to the church, served him at dinner in the imperial palace, and were each given gifts as symbols of their considerable autonomy. To secure Church loyalty, Otto made the Archbishop of Mainz an imperial prince, installed his own brother as Archbishop of Cologne, and similarly ennobled other archbishops, granting them tax immunities on their vast land holdings. When the ungrateful Archbishop of Mainz rebelled, he was replaced by Otto's son Wilhelm.

This political infighting between Otto and his successors had little impact on the everyday life of the people. Land was entirely in the hands of the nobility, secular and ecclesiastic. The peasants worked the farms in virtual serfdom, leaving their lords free to pursue the more honourable art of war—not so very different from what Tacitus had observed among the Germanic tribes 1,000 years earlier. For minimal protection against arbitrary landlords, the peasants formed guilds, regularly renewing their oath of friendship with a communal meal—surviving to this day as the *Stammtisch* (table for regulars) in taverns all over Germany.

In the 12th century, bloody dynastic rivalries for the German throne pitted the Swabian Hohenstaufens against the Welfs (or Guelphs). Finally, the dukes made the conciliatory choice of Friedrich (Frederick) I, son of a Hohenstaufen father and Welf mother. Barbarossa (his Italian nickname) preferred to expand and consolidate his empire outside Germany and left home affairs in the hands of his cousin, the Duke of Bavaria.

After founding Munich in 1158, Henry the Lion (Heinrich der Löwe) concentrated on northern and eastern Germany, making his capital in Brunswick. He founded Lübeck to encourage Baltic trade and promoted German eastward expansion. A clash with Barbarossa drove him into exile, and dynastic struggles for the imperial crown resumed.

The success of Friedrich II (1212–50) consecrated the German particularity of monarchs being chosen by prince-electors (*Kurfürsten*). These were the Archbishops of Mainz, Cologne and Trier, Count Palatine of the Rhine, Margrave of Brandenburg, Duke of Saxony and King of Bohemia, who consulted other German princes to arrive at a consensus. To get their vote, candidates had to guarantee the princes' privileges. But with sons not succeeding their fathers, the throne moved from region to region and prevented the emergence of a national capital. (Like Barbarossa, Friedrich II found Italy more manageable than Germany and established his capital in Palermo.)

Matters of Life and Black Death

From the 11th to the 14th centuries, land development, growth of cities and eastward migration were accompanied by a sharp population increase (to 14 million by the time of the great plague of 1348). In exchange for greater freedom and material benefits, peasants from the Rhineland, Flanders and the Netherlands settled

The treasures of Cologne cathedral underlined the prominence of the town—the largest in medieval Germany.

in Holstein, Mecklenburg and most of eastern Germany. The next generation moved on to Pomerania, Silesia and eastern Prussia. With the Crusades in the Holy Land coming to an end, German knights found a new vocation Christianizing the eastern territories, more often with the sword than with the Bible. Remote from the western centres of power, these lands were governed as regular colonies by local German lords, who made the laws and used a distinctive court life and costume to assert their authority.

The lack of an effective central power made Germany's cities vitally important for day-to-day government. The way they mushroomed around the country was a tribute to a handful of enterprising lords and a dynamic merchant class. Freiburg, founded as a base for trade in 1120 by Duke Conrad of Zähringen, was a landmark of urban planning. Rather than growing out of a country village, it sprang up from scratch when merchants were granted land and trading rights in exchange for building a house in town. Henry the Lion deliberately chose trading crossroads as sites for Munich and Lübeck. Similarly, the Wittelsbachs built 16 towns in Bavaria between 1180 and 1347, all at key frontier locations. Nuremberg, for example, grew up around the lord's residence and adjoining merchants' quarters. The Roman garrison town of Cologne had become, with a population of 40,000, the biggest in Germany.

Town councils asserted citizens' rights and imposed their choice for mayor rather than accepting a lord's appointee. Guild membership was obligatory for merchants and craftsmen to practise their profession. The guilds excluded servants, day-labourers, apprentices, clerics, beggars and Jews—all non-citizens. The council was chosen from leading members of the guilds who handed on their posts from generation to generation.

In these years of expansion, trade prospered in linen and woollen textiles from Augsburg and Ulm, and silk from Cologne. Wine went out from the Rheingau and Alsace (an undisputed German territory until the 17th century). The brewing of beer was already a major German industry. Hamburg was the export centre for two-thirds of national production, principally to England, the Netherlands and up the Rhine, while Lübeck and Wismar took care of shipments to Scandinavia. Baltic ports also traded in furs, wax and amber in exchange for oil and fruit from southern Europe and spices from the East. The key financial centre for trade with eastern Europe was Nuremberg, which by the 14th century had become an international currency exchange for the whole of Europe.

The insecurity of foreign markets and overseas travel prompted merchants to band together in the Hanseatic League. The first German merchants' guild (*Hanse der Deutschen*) was founded in London in 1282, grouping companies from Lübeck, Hamburg, Westphalia and Cologne. Other offices opened in Bruges, Novgorod and Bergen, with activities coordinated at headquarters in Lübeck.

The league had its own court, church, social meeting places and private armed force. Despite internal rivalries, the companies united to wage war against foreign powers and piracy, erecting a trade blockade in 1358 to defend the league's interests in Flanders.

Not everybody prospered. The masses were constantly subject to famines—the worst in 1315—caused by violent fluctuations in harvests and food prices. In 1348, the Black Death, a disease brought from the east by flea-ridden rats, decimated Germany's population (which fell from 14 million to 10 million over the course of the next century).

Coping with the Unruly Reich

The ill wind of the Black Death was not bad for everybody. Skilled craftsmen were at a premium. Tenant farmers struggled along at subsistence level, but free peasants prospered, as did the merchants, high clergy and nobility. Indeed, middle-class merchants did so well that laws were passed to stop them dressing with an ostentatious luxury that threatened the prestige of the nobles. Bishops had to cope with new religious communities that propagated the heresy that the Church should return to Christ's vows of poverty.

As the imperial crown bounced back and forth between Habsburgs (originally from Alsace and Switzerland), Luxemburgs and the Bavarian Wittelsbachs, each emperor trying to impose a little order in the Reich. At the Worms Reichstag (imperial assembly, or Diet) of 1495, the Habsburgs' Maximilian I had to deal with the rival claims of some 350 fiefdoms under princes, dukes, counts, bishops and abbots. Declaring a "perpetual truce", the lords agreed to settle disputes in court rather than by the summary justice of feud. An imperial law court was set up, but the lords resisted a nationwide system of taxation.

The election of Emperor Charles V (1519–56) was preceded by a massive "auction" because of the French candidacy of François I, who offered the prince-electors huge bribes. Although Charles had not yet set foot on German soil, the Flemish-Spanish prince argued his German origins as a Habsburg. He promised he would fill court posts only with German appointees and would not wage war without consulting the German princes, nor bring foreign troops onto German soil without warning. These went the way of all election promises, but added to counter-bribes of 1 million guilders underwritten by the Fugger banking family of Augsburg, and they were enough to swing the vote.

Reformation and Peasants' War

Charles V's coronation in 1520 was the biggest bash Aachen had seen since Charlemagne. Three months later, the man who was to become the dominant ruler of Renaissance Europe presided over the Reichstag in Worms. The assembly bolstered his imperial ambitions by raising an army to accompany him to Rome, but also gave him the headache of dealing with a troublemaker named Luther.

Born in Saxony in 1483, Martin Luther, the son of a copper-mining foreman who wanted him to go into law, had become instead a doubt-ridden monk of the Augustine order. He was burdened by a deep sense of sin but, distrusting the cavalier way in which the Church granted pardons, he turned to the Bible. His meticulous study of the texts convinced him that God granted grace to all who acknowledged sin by good works and free will, but not according to merits as determined by the Church. Luther's emphasis on the Bible as the sole source of individual revelation threatened Church authority. What hurt most, however, was his attack on the sale of indulgences, a major source of Church revenue. This was the central point of the celebrated "95 Theses" that he nailed to the church door in Wittenberg in 1517.

He did this quite unaware of what was at stake, both politically and financially, for his German superior, the Archbishop of Mainz. To raise money for the rebuilding of St Peter's in Rome, the Pope had announced a special indulgence for sinners to buy a way out of purgatory, not just for themselves but also for relatives who had neglected to pay up before they died. Sharing fifty-fifty with the Pope, the Archbishop of Mainz needed the revenues to reimburse a Fugger bank loan with which he had bought the archbishopric in the first place. Luther knew nothing of these shenanigans, but he did see Johannes Tetzel, a fanatical Dominican preacher from Leipzig, drumming up trade among rich and poor alike for jubilee medallions certifying eternal salvation.

Luther's theses, sent first in the form of a letter to the Archbishop of Mainz, contested the Pope's right to pardon anything but offences against the Church, grace for sin remaining the exclusive domain of God. In 1520, Rome branded Luther a heretic. Luther burned a papal order ordering him to retract and was excommunicated, but his protector, Duke Friedrich of Saxony, refused to publish the papal bull in his territory. He was followed by other lords, notably in Hesse, Brunswick and Mecklenburg, where popular uprisings were feared if they bowed to the Pope and condemned Luther. Charles V promulgated the Edict of Worms in 1521, outlawing Luther and forbidding the sale of his books, but as the emperor left Germany to pursue his European adventures, the edict was not enforced until his return, nine years later. The Rhineland and Bavaria remained faithful to Rome. In northern and eastern Germany, Church lands were secularized and services reformed, with Luther's new catechism for pastors and simple prayer books for the congregation. The Protestants took their name from the 1529 "Protestation" of reformist princes against a Catholic injunction on further changes to doctrine and confiscation of Church property.

The peasants responded to the attacks on Church abuses and corruption more vehemently than Luther really wanted. They drew parallels between the injustices of the higher clergy and those of their landlords in general. The population explosion of the 15th century had caused a land crisis, particularly in southern Germany where farms were divided into ever smaller unproductive parcels. To compensate for the lower profits, landowners cut back on grazing, hunting and fishing privileges. To defend what they called their God-given rights, the peasants quoted the Old Testament. This was not at all what Luther had in mind. He called on the peasants to obey secular laws and authority.

The first revolts of the Peasants' War broke out in 1524 in Stühlingen in the

---

FROM GUTENBERG TO SONY

Luther had gauged precisely the vital role to be played by popular opinion in strengthening his position against the Pope. Though he wrote in Latin to his fellow churchmen, he was careful to use a simple, forceful German vernacular to communicate with the people, most brilliantly in his translation of the Bible. The printing press built by Johannes Gutenberg in Mainz in the 1450s came into its own with the mass-production of Luther's sermons—500,000 copies in print by the time of the Diet of Worms, several million only four years later. "The Word did it all," said Luther—as long as it could be spread far and wide. Printed pamphlets were as important to Luther in Wittenberg as was the minicam TV news camera for the quiet revolution in Leipzig in 1989.

Black Forest, spreading quickly through Württemberg and Swabia. By the end of 1525 the fighting stretched from Alsace to the Tyrol and from Thuringia to Switzerland. Preacher Christoph Schappeler and furrier Sebastian Lotzer drew up 12 Articles proclaiming peaceful intentions and demanding an end to feudal injustices, but the rage quickly translated into burning, robbery and violence. Luther wrote a pamphlet *Against the Murdering, Thieving Hordes of Peasants,* adding later his fear that "if the peasants became lords, the devil would become abbot." To protect their lands and privileges, Catholic and Protestant princes found common cause in crushing the revolt with massive brutality, their armies slaughtering 75,000 peasants.

The lesson the Protestant princes drew from this scare was to give the Reformed Church a strong framework, scarcely less authoritarian than the Catholic model they had rejected. They took over the ecclesiastic courts and hand-picked the clergy. Church funds were redistributed to the poor, to new schools and to their own treasuries.

In 1530, Charles V found time to return to Germany, but efforts to impose religious unity were ultimately resisted as much by his fellow Catholics as by the Protestant princes. What still mattered most was local autonomy, consecrated in a truce reached at Augsburg in 1555. Its principle became known as *Cuius regio, eius religio,* "the prince's religion is the religion of his dominions."

After the shake-up of the Reformation, Catholic morale was boosted by the Council of Trent. A Collegium Germanicum was set up to train a tougher breed of German Catholic priests. The Jesuits moved into Bavaria in 1556 and established a college (*Gymnasium*) in Munich four years later. Papal nuncios were sent to Munich and Cologne to make sure Counter-Reformation measures were carried out. Duke Wilhelm V of Bavaria built in Munich the Jesuit church of St Michael, completed in 1597 as a grand baroque "trumpet blast" to champion the Church revival.

Thirty Years' War

Banding together in the Protestant Union on one side and the Catholic League on the other, the German princes resumed their fight for control of Church lands. Tempted by the rich spoils, foreign powers joined in on the side of their co-religionists; Catholic Spain and the Netherlands, Protestant Sweden, Denmark and even, for a time, England. Conversely, Richelieu's Catholic France, interested above all in countering the Habsburgs, sided with the Protestants. The belligerents turned Germany into one vast blood-drenched battlefield.

In 1620, a Spanish army allied with Bavaria routed the Protestants in the Palatinate. Over the next three years, the Catholics dominated Germany all the way north to Lower Saxony. In the east, the imperial general, Wallenstein, swept through the Duchy of Mecklenburg to the Baltic. The huge personal fortune and power he amassed on the way posed a direct threat not only to Sweden but also to his own master, the Habsburg emperor, Ferdinand. The German Catholic princes insisted that Wallenstein be dismissed and the too-mighty imperial army reduced.

Gustavus Adolphus of Sweden landed in 1630 on the German Baltic coast with an army of 13,000 men, later increased to 40,000. The French offered him a subsidy, but Protestant Brandenburg and Saxony

59

joined him only after Magdeburg had fallen to the Catholics. The tide turned. The Swedes and Saxons cut a broad swathe through southern Germany, marching across Bavaria to Frankfurt and the Rhine. For centuries after, in rural Rhineland communities, naughty children heard the ultimate parental threat: *"Die Schweden kommen!"* ("The Swedes are coming!"). In fact, the civilian population suffered regardless of whether the army passing through was "friendly" or "hostile". Commanders used army marches to exhaust local resources, living off the land and leaving nothing for the enemy, rather than engaging in costly battles.

The Swedish king died in battle at Lützen in Saxony in 1632, but the embittered Swedes remained in southern Germany two more years until defeated at Nördlingen. The German Protestant princes negotiated a truce with the emperor in 1635, and Richelieu decided it was time for France to wage open war on the Habsburgs. Military operations and diplomatic negotiations continued hand in hand until the final Peace of Westphalia was signed in 1648. The big losers were the emperor and the German people. The princes of the Reich strengthened their autonomy. France won Alsace and the emperor had to relinquish claims to Lorraine. Sweden occupied Bremen, Wismar and Stettin, controlling the important customs duties of their port traffic. With the population dropping from 16 million to 10 million, the Thirty Years' War proved proportionally more costly to the German people than both world wars of the 20th century.

The Emergence of Prussia

It took over a century to regain the lost population, but the economy was back to pre-war levels within 20 to 30 years. Frankfurt and Leipzig thrived on their international trade fairs. With the Habsburg emperors firmly entrenched in Vienna, the main centres of culture, power and prosperity had switched from the imperial cities of Augsburg and Nuremberg to such princes' capitals as Munich, Dresden and Hanover. There was an explosion of creative talent. Baroque architects such as the Asam brothers were active in Munich, Matthäus Pöppelmann in Dresden, Balthasar Neumann in Würzburg. Johann Sebastian Bach was concert master at Weimar and later Leipzig. The Duke of Hanover's court musician Georg Friedrich Händel moved to London, followed by his

*F*rederick the Great intended his ceremonial avenue of Unter den Linden to be the most fashionable address in Berlin.

former master when the duke became King George I of England.

Amid the rivalries of the German states, Friedrich Wilhelm of Brandenburg-Prussia played one party against another to turn his duchy into a sovereign state on its way to becoming a fully-fledged kingdom. He sided with Louis XIV against the Rhineland but was also quick to welcome 200,000 Protestant Huguenots fleeing French persecution. They founded prosperous colonies throughout Prussia and Brandenburg. Tough, authoritarian, the Great Prince-Elector (*der Grosse Kurfürst*) gave total priority to building a strong army as the best guarantee of his state's autonomy. He imprisoned any aristocrat daring to question his decisions and kept his peasants in feudal submission. In 1701, his son crowned himself in Königsberg (now Kaliningrad) King Friedrich I *in* (not yet *of*) Prussia (part remained in Polish hands). Lacking the statecraft and military preoccupations of his father, the king did inject a certain culture into the hitherto philistine Prussian state. The baroque master Andreas Schlüter was commissioned to build the royal palace.

However, it was the Great Prince-Elector's grandson who instituted the qualities and style that came to be known as quintessentially "Prussian". Friedrich Wilhelm I (1713–40) was a superb, hardworking administrator. Despising the baroque glitter of his parents' court, he set his mind to making the military and bureaucratic state that would one day control the destiny of modern Germany. He built a great army with disciplined training. Military schools replaced law faculties as the training ground for the highly centralized royal administration.

Of the rulers who brought Prussia to the forefront of German and European

YOU'RE IN THE ARMY NOW

The Sergeant King, as Friedrich Wilhelm I was nicknamed, went everywhere in uniform, and his courtiers followed suit. Irascible and deeply religious, he was simple in his personal tastes, finding his pleasure in tobacco and beer, in strictly male company. By making it the duty of all nobles' sons (*Junkers*) to serve in the royal army, he kept the officer class strictly aristocratic—except in the artillery, where only bourgeois officers had the necessary knowledge of mathematics. Infantrymen press-ganged from among the sons of peasants and handworkers were granted prolonged leave to work on the land and in factories, with a new military discipline.

politics, Friedrich II (1740–86) was the most capable. His political intelligence at home and military talent and statesmanship abroad earned him the title of Frederick the Great (Friedrich der Grosse) even beyond Germany's borders. He was an intellectual charmer but not an especially nice fellow. The tough upbringing he received from an overbearing father left him rational and unemotional, cold and hypocritical in human relationships. Supremely pragmatic, he was interested in the Enlightenment of his century, but without its idealism. The welfare of his subjects was less a humane objective than a warrant of domestic peace and tax revenue. In unifying the court system and legal code, he felt people would work better if he also abolished torture and eased the harsher punishments. In reaction to his father's bigotry, he was tolerant in religion, but mostly out of indifference. When seizing Silesia in a war against Austria, Prussia acquired a million new subjects, Catholics whom Friedrich could more easily pacify by guaranteeing their freedom of worship.

In his beloved Potsdam, he provided the overall design for Sanssouci Palace, built with architect friend Georg von Knobelsdorff. The favoured language at court and the revived science academy was French. The king invited Voltaire to stay, hoping to get help in writing a royal political testament, *Rêveries Politiques,* but the French thinker thought too independently.

In the Seven Years' War (1756–63), a worldwide struggle of European alliances, Prussia challenged Austria for control of the German nation. At the outset, Friedrich's pre-emptive strike against Saxony demonstrated his capacity for bold military initiative. He also showed dogged courage in holding out when the prolonged fighting exhausted Prussia's resources, having even to drive the Russians out of Berlin. By the end of the war, his military prowess and tough diplomacy brought Prussia closer to undisputed German leadership. He became at last King *of* rather than *in* Prussia with the 1772 annexation of the Polish-held part. The name now covered possessions all the way to the Rhineland.

The French Revolution

Seduced by the French model, the German princes built miniature versions of Versailles and tried to apply the Enlightenment's ideas of rational, humanitarian reform without slackening their grip on power. Some German princes copied Prussian militarism in miniature. Rococo tyrants like the Duke of Württemberg and Count of Hessen-Kassel sold their armies for mercenary service in the American Revolution.

The Palatinate's Prince-Elector Karl Theodor was, at least until the French Revolution, a model progressive. He

founded in Mannheim a music school, national theatre and science academy, and promoted porcelain manufacture in Frankenthal. Great writers were everywhere in demand. In Baden, Count Karl Friedrich, the first German prince to end feudal control of the peasantry, conferred with Voltaire, Herder, Klopstock and Goethe. In the Weimar of Duke Karl August, Goethe was finance minister, Herder worked on school reform, and Schiller and Wieland found the court atmosphere congenial to their poetry.

All over the country, political newspapers sprang up in the fertile new soil of German nationalism. During the Seven Years' War, Friedrich Carl von Moser wrote *On the German National Spirit* and Thomas Abbt *On Dying for the Fatherland.*

The French Revolution of 1789 was not greeted with great popular enthusiasm, apart from a few pockets of unrest in the Rhineland and Saxony. The ideals of liberty, equality and fraternity appealed to German intellectuals, notably Schiller, Kant and Hölderlin, but Goethe shied away from the accompanying chaos. In 1792, the princes rallied to their fellow monarch in danger, invading France with a coalition army of Austrian and German forces. Its commander, the Duke of Brunswick, threatened to level Paris if the French royal family were harmed, but the Revolutionary army drove the invaders back to the Rhine and Palatinate, capturing Speyer, Mainz and later Aachen. The Rhineland remained in French hands for the next 20 years.

For Napoleon, conquered Germany served as a buffer against Russia and a source of military and economic strength with which to resist Britain. He was greeted with mixed feelings. His self-coronation prompted Beethoven to remove his name from the title-page of the *Eroica* Symphony, but the princes were mostly delighted with his dismantling of the Reich in 1803. Church property was secularized and 112 states abolished. Bavaria, Württemberg, Baden and Hessen were big winners in the share-out. The price was to join the Rhine League, a military alliance with Napoleon that cost them dearly by the end of the war. The redrawn map of Germany remained practically unchanged till 1945. The woefully misnamed "Holy Roman Empire" founded under Charlemagne in 800 effectively came to an end when its last emperor, Franz II of Habsburg, had to adopt the new title of Emperor Franz I of Austria. Prussia's Friedrich Wilhelm III was unhappy about having to introduce Napoleon's social reforms and abolish ancient aristocratic privileges. Peasants were delighted to see the end of feudalism, and Jews were pleased to be emancipated.

The disaster of the military alliance with Napoleon became apparent when 100,000 German troops joined the Grande Armée, one-third of the total force, on its fatal 1812 campaign in Russia. Rhine League regiments were practically wiped out, only Prussia, with its smaller contingent, escaping relatively unscathed. Napoleon's defeat turned popular German feeling against him and fired the movement for national liberation. In 1813, Prussia allied with Austria and Russia to defeat the French at Leipzig in the Battle of the Nations. Jumping on the bandwagon, Saxony and Württemberg rallied to the victors, as did Bavaria, deserting the Rhine League to drive Napoleon out of Germany. Prussian Field Marshal Blücher, the future hero of Waterloo, led the invasion into France.

German patriotism had become a reality in the Napoleonic Wars. In French-occupied Berlin, philosopher Johann Gottlieb Fichte had called on the people to assert their national identity, their "Germanness" in his momentous "Speech to the German Nation". Students, factory workers, doctors, lawyers and teachers volunteered for the armies of liberation, and one of their corps created the black, red and gold banner that was to become the German national flag. Journalist Ernst Moritz Arndt exalted the Germans as "sacred people" whose frontiers extended "as far as the German tongue is heard". Countering the intellectuals, teacher Friedrich Ludwig Jahn had great success with gymnastics clubs, where the bourgeoisie worked off its fat to the slogan "Germany awake!"

At the Congress of Vienna that carved up post-Napoleonic Europe in 1815, German national unity got nowhere. Austrian Chancellor Metternich imposed his principle of "legitimacy" over the revolutionary spirit of "freedom". This kept Germany divided into several small states dominated by Austria and Prussia. A loose German Confederation (*Deutscher Bund*) of 41 states and free cities held its federal assembly (*Bundestag*) in Frankfurt, attacked by nationalists and liberals for its conservative monarchist bias.

Unification of Germany (1815–71)

The old guard had to be dragged kicking and screaming into a national unity that threatened time-honoured prerogatives. Prussia had nominally abolished the serf-like status of its peasants, but the *Junker* gentry continued to exercise local police powers, to hunt on peasant land and to enjoy tax exemptions. The aristocracy controlled the civil administration and still dominated the army officer corps. Southern Germany was more democratic, but factory owners were worried by manual workers returning from abroad with dangerous ideas of social protest.

Prominent in the German unity movement were the nationwide student fraternities (*Burschenschaften*) whose members dressed in black tunics with red epaulettes, gold oak leaves and a sash of black, red and gold. Their ideals ambiguously combined freedom and democracy with a xenophobic nationalism—no foreigners, no Jews allowed. At an impassioned 1817

"DEUTSCHLAND, DEUTSCHLAND ..."

The German national anthem was originally a drinking song, written on British soil. Professor Heinrich Hoffmann von Fallersleben wrote it on the North Sea island of Heligoland, then a British possession. The professor offered as its last two lines:

"Clink your glasses and cry as one: Hurrah for the German fatherland!"

But it is the anthem's first line that has caused the most confusion. *"Deutschland, Deutschland über alles,"* (Germany, Germany above all) has always been taken to champion a national supremacy over all other countries. In fact, at a time of continuing rivalries between Prussia and other German states, the professor wanted to exhort the people to place Germany, Germany above all claims of merely regional allegiance. It became the official anthem only in 1922, was dropped during the Nazi era, and then retrieved by West Germany in 1952. To avoid any misunderstanding, it is now sung beginning at the third verse with the unimpeachable *"Einigkeit und Recht und Freiheit"* (unity, justice and freedom).

---

meeting in Thuringia's Wartburg Castle, they called for equality before the law and freedom of opinion and of the press, and saw no contradiction in then proceeding to burn conservative history texts and law books. The assassination of conservative writer August von Kotzebue by a student two years later brought about a massive police crackdown.

Bourgeois liberals worked out progressive constitutions for Bavaria, Württemberg, Baden and Brunswick. Popular revolts imposed similar reforms on Saxony and Hesse. At the University of Göttingen, Jakob and Wilhelm Grimm set aside their study of fairy tales to join a protest movement forcing the reactionary King Ernst August of Hanover to introduce a semblance of constitutional government.

Repression was tougher than ever. Many free spirits, including the poet Heinrich Heine, were forced to emigrate. After students freed prisoners in Frankfurt as part of a plan to raid the Bundestag in 1833, 204 *Burschenschafter* in Berlin were imprisoned for high treason. Ignored by liberals and student nationalists, the new industrial proletariat found a champion in Trier-born journalist Karl Marx. His ideas to rid the workers of their chains were developed in the columns of the Cologne *Rheinische Zeitung* before he was exiled to Paris in the 1840s, and then to Brussels and London. Meanwhile, national unity was furthered physically by the expanding traffic on roads, rivers, canals and railways. A German Customs Union abolished the centuries-old system of multiple customs frontiers between German states. Otherwise patriots had to rely on symbols. In 1842, completion of the two great spires on Cologne cathedral (700 years after its foundation) provided the occasion for a national celebration. At the inauguration, Prussia's

King Friedrich Wilhelm IV declared it a "work expressing all Germans' sense of brotherhood". Back in Berlin he continued to resist any constitutional reforms which might make that German sense of brotherhood a reality.

It took another French revolution, in 1848, to spark open revolts in favour of democratic parliamentary government. In Berlin, popular rallies in cafés and beer halls around the Tiergarten park began peacefully but turned violent with news of arch-reactionary Metternich's fall in Vienna. The Prussian king tried to pacify a crowd in front of his palace by promising press and other freedoms, but a nervous military response to demonstrators ended in riots with 97 dead and 1,000

Prophet without honour. The city of Trier was never quite sure how much to make of the fact that Karl Marx was born there.

prisoners. Parliament elected a liberal government, rendered impotent by an army enraged by laws ending the death penalty and aristocratic privileges. In Frankfurt, left-wing democrats pushed for an American-style republic, but lost out to the moderate liberals' proposal for a Prussian-led constitutional monarchy. At the end of the year, the bourgeois-dominated National Assembly in the Paulskirche voted a charter of basic rights.

Four months later, the Prussian king spurned the German crown as "a dog-collar to chain me to the revolution of 1848". Friedrich Wilhelm IV wanted none of this parliamentary democracy and was ready to use force to stop it. He withdrew the Prussian delegation from the assembly and sent in his army to help crush revolts in Saxony, the Bavarian Palatinate and Baden. A new lullaby was heard in the cottages:

*"Sleep, my child, sleep tight,
The Prussians pass tonight."*

Finally a man appeared on the scene who decided that if a Prussian-led Germany was inevitable, it must be achieved on Prussia's own terms. Recalled in 1862 from the embassy in Paris, Otto von Bismarck became prime minister to the new king, Wilhelm I (1861–88). The no-nonsense Pomeranian *Junker* immediately declared the new rules of the game: "The great questions of the day will not be decided by speeches and majority resolutions—that was the error of 1848 and 1849—but through iron and blood." This was the argument with which he pushed the king's military reforms through the Prussian budget committee. It became his principle in dealing with the rest of Germany—and Europe.

Austria and Prussia had been vying for German leadership since the Congress of Vienna. In 1864, Bismarck forced a showdown after a dispute with Denmark for control of the two border provinces of Schleswig and Holstein. Denmark's claim to the territories (despite a pre-

COLD IRON AND WARM BLOOD

Behind Bismarck's tough, ruthless exterior was a sentimental softy, if not exactly struggling to get out, then at least making an occasional squeak. He was not much of a soldier. When obliged to enlist for a year at Potsdam, the future Iron Chancellor complained, "I have told them I feel pain when I raise my right arm."

He was an unashamed snob. At university he left his fraternity because he could not bear all those bourgeois radicals, preferring the frivolous but at least aristocratic company of the *Studentenkorps*. His king's Hohenzollern origins were to Bismarck just those of "a Swabian family no better than mine".

In fact, he hated country life among the landed gentry, relieving the boredom by seducing the daughters of his peasants. As a civil servant in Aachen, he pursued a series of English girls, notably a Leicestershire lady for whom he gave up his job in a wild chase across Germany. At Biarritz, he fell in love with a Russian ambassador's wife— Katharina was 22 and he pushing 50. Without ever compromising his solid marriage to the pious Lutheran Johanna, he carried Katharina's onyx medallion on his watch chain for the rest of his life.

Four times he wept in public—after his first public speech, after victory over the Austrians at Sadowa, after being named prime minister, and after being dismissed 28 years later.

His life's ambition anticipated Frank Sinatra: "I want to make music, but I want to do it my way or not at all."

dominantly German population) ended in capitulation to a joint invasion of Prussian and Austrian armies. Rather than accept a docile share-out of the spoils, Bismarck suddenly turned revolutionary. He terrified Austria by proposing universal suffrage to elect a new German parliament that would decide who got what. Austria's protest was met with an aggressive Prussian march through Holstein. As the Habsburg troops sailed from Kiel, a Prussian brass band played Austria's national anthem on the harbour.

By 1866, Bismarck's provocative bluff made war inevitable. The bulk of the German Confederation, led by Saxony, Hanover and Hesse, sided with Austria. However, in Austrian Bohemia, the Prussian army won the decisive battle of Sadowa (*Königgrätz*) against Austria and its allies. Bismarck ended Austrian claims to German hegemony, but resisted King Wilhelm's desire to humiliate the

Otto von Bismarck in proud, military pose (see *opposite*).

Habsburgs by marching into Vienna. While the south German states signed mutual defence treaties with Prussia, the rest formed a North German Confederation (*Norddeutscher Bund*) with Bismarck as its chancellor.

Finishing touches to German national unity were provided by Napoleon III. Fearing German encirclement, he insisted that Prussia refuse to support a Hohenzollern candidate for the Spanish throne. Taking the waters at Bad Ems in July 1870, Wilhelm politely told the French envoy he could not submit to such browbeating. Back in Berlin, Bismarck published an edited version of the Bad Ems telegram that made the terms of the king's refusal much less polite. France declared war.

What is frequently known as the Franco-Prussian War should more properly be called Franco-German, because the war at last brought the German states together. The challenge of their historic enemy created the necessary national solidarity. Military strategists agree that the Germans won the war because their generals had learned to study railway timetables. Logistics were revolutionized. Trains from all over Germany moved 500,000 troops to the front in 18 days. The French were slower to mobilize their 290,000 men and let the Germans take the initiative. They swept through Alsace and Lorraine to crush the bulk of the French army at Sedan on 2 September, six weeks after crossing the frontier. Victory was complete by the end of January, 1871.

The German Reich (1871–1918)

Ten days before the ceasefire, the German Reich was proclaimed in the Galerie des Glaces at Versailles, with Wilhelm I as its Kaiser. The French contribution to the new Germany included Alsace, Lorraine and war reparations of 5 billion francs.

The southern states were hesitant in accepting Prussia's dominant role. Chancellor Bismarck bought the support of Bavaria's Ludwig II by paying him a secret pension from the confiscated fortune of the deposed King of Hanover.

Prussia's effective veto in the ruling council enabled it to block constitutional change in the direction of parliamentary democracy. Thus, on the Prussian model, the chancellor and his government were chosen at the pleasure of the Kaiser, not by parliamentary vote.

The new Reich's early years were dominated by a struggle between Church and state (*Kulturkampf*). Catholics opposed Protestant-controlled state interference in matters of schooling, marriage and Church appointments. Bismarck wanted to eliminate Church influence in politics. In the end, politics forced him into concessions to gain Catholic central party votes for protectionist customs duties during an economic recession. The struggle left a scar on Catholic–Protestant relations.

Politically, the major challenge to Bismarckian conservatism came from the rise of the Social Democratic Party (SPD). Founded by August Bebel in 1869, it was garnering half a million votes by 1877 and giving Bismarck what he called "nightmares of revolution". He imagined the socialists to be the barricade radicals of 1848, not the rather staid trade unionists they had in fact become. Two assassination attempts on the Kaiser in 1878, neither of them by socialists, provided the pretext for anti-socialist laws banning meetings and publications. Over 1,500 party members were jailed for activity threatening to "overthrow the state and social order". Bismarck tried to win over the workers with social reforms—pensions, medical and accident insurance—but strikes increased and the SPD vote grew to 1,427,000 by 1890. Only an obstructive voting system and liberal–conservative coalition kept Germany's largest party from proper representation in parliament. Bismarck tried to resurrect the spectre of socialist revolution as an excuse for revoking the constitution and destroying the SPD. The new Kaiser Wilhelm II (1888–1918), resolutely his own man, refused the Chancellor's advice. Bismarck resigned. With all imperial dignitaries except the Kaiser there to see him off, Bismarck described his departure by train from Berlin as "a state funeral with full honours".

German expansionism was driven by its fast-growing economy. Krupp, AEG, Siemens, IG Farben and Hamburg-America Shipping all needed new trade outlets and more raw materials. Germany had to move fast to catch up with other colonial powers—France, Britain, the Netherlands and Belgium. Chancellor Bülow expressed his master's ambitions: "We also want our place in the sun." Bismarck had been reluctant to get involved in overseas colonies, leaving them to fly-by-night charter companies. Under Wilhelm II, government officials and army units brought a little Prussian order to African Togo, Cameroon, South-West Africa and Tanganyika, and to Pacific New Guinea, known then as Kaiser-Wilhelms-Land and the Bismarck Archipelago. The Germans were very active in China, but made themselves especially unpopular by their over-enthusiastic role in the international force that crushed the Boxer Rebellion of 1900.

Seeking a Mediterranean port for his navy, the Kaiser aggravated relations with France by challenging its privileged position in Morocco. After a provocative visit to Tangiers in 1906, he sent a gunboat to Agadir five years later to protect German merchants against the French military presence, despite the fact that there were no German merchants in Agadir.

Yet Germany, allied now with Austria, was no more aggressive than its European rivals. The Anglo-French Entente Cordiale linked to Russia looked to Germany like a less than cordial encirclement. In the arms race, to counter the German challenge to its naval supremacy, Britain's new *Dreadnought* class of battleship was clearly aimed at Germany.

At home, very few seemed willing, let alone able, to stop the rush to war. Army chief-of-staff Helmuth von Moltke, Jr. expressed succinctly the army's position in 1912: "War is inevitable; the sooner, the better." Conservatives in a united front with Pan-German nationalists saw war as a healing factor to purge the socialist disease and resolve social conflicts in a wave of patriotism. Conquering new territories would open up broader horizons. Out of national solidarity, the SPD voted for the military budget in 1913. Only a few radical socialists led by Polish-born Rosa Luxemburg campaigned against war.

In the summer of 1914, the murder of the Austrian archduke in Sarajevo brought what many in Europe seemed to want. Germany sided with Austria against Russia, whose French and British allies joined the fray. Apart from the battles in the annexed territories of Alsace-Lorraine and a shortlived Russian invasion of East Prussia, World War I was waged entirely outside Germany, but even so, German casualties numbered 1,808,000 dead (French 1,385,000, British 907,000). Supreme Army Command dominated by General

Erich Ludendorff exercised a virtual dictatorship in continuing the war regardless of the government back home. Even as armistice was being negotiated in November 1918, the navy based at Kiel, desperate to redeem its honour, wanted to steam out for one last suicidal battle, but the sailors rebelled against their admirals. Elsewhere soldiers deserted *en masse* and a wave of rebellion that spread across the country brought down the Reich and paved the way for a republic.

The Weimar Republic (1918–33)

Between World War I and the Nazi dictatorship, Germany's first attempt at democracy was both exhilarating and desperate. The Weimar Republic that followed the abdication of the Kaiser was ultimately doomed as much by the hesitancy of its supporters as by its enemies' cynical brutality. Weimar culture was brilliantly creative: the boldness, even brazenness of its artists contrasting sharply with the timidity of most of the political leaders.

Reforms were implemented—the women's vote, an eight-hour day and other trade union demands—but not for long. In the revolutionary atmosphere following the war, SPD leader Friedrich Ebert, the first chancellor of the new republic, gave priority to order over social justice. A year after the Russian Revolution, revolts in Hamburg, Cologne, Berlin and Munich followed the Bolshevik model in forming workers' and soldiers' councils (soviets). Ebert called out the army to crush them. Leaders were assassinated, Karl Liebknecht and Rosa Luxemburg in Berlin, Kurt Eisner in Munich. The killings became for the Communists symbols of the SPD's betrayal of the workers, a major obstacle to

any left-wing alliance against the Nazis, and evoked again in 1945 in the Communist–SPD antagonism in East Germany.

The republic's constitution was drawn up in Weimar not only because, as the home of Goethe and Schiller, it represented the best of German civilization, but because it was also safely remote from troublesome Berlin and Munich. Sadly, the document did not provide the necessary protection for the republic's noble democratic aims. A surfeit of small parties elected by proportional representation prevented a clear majority. Plebiscites enabled unscrupulous minorities to obstruct social reforms voted by parliament. The president's sweeping powers included calling out the army and suspending civil rights in time of unrest, imagined in 1919 to be an exception but, in fact, routine by 1930.

Things were not made easier by the vindictive Versailles peace treaty. The victors attributed to Germany and Austria sole responsibility for World War I. "*Le Boche paiera tout*" ("The Hun will pay for everything"), said French prime minister Georges Clemenceau. He took uncommon pleasure in having the treaty signed in the same Galerie des Glaces in which the German Reich was proclaimed in 1871. Reparations included 60 per cent of its coal production, 25 per cent of its pharmaceuticals, plus shipping, railway stock, construction material and cattle. Germany gave up all its colonies, ceded Alsace and Lorraine back to France, parts of Silesia and Prussia to Poland and Danzig (now Gdansk) to the auspices of the League of Nations as a Free City.

The treaty's harsh conditions further shocked a German people already traumatized by the gap between pre-war euphoria and post-war reality. Ignoring their responsibility for those earlier hopes, conservatives attacked the social-ist–liberal coalition for signing a "peace of shame" (*Schandfrieden*). They nurtured the "stab-in-the-back" legend of a fatherland betrayed by left-wing revolutionaries in a war that could have been won—a major argument in Hitler's rise to power.

In 1923, economic crisis highlighted by rocketing inflation made it increasingly difficult to pay war reparations. The French refused concessions and its army occupied the Ruhr to enforce industrial deliveries. Workers went on strike. The French confiscated German funds and arrested strike leaders. Right-wing groups retaliated with sabotage and violence. Cut off from the Ruhr supplies, Germany suffered crippling unemployment, and inflation reached surreal proportions. Less than 30 per cent of the total labour force was fully employed. A dollar worth 9 Marks in 1919 rose to 17,972 Marks by January 1923 and 4,200 million Marks by November. Black market profiteering was rife, as was ruthless speculation by men like industrialist Hugo Stinnes who accumulated 4,554 companies. At all levels of society, people responded to the crisis with a frantic spree of dancing—lunchtime, teatime and all night long. In November, the national Reichsbank issued a new Mark equal to 1 billion inflationary Marks, pegging its dollar value to 4.2 Marks. The crisis receded but left an indelible scar on the national consciousness. To this day, the people will accept any effort or sacrifice rather than face inflation.

At the height of the hysteria a collection of rabid nationalists and disillusioned army veterans met in the Bürgerbraükeller, a Munich beer hall. Inspired by Mussolini's fascist March on Rome a year earlier, the National Socialist Workers Party of Germany (Nationalsozialistische Arbeiterpartei Deutschlands) prepared a march to seize power in Berlin. With the support of wartime leader General Ludendorff, the Nazis of Adolf Hitler were entering history. However, their Beer Hall Putsch ended almost before it had begun in an armed clash with Munich police, killing 16 "martyrs" and 3 police. Ludendorff gave himself up. Hitler fled and was captured hiding in a clothes cupboard. Had the trial judge applied the law to deport this Austrian citizen for high treason, his career might have ended in personal farce rather than global tragedy, but judges viscerally hostile to the republic habitually treated right-wing radicals as "patriots" and left-wing agitators as "criminals". Hitler was permitted to use his trial to launch a violent tirade against the Weimar Republic. He served nine months in jail and in December his followers won 14 seats in the national elections. The real march had begun.

From 1924 to 1930, Gustav Stresemann, the republic's outstanding statesman, skilfully negotiated reduction of war reparations and evacuation of French forces from the Rhineland. For his pains, this pillar of the liberal establishment won the Nobel Peace Prize and the hatred of right-wing opponents for "anti-national Europeanism". At home, he streamlined industrial production, but the subsequent rise in unemployment alienated the far left. Making friends in the Weimar Republic was not easy.

Amid the world economic crisis of 1929, with unemployment at 3 million, the Nazis made their political breakthrough. Blaming Germany's woes on Jews, freemasons and Communists, they scored important successes in regional elections, entering government for the first time with Wilhelm Frick as Thuringia's interior minister. In national elections a year later, they became the country's second largest party, winning 6,400,000 votes. The SPD was still the largest party, but its resistance to the Nazi surge was weakened by the Communists' refusal to form a common front.

Successive conservative governments under Heinrich Brüning and Franz von Papen consistently underestimated the Nazi threat. After a first meeting in 1931, the President, Field Marshal Paul von Hindenburg, complained Hitler had talked his head off, a decidedly queer fellow who could never become chancellor but might be able to run the post office. A few months later, Hitler won over 13 million votes in his presidential challenge to the old soldier. Financed by Ruhr industrialists like Fritz Thyssen, Hamburg shipping magnates, insurance companies and the Deutsche Bank, the Nazis won 230 seats in the 1932 Reichstag elections. Hitler's deputy, Hermann Göring, became Speaker. It proved impossible to form a coalition government without the Nazis, and on 30 January 1933 Hindenburg was obliged to name Hitler chancellor. Only two other Nazis were in the cabinet, Frick and Göring. With Papen as vice-chancellor and conservatives in key economics, labour and defence ministries, financier Alfred Hugenberg, holding the economics portfolio, felt able to comment: "This way we have Hitler fenced in."

The Third Reich

One of the many myths surrounding Hitler's dictatorship is that it began, to use the commonly accepted term, with a "seizure of power" (*Machtergreifung*). Not at all. Power was handed to him in 1933 by the constitution. Voters had made the Nazis the biggest, but not yet totally dominant party. To escape the conserva-

tive straitjacket in his cabinet, Hitler persuaded President Hindenburg to dissolve parliament and call new elections in March. A week before the vote, the Reichstag was set on fire. Dutch Communist Marinus van der Lubbe was arrested on the spot. He confessed but insisted he had acted alone. No conclusive proof has been offered for either a Nazi or a Communist plot, but Hitler had a perfect excuse to eliminate his political enemies. In the tense pre-election atmosphere, he presented the fire as part of a wider national threat, justifying a presidential emergency decree to protect the people and state. The government was empowered to arrest 4,000 Communists, most of them sent off to the first concentration camps—Dachau, near Munich, and Oranienburg, outside Berlin. Others fled into exile. The decree providing a legal basis for the Nazi totalitarian state was in force "till further order", that is, until 1945.

The last semblance of a free election gave the Nazis "only" 44 per cent of the vote, imposing another coalition with the conservatives, but Hitler's personal ascendancy over Hindenburg removed all further obstacles to absolute power. His propaganda impresario Joseph Goebbels brilliantly staged the passage of powers in a crypto-religious ceremony of national unity. With the Reichstag gutted, the new parliament met in the Potsdam Garrison Church where Hindenburg grasped Hitler's hands across the tomb of Frederick the Great. The torch of Prussian-German tradition was symbolically handed to the Nazis.

Two days later, the parliament voted itself out of existence by giving Hitler's government an Enabling Act (*Ermächtigungsgesetz*) to legislate without parliament. As storm troopers patrolled the assembly during the vote, the conservatives and liberals supported the Nazi proposal, with only the SPD voting against—the Communists having been excluded. One of the first laws banned the SPD, while the other parties dissolved themselves. By July 1933, another law had forbidden formation of any new parties. Germany was declared a one-party state.

After an impressively violent role in the March election campaign, the million-strong SA storm troopers felt they had not been properly rewarded. Impatient for the spoils of their "national revolution", they ran amok, helping themselves in raids on banks and shops. To satisfy conservatives' complaints, Hitler sent in the SS to round up and kill dozens of SA leaders. Hitler profited from the "Night of the Long Knives" (30 June 1934) to settle a few personal scores, the 83 murders including renegade ex-Nazis and politicians who had nothing to do with the party at all. The SA was reduced to paramilitary training activities, and the SS of Heinrich Himmler became the Nazi state's most powerful organization. Hindenburg congratulated Hitler on restoring law and order. The president died a month later, succeeded by Hitler with the new title of *Führer*.

The Nazis won popular support, less with the nebulous new sense of national identity, pride and purpose than with jobs. Public works on the new highways, housing construction, rearmament and military conscription cut unemployment from 26 per cent in 1933 to 2 per cent by 1938 (at a time when the US figure was still at 26 per cent). Relations with the Church were more delicate. Hostile to the Weimar Republic and its atheist Marxists, the Protestant Church had high hopes for the new regime. Scepticism set in with Hitler's imposition of army pastor Ludwig Müller as Reich Bishop, but protest remained muted. Catholics were also ambivalent. At first the Church excommunicated Catholic Nazis, but it dropped its hostility after the Concordat between Reich and Vatican (July 1933). This safeguarded the German Catholics' churches, property and schools in exchange for their abstention from politics. Pope Pius XI commented: "The new Germany has waged a decisive battle against Bolshevism and the movement of the godless." The universities were not exactly hotbeds of resistance. Anti-semitism had long been rife in student fraternities, and if many professors were dismayed by the cultural philistines running the country, others were ready to denounce Jewish or left-wing colleagues to further their own careers. Students and professors participated

---

STORM TROOPS

Paramilitary groups of all political colours loved marching—and bashing their opponents. The Nazis had their SA storm troopers (*Sturmabteilung*) and SS "defence squadron" (*Schutzstaffel*). Troops of the conservatives' *Stahlhelm* (Steel Helmet) were marginally less brutal, but just as hostile to the republic. The Communists responded with their Red Front-Fighters (*Roter Frontkampfer*), while the SPD sought to defend its meetings with the more mild-mannered groups of the *Reichsbanner*.

*B*erlin's Kaiser-Wilhelm memorial church, left a bombed-out shell after World War II. The modern church beside it symbolized hope for the city's isolated western sector.

in the nationwide book-burning of May 1933, when bonfires were made of works not only by Jewish authors like Heine, Freud and Zweig, but also Voltaire, H G Wells, Thomas and Heinrich Mann. A century earlier, Heine had noted: "They begin by burning books and end by burning people."

FOR BLOOD AND HONOUR

In contrast to the brutal elimination of his Marxist enemies, the Communists and SPD, Hitler's treatment of his major obsession, the Jews (503,000 in Germany in 1933, highly integrated, often through intermarriage) was at first quite moderate. In April 1933, the Nazis started a national boycott of Jewish companies, lawyers and doctors. Jews were excluded from the civil service and then stripped of German citizenship. Anti-semitic practices were formulated in the Nuremberg Laws of 1935 on Reich citizenship and racial purity: "for the protection of German blood and German honour". Beyond outlawing "Aryan" marriage with Jews, the sexuality of the racist obsession was underlined in the ban on Jewish employment of "Aryan" female servants under 45. On 9 November 1938 the hatred exploded into widespread violence. The pretext was the assassination of a German diplomat by a young Jew protesting against the deportation of his Polish parents living in Germany. Like the Reichstag fire, this served Hitler as evidence of a wider plot, the work of "world Jewry". Party leaders meeting with Hitler and Göring in Munich to commemorate the 1923 Beer Hall Putsch were urged to stir up the people's righteous anger. Jewish shops across the country were demolished, 250 synagogues burned down, 90 Jews murdered, 25,000 others sent to detention camps and Jewish property confiscated to "pay" for the damage of Kristallnacht (Night of Crystal, because of the broken glass). Henceforth, no one could claim ignorance of Nazi intentions.

The main aim of Hitler's foreign policy was to give the German people appropriate living-space (*Lebensraum*) by reconquering lands lost in the Treaty of Versailles and expanding further east. France gave him a green light by letting the German army breach the treaty with its occupation of the Rhineland in 1936. In the same year, the army tried out its new artillery and aircraft in the Spanish Civil War. It marched into Austria in 1938 (where Hitler was welcomed home as a conquering hero) and Czechoslovakia a year later. France and Britain protested. In August 1939, Hitler made a non-aggression pact with Stalin, initially to gain a free hand in Poland. The Germans crossed the Polish border on 1 September, unleashing the bloodiest war mankind had ever known.

World War II

By the summer of 1941, Hitler was at the height of his popularity in Germany, projecting the image of a worthy successor to Frederick the Great and Bismarck. The rapid victory in Poland, followed by the occupation of Denmark and Norway and then the sweep through Belgium to take France, made the German war machine look invincible. Even the air force's failure to open up Britain to naval invasion seemed only temporary. Three weeks after attacking the Soviet Union in June 1941, spectacular victories promised another quick success, but Russia's vast spaces and the courage of its people slowed Germany's *Blitzkrieg* to a halt in the snows of winter, almost within sight of Moscow. At this moment Japan chose to start a Pacific war by bombing the US fleet at Pearl Harbor. Remarkably, Hitler now declared war on the United States. At the same time, he returned to his old obsession, the destruction of the Jews. Security police chief Reinhard Heydrich was given the Führer's order to organize the "final solution for the Jewish question". Himmler had already prepared the gassing facilities at Auschwitz. The extermination of millions of Jews, Slavs, gypsies and other "enemies of the Reich", conducted mostly outside Germany in Eastern European camps, became fully operative at a time when the war began to be lost.

Back home in the winter of 1942–43, news of Rommel's defeat in the African desert and the catastrophe of Stalingrad shocked the people lulled by months of propaganda promising victory. At the University of Munich, two students and a professor were executed for distributing anti-Nazi tracts, but this White Rose (*Weisse Rose*) movement was an isolated instance at a time when opposition to Hitler was seen as betrayal of the nation at war. On 20 July 1944, with the western Allies liberating Italy and France and the Russians on the counter-offensive, German army officers led by Count Schenk von Stauffenberg made an abortive attempt on Hitler's life. Over 200 implicated in the plot were executed and some 7,000 others arrested. Hitler retreated to his bunker as the Russians closed on Berlin, and British and American bombers devastated German cities. Among the worst hit were Dresden, Cologne, Düsseldorf, Bremen, Kiel, Hamburg and Berlin itself. On 30 April 1945, Hitler committed suicide. Germany capitulated eight days later.

The Road Back to National Unity

Amputated in 1918, Germany seemed at first to be hung, drawn and quartered in 1945. The Allies cut the land up into four occupation zones—and Berlin, too, situated inside the Soviet zone. The national map was drawn afresh to return, yet again, Alsace and Lorraine to France and cede territories east of the Oder and Neisse rivers to Poland and the Soviet Union. An International Military Tribunal at Nuremberg hanged the major surviving Nazi leaders (Goebbels, Himmler and Göring had all, like Hitler, committed suicide). However, the United States persuaded Britain and France not to repeat the mistake of Versailles in leaving the vanquished Germany totally destitute and resentful. The western zones gradually coordinated their economic activities, allowing West Germany to rebuild with the aid of the Americans' Marshall Plan of 1947. Stalin refused the same aid offered to East Germany (and his other Eastern European satellites) as an attempt to incorporate the region into the American capitalist system. The front line of the Cold War ran through the middle of Germany. Resenting the rapid resurrection of the Ruhr, the industrial backbone of Germany's military potential, Stalin countered in 1948 by isolating West Berlin. He blocked the land routes from West Germany and cut off all supplies of electricity and coal. The Western Allies broke the blockade with an "air lift", flying in vital supplies. The blockade hardened anti-Communist feeling in the West and ended French resistance to uniting the three western zones in one West Germany.

The Federal Republic of Germany was created in May 1949 with a democratic constitution drawn up under the strong influence of US and West European political scientists and advisors, correcting the weaknesses of the Weimar Republic and avoiding the abuses of the Third Reich. It instituted a federal chancellor answerable directly to a strong parliament, the president's role honorific and moral rather than political, and 11 states (*Länder*) with a healthy autonomy in local affairs. The first chancellor was Konrad Adenauer, a crusty 73-year-old Christian Democrat who was the former mayor of Cologne and had once before been candidate for the post, back in 1923. A champion of Rhineland separatism under the Weimar Republic, he now anchored the new federal republic firmly to the Western alliance, distrustful of any attempts to promote unification with Communist East Germany.

In October 1949, the Soviet zone became the German Democratic Republic. Stalin had made of it a buffer against the capitalist West. To rebuild its own economy, the Soviet Union appropriated East German industrial equipment, raw materials and food. The country was led by Walter Ulbricht, a hard-line Stalinist formed by wartime exile in Moscow. The SPD was swallowed by his SED (Sozialistische Einheitspartei Deutschlands—German Socialist Unity Party), and other Christian, liberal and peasants' parties were lumped together in an impotent National Front. In the political uncertainty after Stalin's death in 1953, East Germans protested against forced collectivization of the farms and harsh productivity demands in the factories. Soviet troops repressed the strikes and street riots.

Motivated to overcome and perhaps forget the horrors of the Third Reich, the West Germans achieved a phenomenal economic recovery. The dynamic banks of Frankfurt, the industrial energy of the Ruhr and the rebuilt ports of Hamburg and Bremen made the country a powerful founder-member of the European Common Market. Central to this was the new Franco-German alliance cemented by the personal friendship between Adenauer and General de Gaulle. West Germany's democracy was functioning healthily enough for a new German army, kept strictly under parliamentary control, to be accepted into the NATO alliance. Military conscription would break away from the old professional army traditions. Old Nazi rocket experts might be working for the Americans and Russians, but there would be no German atomic weapons.

West German prosperity was visible on television programmes picked up inside East Germany, and especially in the ostentatious shop-window of capitalism that West Berlin had become. Hundreds of thousands of refugees were leaving East Germany each year through the open frontier between East and West Berlin. They numbered 2,700,000 by 1960, and increasingly included engineers, doctors and other professionals. The drain had become economically unacceptable. Ulbricht persuaded the Soviet Union to let him build the Berlin Wall on 13 August 1961.

However, the prosperity also had its impact on West German politics. The Adenauer years had been marked by anti-Communism, bourgeois virtues of hard work and efficiency and a certain conservative conformism. The 1960s brought a new rebellious spirit to the consumer society. Germans could afford to think about social equality and women's emancipation, and devote some of their national wealth to helping the Third World.

Representing these values, the SPD under Willy Brandt joined a coalition with the Christian Democrats in 1966. Three years later, Brandt became chancellor, drawing on his experience as mayor of West Berlin to ease relations with Eastern Europe, his celebrated *Ostpolitik*. In 1970 he signed the Warsaw Treaty guaranteeing Poland's Oder-Neisse frontier and renouncing German claims to territories ceded to Poland in 1945. Just as significant was his gesture of kneeling at the monument to Jews killed in the Warsaw Ghetto by the Germans in 1943. He brought the two Germanys closer together by his 1970 visit to Erfurt, negotiating increased trade and more contacts for families divided by the Wall. In 1974 he also signed a conciliatory treaty with Czechoslovakia.

At home, the spirit of revolt hardened against the continuing materialism of the 1970s. Verbal violence deteriorated into terrorism, most notably the Baader-Meinhof gang striking at bankers, industrialists and government officials. Police cracked down hard to break up the groups. Protest then took a milder form with ecological campaigns in which the old German mystic attachment to nature was translated into a modern political party, the Greens. In the 1982 parliament which elected Christian Democrat Helmut Kohl as the new chancellor, the Greens brought a breath of fresh air with their open-necked shirts, jeans, anoraks and flowers for everybody. Less attractive were the neo-Nazi Republicans making an impact at the end of the 80s, but West German democracy seemed strong enough to resist.

However ugly a symbol the Berlin Wall had been—the sour admission of ideological failure—halting the flow of refugees did stabilize East German society. Under Erich Honecker, desperate hostility turned into sullen acceptance. To cheer people up, investment in steel, mining and chemicals was reduced in favour of housing, cars and other consumer goods. This was made possible in part by heavy West German subsidies, but also by an economy that, for all its failings, had become the strongest in the Eastern bloc. From 1972, Western embassies were established in East Berlin. East Germans made an effort to win respect by spectacular success in sport, particularly at the Olympic Games where they almost overdid it by threatening Soviet supremacy.

Freedom of expression was still not possible. Dissident intellectuals like singer-poet Wolf Biermann were expelled. Art remained stultifyingly official. In 1987, a Western rock concert near the Wall loudly amplified eastwards attracted East Berlin youths who chanted: "The Wall must fall! The Wall must fall!" An ecological group began meeting in Leipzig to campaign against industrial pollution and nuclear weapons. In May 1989, East German holiday-makers took advantage of Hungary's newly opened borders to flee via Austria to West Germany. In the summer, others took refuge in West Germany's embassies in Prague and Warsaw. East Germany was swept up in the wave of Eastern European liberation unleashed by the reforms of Mikhail Gorbachov. His October visit to East Berlin for the German Democratic Republic's 40th anniversary left it clear that Soviet troops would no longer support its moribund regime. On 9 November 1989, the Berlin Wall was opened.

In 1990, politically and economically bankrupt, East Germany bowed off the world stage and West Germany braced itself to foot the huge financial bill of unification. Euphoria gave way to grim realism as the scale of the task became clear. To bring anything like Western levels of prosperity to the "former East" would take decades. It was decided that Berlin would again be the capital, although no date was fixed for the move from Bonn. In the first free elections as one united country since 1932 the Germans had at last won the right to determine their own national destiny.

HISTORICAL LANDMARKS

Prehistory	600,000 BC	*Homo heidelbergensis* hunting in Rhineland.
	50,000 BC	Neanderthal man.
	700 BC	Germanic tribes from Scandinavia occupy N Germany.
Roman Times	58 BC	Julius Caesar sets empire frontier at Rhine.
	AD 9	Hermann's Germans defeat Romans at Teutoburger Wald.
	314	First German bishopric founded at Trier.
Middle Ages	800	Charlemagne (Karl der Grosse) crowned Holy Roman Emperor.
	936	Otto I crowned King of Germany at Aachen.
	12th c.	Munich, Lübeck and other major cities founded.
	1211	German princes assert authority in electing Emperor Friedrich II.
	1282	Merchants found Hanseatic League.
	1348	Black Death decimates German population.
	1448	Gutenberg sets up printing press in Mainz.
	1495	Worms Reichstag creates imperial law court.

Reformation and Counter-Reformation

	1517	Martin Luther nails 95 Theses to Wittenberg church door.
	1521	Luther excommunicated.
	1524–25	Peasants' War against feudalism, opposed by Luther.
	1529	Movement named Protestant after princes lodge "Protestation" against Catholics.
	1555	Augsburg truce between Protestant and Catholic princes.
	1556	Jesuits move into Bavaria.
Thirty Years'	1620	Palatinate Protestants routed by Spanish.
War	1630	Invasion of Gustavus Adolphus of Sweden.
	1648	Germany loses Alsace and Lorraine by Peace of Westphalia.
Emergence of	1701	Friedrich I crowns himself King *in* Prussia.
Prussia	1713–40	Prussian army built by Friedrich Wilhelm I.
	1740–86	Frederick the Great (Friedrich der Grosse) challenges Austrian domination of Germany.
French Revolution	1792	French repel Austro-German army and occupy
and Napoleon		Rhineland.
	1803	Napoleon dismantles Reich; princes expropriate Church lands.
	1812	100,000 German troops join Grande Armée's disastrous campaign in Russia.
	1813	Napoleon defeated at Leipzig "Battle of the Nations".
Towards	1815	Congress of Vienna creates German Confederation.
Unification	1842	Festival of national unity for completion of Cologne cathedral.

	1848	Revolts against absolutist monarchies.
	1862	Bismarck prime minister of Prussia.
	1864	Schleswig-Holstein seized from Denmark.
	1866	Prussia defeats Austria at Sadowa (Bohemia).
	1869	Social Democratic Party (SPD) founded.
	1870	Prussian-led German armies invade France.
German Reich	1871	Prussian king Wilhelm I proclaimed Kaiser at Versailles.
	1882–85	Colonies founded in Africa and Pacific.
	1890	Wilhelm II dismisses Bismarck.
	1898–1912	Navy built to challenge British naval supremacy.
	1906–11	Kaiser provokes France over Morocco.
	1914–18	World War I.
Weimar Republic	1918	November revolutions force Kaiser to flee.
	1919	Versailles Treaty returns Alsace-Lorraine to France, cedes eastern territories to Poland.
	1923	Hyper-inflation crisis; Hitler's Beer Hall Putsch.
	1924–30	Stresemann's negotiations ease reparation payments; French withdraw from Rhineland.
	1932	Nazis largest party in Reichstag.
Third Reich	1933	Hitler chancellor, becomes dictator after Reichstag fire.
	1935	Nuremberg race laws.
	1936	Berlin Olympics; German army reoccupies Rhineland.
	1938	Full employment achieved; Austria annexed; *Kristallnacht* pogrom against Jews.
	1939	Invasion of Czechoslovakia; Hitler–Stalin pact.
World War II	1939	1 September, Germany invades Poland.
	1940	Denmark, Norway, Benelux and France occupied.
	1941	Operation Barbarossa against Soviet Union; order to complete extermination of Jews; Hitler declares war on United States.
	1943	Defeat at Stalingrad.
	1944	German armies driven back in E Europe and Italy; Allies land in France to begin liberation of W Europe.
	1945	Massive Allied bombing of Dresden, Cologne, Hamburg; Russians take Berlin; Germany capitulates.
Division and Unification	1945	Potsdam summit divides Germany into four zones.
	1947	Marshall Plan for economic recovery.
	1948	Stalin's blockade of West Berlin broken by Western Allies' air-lift.
	1949	Creation of Federal Republic of Germany and German Democratic Republic.
	1953	Soviet troops suppress East German uprising.
	1961	Berlin Wall built to stop flow of refugees.
	1970	Brandt launches *Ostpolitik* in Warsaw.
	1982	Green Party enters West German parliament.
	1989	Berlin Wall opened.
	1990	East and West Germany united on 3 October.

Just the Essentials

On a first-time visit to Germany, you may be overwhelmed by the sheer wealth of choices you have wherever you start. We propose here a few major landmarks to help you establish your priorities.

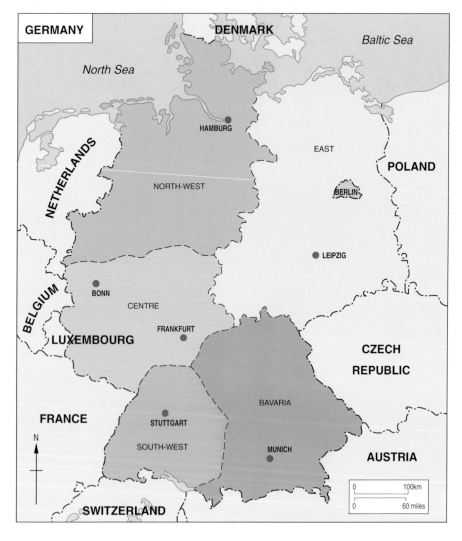

Bavaria

Ottobeuren: baroque masterpiece
Hohenschwangau, Neuschwanstein: royal
  castle follies in Alpine setting
Garmisch-Partenkirchen: great Alpine
  resort
Chiemsee: lake and castle
Romantische Strasse: drive through
  medieval and Renaissance Germany
Würzburg: baroque palace,
  Riemenschneider sculptures
Bamberg: cheerful Gothic and baroque
Nuremberg: home of Dürer
Munich
—Marienplatz: bouncing town centre
—Hofbräuhaus: world's most famous
  beerhall
—Schwabing: lively artists' district
—Englischer Garten: delightful park
—Alte Pinakothek: top art museum
—Deutsches Museum: science made fun

The South-West

Heidelberg: famous university town
Black Forest: woodland rambles,
  chocolate cherry cake
Baden-Baden: spa, casino, horse races
Freiburg: Gothic cathedral
Furtwangen: cuckoo clocks
Stuttgart: culture, Mercedes, Porsche
Ulm: old town charm on Danube
Lake Constance: boat cruises, mellow wine
Reichenau: Romanesque churches
Mainau: sub-tropical gardens
Birnau: baroque abbey-church
Lindau: quaint old streets

The Centre

Cologne: cathedral, art museums
Rhine Valley: castle ruins and Lorelei
Rheingau: best Rhine wines
Mainz: Romanesque cathedral, Gutenberg
  museum
Frankfurt: Goethe's house, cider-taverns
Lahn Valley: romantic river trip to
  Wetzlar and Marburg

The North-West

Hamburg: harbour cruises, elegant water-
  side villas
Lübeck: redbrick Gothic
Sylt: queen of Frisian island resorts
Bremen: fine Renaissance city centre
Walsrode: bird sanctuary
Hildesheim: Romanesque churches
Hamlin: celebrates Pied Piper in
  Renaissance setting
Düsseldorf: fashion centre

Berlin

Kurfürstendamm: city's heartbeat
Tiergarten: "culture in the park"
Reichstag: historic parliament building
Schloss Charlottenburg: Hohenzollerns'
  graceful residence
Egyptian Museum: Nefertiti
Grunewald and Wannsee: forest and lakes
Dahlem museums: major European
  painting and Brücke Expressionists
Brandenburg Gate: symbol of city's unity
Unter den Linden: grand baroque and
  neoclassical avenue
Pergamon Museum: Babylonian
  processional street and Pergamon Altar
Märkisches Museum: eloquent view of
  proletarian Germany

Eastern Germany

Potsdam: Sanssouci, Cecilienhof
Dresden: baroque, porcelain museum,
  opera, European painting
Meissen: cathedral, castle, porcelain
Weimar: Goethe's home, Cranach
  paintings, Bauhaus
Eisenach: Wartburg castle, homes of Bach
  and Luther
Thuringian Forest: ramble along Rennesteig
Harz mountains: witches' Brocken,
  medieval towns
Wittenberg: Luther house and museum,
  Cranach paintings in church
Naumburg: cathedral's landmark Gothic
  sculpture
Baltic Coast: Wismar, Stralsund, Rügen

Going Places with Something Special in Mind

As you travel around the country, you will often notice road signs indicating a route (*Strasse*) of special interest. The best known of these are the *Romantische Strasse* between Würzburg and Füssen and the panoramic *Deutsche Alpenstrasse* along the German Alps. Many more follow, for instance, the vineyards or castles. We propose here a series of Leisure Routes that incorporate a few of the official *Strassen,* but many more of our own concoction. They cater for all kinds of cultural, or simply picturesque tastes. Some can be followed as an itinerary, others show where you can pursue your pet interest in a particular region.

Wine Routes

Germany's vineyards are often beautifully situated on the slopes of river valleys. In towns like Mainz, Rüdesheim, Neustadt or Würzburg, tourist offices can advise about guided tours, wine-tasting or buying wine.

Rheingau

1 RÜDESHEIM
Half-timbered taverns, wine museum.

*G*arrison town for the Romans in the Neckar Valley, imperial citadel for Friedrich Barbarossa, Bad Wimpfen is now a tranquil spa.

2 JOHANNISBERG
Wine cellars in the castle.

3 OESTRICH-WINKEL
Charming old houses.

4 ELTVILLE
Produces champagne-like *Sekt* in a medieval atmosphere.

5 KLOSTER EBERBACH
Monastery that claims to have founded German wine making.

Left Bank

6 MAINZ
Cathedral city; major wine distribution and tasting centre.

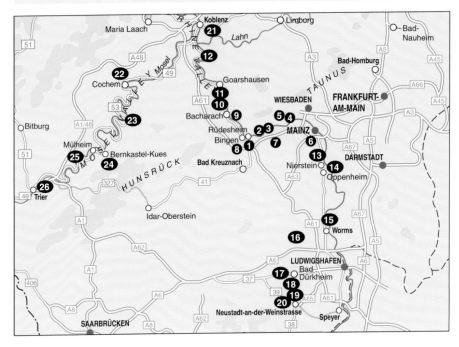

7 INGELHEIM
Rare red-wine vineyards.

8 BINGEN
Good wine-tasting town.

9 BACHARACH
Claims name comes from Bacchus.

10 OBERWESEL
Red and white churches, but wine strictly white.

11 ST GOAR
Castle ruin above vineyards.

12 BOPPARD
Cheerful town with Renaissance church.

Palatinate

13 NIERSTEIN
Connoisseurs' favourite.

A selection of wine routes in central Germany (Rheingau 1–5, Left Bank 6–12, Palatinate 13–20 and Mosel Valley 21–26).

14 OPPENHEIM
Good wines, fine Gothic church.

15 WORMS
Historic cathedral city; first home of popular Liebfraumilch.

16 BOCKENHEIM
North end of Deutsche Weinstrasse.

17 BAD DÜRKHEIM
Drink inside the world's biggest wine barrel.

18 WACHENHEIM
Boasts the region's best wine.

84

19 DEIDESHEIM
Handsome town claims close second.

20 NEUSTADT
Main distribution centre; harvest festival.

Mosel Valley

The wines in this cheerful region enjoy a reputation for delicate bouquet. They come in green bottles to distinguish them from the Rhine wines' brown ones.

21 KOBLENZ
Gateway to compare Mosel and Rhine vintages.

22 COCHEM
View this popular wine-tasting centre from Pinnerkreuz hill.

23 ZELL
Celebrated vineyards visible from Marienburg convent.

24 BERNKASTEL-KUES
Picturesque twin towns straddling river. Romantic market-place and ruins.

25 PIESPORT
Wine famous for its bouquet.

26 TRIER
Romans' distribution centre; see their wineship in the museum.

Franconia

The *Bocksbeutelstrasse* is named after the pleasant Franconian wines' distinctive pot-bellied bottles.

1 WÜRZBURG
Vineyards surround Marienberg citadel; see Baroque palace, too.

2 SOMMERHAUSEN
Fine 16th-century town hall.

3 FRICKENHAUSEN
Medieval ramparts.

4 KITZINGEN
Good place to buy; carnival museum.

5 DETTELBACH
Bristles with rampart towers; try local spicy biscuits with wine.

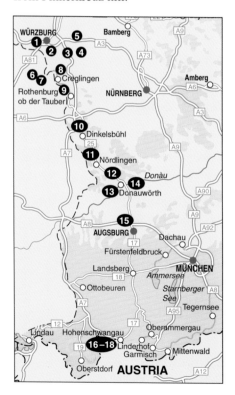

The Franconian wine route (1–5) and the famous Romantische Strasse *tourist route (6–18).*

Romantische Strasse

The most famous of Germany's tourist routes presents a picture-book image of medieval, Renaissance and baroque towns between the Main river and the Alps. Here are some of the highlights.

6 BAD MERGENTHEIM
Renaissance palace with Grünewald painting in nearby Stuppach.

7 WEIKERSHEIM
Baroque castle and pretty gardens.

8 CREGLINGEN
Riemenschneider masterpiece in Herrgottskapelle.

9 ROTHENBURG
Archetypal picturesque town with medieval ramparts.

10 DINKELSBÜHL
Grand half-timbered houses, Gothic "Daniel" tower.

11 NÖRDLINGEN
Superb medieval fortifications.

12 HARBURG
One of the greatest castles in Germany, begun in the 12th century.

13 DONAUWÖRTH
Old fortified town where the Wörnitz river meets the Danube.

14 LEITHEIM
Rococo castle near Donauwörth.

15 AUGSBURG
Home of Fugger merchants, Renaissance town hall.

16 FÜSSEN
Spa with sulphur springs and mud-baths, old houses, castle turned bishop's palace.

17 HOHENSCHWANGAU
Maximilian's neo-Gothic pile where Ludwig II of Bavaria spent his childhood.

18 NEUSCHWANSTEIN
Silvery castle built by Ludwig II as a pinnacled Wagnerian fantasy.

Riemenschneider's Masterpieces

Sculptor Tilman Riemenschneider stood at the transition from late-Gothic to Renaissance art. His work, which can be seen in the churches and museums of northern Bavaria is charged with deeply felt emotion and energy.

1 WÜRZBURG
Elected him mayor in 1520. See his works in the cathedral, Franciscan church and Mainfränkisches Museum.

2 BAMBERG
Tombs of Heinrich II and wife Cunegund in cathedral.

3 CREGLINGEN
Assumption of Mary altar in Herrgottskapelle.

4 ROTHENBURG
Last Supper altar, St Jakobskirche.

5 DETWANG
Altar in the Romanesque village church.

6 HARBURG
Two sculpture groups in castle museum.

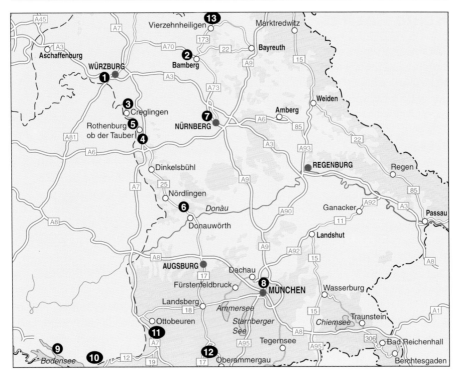

7 NUREMBERG
Rich collection in Germanisches Nationalmuseum.

8 MUNICH
Bayerisches Nationalmuseum has fine statues.

South German Baroque Churches

The most spectacular of the churches in Bavaria and around Lake Constance were commissioned by the monasteries or for pilgrimages. They expressed an assertive resistance to the Protestant Reformation.

9 BIRNAU
Cistercian pilgrimage church with exuberant interior by Feuchtmayer.

The genius of Riemenschneider (1–8) and southern baroque churches (9–13).

10 WEINGARTEN
Massive Benedictine abbey basilica, frescoes by Cosmas Damian Asam.

11 OTTOBEUREN
Biggest German baroque church, Johann Michael Fischer's masterpiece.

12 WIESKIRCHE
Pilgrimage church by Dominikus Zimmermann; exquisite location.

13 VIERZEHNHEILIGEN
North-east of Bamberg. Balthasar Neumann's pilgrimage church, Altar of Grace.

Rhine Castles

The castles looming over the river are the stuff dreams are made of, haunts of rob-ber-barons, redoubts of belligerent bish-ops. The most spectacular series is be-tween Koblenz and Bingen.

1 EHRENBREITSTEIN
Outpost for Archbishop of Trier.

2 STOLZENFELS
Fanciful reconstruction by Friedrich Wilhelm IV of Prussia.

3 MARKSBURG
13th century castle, now the home of the Museum of Castles.

4 BURG MAUS
Toll-collecting rival to …

5 BURG KATZ
… 14th-century fortress of Count Katzen-elnbogen.

6 BURG RHEINFELS
Fine 13th-century pile.

7 PFALZGRAFENSTEIN
Built in mid-river.

8 SOONECK
13th-century fortress restored as a hotel.

9 RHEINSTEIN
Collections of arms and armour.

10 EHRENFELS
Once a fortress of the Archbishop of Mainz.

11 MÄUSETURM
Where mice ate the Bishop of Bingen.

Castles guarding the River Rhine.

Gardens

The princes had gardens laid out in geo-metric French, formal Italian or more "nat-urally" landscaped English manner. They all offer a delightful refuge from the city bustle.

1 MUNICH
Englischer Garden designed by Yankee refugee from Rumford, New Hampshire.

2 LINDERHOF
Alpine garden for Ludwig's castle folly.

3 ASCHAFFENBURG
Pretty park at Schönbusch.

4 STUTTGART
Haven from modern city in Schlossgarten.

5 KASSEL
Spectacular fountains in Italian-style Wilhelmshöhe gardens.

6 HANOVER
Palace has gone but Herrenhausen gardens remain for walks and concerts.

7 BERLIN
Tiergarten is now both park and cultural forum.

8 WÖRLITZ
Fantasy 18th-century gardens near Dessau.

Taking the Waters

*T*he *best of German gardens (1–8) and spa resorts (9–17), and marvels of German engineering (18–25).*

Spa resorts are a venerable institution, here where rulers decided affairs of state, the Russians gambled away fortunes and the French "hid" their mistresses. You can

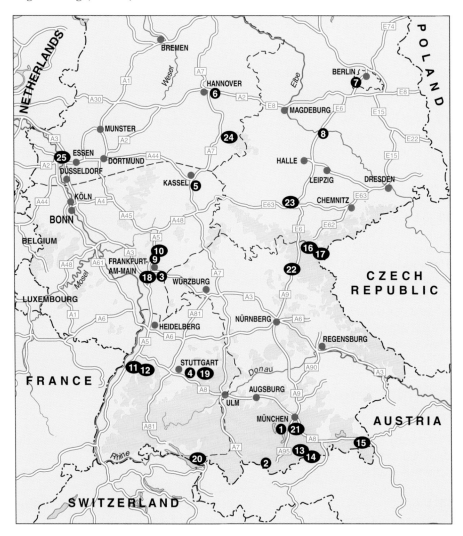

still do all of that while easing your aching back.

9 BAD HOMBURG
Europe's first casino, a haven for Frankfurt businessmen.

10 BAD NAUHEIM
Unique *Jugendstil* décor.

11 BADEN-BADEN
Promenade on elegant Lichtentaler Allee; excursion into Black Forest.

12 WILDBAD
Major resort on Black Forest spa route—*Schwarzwald Bäderstrasse*.

13 BAD TÖLZ
On banks of rushing Isar river.

14 BAD WIESSEE
Chic spa on Tegernsee lake.

15 BAD REICHENHALL
Alpine setting with old salt mine.

16 BAD BRAMBACH (SAXONY)
Medicinal springs among wooded hills.

17 BAD ELSTER (SAXONY)
Mineral and mud baths; beautiful setting near Czech border.

German Engineering Genius

The country's technological talent has long commanded the world's admiration. See where it all began.

18 MAINZ
Gutenberg printing museum.

19 STUTTGART
Car museums of Mercedes Benz and Porsche.

20 FRIEDRICHSHAFEN
Zeppelin flying-ship museum on Lake Constance.

21 MUNICH
Deutsches Museum's cheery survey of national achievement, and BMW car museum.

22 BAYREUTH
Typewriter museum.

23 JENA
Precision glass pioneer Carl Zeiss founded a new industry here. Optical Museum.

24 CLAUSTHAL-ZELLERFELD
Harz mountain mining.

25 ESSEN
Ruhrland museum of factory life and Haus Industrieform on industrial design.

The Alps

No spectacularly high peaks, but plenty of pretty mountain vistas, rushing streams, placid lakes and Alpine meadows. The mountain villages have lovely baroque chapels and half-timbered houses with gaily painted façades.

1 OBERAMMERGAU
Home of wood carving and ten-yearly Passion Play.

2 LINDERHOF
Ludwig II's exquisitely located vanilla-coloured Trianon-in-the-Alps.

Colourful spots in the German Alps.

Walkers' Country—the Harz Mountains

Unification makes it possible at last to ramble the witches' mountains and forests east and west of the old border.

GOSLAR
Renaissance houses in old mining town make this attractive "base camp". Doll and musical instrument museum.

OKERTAL
Pretty wooded valley with fishing lakes.

BRAUNLAGE
Mountain resort.

BROCKEN
Peak where witches danced.

WERNIGERODE
Retains medieval charm.

HALBERSTADT
Great Gothic cathedral.

QUEDLINBURG
Medieval streets around Renaissance castle.

3 GARMISCH-PARTENKIRCHEN
Most fashionable resort.

4 MITTENWALD
Colourfully painted façades.

5 TEGERNSEE
Smart resorts for Munich weekenders.

6 WENDELSTEIN
Cable-car to mountaintop view.

7 CHIEMSEE
Resort lake with island castle of Herren-chiemsee, Ludwig II's last fling.

8 REIT IM WINKEL
Rustic village.

9 RUHPOLDING
Mountain resort with folklore museum.

10 BAD REICHENHALL
Spa with old salt mine.

11 BERCHTESGADEN
Highly popular Alpine resort.

12 KÖNIGSSEE
Almost unbearably picturesque.

Scenic Diversions

The Lahn Valley ...
This itinerary among ruined castles and monasteries was much favoured by poets, not the least of them Johann Wolfgang von Goethe.

1 MARBURG
University and market town; shrine of St Elizabeth of Hungary.

2 WETZLAR
Baroque town of Goethe's *Werther*.

3 WEILBURG
Renaissance and baroque ducal residence.

4 NASSAU
Only ruin remains of original home of Holland's House of Orange.

5 BAD EMS
Sleepy spa where dispatch started Franco-Prussian War.

6 LAHNSTEIN
Castle guards entrance to Rhine.

Sites not to miss in the Lahn Valley (1–6) and Hunsrück (7–12).

... and Hunsrück
This wooded plateau south of the Mosel Valley offers broad sweeping vistas and sudden dramatic gorges.

7 HUNSRÜCK HÖHENSTRASSE
Start along wooded ridge from Morbach.

8 ERBESKOPF
Good hilltop view of surrounding region.

9 IDAR-OBERSTEIN
Gem-cutting town spectacularly situated in river gorge.

10 DHAUN
Castle ruin.

11 MONZINGEN
Pretty wine village.

12 BAD KREUZNACH
Attractive spot to take the waters or wine.

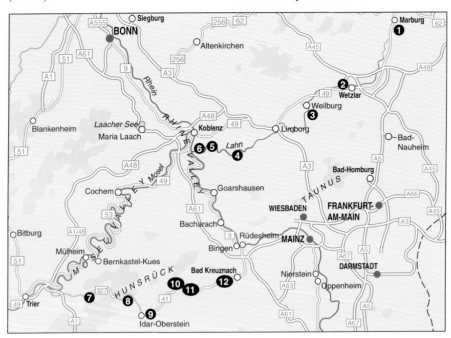

Baltic Coast and Islands

Eastern Germany opens up new possibilities for its old Baltic ports, resorts and islands, with as yet unspoilt coastlines.

1 WISMAR
Picturesque old Hanseatic port with many fine restored 14–16th-century buildings.

2 BAD DOBERAN
Huge former Cistercian monastery. Nearby Baltic resorts are the oldest and biggest.

3 WARNEMÜNDE
Fishing and ferry port, sailing and holiday centre; broad sandy beach.

4 ROSTOCK
Many fine surviving or restored medieval buildings.

5 FISCHLAND-DARSS-ZINGST
Wooded sand-dunes and tranquil marshland for poets and painters.

6 STRALSUND
Handsome historic town centre.

Islands along Germany's only coast.

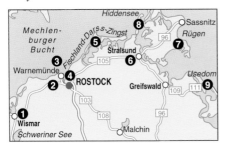

7 RÜGEN
Island's rugged shores attracted Romantic painter Caspar David Friedrich. Sandy beaches and sheltered inlets.

8 HIDDENSEE
Artists' colony and later East German bosses' retreat. No cars.

9 USEDOM
Popular summer resort island; long beaches and sheltered lagoon.

Albrecht Dürer

See the home and major works of Germany's greatest Renaissance painter. His gigantic talent drew inspiration from, and transcended, the art he had seen on his visits to Italy.

1 MUNICH
Masterpieces in Alte Pinakothek.

2 AUGSBURG
Great portrait of Jakob Fugger in Schaezler Palais.

3 NUREMBERG
His house restored and works in Germanisches Nationalmuseum.

4 FRANKFURT
Städelsches Kunstinstitut collection has Dürer's *Mocking of Job*.

5 COLOGNE
Wallraf-Richardz Museum includes his *Piper and Drummer*.

6 BERLIN
Far from home, major paintings in Dahlem Gemäldegalerie.

The masterpieces of
Albrecht Dürer.

7 DRESDEN
The great *Wittenberg Altar* in Old Masters Gallery.

Porcelain

The 18th century was the golden era of Germany's porcelain manufacture. The tradition is still maintained in its historic centres around the country.

1 MEISSEN
See the country's most famous factory in operation.

2 DRESDEN
Superb collection in Zwinger palace.

3 MUNICH
Nymphenburg collection displayed in palace after which it is named.

4 SCHLOSS SCHLEISSHEIM
Near Munich. Spectacular collection of Meissen in the Schloss Lustheim hunting lodge.

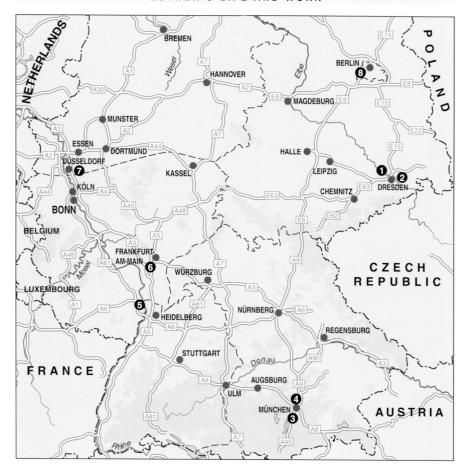

*H*istoric porcelain centres.

8 BERLIN

Prestige KPM brand. Fine collections in Kunstgewerbemuseum.

5 FRANKENTHAL

Exquisite tableware launched by Palatine princes still manufactured.

6 FRANKFURT

Superb collections in the Museum für Kunsthandwerk (Applied Arts).

7 DÜSSELDORF

International ceramics collection in Hetjens Museum.

Luther's Life and Work

The founder of German Protestantism travelled all over Germany, but died where he was born, Saxon Eisleben. You can visit his homes and churches where he preached.

1 EISLEBEN (SAXONY-ANHALT)

The houses where he was born and died.

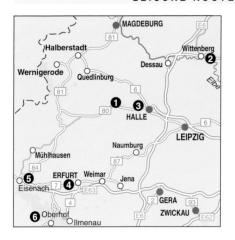

Jugendstil ...

Also known as Art Nouveau, the popular 1900s decorative style took its German name from the magazine *Die Jugend* which promoted the design. You will find it in architecture, book-binding, porcelain, glassware, mirror frames and even in ornate plumbing.

1 DARMSTADT
Artists' colony at Mathildenhöhe, collection in regional museum.

2 BAD NAUHEIM
Jugendstil artists designed spa installations, bath fixtures.

In the footsteps of Luther.

3 FRANKFURT
Superb collection in Arts and Crafts Museum.

2 WITTENBERG
Main home, Schlosskirche, where he nailed the 95 Theses, and the tomb where he lies buried. He preached in Marienkirche.

4 DÜSSELDORF
Glassware in Kunstmuseum.

3 HALLE
Where Luther preached, and Händel was born.

5 BREMEN
Unique architecture in brick buildings of Böttcherstrasse.

4 ERFURT
Augustine monastery for which he gave up law school.

6 BERLIN
International collection in Arts and Crafts Museum.

5 EISENACH
Refuge in Wartburg Castle, house in town.

... and Bauhaus

This enormously influential school of artists and architects began in eastern Germany and spread throughout the Western world.

6 SCHMALKALDEN (THURINGIA)
Where Protestant Association met, precipitating decisive break with Catholic church.

7 BERLIN
Bauhaus-Archiv museum, Mies van der Rohe's Nationalgalerie.

7 WORMS (OFF MAP)
Where he pleaded his case to Emperor.

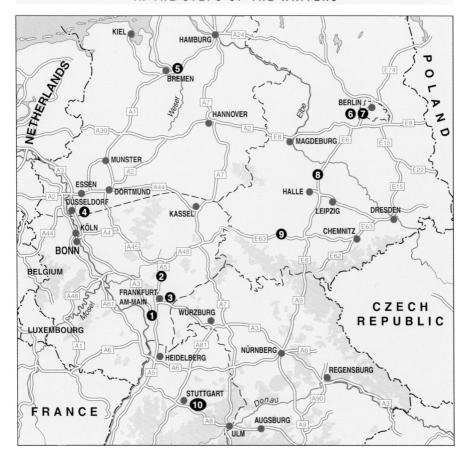

German artistic styles: Jugendstil *(1–6)* and Bauhaus *(7–10)*.

8 DESSAU

Gropius's Bauhaus building, model housing development.

9 WEIMAR

Van de Velde's school where it began, Georg Muche's model house in park.

10 STUTTGART

Weissenhof Siedlung houses, Schlemmer paintings in Staatsgalerie.

In the Steps of the Writers

Germany reveres its men of letters. Their houses have become shrines, in which are contained their sacred memorabilia.

1 DÜSSELDORF

Modern monument and museum to Heine.

2 WETZLAR

Setting of Goethe's romance with Charlotte and *Werther* novel.

3 FRANKFURT

Goethe's house.

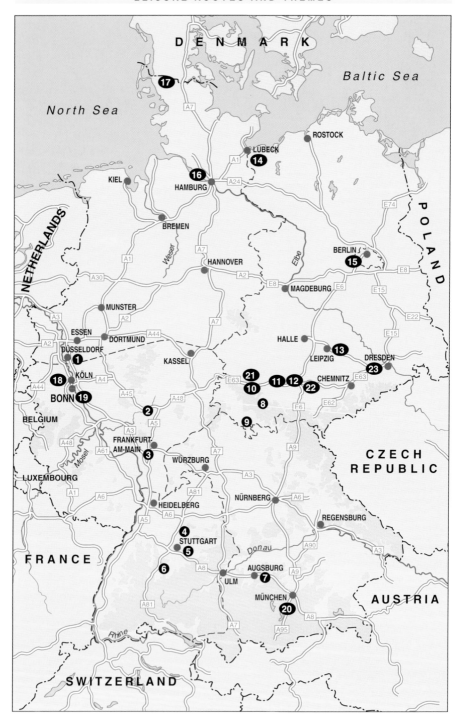

4 MARBACH
Where Schiller grew up.

5 STUTTGART
Square and monument to Schiller's university days.

6 TÜBINGEN
Hölderlin's student home in tower by Neckar river.

7 AUGSBURG
Museum in Brecht's birthplace.

8 ILMENAU
At edge of Thuringian Forest, Goethe's hunting lodge and botany trail.

9 MEININGEN
Bauerbach estate where Schiller worked; his rooms preserved as a museum.

10 ERFURT
Goethe's meeting-place with Napoleon on Futterstrasse.

11 WEIMAR
Where Goethe spent much of his life. Town-house museum and garden-house in park.

12 JENA
Cottage where Schiller wrote *Wallenstein.*

13 LEIPZIG
From Goethe's student days, Auerbach's Keller inspired Faust-and-Mephisto scene.

*H*omes of the German writers (1–14) and where to see examples of German Expressionism (15–23).

14 LÜBECK
Thomas Mann's *Buddenbrooks* house, memorabilia of him and brother Heinrich.

Expressionists

In the first decades of the 20th century, Nolde, Kirchner, Macke, Dix and company produced a vigorous body of work in intense contrast to the rigidity of previous generations.

15 BERLIN
Collection in Nationalgalerie plus Schmidt-Rottluff's Brücke Museum.

16 HAMBURG
Fine range in Kunsthalle.

17 SEEBÜLL (OFF THE MAP)
Near Neukirchen, Schleswig-Holstein. Emil Nolde's home-turned-museum.

18 COLOGNE
Outstanding Museum Ludwig.

19 BONN
Städisches Kunstmuseum.

20 MUNICH
Franz Marc's Blauer Reiter group in Städtische Galerie.

21 ERFURT
Outstanding Brücke works in Angermuseum, notably Erich Heckel.

22 GERA
Birthplace of Otto Dix; collection of his work in the Orangerie.

23 DRESDEN
Gemäldegalerie's New Masters.

Baroque Churches and Lakeside Castles, not Forgetting Beer and Sausages

The good people of Bavaria apparently owe the beauty of their land to their natural modesty. God had parcelled out the whole earth before the Bavarians came forward for their portion. Moved by their humility, he gave them the piece he had reserved for himself. In gratitude, they adorn the valleys and lakes with some of Germany's finest churches and fairy-tale castles, and celebrate their good fortune with a modest little party known as the Oktoberfest.

Actually, there is nothing modest about the Bavarians. They set themselves proudly apart in a fervently Catholic and largely conservative Free State that asserts a maximum of autonomy within Germany's federal system. Good-natured local chauvinism regards the rest of the country with a certain condescension, reserving its sharpest barbs for cool, stiff-necked northerners. Although most Bavarians prefer an easy, relaxed approach to life, their region is prosperous and well organized.

*B*avarians are a friendly lot but it's sometimes difficult to get them to put down their beer long enough to shake your hand.

They manage to combine the Germanic talent for getting things done with a specifically Bavarian need to do them pleasantly. In Munich, the capital, business lunches seem to last a little longer, office hours seem a little shorter. However, its dynamic car industry and other concerns, splendidly arranged museums, and the creativity of its performing arts offer convincing proof that this casual attitude is far from unproductive.

The old clichés, occasionally updated, endure as part of Bavaria's reality. Munich's great beer tavern, the Hofbräuhaus, continues to draw the throngs, even if foreigners often outnumber the locals. Edelweiss still blooms high in the Alps. The ghosts in Ludwig's dream castles stay away until winter, when the tourist crowds have thinned out.

101

The state can be divided into two parts. The region surrounding Munich and south to the Alps takes in the lakes, the royal castles, baroque gems such as Ottobeuren Abbey and the church of Wies, and the mountain resorts of Berchtesgaden and Garmisch-Partenkirchen. Northern Bavaria includes the famous Romantic Route of medieval towns stretching from Augsburg north to Aschaffenburg, the proud Franconian cities of Würzburg, Bamberg, Nuremberg and Bayreuth, and east to the Austrian border at Passau.

Munich (*München*)

To northerners seeking the more carefree life of southern Europe, Munich seems almost Mediterranean. This last main stop before the Alps provides, for many, a first breath of Italy. By the same token, for southern Europeans heading towards the prosperous efficiency of the cooler north, the Bavarian capital—more baroque than Gothic, more green than grey—makes the transition less abrupt. A lot of them— Greeks, Italians and Turks—decide quite

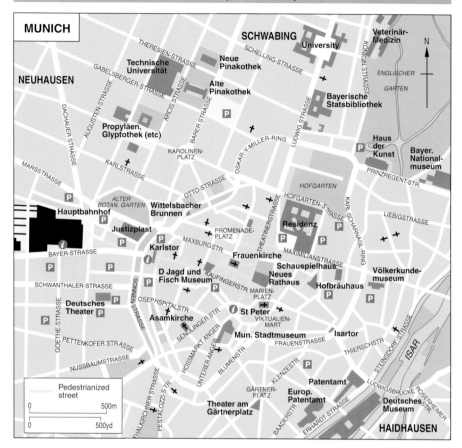

simply to stop in Munich and enjoy the best of both worlds. Munich's gain. Italians themselves will tell you that the city has the best Italian restaurants north of the Alps.

The poet Heinrich Heine said on a visit: "Between art and beer, Munich is laid out like a village between two hills." The town is in fact mostly flat but best enjoyed if you wander from one "hill" to the other. Beer halls in the winter and beer gardens in the summer make delightful temples of that untranslatable German feeling of warm fellowship known as *Gemütlichkeit*. There is also *Kultur*. During the post-war division of Berlin, Munich staked a serious claim to being the arts capital of West Germany. Its leading role in German cultural life remains. The opera house and concert halls provide magnificent homes for traditional classical works and the avant-garde. Painters cluster in the bohemian district of Schwabing, which exploded on the international scene in the 20th century as a focus for the Blaue Reiter school of Vasili Kandinsky, Paul Klee and Franz Marc. Munich galleries are still among the most innovative, while classical and modern collections of the Alte and Neue Pinakothek museums are richly endowed and superbly displayed.

Fiercely loyal to its traditions, the town has done a heroic job of reconstructing its

monuments after the 71 bombing raids in World War II. The Frauenkirche cathedral, and St Peter's and St Michael's churches were heavily damaged, as were large sections of the Residenz palace and Alte Pinakothek. Luckily, most of the art collections and other treasures were safely stored away.

Getting Around

Conveniently for the visitor, a majority of museums, monuments, palaces and churches are concentrated in the inner city (Innenstadt). Aided by a broad area of pedestrian zones, this makes Munich a great place for walking. Secondly, the superb public transport system of buses, trams, underground (U-Bahn) and surface trains (S-Bahn) brings all the other sights within easy reach.

If you are driving, find a good parking place and save the car for excursions and the occasional night out. By walking wherever you can, you will see more of the town's bustling street life and drop in more easily on the outdoor cafés. Discover, too, the many unexpected courtyard vistas and hidden alleyways, little bars and shops tucked away in corners you would completely miss in a car. So we offer you Munich as a series of walks.

The Inner City

The old city wall that once defined Munich's medieval boundaries has long since disappeared. However, the sturdy

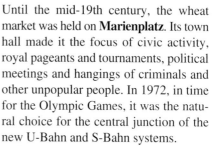

*M*unich's north-German-style, neo-Gothic, 19th-century town hall made Thomas Mann feel quite at home when he came down here from Lübeck.

remains of three gates survive to indicate the perimeter of the inner city—Isartor, Karlstor and Sendlinger Tor—as does Odeonsplatz, a rendezvous for salt traders setting off in the 14th century for northern Germany. Since the city's beginnings, Marienplatz has been at the heart of it all.

Marienplatz to Theatinerstrasse

Until the mid-19th century, the wheat market was held on **Marienplatz**. Its town hall made it the focus of civic activity, royal pageants and tournaments, political meetings and hangings of criminals and other unpopular people. In 1972, in time for the Olympic Games, it was the natural choice for the central junction of the new U-Bahn and S-Bahn systems.

Graced with tubs of flowers and outdoor cafés, Marienplatz today forms part of an attractive pedestrian zone. The **Mariensäule** (Column of the Virgin Mary) was inaugurated in 1638 by Maximilian I in gratitude for the town's deliverance from the Swedes in the Thirty Years' War. Notice at the column's base a basilisk, dragon, serpent and lion—symbols respectively of plague, hunger, heresy and war—each being vanquished by heroic child-angels. From the top of the monument, the majestic figure of Mary watches over Munich. Holding Jesus in her left arm and a sceptre in her right, the figure became a pioneer for such votive columns all over southern Germany and Austria.

The square's other, more modern, monument is the 19th-century **Fischbrunnen**. Young butchers used to leap into this bronze fountain after completing their apprenticeship, but now the tradition is kept up only by an occasional *Fasching* (carnival) reveller or happy soccer fan.

At the east end of Marienplatz stands the almost too picturesque **Altes Rathaus** (Old Town Hall), a gay example of Munich's efforts to reconstruct rather than simply replace the vestiges of its venerable past. This Gothic-style edifice, with its dove-grey façade, amber-tiled steeple and graceful little spires, captures the spirit of the 15th-century original that was designed by Jörg von Halsbach (also called Ganghofer), though it is not an exact replica. In any case, with the addition over the centuries of a baroque onion-shaped cupola and then a too-conscientious "re-Gothification", the building destroyed by bombs was probably further from the original than what you can see today. The steeple houses a charming **Toy Museum** (*Spielzeugmuseum*). It displays two centuries of dolls, soldiers and cowboys, medieval castles, doll houses and menageries, and a great array of cars, planes, ships and trains. The rest of the building fulfils a largely decorative function.

The real business of city government is conducted at the **Neues Rathaus** (New Town Hall) on the northern side of Marienplatz. This is a classic piece of 19th-century neo-Gothic—proud, assertive, but in architectural spirit more "northern" than Bavarian. Its façade is elaborately decorated with statues of kings, princes and dukes, saints, allegorical figures and characters from Munich folklore. The tower is 80m (262ft) high. Its main attraction—apart from the splendid view if you want to take the lift to the top—is the 43-bell **Glockenspiel** (carillon) which goes wild every day at 11 a.m. Two groups of figures appear, one re-enacting the tournament held on Marienplatz in 1568 during the wedding of Duke Wilhelm V and Renata of Lorraine and the other, underneath,

re-creating the cooper's dance (*Schäfflertanz*) performed to exorcise the plague of 1517. At 9 p.m., a nightwatchman with his lantern blows his horn, and an angel of peace blesses the little monk that has become the city's talisman, the *Münchner Kindl*.

Now, around the corner at the west end of the Neues Rathaus, go up Weinstrasse and left along Sporerstrasse to the **Frauenkirche**, its full title being Domkirche zu Unserer Lieben Frau (Cathedral Church of Our Beloved Lady). With its gold-tipped bulbous domes on twin brick towers dominating the skyline, this building is the city's dominant symbol. (There is a good view from the top of the south tower, 99m/325ft by lift.) The church, an austere, unadorned Gothic structure was built by Jörg von Halsbach from 1468 until his death in 1488, when Lukas Rottaler took over. The Italian Renaissance domes are an addition of 1524. The stark interior is the work of painful reconstruction from wartime rubble. The original Gothic windows in the choir, prudently stacked away before the bombardments, give some idea of the church's former glory. The choir has also preserved Erasmus Grasser's fine sculptures of the Apostles and Prophets (1502). An admirable altarpiece of 1483 by Friedrich Pacher, the *Baptism of Christ*, hangs in the north chapel. It is flanked by Jan Polack's panels depicting Jesus on the Mount of Olives and his arrest, crucifixion and burial. Notice, too, the imposing 17th-century funerary monument of Emperor Ludwig the Bavarian, who died in 1347. The Pope had always referred to the emperor, mockingly, as "the Bavarian". Ludwig and his compatriots took it as a badge of honour.

At the western end of Frauenplatz, the cathedral's square, Augustinerstrasse

The colourful figures of the Glockenspiel in the tower of Munich's Neues Rathaus commemorate two 16th-century events: a wedding and the end of the plague.

Alps after the Council of Trent marked the determination of Bavaria's Duke Wilhelm V to resist the spread of Lutheranism. Prompted by the newly arrived Jesuits, he commissioned a forceful transition from Italian Renaissance to baroque. The elegant gabled façade portrays Germany's secular defenders of the faith. Among the emperors and Wittelsbach dukes, you will see Wilhelm V holding a scale model of the church (above the entrance, third figure from the right). Il Gesù, the Jesuits' church in Rome, inspired St Michael's baroque interior, which many feel surpasses the former in its masterful lighting.

Karlstor, a city gate dating from the 14th century, links Neuhauser Strasse to the busy commercial Karlsplatz, popularly known as the **Stachus** after the innkeeper Eustachius Föderl. The Stachus conceals a veritable city of underground shops extending from the exit of the S-Bahn station. Walk north to Lenbachplatz and the city's loveliest fountain, the neo-baroque **Wittelsbacher Brunnen**. Signally unromantic in origin, it was built by Adolf von Hildebrand in 1895 to celebrate completion of the new municipal plumbing.

On Pacellistrasse east of Lenbachplatz is the distinctively faceted façade of the **Dreifaltigkeitskirche** (Trinity Church). In 1704, a local lass, Maria Anna Lindmayr, dreamed the city would be invaded and

leads to what was once the church of the Augustinians. Transformed into a customs house under Napoleon, it is now a hunting and fishing museum, the **Deutsches Jagd- und Fischereimuseum**, displaying trophies, skeletons and weapons beneath elegant baroque vaults and stucco work.

Further along Neuhauser Strasse is the 16th-century **St Michael's Church**, which is an architectural landmark in the German Counter-Reformation. This was the first major edifice built north of the

destroyed unless a new church were built. The next year, during the War of the Spanish Succession, a hostile Austrian army arrived. They did not destroy the city, but the close shave persuaded city elders to build the church anyway. Inside, in the cupola, the Trinity is depicted by an early fresco of Cosmas Damian Asam, a member of Munich's celebrated family of baroque painters.

Promenadeplatz is noted for the elegance of Palais Montgelas, the residence of the Bavarian minister who negotiated with Napoleon Bavaria's transformation from duchy to kingdom. This neoclassical building today forms part of the expensive Bayerischer Hof hotel, where you can refresh yourself with an expensive drink at the bar. Or else continue north along Kardinal-Faulhaber-Strasse past the Palais Porcia, one of Munich's first baroque palaces and now a bank, to the **Erzbischö-fliches Palais** (Archbishop's Palace) at number 7. This 18th-century triumph of rococo harmony with especially fine stucco work is the only palace by François

---

THREE LUDWIGS AND A LOLA

The Wittelsbach dynasty that ruled Bavaria for over 700 years had a strange 19th-century swansong. Enriched by church property confiscated during the Napoleonic Wars, the duchy became a kingdom in 1806. The people clamoured briefly for a democratic constitution, but the monarchy showed it knew its Bavarians by contenting them with the Oktoberfest, commemorating the wedding anniversary of Crown Prince Ludwig.

As King Ludwig I (1825–48), he was obsessed by all things Greek. Determined to make Munich a "German Athens", he built a Propylaeum to emulate the gateway on the Acropolis, beside a neo-Grecian Glyptothek for ancient sculpture. To spearhead his new German Renaissance, he brought the state university from Landshut to Munich and founded the Alte and Neue Pinakothek for the royal art collections.

So what could have made him happier than to see his son Otto enthroned as King of Greece in 1832? Well, how about the arrival in Munich 14 years later of Maria Delores Eliza Rosanne Gilbert, better known as Lola Montez? The "Spanish dancer" born in Limerick, Ireland, in fact danced terribly but was beautiful enough to be the mistress of Franz Liszt and Alexandre Dumas before ensnaring Ludwig. He was so crazy about her that he made her Countess of Landsberg. Dubbed the "Bavarian Pompadour", she got involved in local politics and brought down the Bavarian government. This, plus the closing of the troublesome university and a sharp rise in beer prices, caused a full-scale revolt and led Ludwig to abdicate.

Ludwig II (1864–86) hated politics. He lived in his own dream world, building fantastic neomedieval castles and promoting the grandiose musical visions of his protégé, Richard Wagner. The Bavarian government feared his follies would empty the state treasury and had him vacate the throne to pursue medical treatment. Four days later, Ludwig II and his doctor were found drowned in the lake at Starnberg, with the mystery of suicide, murder or accident never solved. The dreamer's extravagant investment today brings in huge profits from tourist receipts at his castles and the annual Bayreuth festival.

With the quiet, unimaginative Ludwig III, the Wittelsbachs ended not with a bang but a whimper. In the Bavarian revolution of November 1918, the Munich mob invaded his palace and roamed around the galleries and ballrooms, hooting to hear the echoes. Ludwig cried: "Oh, oh, the revolution—and here am I, still in my uniform!" He changed into civilian clothes, packed a few bags into his car and fled with his family, never to return.

de Cuvilliés to have survived intact to the present day.

The chic shopping arcades of **Theatinerstrasse** make a pleasant end to this walk. Spoil yourself with a delicious pastry and coffee at a sumptuous *Konditorei*.

Isartorplatz to Hofbräuhaus

The massive **Isartor** in its restored form is the only city gate which retains its 14th-century dimensions. Erected in the days of Emperor Ludwig the Bavarian, the gate's arch has been embellished with a fresco of 1835 showing him returning triumphantly from victory over the Habsburgs. The Isartor now serves as an outsize traffic island, but one of the towers houses a rooftop café and the Valentin Museum, devoted to the great cabaret comic of 1920s Munich, Karl Valentin.

From Isartor, go along Tal, a shopping street that runs to the **Heiliggeistkirche** (Church of the Holy Spirit). This 14th-

century Gothic structure has been extensively baroquified, but the two styles come together in the *Marienaltar*—a beautiful wooden sculpture of 1450, the *Hammerthaler Muttergottes* (Hammerthal Madonna) from the Tegernsee monastery, set in an opulent gilded baroque framework. The reconstructed high altar preserves a fine pair of *Adoring Angels* by Johann Georg Greiff (1730).

West of the Heiliggeistkirche, with an entrance on Rindermarkt, is **St Peter**, the oldest church in Munich. It dates from before the founding of the city itself in 1158. It underwent constant transformation from Romanesque to Gothic to Renaissance in the 17th century, when a single steeple replaced the original twin towers. Destroyed in World War II, the church has been faithfully reconstructed, down to the asymmetrically placed clocks on the tower. (On days when the *Föhn* is blowing, the tower-top observatory offers a wonderful view of the Alps.) Crowning glory of the light, bright interior is the **high altar** celebrating Peter and the Fathers of the Church. It was restored from the remains of the 18th-century original designed by Egid Quirin Asam, who drew his inspiration from Bernini's altar for St Peter's in Rome. The centrepiece is Erasmus Grasser's great wooden sculpture of Peter of 1492, while Asam worked with Johann Georg Greiff and Andreas Faistenberger on the masterly gilded wood carvings of the Church Fathers. Notice in the choir the

*T*he brick towers of Munich's Frauenkirche (Cathedral Church of Our Beloved Lady) dominate the skyline of the city.

splendid rococo stalls and five paintings of Peter's life by Jan Polack (1517), part of the high altar in its Gothic form. On the north side of the church is the early 15th-century Schrenk-Altar, a sandstone relief of the Crucifixion and the Day of Judgement.

Now duck along the little Burgstrasse past the Altes Rathaus, stopping at number 5 to admire the **Weinstadl**. Once the home of the town clerk and now a tavern, it is one of Munich's few remaining Gothic houses, enhanced with Renaissance detail on its painted façade. Take a peep at the neatly restored leafy courtyard with its spiral staircase tower.

A miracle of inner-city tranquillity pervades the Alter Hof. The tree-shaded square offers an exquisite panorama of medieval buildings. The reconstructed Burgtor (City Gate) and quaint little Affenturm (Monkey Tower) recapture something of the atmosphere of the Wittelsbachs' first Munich residence as it was in the 15th century. The heraldic painting on the tower was uncovered only in the 1960s.

You will find another island of peace at the old mint, **Münzhof**, tucked away in the interior of Hofgraben 4. The state office for preserving monuments has shown great taste in making its home in this three-storey Renaissance building with its handsome arcaded courtyard.

Take Pfisterstrasse over to the Platzl (Little Square), the site of a building of no great architectural distinction but nonetheless the most famous building in Munich, the **Hofbräuhaus**.

Duke Wilhelm V founded a brewery in the Alter Hof in 1589 to avoid paying the high prices for the imported stuff from Hanover—beer always having been just as much an aristocratic as a plebeian drink in

---

VALENTIN'S DAY

Although little known outside Germany, Karl Valentin was regarded by connoisseurs such as dramatist Bert Brecht as a comic genius equal to Charlie Chaplin. While resident in Munich in the early 1920s, Brecht went almost every night to watch Valentin's portrayal of the clownish working-class characters of peasant origin peculiar to the city.

Valentin started out in beer halls, but he quickly attracted the attention of Schwabing's artists and intellectuals, who loved his insane, surreal logic. One of his most celebrated sketches involved his efforts to house birds in an aquarium and fish in a bird-cage.

Bavaria. It replaced wine as the staple alcoholic beverage after the Bavarian vineyards were destroyed during the cruel winters of the 13th and 14th centuries, making way for the sturdier hop and barley crops.

The brewery was first set up in the royal bath-house, moving to more spacious quarters on the Platzl in 1644. The Hofbräuhaus itself was built in 1896, after the brewery had been transferred to the other side of the Isar river. It soon became the most prestigious of Munich's political beer-hall arenas. In fact, in November 1921, Hitler's storm troops first gained notoriety in what became known as the *Schlacht im Hofbräuhaus* ("Battle of the Hofbräuhaus"). Today, the huge beer hall, with its long tables and oom-pah-pah music, tends to attract more foreigners than locals. Most customers seem to know at least the first two lines of its signature tune: *In München steht ein Hofbräuhaus, Eins, zwei, gsuffa!* ("In Munich, there's a court brewery, One, two, drink up!"). The important thing is to be able to sway in unison, arms locked with your neighbours', a movement technically known as *schunkeln*. Some Bavarian purists insist this is a barbarian custom imported from the Rhineland.

Odeonsplatz to Maximilianstrasse

Odeonsplatz links the inner city to Schwabing and the university. It is the point at which Ludwig I opened up the crowded city centre to the more spacious **Vorstadt**, Schwabing then being just a suburb.

This emphatically airy and "liberating" walk begins in the Italian Renaissance-style **Hofgarten** (Court Garden), restored and replanted with the chestnut trees, flower-beds and fountains specified in the original 17th-century plan. In the centre stands a 12-sided temple to Diana topped by a rather sexy bronze allegorical statue of Bavaria. Art galleries and cafés line the arcades, decorated with historic frescoes of the Wittelsbachs. On the north side is a fascinating little **Theater-museum** (Galeriestrasse 4) displaying set designs from Munich's grand theatrical past.

Turn and look south-west across the Hofgarten to capture a delightful vista evoking Munich's peculiarly Mediterranean flavour—the twin towers and dome of the 17th-century **Theatiner-kirche**. Agostino Barelli and Enrico Zuccalli built this spirited Italian baroque church to celebrate the birth of a Wittelsbach prince—with a rococo façade added by Cuvilliés. A feeling of jubilation animates the richly decorated interior—ornamental vines, acanthus leaves and rosettes, with superb grey-and-white stucco detail embellishing the cupola.

Across the street, facing Odeonsplatz, is the **Feldherrnhalle** (Hall of the Generals), a 19th-century monument to military heroes modelled, somewhat heavily, after Florence's Loggia dei Lanzi. The statues include Johann Tilly, the commander of Catholic forces in the Thirty Years' War, and Karl Philipp von Wrede, who was victorious over the French in 1814. Less gloriously, it was the rallying point for Hitler's storm troops in his abortive Beer Hall Putsch in 1923 and a focus for commemorative marches thereafter.

Next door in the Residenzstrasse stands **Preysing-Palais**, a lovingly restored rococo palace. Take a look inside at its majestic ceremonial staircase. At the other end of Residenzstrasse is another jewel of 18th-century architecture, the **Hauptpostamt** (Main Post Office) occupying the Palais Törring-Jettenbach. You will never buy a postage stamp in a more beautiful setting. The northern façade was reworked in the 19th century to match the neoclassical appearance

---

WORRISOME WIND

Strange things can happen in Bavaria when the *Föhn* blows, most often in springtime. As a messenger from the Mediterranean on the other side of the Alps, this warm dry wind gusts down the mountains' northern slopes. It so clears the air that people in Munich get the optical illusion that the Alps have moved right up to the southern suburbs. If it gives some people migraine, others, often artists, claim phenomenally clear creative insights reminiscent of drug-induced conditions. Some surgeons refuse to operate because of the *Föhn*'s influence on blood pressure and other factors. Criminologists have also observed an increase of violence between husband and wife when the *Föhn* blows in through the kitchen window.

of the Residenz and Nationaltheater on Maximilianstrasse, but the original baroque doorway can be seen inside.

Bavarian traditionalists rebuilt the **Nationaltheater** in 1963 as a copy of the original 1818 Greek-temple design of Karl von Fischer.

The spacious **Max-Joseph-Platz** is named after the first Wittelsbach, by the grace of Napoleon, to bear the title of king, honoured here with a seated statue. Max wanted a more dignified standing pose, but he died before the statue was completed, and his son Ludwig I accepted the seated version.

The statue was placed alongside the Wittelsbachs' **Residenz**. In 1385 the citizenry revolted, driving the dukes to construct safer lodgings than the Alter Hof. Over five centuries later another revolt, creating the short-lived Bavarian Republic, drove the family out for good. In contrast to many of the myriad German principalities that were downright futile, the Residenz palace, now a magnificent museum, shows how powerful and immensely wealthy the Bavarian monarchy grew to be (*see* page 121).

To view the palace exterior, enter from Residenzstrasse and walk through the seven courtyards to the **Cuvilliéstheater**, within the Residenz but not included on museum tours. The Altes Residenztheater, as it is also known, is one of the most enchanting playhouses in the world. Like its architect, François de Cuvilliés, a dwarf from the Spanish Netherlands, the theatre is tiny, seating only 450. However, its festive intimacy makes every performance a cosy gala. The four-tiered horseshoe-shaped auditorium basks in a gilded rococo décor that manages to unite Bacchus,

The German flair for architecture and design is demonstrated in the construction of this palace, situated in northern Munich.

Apollo and Diana with an American Indian girl complete with feather headdress, bow, arrows and cactus. The acoustics are correspondingly warm and golden—totally appropriate to the Mozart works that have been played here for the past 200 years.

The theatre was preserved to the present day by an inspired stroke of foresight. In 1943, the stucco ornamentation and sculpture were dismantled bit by bit. Some 30,000 separate pieces were stored away in the vaults of various castles around Munich. Six weeks later the theatre was gutted by fire bombs. Fifteen years elapsed before the fragments were brought out of hiding and put together again.

Sendlinger Tor to Viktualienmarkt

The busy shopping area of Sendlinger Strasse takes you past the municipal museum to the open-air market beside St Peter's church.

Only two hexagonal towers remain from the picturesque medieval city gate **Sendlinger Tor**. Take Sendlinger Strasse to the **Asamhaus** (number 61) where Egid Quirin Asam, master sculptor and architect of the 18th century, had his home. He decorated the building with his brother, Cosmas Damian, who specialized in fresco painting. The ornate forenames—probably their father's revenge for his own mundane Hans Georg—go with the brothers' rich baroque style. Stand on the opposite side of Sendlinger Strasse to see the house's marvellously intricate façade, dated 1733. Secure in their Catholic faith, the Asams happily mixed pagan and Christian figures in their decorative schemes. Just below the roof to the right (directly above the doorway) is a representation in stucco of

heaven and the monogram of Christ, and below that, the seated figure of Mary. To the left is vine-bedecked Olympus with Apollo and the triumphant gods of Fame and Fortune. Pegasus, the flying horse, leaps up towards them while a riot of nymphs and satyrs dance below, around the Muses of painting, sculpture and architecture.

The brothers' light-hearted devotion to the good life and the inspiration of their religion can be seen in the Asams' exquisite private chapel next door. A special entrance once linked the family house to this church of St John of Nepomuk, more commonly known as the **Asamkirche**. The variegated marble façade serves as a street-altar for passers-by on busy Sendlinger Strasse. It incorporates unhewn rocks originally intended for a fountain; a statue of John of Nepomuk, a Bohemian saint popular in 18th-century Bavaria, presides over the porch. Built in 1746 at Egid Quirin's own expense and so liberated from the constraints of a patron's demands, the interior is a very personal celebration of faith and life. The two-tiered **high altar** carries the eye upwards to a towering Crucifixion dominated by God the Father wearing the papal crown. Around this formidable monument, all is movement and light, still aglow with the Asams' enthusiasm despite the ravages of wartime destruction.

On the corner of Hackenstrasse is the imposing four-storey **Altes Hackenhaus**, a rare surviving example of a private house in the classical style. A succession of nine Doric, Ionic and Corinthian pillars run along each façade. Look inside at the charming courtyard. Further along Hackenstrasse is Munich's oldest operating tavern, the **Gaststätte zur Hundskugel**, serving beer since 1440.

Double back across Sendlinger Strasse to St-Jakobs-Platz and the remarkable **Münchner Stadtmuseum** (Municipal Museum; *see* page 123). East of the museum is one of the town's most colourful spots, a rendezvous for all with a fine nose or palate, the **Viktualienmarkt**—what Charles Dickens would have called a "vittles market". The city's central food market has stood here since 1807. Stroll around the enticing stalls with their scores of cheeses and exotic spices, meats and endless varieties of bread. The cornucopia of vegetables and fruit offers most convincing proof that Munich is a crossroads of northern and southern Europe, and a gateway to the East, too. The atmosphere is always cheerful, but at its most uninhibited when the marketwomen let down their hair at the end of the carnival season on Shrove Tuesday for the Marketwomen's Dance, and again around the flower-bedecked maypole.

Around Königsplatz

Over the last two centuries, Munich realized on **Königsplatz** the noblest and basest of its aspirations. Ignoring the protests of his urban planners, Ludwig I imagined the square as a second Acropolis, a vast open space to be surrounded with neoclassical temples. With Leo von Klenze as his architect, the king made the square a grassy tree-lined haven of peace. A hundred years later, Hitler cut down the trees and paved over the grass for the troops and armoured cars of his military parades. Today, Königsplatz is returning to its original serenity, and the greenery is back. It is the focus of Munich's major art collections (*see* page 117).

The U-Bahn station brings you out beside the **Propyläen** (Propylaeum), modelled after the gateway on the Acropolis in Athens. In fact, epitomizing Ludwig's sublime imperviousness to functional considerations, this entrance leads nowhere, closing off Königsplatz rather than providing access to the square. Despite the Doric columns, even its "Greekness" is diminished by the two Egyptian-style towers flanking the central gateway. Their friezes depict the Greek War of Independence and the Greek people paying homage to Ludwig's son Otto when he was made their king in 1832.

Before visiting the square's other monuments, continue past the Propyläen to the **Lenbachhaus** on Luisenstrasse, an elegant ochre-coloured villa of the 1880s built in the style of Renaissance Florence and reconstructed after World War II. More successful than talented, the academic painter Franz von Lenbach built himself this town palace with a fortune accumulated from his portraits of the German aristocracy. Today, the villa houses the excellent **Städtische Galerie** of 19th- and 20th-century art. Coffee is served on the terrace or in its pleasant garden. In the little park opposite, open-air chess is played on big stone boards.

On the south side of Königsplatz, the neo-Corinthian home of the **Staatliche Antikensammlungen** (Classical Art Collections) by Klenze's successor, George Ziebland, is decidedly clumsy compared with its companion, the **Glyptothek** (Sculpture Museum) across the square. Klenze's elegant structure of 1816 for Ludwig I's personal collection of Greek and Roman sculpture was the first public edifice expressly designed as a museum. Klenze chose the style of an Italian Renaissance palace for the **Alte Pinakothek**, one of the world's great art collections, across Gabelsberger Strasse. Behind it, on Theresienstrasse, is the resolutely post-modern **Neue Pinako-thek** devoted principally to art of the 19th century. With moat, turrets, stairways and ramps in granite, sandstone and glass, it makes a witty architectural comment on the historicism of its elder sister across the way.

Less amusing are a couple of bunker-like survivors from the Hitler era designed by Paul Ludwig Troost at the east end of Königsplatz. In the **Führerbau** (Führer Building) at Arcisstrasse 12, now a music academy (*Staatliche Hochschule für Musik*), Hitler received Chamberlain, Daladier and Mussolini for the 1938 agreement that sold out Czechoslovakia. Along the road at Meiserstrasse 10, the Nazi Party had its administrative centre (today the *Haus der Kulturinstitute*, important institutions of archaeology and art history).

Schwabing

Schwabing belongs to that select group of districts around the world—New York's Greenwich Village, Paris's Montparnasse and London's Chelsea are also included—of which it is said, perhaps glibly but nonetheless accurately, that it is less a place than a state of mind. Begin your walk symbolically at the **Siegestor**, a less than triumphal arch of victory marking the neighbourhood's southern boundary. Erected under Ludwig I to celebrate the Bavarian army, it was bombed in 1944 and left with the scars of war and a new inscription on the south side: *Dem Sieg geweiht, im Krieg zerstört, zum Frieden mahnend* ("Dedicated to victory, destroyed in war, exhorting to peace"). Schwabing epitomizes a break with military tradition. Walk to the entrance of the university at the little square named Geschwister-Scholl-Platz after two students, brother and sister, who were both

> **FREE FOR ALL**
>
> Schwabing's heyday was the turn of the 20th century, when artists, writers and hangers-on flocked here from all over Germany and eastern Europe. Thomas Mann and Frank Wedekind moved here from the cold north, Rainer Maria Rilke from Prague and Bert Brecht from nearby Augsburg. Local painter Franz Marc welcomed Paul Klee from Berne and Vasili Kandinsky from Moscow. Another Russian exile wrote to his mother of the crazy carnival, admiring how "people know how to live in public here, how to amuse themselves in the streets!" It was in Schwabing that he changed his name from Vladimir Ilyich Ulyanov to Lenin.
>
> A countess-turned-bohemian, Franziska zu Reventlow, chronicled the neighbourhood's free love, free art, freedom for all and everything; her apotheosis was to die penniless of the fashionably romantic illness of tuberculosis. Schwabing was the home of the biting satirical weekly *Simplicissimus* and the art magazine *Jugend*, which gave its name to the German version of Art Nouveau—*Jugendstil*.
>
> A last moment of glory came in 1919 when the "Coffeehouse Anarchists", dramatist Ernst Toller and poet Erich Mühsam, took power after the assassination of prime minister Kurt Eisner. For all of six days— till the Communists pushed the poets out— Schwabing ruled Bavaria, proclaiming the republic a "meadow full of flowers".

executed for mounting a rare resistance movement to Hitler in 1943.

At night, Schwabing's bohemian spirit, somewhat commercialized at weekends, animates wide and breezy **Leopoldstrasse**, stretching north from the Siegestor. Here, and in side streets, the cafés and art galleries still attract writers and painters, but also the talents of the new German cinema. At the major traffic intersection of Münchener Freiheit, cut down Feilitzschstrasse to **Wedekindplatz**, a centre of the theatre, cabaret and café life that in its best moments recaptures the golden past.

Englischer Garten Area

From Schwabing, head east to the **Englischer Garten**. Opened in 1793, the park was the brainchild of an American-born adventurer, Benjamin Thompson, better known to Bavarians as Count von Rumford (in New Hampshire). He drew on the ideas of the great English landscape gardeners, Capability Brown and William Chambers. The **Chinesischer Turm** (Chinese Tower) that serves as bandstand for a popular beer garden was inspired by Chambers' Cantonese Pagoda in London's Kew Gardens.

Breaking with the French tradition of geometric avenues, and intricately sculpted trees and hedges favoured by the Bavarian aristocracy, Rumford went for a more "natural" group of hills, dells and babbling brooks. In the revolutionary spirit of the times, Rumford and his German associate Friedrich Ludwig von Sckell created a park for Munich's poor. Their royal patrons had imagined the Englischer Garten would be an elaborate extension of the Hofgarten, until they saw pigs rooting and cattle grazing where once they had hunted pheasants and stags, and potato patches in place of exotic flowers. Potatoes turned up in the American maverick's other great legacy, a barley soup served in his popular soup-kitchens and known to this day as *Rumfordsuppe*. (He is honoured with a monument in the park's south-east corner.)

Today the pigs and potatoes have gone, but the natural landscaping is still a joy for picnickers, lovers and other usually ami-

The Chinese Tower in Munich's Englischer Garten combines the functions of landmark, bandstand, meeting point and beer garden.

able loiterers. The **Monopteros** (love temple) atop a grassy mound south of the Chinese Tower attracts the more colourful residents of Schwabing. They bask in a haze of exotic Oriental herbs, smiling at the splendid view of the old city.

Walkers and joggers enjoy the park's 5km (3-mile) stretch of the swiftly flowing Isar river. Row-boats can be rented on the **Kleinhesseloher See**. The little Eisbach stream, a branch of the Isar, tumbles under Tivoli Bridge like a veritable mountain rapid, encouraging a somewhat breakneck version of windsurfing. More relaxing, in the park's south-west corner, is the **Japanese Tea House**, which Japan donated for the 1972 Olympic Games.

Just beyond the Tea House, at Prinzregentenstrasse 1, stands the formidable **Haus der Kunst** (House of Art), home of the State Modern Art Gallery (*see* page 125) and special contemporary exhibitions. Many art lovers cannot forgive the Allied bombers for missing this monstrosity built as a temple to Hitler's personal vision of a truly German art. Today trees and ivy vainly try to camouflage the grotesque neoclassical blockhouse variously nicknamed *Münchner Kunstterminus* ("Munich Art Terminus"), *Palazzo Kitschi* and *Weisswurstallee* ("White Sausage Alley", for its monotonous row of Doric columns).

Further along Prinzregentenstrasse is the **Bayerisches Nationalmuseum** of German cultural history (*see* page 123). Cross the bridge over the Isar to the winged **Friedensengel** (Peace Angel, 1896). High on her column over a pleasant Florentine terrace, the monument celebrates the 25 years of peace following the German defeat of the French in 1871. Portraits of the architects of that peace—Bismarck, and Kaisers Wilhelm I and II and their generals—decorate the monument. But the allegorical mosaics of *Peace, War, Victory* and the *Blessings of Culture* are decidedly more belligerent than pacific.

The opulent **Villa Stuck** (Prinzregentenstrasse 60) was built in 1898 for the last of Munich's painter-princes, Franz von Stuck. His fortune rivalled that of Lenbach by astutely combining the new trends of *Jugendstil* symbolism with the fashionable salon taste for a certain luxury spiced with a dash of decadence. The villa's museum is decorated with furniture and ornaments of the 1900s.

Olympiapark

Munich's Olympic centre north-west of Schwabing is a *tour de force* of virtuoso engineering and aesthetic panache. Built by Günther Behnisch and partners for the 1972 Games, the stadium, sports hall and swimming pools are linked by a swooping tent-like roof of transparent pre-stressed cable-net acrylic. The surrounding park, now used for summer theatre and arts festivals, has a man-made lake and grassy hillocks. There is a revolving restaurant and observation deck two-thirds of the way up the 290m (950ft) Olympic Tower.

North-east across the Petuelring Autobahn is the "four cylinder" aluminium skyscraper built as headquarters for the Bavarian Motor Works. Alongside, in the upturned dome, the **BMW Museum** displays the cars, motorcycles and aircraft engines that made the company famous. The classic originals are placed in their historical context of the Weimar republic, Third Reich and modern era of space technology and rock'n'roll.

Three Major Museums

Munich boasts an amazing variety of museums—classical, historical and downright frivolous. We begin with three "musts".

Alte Pinakothek (Barer Strasse 27)

This is one of the world's great museums, ranking with the National Gallery of London, Louvre of Paris, Prado of Madrid or New York's Metropolitan. The Bavarian royal collections assemble here not only German masters but also the highest achievements of the Flemish, Dutch, Italian, Spanish and French. To help you find your way around, the museum provides a good ground-plan of the rooms organized by country and period.

We recommend that you start upstairs with the Dürers, Rembrandts, Rubens and Italian masters before tackling the other great Germans and Brueghels on the ground floor. The following are among the highlights. **German** By the leader of the 15th-century Cologne school, Stefan Lochner, see two exquisite little paintings, *Maria im Rosenhag* (Mary in the Rose Garden) and *Anbetung des Christkindes* (Adoration of the Christ Child).

The *Kirchenväteraltar* (Altar of the Church Fathers, 1480) is a glowing polyptych by the South Tyrolean, Michael Pacher, depicting Jerome, Augustine, Gregory and Ambrose.

Among several works by Albrecht Dürer, his *Vier Apostel* (Four Apostles, 1526) is a noble portrayal of John with Peter, and Paul with Mark. In his idealized self-portrait (1500), many object to his Christ-like pose, but for others, his genius justified his vanity.

His contemporary, Matthias Grünewald, is more down-to-earth, both in his gentle *Hl. Erasmus und Hl. Mauritius im Gespräch vertieft* (St Erasmus and St Mauritius Deep in Conversation) and in the brutal but moving *Verspottung Christi* (Mocking of Christ).

The grandiose *Alexanderschlacht* (1529) by Albrecht Altdorfer depicts Alexander's victory over Darius of Persia in 333 BC. This celebration of the

*T*he four gleaming aluminium cylinders of the Bavarian Motor Works' skyscraper dominate northern Munich from the edge of the Olympic sports complex.

Western world's triumph over the Orient was retrieved from Napoleon's apartments in France.
Flemish and Dutch The 15th-century master Rogier van der Weyden achieves a high spirituality with the pure artistic harmony of his *Adoration of the Magi* (1460).

Fool's Paradise (1567) by Pieter Brueghel may look playful enough, with a soldier, peasant and scholar sprawling on the ground, but Brueghel was trying to alert his countrymen to the evils of Spanish military occupation.

The prolific Peter Paul Rubens is represented here by some gigantic canvases, notably the formidable *Great Last Judgement* (1615) with its huge riot of damned and saved. He can also be intimate, with his loving portrait of wife Hélène Fourment in her wedding dress.

An intriguing self-portrait of Rembrandt catches him as if by surprise, a young man of 23 in 1629. The face appears again in his *Removal of Christ from the Cross* (1633)—the young man next to the ladder.
Italian Despite heavy-handed restoration, the *Virgin and Child* (1473) of Leonardo da Vinci still has enough of the master's nuanced serenity to be worth our attention. A magnificent *Virgin of the Annunciation* of the same period by Antonella da Messina needs less apology.

Among several works by Raphael are the tender *Madonna from the Tempi House* and a *Holy Family*.

We see Titian at his most powerful with the piercing portrait of *Emperor Charles V* and the passionate *Christ Crowned with Thorns*, completed around 1570 when the painter was almost 90.

Bedroom farce becomes high art in Tintoretto's *Vulcan Surprises Venus and*

Mars, with the war god hiding under a couch, still wearing his helmet.

Spanish Characteristically, El Greco evokes a disturbing melancholy in his *Disrobing of Christ* (1590). The portrait of a young Spanish noble by Velázquez is unfinished, but splendid nonetheless.

One of the great museum favourites is Murillo, for the young rascals he portrays in *Domestic Hygiene*—grandmother delousing a boy more interested in his dog— and *Melon- and Grape-Eaters*.

French A romantic sunrise by Claude Lorrain, a portrait of *Madame de Pompadour* by François Boucher and a Nicolas Lancret shepherdess characterize the rosy view of the 18th century that prevailed in France before the revolution. Artistically more impressive are works by Nicolas Poussin—the beautifully stylized *Midas and Bacchus* and *Lamentation of Christ*.

Residenzmuseum (Max-Joseph-Platz)

The Wittelsbachs' palace is so huge—112 rooms, halls and galleries, plus the ten rooms of the Schatzkammer (Treasure Chamber)—that two separate itineraries are organized on different days. Since the more important rooms are included in both, one tour is enough for a good overall impression. Following are some of the main stops on the way.

Ahnengalerie The Ancestors' Gallery introduces you to no less than 121 Wittels-

This priceless porcelain collection was given its own specially designed room when the Residenz was enlarged in the 18th century.

bachs going all the way back to Duke Theodor around 700.

Antiquarium Duke Albrecht V's library, 68m (225ft) long, is the biggest Renaissance room outside Italy. The busts of Greek and Roman heroes are works of the 16th century.

Porcelain Collection Cuvilliés designed this exquisite room for French, English and German porcelain, including delicate Meissen ware and locally manufactured pieces from Nymphenburg.

Grottenhof This most elegant of the Residenz courtyards was the work of

In The Mocking of Christ, Matthias Grünewald painted Jesus blindfolded so that he would not see his tormentors. The painting is in the Alte Pinakothek.

Netherlands architect Friedrich Sustris in 1581. In the middle is a handsome Perseus bronze by Hubert Gerhart. The courtyard takes its name from the Grotto Wall's elaborate Mercury fountain, set in an alcove encrusted with thousands of mussel, scallop and winkle shells.

Reiche Zimmer The State Rooms form the summit of Cuvilliés' art and the most admired rococo ensemble in Germany. Designed in 1729, the finest of these jewels is the Grüne Galerie (Green Gallery). Spare time, too, for the enchantment of the Spiegelkabinett (Cabinet of Mirrors), Miniaturenkabinett and Chinesisches Kabinett.

Hofkapelle and Reiche Kapelle Maximilian I built the first of these intimate chapels in the early 1600s for his courtiers, the second for his family.

Schatzkammer The Treasure House has a separate tour all to itself to show the Wittelsbachs' dazzling crystal and gold, silver and enamelware jewellery amassed over the course of 1,000 years. One of the earliest heirlooms is Arnulf's Ciborium, a communion goblet dated around 890.

Deutsches Museum

Zweibrückenstrasse takes you to the museum on its own little island in the Isar, where children (that is to say, everybody) have all the fun. This is reputedly the biggest scientific and technological collection in the world—19km (12 miles) long if you faithfully followed the lines guiding you to each and every exhibit, but do not let that put you off. Displays have been laid out with delightful attention to the comfort and enjoyment of the visitors. Most often, you yourself can push buttons, turn wheels and pull levers on the models, experimental machines and audio-visual systems. In a land that takes its science

and technology very seriously, this place reassuringly presents the most complex machines as monster toys. Exhibits range from printing and musical instruments to nuclear energy and the space sciences. See the first-rate planetarium and the old wooden bridge built when Munich was a tiny 12th-century settlement.

Setting the tone in the courtyard is "the world's first vertical take-off jet transport plane", the **Dornier Do 31** of 1967. This is no model, but the actual aircraft, an endearing object that belies its forbidding title.

In the transport halls, the **shipping section** (*Schiffahrt*) brings together every kind of boat from an Indian canoe, Arab dhow and Irish curragh to a splendid black velvet upholstered gondola and magnificent 19th-century 60m (200ft) German sailing ship. Remember that these are the real thing, not scale models.

Machinery devoted to **energy production** (*Kraftmaschinen*) takes on the beauty of sculpture—windmills, watermills, a wind turbine of 1900 from Dresden and a grand steam-powered fire-engine of 1893 from Nuremberg.

Railway enthusiasts will love the first German "Lokomobil", built in 1862 and still operating with the gentle hiss of a domestic steam iron. British patriots will approve the Germans' perfect copy of *Puffing Billy*, one of the earliest British locomotives (1813). The star attraction for youngsters is the model railway (*Modelleisenbahn*), 240m (790ft) of track with over 100 curves, a vast station and shunting yard for nine parallel tracks.

The **cars** on display range from Karl Benz's superb "Automobil Nummer 1" of 1886 to an unpainted stainless-steel Porsche made in 1967, immaculate after

155,000km (nearly 100,000 miles). They stand alongside Ludwig II's gilded super-rococo *Prunkwagen* (State Coach) designed just eight years before the first car. The technical data note: *"Bremsen fehlen"*—"No brakes".

Other Museums

Try to find time, too, for the excellent **Bayerisches Nationalmuseum**, Prinzregentenstrasse. Built in 1900, the exterior's different architectural styles reflect the artistic movements shown inside—a Romanesque east wing, Renaissance western façade, baroque tower and rococo west wing. The panorama of German cultural history from Roman times to the 19th century emphasizes both religious and secular arts and craftsmanship.

With the sweeping baroquification of Bavaria's churches and abbeys, this museum offers a rare occasion to see the splendid Romanesque and Gothic sculpture and painting that were discarded. A highlight is the **Tilman Riemenschneider room** of Gothic sculptures by the great Wurzburg master. Among the most powerful of his wooden statues are Mary Magdalen, St Sebastian and the Apostles, carved around 1500.

Look out for a chiming clock from the Heilbronn Monastery, giving *tempus fugit* awesome implications with its furious figure of Death riding a frantic lion.

Admirable secular exhibits include the **Augsburger Weberstube**, a room decorated with the original medieval furnishings and carvings of the Augsburg Weavers' Guild, and the superb doors carved with Old and New Testament scenes for the Asam house on Sendlinger Strasse (*see* page 113).

The **Müncher Stadtmuseum** (Municipal Museum, St-Jakobs-Platz) traces the

---

DEGENERATES FOREVER!

Hitler's speech inaugurating his new national art museum in 1937 attacked the "obscenities" of avant-garde art and expressly forbade any painter to use colours that the "normal" eye could not perceive in nature. Two exhibitions were staged to distinguish the good from the bad: one of great, that is officially sanctioned, German art; the other of "degenerate art".

The trouble was that people preferred the "degenerate" stuff exhibited in the nearby Hofgarten, where 2,009,899 spectators turned up, five times as many as for Hitler's favourites. Afterwards many of the officially despised paintings were auctioned off or hidden away. Back in the Haus der Kunst today, they include works by Kandinsky, Klee, Kokoschka and Chagall.

Kandinsky: Romantic Landscape.

---

town's history and folklore. The Moriskenraum displays Erasmus Grasser's wooden carvings of the Morris Dancers (1480) from the Old Town Hall's council chamber. Twenty kitchens, bedrooms and living rooms have been reconstituted, ranging from the frugal medieval to sumptuous rococo and cosy 19th- and early 20th-century bourgeois,

both heavy Biedermeier and more delicate *Jugendstil*. Highlights include a very inviting 18th-century wine tavern and an opulent artist's studio. The costume collection emphasizes Munich's role in German fashion design, with a poignant effort to bring a light touch to the display of wartime fashions. Other collections are devoted to film and photography and musical instruments, especially beautiful harps.

Up on the third floor is a charming collection of **Marionette Theatres** (*Puppentheatersammlung*), featuring glove puppets, shadow plays and mechanical toys. Munich would not be Munich if it did not have, on the ground floor, the **Deutsches Brauereimuseum** (German Brewery Museum) devoted to the German national drink. It begins in the year 3000 BC with the sculpture of an Egyptian brewery worker. You will find, too, the first-known literary allusion to the noble beverage in

With strings attached— marionettes in the wonderful Munich Puppet Theatre museum collection.

the Sumerian *Epic of Gilgamesh*. The hero's advice applies equally to Babylon and Bavaria: "Eat bread, you need it to live. Drink beer, it's the local custom."

The Ionic-columned **Glyptothek**, the museum of Greek and Roman sculpture on Königsplatz, was the glory of Ludwig I's "German Athens". Its greatest treasures are the Aegina friezes from the Temple of Aphaia, that date back to 505 and 485 BC. The well-preserved marble carvings show shielded warriors defending the island of Aegina's patron goddess, with that Ancient Greek smirk about her lips. Other major works include the *Apollo* *of Tenea, a Medusa*, the goddess of peace *Irene* and the *Barberini Faun.*

On the other side of the square, the highlights of the **Antikensammlungen** (Classical Art Collections) are a fine display of Greek vases and urns, and the Etruscan gold and silver donated by James Loeb. The German-American benefactor is known to classical students for the famous Loeb's Classical Library of Greek and Latin texts.

The **Neue Pinakothek** on Theresienstrasse is the pendant to the Alte Pinakothek opposite. It places 18th- and 19th-century German painting and sculpture, with an emphasis on Bavarian artists, in a historical context of European art. Caspar David Friedrich captures the essence of mystical German Romanticism in his foggy mountain landscapes. Munich's witty genre painter Carl Spitzweg spoofs the Romantic view of artistic squalor in his *Armer Poet* (Poor Poet). Max Liebermann, Max Slevogt and Lovis Corinth are tough exponents of realism, while Austria's Gustav Klimt and Egon Schiele contribute their respectively decorative and melancholy *Jugendstil.*

The Germans' European contemporaries found here include Goya, Gainsborough, Turner, Cézanne, Manet and Van Gogh.

JUST LIKE HOME

His royal parents celebrated Max Emanuel's birth in 1662 by building both the Theatinerkirche and Nymphenburg. All this attention went to Max's head and he tried to turn what was just a summer villa into a second Versailles. Bavarians were amused by his presumption, but in 1800 invading French armies found the surroundings familiar enough to make the castle their barracks.

The **Städtische Galerie** in the Lenbachhaus, Luisenstrasse, extends the city's art treasures into the 20th century. It is most notable for its unrivalled collection of works by Vasili Kandinsky, plus important canvases by Franz Marc, August Macke and Paul Klee. These four formed the nucleus of Munich's Blaue Reiter school of painting (*see* page 105). Look out, too, for its often controversial exhibitions of contemporary art.

The **Staatsgalerie moderner Kunst** exhibits Picasso, Braque, Dali, Italian Futurists and German Expressionists in Hitler's Haus der Kunst. Hitler would undoubtedly not appreciate the fine collection of American Abstract Expressionist, Pop, Op and Minimal Art.

Royal Retreats

Inside the city limits, **Schloss Nymphenburg** was the Wittelsbachs' summer refuge from the downtown heat of the Residenz. Follow their lead for a refreshing stroll around the gleaming palace's spacious grounds, ponds, fountains and garden pavilions.

It is an 8km (5-mile) drive or leisurely No. 12 tram ride from the Sheidplatz U-Bahn Station.

Leading to the palace, a canal passes a semicircle of lawns, the Schlossrondell, site of the **royal porcelain factory** (*Porzellansammlung*). The central edifice of the palace proper has galleries of fine 18th-century stucco work and ceiling frescoes. Johann Baptist Zimmermann has decorated the majestic **Steinerner Saal** (banquet hall) with nymphs epitomizing the palace's light-hearted ambiance when compared with the more formal Residenz. In the first pavilion to the south is Ludwig I's famous **Schönheitengalerie** (Gallery of Beauties). Joseph Stieler's paintings are said to portray the king's many mistresses. One at least, a ferocious lady with a belt of snakes around her waist and whip in her hand, can be identified as the notorious Lola Montez (*see* page 108).

The royal stables in the south wing now house the **Marstallmuseum**, a dazzling collection of state coaches. From the extravagance of Karl Albrecht's 18th-century coronation carriages, the vehicles went into a state of ornamental delirium under Ludwig II. Look at the Nymphen-schlitten (Nymph sleigh) used for his escapades into the foothills of the Alps.

After a subdued Italian period and the grand French geometric style, the **gardens** have ended up as a less formal English-style park, designed by Sckell, Rumford's associate on the Englischer Garten. The baroque and rococo pavilions seem a little isolated now, like original tenants who stayed on in the house while new owners changed all the furniture around them. They are left only with a few Grecian statues and a little classical geometry in the Schlossrondell and the rectangular Grosses Parterre immediately west of the central edifice.

To the left, **Amalienburg** (1734) is a delightful hunting-lodge by the designers of the State Rooms in the Residenz; architect François de Cuvilliés, sculptor Joachim Dietrich and stucco artist Johann Baptist Zimmermann. Wander through the rooms where the dogs and rifles were kept, the Pheasant Room next to the blue-and-white, Dutch-tiled kitchen, and the brilliant silver and pastel yellow Hall of Mirrors.

Continue west to the **Badenburg** (Bath Pavilion), which is fitted with Delft china fixtures that are an interior decorator's dream. On a promontory across the island-dotted Grosser See is the little Monopteros, a temple for trysts and picnics.

Skirt the central canal and its spectacular cascade to another, smaller pond and the **Pagodenburg**, an octagonal tea pavilion, with exotic black-and-red-lacquered Chinese chambers upstairs.

On your way back to the palace, visit the curious **Magdalenenklause**. Prince Max Emanuel built it as a hermitage for his meditation but died before it was completed. Its melancholy crumbling ruin is a deliberate architectural effect, and penitence is the dominant theme of its sculpture and paintings.

North of the park is the fine **Neuer Botanischer Garten**, entrance on Menzinger Strasse. The Arboretum is cleverly landscaped to resemble different climatic regions of the world with their appropriate flora—pine forest, Arctic tundra, moorland, desert dunes, the steppes and Alpine country alongside an artificial pond.

After Nymphenburg's flamboyance, drive west (or take No. 73 tram from Menzinger Strasse) to the refreshing simplicity of **Schloss Blutenburg**, now a convent. It is worth visiting if only for the palace chapel, a superb Gothic structure rare in this part of Bavaria. See three splendid altar paintings by Jan Polack (1491): the *Holy Trinity* on the high altar with *Christ Enthroned* on the left and the *Annunciation* to the right. Note, too, on the walls the polychrome wooden sculptures of the Apostles, Mary and a resurrected Christ.

Finish your tour in nearby Pippinger Strasse with a visit to **Pfarrkirche St Wolfgang**. The parish church's serene interior has frescoes by Polack (1479) and fine carved wooden altars from the same period. The perfect place to meditate at the end of a long day.

Excursions from Munich

At the weekend, many Munich residents head for the resort lakes and sparkling baroque churches south-west of the Bavarian capital. Go on a weekday; you will not have the place to yourself, but the roads will be less crowded, particularly the infernal Autobahn ring-road. A day trip to Munich's northern outskirts takes in the lightest and most sombre aspects of Bavaria's past. You will probably prefer to start with the dark and relax afterwards in the light.

Dachau

This pretty village, 17 km (9 miles) north-west of Munich on the B304, was once just a sleepy place much favoured by painters. People came to see the remains of its baroque palace. Then, on 20 March 1933, a mere 48 days after Hitler came to power, Dachau was designated as the site of the first Nazi concentration camp. Munich police chief Heinrich Himmler chose a disused gunpowder factory. Today you can still admire the palace and the attractive 17th- and 18th-century houses around their Renaissance parish church of St Jakob, but the concentration camp has become the main attraction. Follow the road sign, just like one shown in a 1930s photo in the camp's museum, to the *Konzentrationslager*.

The **museum** was built on the camp site by the International Dachau Committee, funded by the Bavarian state government. Exhibits document the camp's history soberly but uncompromisingly, without unnecessary pathos. You will see photos, uniforms, and the insignia that distinguished inmates—black for political prisoners, pink for homosexuals, yellow for Jews, and so on. Dachau was not one of the leading centres for extermination—31,951 deaths were recorded from 1933 to 1945—but it served as a hard labour camp and as a research station for experiments that were carried out in Auschwitz. Some 100,000 prisoners, principally political, were kept here. Apart from the museum, the original crematorium and a reconstructed prison barracks still stand. Chapels and a synagogue are provided for prayer. A Carmelite convent, **Sühnekloster Heiliges Blut**, uses a camp watch-tower as its entrance.

Schloss Schleissheim

East on B471, re-enter the sunny baroque world of Max Emanuel. The Neues Schloss has a glorious staircase with frescoes by Cosmas Damian Asam. Fine stucco work ornaments banquet halls and the grand **Barockgalerie**. Its art collection is particularly strong in Flemish and Dutch painters—Rubens, the younger Brueghel and Van Dyck—but also boasts fine works by Poussin and Ribera.

The **palace gardens** are a triumph of the French style of landscaping. It is a sheer joy to walk around the waterfall, canals and flowerbed designed by Dominique Girard, disciple of the Versailles master André Le Nôtre. At the far east end of the gardens is the **Schloss Lustheim**, a hunting-lodge now housing Germany's biggest collection of Meissen porcelain.

Fürstenfeldbruck

The town's former Cistercian monastery makes a worthwhile stop if, rather than returning to Munich, you are heading south-west towards the lakes of Ammersee and Starnberger See. The monastery itself is now used as a police training academy, but the imposing **Klosterkirche Mariae**

Himmelfahrt (Church of the Assumption) has been preserved as a masterpiece of 18th-century baroque. After working on Munich's Dreifaltigkeitskirche and Schloss Nymphenburg, Giovanni Viscardi achieved here a synthesis of Italian grace in its interior with a more Bavarian tone to its lofty façade. The Asam brothers did the ceiling frescoes. In the sacristy are paintings by Gabriel Mälesskircher, an important contemporary of Matthias Grünewald.

Starnberger See

This lake, some 25km (15 miles) southwest of Munich, is a sportsman's delight. Anglers come for pike and tasty *Renken* (whitefish). Water sports enthusiasts enjoy the windsurfing or sailing against an idyllic Alpine backdrop. Near every resort town, particularly on the west shore, is a beach for a bracing swim. Golfers make straight for the 18-hole course at **Feldafing**. Further south, music lovers come for the summer concerts at **Tutzing**. Just inland, you get a fine view of the whole lake from the beer garden up on **Ilkahöhe** at a height of 728m (2,388ft).

The town of **Starnberg** has many elegant villas for the élite of Bavarian society. They go to Sunday mass at the 18th-century parish church of St Joseph, which boasts a fine baroque altar by Ignaz Günther. The lake visitors love its darker side, too. On the north-east shore near **Schloss Berg** (a private palace still owned by the Wittelsbachs), a cross rises from the water marking the spot where Ludwig II died in 1886. (Across the lake at Possenhofen was the childhood home of his niece Sissi, Empress Elisabeth of Austria.)

Ammersee

For your first view of the lake surrounded by its wooded green hills, visit the Benedictine abbey of **Andechs** to the south-east. The monastery includes a restaurant, shops and old apothecary. The simple, almost austere exterior of the abbey's pilgrimage church, **Mariae Verkündigung** (Annunciation), is in sharp contrast to the bright and airy rococo décor created by Johann Baptist Zimmermann. Stroll in the charming 17th-century arcaded cloisters.

Like Starnberger Lake, the Ammersee is much appreciated for its fishing and water sports, with half a dozen beaches lining the western shore. The principal resort, **Diessen**, has a good sailing school. The elegant 18th-century **St Maria Stiftskirche** (abbey church) is by Johann Michael Fischer. The richly endowed interior has a graceful high altar by François de Cuvilliés, pulpit by Johann Baptist Straub, altar painting of St Sebastian by Giambattista Tiepolo on the south wall and, in the sacristy, a sculpture of St Peter by Erasmus Grasser.

THE LAST WALK

The Bavarian government had declared Ludwig II mad and incompetent and placed him under house arrest at Schloss Berg, where he had spent much of his youth. Despite the pouring rain on that Whit Sunday evening, 12 June 1886, Ludwig asked his doctor, Bernhard von Gudden, to join him for a walk down by the lake. They never returned. Later that night their corpses were found in the water, the doctor's face scratched and bruised and strangulation marks around his neck. Was the king murdered? And the doctor? Both by an unknown third party, as a recent documented theory suggests? Or did they both drown accidentally after a struggle? At any rate, the king's death, like his life, was the stuff dreams and nightmares are made of.

Landsberg

This proud old town on the Lech river was founded in 1160, just two years after Munich, and still has its medieval ramparts with towers and gate houses. The battlemented **Bayertor** (1425) is one of Germany's most handsome Gothic fortifications. Local architect Dominikus Zimmermann worked on four churches here, boosting his budgets by becoming mayor. Note his interior baroquification of the big Gothic parish church **Mariae Himmelfahrt** (Assumption). Tall Renaissance and baroque houses, including the town hall, give a fine allure to the market square, Hauptplatz.

Ottobeuren

In the gently rolling wooded foothills of the Allgäu Alps, the heart of Bavarian Swabia, stands one of southern Germany's grandest monasteries. The Benedictine abbey, founded under Charlemagne in 764, was spared the assaults of the Reformation and Peasants' War and sustained a great scholarly reputation for its manuscripts and music. Its church, **Heilige Dreifaltigkeit** (Holy Trinity, 1748), is a masterpiece of baroque architecture, and is the supreme achievement of Johann Michael Fischer. The towers are 82m (269ft) high. Unusually, the nave, 90m (295ft) long, runs north–south, creating a unique play of light and colour. The interior shines with rose tints from the columns and pilasters, and with ochres and mauves from the rococo decoration of Johann Jakob Zeiller's frescoes and Johann Michael Feuchtmayer's stucco and sculpture. The cupola fresco over the transept depicts the Pentecost Miracle. Side altars at the crossing of nave and transept portray four saints—Michael, Raphael, Joseph and John the Baptist. Notice, too, the pulpit, splendid walnut choir stalls and the magnificent organ with dazzling panoply of modern pipes added in 1957.

The abbey of 250 rooms and halls is now shared by the monastery and a boarding school. The buildings include not only the abbot's palace, an opulent library and a museum of local Gothic wood sculpture but also, a rarity for a religious institution, a baroque theatre.

South to the Royal Castles

This is an excursion into Bavaria's fantasy land. Though you will pass some other genuine architectural jewels on the way, suspend all serious aesthetic judgment for Ludwig's castle follies. Guided bus tours are available direct from Munich or from nearby Füssen. It's difficult to avoid the crowds for this year-round attraction, but try the heart of the winter when the snow doubles the castles' fairy-tale effect.

Highway 17 down from Landsberg is the southernmost section of the Romantic Route (*Romantische Strasse, see* page 142). **Steingaden** has kept intact the 12th-century Romanesque exterior of its parish church, **St Johann Baptist**, though the interior has undergone the customary baroque changes of Bavaria's Counter-Reformation. In the cloisters, the western arcade's sculpted pillars and Gothic vaulting have escaped unscathed.

To enjoy baroque architecture's unfettered luminosity, pay a visit to the nearby **Wieskirche**. With an exterior simple as a country barn, Dominikus Zimmermann's pilgrimage church fits perfectly into the exquisite landscape of wooded hills and flowery meadows. Inside, his brother Johann Baptist Zimmermann enhances the

festive spirit with a ceiling fresco of bright heaven ringed by trumpeting angels and adoring saints. Almost forgotten is the grim object of the faithful's pilgrimage, a crude chained wooden image of Christ flagellated, which miraculously shed tears before a local peasant girl back in 1738.

Füssen is a spa resort with sulphur springs and mud-baths for all kinds of aches and pains. Its 15th- and 16th-century gabled houses are a handsome testimony to its prosperous civic past on the trade route between Bavaria and Lombardy. Rising high above the rooftops of the old town, the **Hohes Schloss**, turned by the Bishop of Augsburg from a 14th-century fortress into a Renaissance residence, shows what a no-nonsense palace should look like. The attractions of the town have made it a popular resort, but the crowds who flock here are drawn by two extraordinary royal castles in the nearby mountains.

Hohenschwangau and Neuschwanstein

Dense pine forests and mountains hug the lakes where the feudal lords of the Schwangau built their fortresses which were impregnable until the invention of the internal combustion engine. Now buses take them by assault to see where the latter-day kings of Bavaria erected their follies. Drivers park their cars at Hohensch-

The gorgeous ceiling of Ottobeuren Holy Trinity abbey church depicts the Pentecost Miracle when "cloven tongues as of fire" descended on the multitude.

wangau and take a shuttle-bus or more romantic horse-and-carriage to Neuschwanstein. The half-hour walk is steep.

Perfectly conscious of the fantasy element in the enterprise, crown prince and future king Maximilian II asked Italian theatre designer Domenico Quaglio to rebuild the 12th-century **Hohenschwangau** as a summer home in 1833. The heavily neo-Gothic four-towered pile imposes a relentless Romantic medievalism. Moritz von Schwind's frescoes depict great moments of German history. The music room displays Wagner memorabilia—the composer was a guest of Ludwig II, whose bedroom has an astounding star-studded ceiling. Swan motifs pay heraldic tribute to the Schwangau lords, culminating in the swan fountain in the park. Amid the crypto-medieval bric-a-brac, the solidly 19th-century Biedermeier furnishings are comfortingly down to earth, but perhaps not enough to anchor Ludwig II to the world of reality when he spent his boyhood here dreaming of troubadours and fairy-tale princes.

After visiting the medieval fortress of Wartburg in Thuringia in 1867, Ludwig was fired with a vision of the *Minnesänger*—minstrels of the 12th century—and decided to build a castle that would recapture the spirit of that romantic era. On a spur in the Pöllat gorge looking down on Lake Forggen, **Neuschwanstein** is the result. Like his father, Ludwig called on a theatre designer, Christian Jank. The silver granite neo-Romanesque fastness thrusts its pointed turrets above the pines and larches, at once massive and strangely slender, even fragile. Inside, all is opulently operatic—and totally unlivable. Sculptural and painted allusions to Wagner's *Tannhäuser, Tristan and Isolde* and *Lohengrin* are everywhere.

Richard Wagner (1813–1883)

The man was extravagant in all things—his art, his public and private life and his money-spending. Always in debt, forever being chased by some irate husband or berated by political opponents, he was applauded and booed in opera houses with equal fervour. He sought in his grandiose operas of German saga to embrace all the arts, uniting music, drama and meticulously designed décor in his concept of *Gesamtkunstwerk* (synthesis of the arts). Writing both music and libretto, he broke with the traditional distinction between aria and recitative, substituting the "endless melody" of his *Sprechgesang* ("speech-song"), as exhilarating for his fans as it was exasperating for his enemies.

He was born in Leipzig on May 22, 1813, six months after the death of his father. His step-father was a painter, singer and actor, and his sisters were opera singers and actresses. He did a quick six months at Leipzig University more for the fun of student life than for any serious work. He relied more on his own studies than a tutor to learn piano and composition and steeped himself in Beethoven's quartets and symphonies and the theatre of Shakespeare, Goethe and Schiller.

Troublesome Beginnings

At 20, he wrote an undistinguished Symphony in C Major and began his opera career working in third-rate provincial theatre companies. He wrote two resounding failures: *Die Feen* (The Fairies) and *Liebesverbot* (Ban on Love), based on Shakespeare's *Measure for Measure*. Between flops, he fell in love with a Magdeburg actress, Minna Planer, and embarked on a stormy marriage beset with jealousies and monumental debts.

In Paris, living in poverty cooped up with a Bohemian German colony, he created two new operas. However, despite the support of composer Giacomo Meyerbeer, the musical establishment closed its doors on him and he had to go to Dresden in 1842 to have them produced. The Romantic *Rienzi* was a success, but *The Flying Dutchman,* the tale of a sea captain condemned to sail forever in which Wagner introduced his new ideas of integrating music and drama, was coolly received. He remained in Dresden as *Kapellmeister* (musical director) to produce *Tannhäuser*, the first of his operas based on a German legend. But the King of Saxony refused to let him stage *Lohengrin* because Wagner wanted control of opera productions to be in the hands of the artists rather than the royal court. His radical ideas were getting him increasingly into trouble, and involvement in the German revolutionary movement of 1848–49 forced him to flee to Switzer-

One of the master's pianos

land. His friend Franz Liszt directed the *Lohengrin* première in Weimar while Wagner was in exile.

Triumph of the Nibelungs

During his exile in Zurich from 1849 to 1858, Wagner expounded his aesthetic ideas for a total synthesis of music and drama, the famous *Gesamtkunstwerk*. He also studied Norse myths and the Siegfried legend, which he developed into his great four-part opera cycle, *Der Ring der Nibelungen*. The mammoth concept of his operatic epic poems *Rheingold* (Rhine Gold), *Walküre* (Valkyries), *Siegfried* and *Götterdämmerung* (Twilight of the Gods), threatened to be impossible to stage.

His progressive social revolutionary ideas grew increasingly dark and nihilistic under the influence of Schopenhauer's pessimistic metaphysics. He also revealed a vehement anti-Semitism, turning on his benefactor Meyerbeer and Felix Mendelssohn in his essay *Judaism in Music* (1850) which declared his "invincible antipathy for the Jewish spirit". Together with his glorification of the Germanic identity, this was to win him the admiration of Adolf Hitler.

Meanwhile, another tempestuous but hopeless love affair with Mathilde Wesendonck, wife of a rich patron and friend, forced Wagner to leave Zurich and inspired him to give grandiose lyrical expression to his new pessimism in *Tristan and Isolde*. Despite 77 rehearsals in Vienna, this, like *The Ring*, proved impossible to stage, and he had to flee his debtors and enemies caused by his growing irascibility.

In 1864, Ludwig II of Bavaria came to Wagner's rescue, inviting him to Munich to complete *The Ring* and stage his other operas in financial and artistic comfort. He promptly fell in love with Cosima, wife of his conductor, Hans von Bülow, and had to move on to Lake Lucerne. *The Ring* was finally ready for production in 1876, triumphantly staged at the new Festspielhaus in Bayreuth in the presence of Emperor Wilhelm I—and Ludwig II despite the composer's broken promise to hold the première in Munich. Personal loyalty was not his strong suit. Friedrich Nietzsche, whom he had befriended and then antagonized, sighed philosophically: "Wagner is a neurosis." The genius's rendezvous was always with his muses.

He died in Venice, February 13, 1883.

The composer's Bayreuth home, Villa Wahnfried

Ettal and Oberammergau

To reach Ludwig's other castle in this region, Linderhof, take the Garmisch-Partenkirchen Autobahn from Munich. Turn off west to Ettal to visit first the lovely abbey church of **St Marien**, in the Benedictine monastery, set in the gently curving Ettal valley. The church, with its baroque shell built around the original 12-sided Gothic dome, has a magnificent fresco by Johann Jakob Zeiller in the cupola, depicting the life of St Benedict.

To visit **Oberammergau**, do not wait until the next (ten-yearly) performance of its famous Passion Play in 2000. As the home town of *Lüftlmaler* (literally air-painter) Franz Zwinck, it is equally proud of its gaily painted 18th-century house

façades, combining religious and rustic motifs with clever *trompe-l'oeil* architectural effects. The frescoes, nicely restored, have the fresh impact of a sketch since they had to be rapidly executed before the wet plaster base dried in the open air. The most important are the Geroldhaus (1778) and Pilatushaus (1784). Boasting one of Germany's leading craft

Anybody in the materialistic 19th century spending millions on a fairy-tale castle like Neuschwanstein was clearly certifiable. Ludwig II of Bavaria was certified.

MOVING WITH THE TIMES

The Oberammergau Passion Play, performed not at Easter but from May to September, was begun in 1634 to give thanks for being spared a plague that ravaged Bavaria the year before. Nearly 2,000 villagers act in the play, preparing for their parts by growing long hair and beards months in advance to conform to the traditional images of Christ and the Apostles. Over the centuries, the day-long performance has been altered, accentuating or tempering, for instance, the role of the Jews in the Crucifixion, to meet the changing spirit of the times. In the more liberal modern era, anti-Semitic passages have been eliminated from the text, but only in 1990 did the town council, which organizes the play, agree to admit the participation of non-virgins over 35. Until then, the mother of 33-year-old Jesus was always played by a teenage virgin.

schools, the town is also renowned for its woodcarvers. See their work in the **Heimatmuseum** (Folklore Museum, Dorfstrasse 8), most notably a monumental Christmas crib created over several generations in the 18th century.

Linderhof

In a remote valley of the Ammergau Alps, this little vanilla-coloured palace was Ludwig's favourite. In the same year that he drew inspiration from Wartburg castle for Neuschwanstein, he visited Versailles. This is his neo-rococo version of Louis XIV's Grand Trianon. After Wagner, the Sun King was Ludwig's major obsession, omnipresent at Linderhof, notably in the

*L*udwig of Bavaria was a fan of syrupy kitsch typified by this Venus Grotto at Linderhof.

luxurious state bedroom; but would Louis have installed a sunken dining table to conjure up only for solitary royal suppers? Or built a Moorish pavilion in which to dress up as a Turkish sultan and smoke a hookah with young boys disguised as palace eunuchs? Standing in the tailored landscape of pond and park, you might imagine that even the romantic Alpine backdrop of the Graswangtal sprang from Ludwig's imagination. The Venus Grotto is man-made, carved out of the mountainside with another motif from Wagner's *Tannhäuser*.

The German Alps

The mountains are not as high as the Swiss or French Alps, but the landscape around the resorts of Garmisch-Partenkirchen and Berchtesgaden is truly spectacular. The scenic route signposted *Deutsche Alpenstrasse* is second in popularity only to the Romantic Route. We have divided it into three sections.

Oberstdorf to Garmisch-Partenkirchen

The mountain resort of **Oberstdorf** in the Allgäu region is popular with hikers and offers a climbing school to budding mountaineers. The town's bracing air is a reputed cure for respiratory ailments. Winter sports facilities are first class, with the bonus of a great ice skating rink. A cable-car gives you a good start for an hour's hike up the Nebelhorn, 2,224m (7,300ft) where, despite its name ("foggy peak"), you may get a fine view of the Zugspitze (*see* page 138) and the Appenzell Alps in Switzerland. Amateur botanists hike among the wild flowers of the Stillach valley, starting out with a cable-car ride to the Fellhorn, 2,037m (6,683ft).

Plentiful sun and snow from November to May make **Garmisch-Partenkirchen** Germany's most popular winter sports centre. Since the 1936 Olympics, it has boasted superb ice rinks and a breathtaking ski-jump. With its casino, health spa and bouncing night-life, the cheerful resort also has much to offer spring and summer visitors. West of the railway on the Loisach river, Garmisch is the bustling town centre. It has an old Italian apothecary on the market square and many fine rustic houses with *Lüftlmalerei* frescoes, one of the best being the Altwerdenfelser house on Bahnhofstrasse. Composer Richard Strauss had his home at Zöppritzstrasse 42; he died there in 1949.

Partenkirchen is the quieter, quainter side of town. On Ludwigstrasse see the Haus zum Langerbeck and the splendid Werdenfelser folklore museum—with Christmas cribs, costumes and farm kitchens. Climb up to the pilgrimage church of St Anton to see the fine baroque fresco by Johannes Holzer.

Out of town, the first and almost obligatory pilgrimage is a ride to the top of Germany's highest peak, the **Zugspitze**, 2,963m (9,718ft). Take the mountain railway (*Bayrische Zugspitzbahn*) from near the Olympic Stadium and then the cable car to the top. The most popular hikes are through the **Höllentalklamm**, a gorge 6km (4 miles) south-west of town, and the **Partnachklamm** 3km (2 miles) to the south-east—take a raincoat for the spray from the gorge's waterfall.

A more ambitious but rewarding hike takes you via the Partnachklamm and Elmau up to another of Ludwig II's hideaways, the **Schachen hunting-lodge**. Here behind an innocent Swiss-chalet façade, above the simple wood-panelled ground floor, is an Oriental palace. As at

Linderhof (*see* page 137), Ludwig put on his Turkish-sultan act, sprawling on the cushions and carpets while dusky young fellows fanned him with peacock feathers.

Mittenwald and Tegernsee

An old trading depot for Venetian merchants, **Mittenwald** is today subject to heavy traffic to and from Austria, but remains a pleasant base for exploring the surrounding countryside. Attracting the leading talents of the day (Matthäus Günther, Franz Zwinck and Franz Karner), Mittenwald can claim some of Bavaria's

best-preserved *Lüftlmalerei* houses. On Obermarkt square, look out for the Neunerhaus, Schlipferhaus and Gasthof zur Alpenrose. Günther also painted the tower façade of St Peter and Paul church. Inside, the excellent baroque stucco work and painting is by Josef Schmuzer. The town's folklore museum (*Geigenbau- und Heimatmuseum*, Ballenhausgasse 3) is devoted mainly to musical instruments. It was once the workshop of 17th-century violin-maker Matthias Klotz, who worked in Cremona with the great Italian craftsman Nicola Amati.

The Alps may not be high by Himalayan standards but they stand like a wall, forming the southern frontier of Germany.

Sailors, windsurfers and fishermen make for the nearby **lakes**: Wildensee, Ferchensee and Lautersee. Hikers and climbers head for the Karwendel mountains. A cable-car takes care of those interested only in looking around the nature reserve.

139

Highway 11 runs north through some grand countryside around the Walchensee, framed by densely wooded mountains. Enquire about summer concerts held at **Benediktbeuern** abbey church; its chapel devoted to St Anastasia was decorated by Hans Asam.

Bad Tölz stands on either side of a bend in the rushing Isar river. Facing a modern spa (its iodized waters are good for the heart), the Old Town is on the west bank, distinguished by a colourfully painted town hall and other old houses on and around Marktstrasse. North of town, a Calvary of 15 chapels marks the Stations of the Cross from the Mount of Olives to the Crucifixion. At the top is the chapel of St Leonard (1718), with chains symbolizing the patron of liberated prisoners— and kept closed because of the risk of theft.

With sailing and boat cruises in summer and skating in winter, **Tegernsee** is a magnet for fashionable Munich society. Beautifully situated among mountains, pine forest and meadows, the Benedictine **monastery** was a centre of culture renowned for its work in gold, stained glass and illuminated manuscripts. Its abbey church of St Quirin is a Gothic basilica reworked in Italian baroque by Enrico Zuccalli. Less celestial, the local folklore museum runs a charming lakeside steam train ride from Tegernsee town to Schaftlach and back.

In the quiet little resort of **Gmund**, see the pretty baroque parish church of St Egidius. Across the lake, **Bad Wiessee** offers sailing for the healthy, as well as iodized, chloride or sulphur baths for the sick and a casino for everybody. From **Rottach-Egern** at the lake's southern end, take a cable-car trip up into the Walberg mountains.

Another popular excursion takes you east to **Schliersee**, a smaller, more peaceful lake. Visit St Sixtus church which boasts three fine pieces of late 15th-century art. Left and right of the high altar are Erasmus Grasser's carvings of St Sixtus and a *Gnadenstuhl* (God's Throne of Grace) and, over the sacristy, a *Madonna* painted by Jan Pollak. Continue on Highway 307 to take the cable-car, signposted *Wendelsteinbahn*, and an easy walk to the top of **Wendelstein mountain**, 1,838m (6,030ft). You get a grand view north-east to Chiemsee and due east to the Berchtesgaden Alps.

Chiemsee to Berchtesgaden

With typical self-parody, Bavarians like to call their biggest lake the "Bavarian Sea". Once a glacier basin and often not much warmer, **Chiemsee** covers 82km² (32 square miles), broad enough to work up some good winds off the Alps for exhilarating sailing and windsurfing. Steer away from the noisy south shore, where the Munich–Salzburg Autobahn passes.

You will find the best beaches at **Chieming** on the east shore. To the west, the main town, **Prien**, is a health resort from which most of the cruises leave for the islands. These are the lake's major attraction. The largest, **Herreninsel**, is the site of a medieval monastery and, since 1885 when the building money ran out, the last and most extravagant of Ludwig II's follies, the unfinished **Schloss Herrenchiemsee**. A walk through the island's woods or a romantic ride in a horse-drawn carriage reveals here the full extent of Ludwig's obsession with his idol, Louis XIV. Challenging this time not some subsidiary Trianon but the grand palace of Versailles itself, the Bavarian king built (though never slept in) a bedroom more opulent than the Sun King's and a gigantic garish Hall of Mirrors to out-dazzle the Galerie des Glaces. The hall has doors with inlaid Meissen porcelain and has, as tourguides love to announce, 1,848 candles, 33 chandeliers and 44 candelabras. Not all, but quite enough, are used for summer candlelit concerts of chamber music. The gardens are at their most magical when the fountains are illuminated at night.

On **Fraueninsel**, a pretty fishing village and the Benedictine convent, which is still active, provide a welcome modest antidote. In the church of St Maria and nearby Michaelskapelle, important fragments of 12th-century and even 9th-century frescoes have been uncovered under the baroque stucco. From the lake, the *Deutsche Alpenstrasse* (Highway 305) crosses the fast-running Tiroler Ache river on the way south to **Reit im Winkel**. This charming mountain village of rustic houses is popular with skiers for the pistes on the nearby Winklmoos Alm. Stop off at the resort of **Ruhpolding**. Its folklore museum has an impressive collection of peasant costumes and ecclesiastic robes from Gothic to neoclassical times, most notably a Renaissance chasuble from Toledo. Visit, too, the little rococo St Georg church with an exquisite Romanesque *Madonna and Child* in a side altar on the south wall.

Bad Reichenhall, an ancient salt-manufacturing town on the Saalach river (now quite a prosperous spa resort) traces its origins back at least to 200 BC. Tour its **Alte Saline** (Old Salt Works) built in 1834, with paddle wheels and pumps installed in astonishing neomedieval marble halls. The salt is derived not from the rock but from highly concentrated saline springs.

By dint of the town's salt trade with Italy, the church of St Zeno was built as a pendant to Verona's famous San Zeno Maggiore. The Italian influence is evident in its Romanesque west porch. Its tympanum shows Zeno to the left of Mary and Jesus—St Rupert is on the right. The church is undergoing extensive renovation to restore the Romanesque interior.

Berchtesgaden, magnificently situated in an arc of formidable mountains, is one of Germany's most popular resorts. In history, it was the Wittelsbachs' eastern redoubt against encroachment by the powerful archbishop of Salzburg. In 1945, faulty intelligence convinced the Allies that Hitler would stage a last stand here, from his country home above the town.

Considering the town's troubled past, its historic centre is marvellously preserved around Schlossplatz, with granary, accounting house and royal castle transformed by the Wittelsbachs from an Augustine monastery. The castle is now a rich museum of weapons, porcelain and tapestries. Wood sculpture of the 15th and 16th centuries are displayed in the monks' two-aisled Gothic dormitory. The medieval cloister has intricately carved capitals on its colonnade. As the lions at the entrance indicate, the abbey church is Lombard Gothic in structure. Notice its fine 15th-century choir stalls. But it is the **Salzbergwerk** (Salt Mines), active since 1515, that are the town's main attraction. For the guided tour, you are given miner's clothes—cap, apron and leggings. You are also provided with a leather "seat" on which to slide 500m (1,640ft) down the mine chute (perfectly safe) to the salt rock below. The salt is manufactured by sluicing the salt rock with fresh water to produce a 27 per cent concentrate of salt brine. Down below, a train takes you through galleries and tunnels of glistening salt crystal. Then there is a boat trip across an illuminated subterranean lake—was it this much fun in the salt mines of Siberia? For an awesome view of the surrounding countryside, drive up to **Obersalzberg**, 4km (2½ miles) east of town. This was the site of Hitler's country home, now destroyed. A shuttle-bus takes you on the last winding stretch with its hair-raising hairpin bend over the Scharitzkehlalm ravine. An elevator completes the climb to the Kehlstein peak, 1,837m (6,025ft).

One of the prettiest excursions out of town is 5km (3 miles) south to **Königssee**. Part of Berchtesgaden National Park, this idyllic lake attracts an uncomfortable mob scene in summer but is well worth the trip out of season. With the sheer mountain walls of the **Watzmann**, 2,714m (8,904ft) towering above, take a quiet electric-powered boat from the village of Königssee to the little 18th-century St Bartholomä church. Its domed chapels form a cloverleaf pattern beside the Wittelsbachs' old hunting lodge amid the maple trees.

The *Romantische Strasse* (Romantic Route)

With half of southern Germany clamouring to be included on this most popular of tourist routes, the official signs for the *Romantische Strasse* stretch from Füssen near the Swiss border right the way up to Aschaffenburg. We have selected the most popular stretch from Augsburg to Rothenburg. It is enough to do full justice to the old image of Romantic medieval Germany.

*P*alatial boat-houses on Königssee near Berchtesgaden shelter the boats that take you cruising on the deep, dark waters of the lake.

142

Augsburg

Proud and independent-minded, more Swabian than Bavarian, the town was founded by the Romans as *Augusta Vindelicorum* in 15 BC. Its golden age was in the 15th and 16th centuries when the Fugger and Welser families were bankers of the German empire, making and breaking its Habsburg rulers. (The Welsers founded Venezuela, Germany's first overseas colony. Descendants of the Fugger family are still shareholders in the bank that today bears their name.) Augsburg was the home, too, of great painters—Hans Holbein, Hans Burgkmair and Martin Schongauer—and of Mozart's father, Leopold. More recently, it was the birthplace of Bert Brecht (museum in his home, Auf dem Rain 7).

The city gate on the southern edge of town, **Rotes Tor**, makes an appropriate entrance to the Romantic Route. The fortified gatehouse encloses a courtyard that serves as an open-air theatre in summer.

On Maximilianstrasse, the town's main street badly hit in World War II, the stately Renaissance façades of its patrician houses have been painstakingly restored. Two **Fugger mansions**, at Nos. 36 and 38, are now in part a science museum. The 18th-century **Schaezler-Palais** at No. 46 houses a state art gallery of Swabian masters Holbein and Burgkmair, and Dürer's portrait of Jakob Fugger. A baroque collection groups works by Matthäus Günther, Johann Baptist Zimmermann and Franz Anton Maulpertsch.

In front of the palace, the bronze **Herkulesbrunnen** is one of three fine Renaissance fountains in the town centre. The **Merkurbrunnen** celebrates the god of commerce at the town's busiest intersection at the top of Maximilianstrasse, and the grand **Augustusbrunnen** stands on Rathausplatz. Notice as you walk around the east side of town its attractive, time-honoured water supply system drawing clean, swift flowing conduits from the Lech river.

Framed by two onion-domed towers, Elias Holl's soaring **Rathaus** (1618) is a splendid expression of Augsburg's civic pride—reinforced by the neighbouring watchtower, the **Perlachturm**, 70m (230ft) high. The town hall's gable is crowned by the Imperial two-headed eagle and Augsburg's pine-cone emblem, a Roman symbol of fertility. Inside, the council chamber (*Goldener Saal*) has a superb coffered ceiling.

The Gothic **St Ulrich and St Afra** parish church stands at the south end of Maximilianstrasse. In its noble, lofty interior, the Kreuzaltar at the crossing between transept and nave has a remarkable bronze Crucifixion group of Jesus with Mary, Mary Magdalen and St John.

Visit, too, the church of **St Anna** (Annastrasse 20), which has been Protestant since the time it gave sanctuary to Martin Luther in 1515. At the west end, the Fuggerkapelle built by Jakob and son Ulrich in 1509 is a grandiose Renaissance monument. On the blind arcade at the chapel rear are Sebastian Loscher's sculpted reliefs of the *Resurrection* and *Samson fighting the Philistines*. Sarcophagus portrayals of Jakob and Ulrich Fugger are based on drawings by Dürer.

However, the most human monument to the bankers' presence in Augsburg life is the **Fuggerei** (1525), Europe's first social housing development. It still provides homes for the needy at the original token rent of one *rheinischer Gulden*, 1.70 DM a year. Built east of the Oberer Graben just off Jakoberstrasse, the 53 two-storey red-brick houses provide 106 apartments,

which have been lovingly restored from their wartime damage. Uniform, but by no means monotonous, many have ivy-covered façades along the eight tree-lined streets. The Hauptplatz attracts local gossips around the bronze Neptune fountain (1550). A museum at Mittlere Gasse 13 shows a house as it was furnished in the 17th century. The little church of St Marx has on its high altar a *Crucifixion* by Venetian painter Palma Giovane.

Donauwörth to Nördlingen

Take Highway 2 north to the confluence of the Danube and Wörnitz rivers. The tranquil fortified town of **Donauwörth** stands on a hill above the rivers. Old houses are built into its moated redbrick ramparts, nestling up to the city gates.

The Romantic Route follows the Wörnitz river on Highway 25. Turn off to visit **Harburg castle,** housing an important collection of Renaissance sculpture, ivories, gold, silver and Gobelin tapestries. Look out for two groups of figures by Tilman Riemenschneider—ladies in mourning and St John.

Encircled by its medieval wall with five sturdy gates and eleven bastions, **Nördlingen** has all the ingredients of Germany's Romantic myth. To get the measure of the town, walk along the parapet from the Reimlinger Gate on the Augsburg road via the massive Alte Bastei (the scene of open-air theatre in the summer) to the Berger Gate in the south-west. Nördlingen's

*R**oman Catholicism tied Bavaria firmly to Western Europe, though the distinctive onion domes of its churches recall the orthodox world to the east.*

enduring symbol is the so-called "Daniel", the 90m (295ft) copper-domed tower of the Gothic **St Georgskirche** (1490), with 365 steps leading to its summit. The sober interior is distinguished by statues of St George and Mary Magdalene around the baroque high altar. The church's beautiful 15th-century altar paintings by Friedrich Herlin are now kept in the town museum (Vordere Gerbergasse 1). In mid-July is staged the **Scharlachrennen,** a horse show and race with a cherished scarlet cloth as the trophy.

Dinkelsbühl

The town prospered in the 15th and 16th centuries from standing at the junction of the Stuttgart–Nuremberg and Rothenburg–Augsburg trade roads. The strategic location is emphasized by the fortifications' four monumental city gates: Rothenburger Tor and Nördlinger Tor north and south, Wörnitz Tor and Segringer Tor east and west. And the prosperity is seen in magnificent flower-bedecked *Fachwerk-häuser,* half-timbered gabled houses, many with gilded wrought-iron insignia. The most handsome are on Dr-Martin-Luther Strasse, notably the 16th-century **Deutsches Haus** (now a hotel and restaurant), five storeys with overhanging balconies. Look, too, for the **Hetzelhof,** Segringerstrasse 7, with pretty flowered balconies in the inner courtyard.

The **Heimatmuseum** (folklore museum) in the Spitalhof traces Dinkelsbühl's history with a model of the medieval town, furniture, textiles, kitchen utensils, instruments of torture and a portrait of Gustavus Adolphus in 1632, just before his death. The town's siege by the Swedish king's army is still re-enacted on Altrathausplatz and fields on the outskirts of town during a festival in late July

A symphony of woods and water at Bavaria Falls.

known as the *Kinderzeche*. The "children's tribute" is free sweets for having saved the town from plunder by going out to beg the Swedes for mercy. For the adults, it is an excuse for a beer garden, wine market, dances, open-air theatre and dancing in the streets.

Baroque decoration has been removed from the 15th-century Gothic **St Georg** parish church with its older, partly Romanesque, tower to restore the noble lofty interior. The rib vaulting by Nikolaus Eseler, the same architect who built Nördlingen's church, is superb. Notice, too, Michael Wolgemut's *Crucifixion* on the high altar.

Rothenburg ob der Tauber

If you cannot take in all the other stops on the Romantic Route, this one remains a must. Even in the massive summer invasion, it is difficult to resist the charm of Rothenburg's tall gabled houses towering over narrow streets with paving polished by the ages, and glimpses of the peacefully meandering Tauber river providing the western ramparts with a natural moat.

The undisputed centre of town is the **Old Town Hall**. It happily marries a Gothic part facing south, gabled with mighty Imperial Hall and belfry (tough stairway to the top for a rewarding view), and to the east a Renaissance façade of arcades with a 17th-century doorway. On the north side of Marktplatz, the clock on the old **Rattrinkstube**, the aldermen's tavern, performs the town's favourite legend, the *Meistertrunk* (Masterly Drink), on the hour from 11 a.m. to 3 p.m. and again at 8, 9 and 10 p.m.

Behind the town hall, **St Jakobskirche** possesses, in the upper chapel of the Holy Blood, one of Bavaria's great art treasures, Tilman Riemenschneider's sculpture revealing all the drama and pathos of the *Last Supper* (1505). The choir has some fine 15th-century stained-glass windows. The sculpture and painting of the high altar constitute a major achievement of late Gothic art, most notably for the work of Nördlingen painter Friedrich Herlin. The **Reichsstadtmuseum** (municipal museum) is housed in an old Dominican convent adjoining the north-east ramparts. You can see Nusch's original tankard here, as well as a good display of medieval kitchens and memorabilia from the old Jewish community.

In the **Herrngasse,** you will pass some charming half-timbered houses. Do not hesitate to peek in at their courtyards. The

Burggarten on the site of a Hohenstaufen castle offers a delightful view of the Tauber valley.

Back at the town hall, take the Obere Schmiedgasse south past the handsome Renaissance **Baumeisterhaus** (1596). Notice the dragons up on the gable steps, and the caryatid statues of the seven cardinal virtues on the first floor and seven deadly sins on the second. The best point from which to view the **ramparts,** intact since the 13th and 14th centuries, is from the old Hospital (*Spital*) and its bastion guarding the south end of town. You can walk the ramparts along the northern parapet from Klingentor over to the Würzburger Tor (also known as the Gallows Gate for an unfortunate few).

Franconia

Once a vast territory all along the Rhine from which its warriors conquered Gaul and gave France its name, the region stretches now from the Main river east to Bamberg, Nuremberg and Bayreuth. It remains a backbone of German tradition, renowned for its artists, fine craftsmen and precision engineers.

Aschaffenburg

Surrounded by the lovely hills and forests of the Spessart region, the town owes its charm to its lovely parks and to the opulent tastes of the archbishops of Mainz and more recently Bavaria's King Ludwig I. The archbishops' 17th-century **Schloss Johannisburg** incorporates a medieval castle keep in a gigantic Renaissance palace built four-square around an inner courtyard with lantern towers at each corner. The palace's art gallery has works by Hans Baldung Grien and Lucas Cranach.

In the grounds west of the palace is the **Pompeianum,** Ludwig I's fanciful replica of the house of Castor and Pollux at ancient Pompeii. In constant pursuit of classical antiquity, the king recreated here a piece of the Mediterranean, setting the house amid cypress, almond and fig trees.

South-west of town, **Schönbusch** is the prettiest of Aschaffenburg's parks, designed in the "natural" English manner by Sckell, who collaborated on Munich's Englischer Garten. The canals, neoclassical pavilions and a rustic hamlet were left by predecessors.

Würzburg

The illustrious bishopric lies in the heart of Franconia's wine country. Vineyards climb the slopes around the **Marienberg** overlooking the town from across the Main river. In its final form, this Renaissance fortress houses the excellent **Mainfränkisches Museum** of regional art and folklore, including some ancient wine-presses. The most cherished works, however, are the Gothic sculptures of Tilman Riemenschneider, who made Würzburg his home from 1483 to 1531. Outstanding are his Adam and Eve, six Apostles and an exquisite Madonna. For a wonderful view across to the Marienberg and over the city, drive up the Nikolausberg to the **Käppele,** a little rococo chapel. Spare a moment for its frescoes by Matthäus Günther.

In the episcopal princes' **Residenz,** designed by Balthasar Neumann and Lukas von Hildebrandt (1744), the city possesses one of the finest baroque palaces in Germany. Start out with an overall view from the attractive gardens. Inside, over the grand ceremonial staircase is the *Europa* fresco of Giambattista Tiepolo. He also did the frescoes for the oval Imperial Hall depicting Würzburg's medieval history,

TIL'S POLITICAL ERROR

Like the painters Albrecht Altdorfer in Regensburg and Lucas Cranach in Wittenberg, Tilman Riemenschneider served as mayor of his city. During the Peasants' War of 1525, the conservative-minded artist surprised his citizens by telling them to open the gates of Würzburg and let the rebels in. After the war, Riemenschneider was imprisoned for a while in a dungeon of the Marienberg, lost his office and fortune, but not—as did 62 other rebels—his head. He reflected his personal misery in the groups of mourners he depicted in his last years. But the only paid commission he received after the war was to repair altars damaged by peasants in a Benedictine convent in nearby Kitzingen—a form of after-sales service.

including the wedding of Friedrich Barbarossa. Neumann's triumph is the **Hofkirche**, the court church flooded with light and colour. Tiepolo contributed an *Assumption* and the *Angels' Fall from Heaven* for two side altars.

Another fine baroque church is the **Neumünster**, its noble façade attributed to Johann von Dientzenhofer. Inside, Riemenschneider's *Madonna* in stone stands in the south-east niche of the rotunda. The church is the burial shrine of St Kilian, the Irish monk martyred in Würzburg in 689 during his Christianizing mission to Franconia. The neighbouring **cathedral** (rebuilt since its destruction in 1945) is dedicated to the monk. On the south side of the transept, three Riemenschneider sculptures of Jesus, Peter and Andrew have been salvaged and placed in a modern stone setting.

Franconia's Wine Country

Take Highway 13 south-east from Würzburg into the heart of the wine country. Sample some respectable dry, earthy Sylvaners and Rieslings served in the characteristic plump green bottle known as a *Bocksbeutel*. Unspoiled villages with medieval ramparts provide an appropriately romantic setting. **Sommerhausen** has a fine 16th-century town hall, as does fortified **Ochsenfurt**, boasting also a Riemenschneider sculpture of the *Adoration of the Magi* in St Andreas parish church. **Frickenhausen** is the prettiest of the trio, with its medieval ramparts, towers and gatehouses all intact and a 16th-century town hall with superb half-timbering in the inner courtyard.

As a centre of the wine trade, **Kitzingen** is a good place to buy if you want to ship some home. In its old bastion, the Falterturm, the wine country emphasizes its festive atmosphere with a **Deutsches Fastnachtmuseum** (carnival museum) tracing the history of the Mardi Gras celebrations.

On the Würzburg–Bamberg road (Highway 22), stop off at the delightful little town of **Dettelbach**. Of the original 52 turrets in its ramparts, 36 still look down on a warren of charming narrow streets. Try the local spicy biscuits, *Muskazinen*, with your wine.

Without leaving the wine country, end on a high cultural note at **Ebrach**. Originally belonging to the town's Cistercian abbey, the sandstone parish church (1285) is one of Germany's finest Gothic structures, built in the Burgundian style. Its rose window was inspired by the transept window of Notre Dame-de-Paris. In the baroquified interior, notice in the northern transept a Renaissance alabaster altarpiece portraying the vision of St Bernard. Impressive reliefs on the choir stalls depict Christ's Passion in alabaster and wood.

The abbey, transformed into a veritable baroque palace, is now a prison, but a polite request to the authorities will gain you access to Balthasar Neumann's splendid ceremonial staircase.

Bamberg

A symphony orchestra of world renown and a harmonious blend of lovingly restored Gothic and baroque monuments make this cheerful town one of the most attractive in southern Germany. The beautiful natural situation in the Pegnitz valley at the eastern edge of the forest of Steigerwald does not hurt either. Historically, the Pegnitz river served to separate the old aristocratic cathedral quarter, to the west, from the civic population housed between the two arms of the river into which it divides as it passes through town. The division is admirably marked by the **Altes Rathaus** (Old Town Hall) standing on neutral ground on a bridged island in the river. The colourful heraldic frescoes on its two façades bear the bishop's arms facing west and the civic arms facing east. The handsome late Gothic structure has among its 18th-century additions a grand rococo archway for the Obere Brücke (upper bridge) traffic, now pedestrian only. North of the Altes Rathaus, on the **Untere Brücke** (lower bridge), notice the lovely rococo statue of St Cunegund, the wife of medieval German emperor, Heinrich II, who lived in Bamberg. The bridge affords a good view of the pretty fishermen's houses with their red roofs and flower-bedecked balconies in the Pegnitz—dubbed, apparently because of their reflection in the river, yet another "little Venice".

On your way up to the cathedral quarter, take a look at the showy **Böttingerhaus** at Judenstrasse 14. An 18th-century privy councillor built this overripe baroque mansion on the model of an Italian palazzo. Its even more ornate

garden side was carted off in 1900 to be reassembled in Munich's Luitpoldpark.

Domplatz beautifully juxtaposes its Romanesque–Gothic cathedral, Gothic–Renaissance castle and baroque palace. The **cathedral** (1237) is a majestic building with four towers 81m (265ft) high, and two chancels, east and west. Facing the palace, the imposing Fürstenportal (Prince's Doorway) has a Romanesque tympanum of the Day of Judgment. Enter through the Adam Door at the south-east corner. The 13th-century sculpture of a knight, the **Bamberger Reiter**, against a corner pillar of the east choir, represents the ideal of medieval chivalry. Nearby in the north aisle is the equally admirable sculptural group of the Visitation. Riemenschneider's monumental tomb of Heinrich II (1513) stands in the nave, portraying the emperor and wife Cunegund. In the west choir is the only papal tomb in Germany, for Clemens II, who was Bishop of Bamberg before serving less than a year as Pope (1047). Note the Gothic choir stalls. In the south transept, the Marien-Altar has a spirited *Nativity* sculpted by Veit Stoss (1523) with midwives bustling around, angels playing music and poor old Joseph lugging in the water.

Left of the cathedral on Domplatz, the **Alte Hofhaltung** (Old Residence) served as the bishop's and emperor's palace up to the 16th century. Beyond the ornate Renaissance doorway is a courtyard of half-timbered Gothic buildings with wooden galleries and dormer windows set in a steeply sloping roof.

The warm golden sandstone **Neue Residenz** is a grandiose baroque palace built by the immensely wealthy bishop-prince Lothar Franz von Schönborn. Its Staatsgalerie has a remarkable collection of Cologne and Westphalian masters and

works by Lucas Cranach and Hans Baldung Grien, and Dutch masters van Dyck and Salomon Ruisdael.

Vierzehnheiligen

A half-hour's drive north-east of Bamberg on Highway 173, this great baroque pilgrimage church of the Fourteen Saints (1741) is considered Balthasar Neumann's masterpiece. With its soaring twin towers, it dominates a hill over the Main valley on the spot where a shepherd had a vision of the child Jesus and 14 saints, calling on him to build a shrine. The basilica interior is divided into linking oval spaces, three down the centre with two smaller pairs at the sides. The saints are painted in the central dome with the *Annunciation* and *Nativity* over the choir. In the centre stands the astounding monumental concave and convex curving Altar of Grace. Under a canopy on which four sculptures of Jesus stand, the saints ward off dangers, particularly for travellers—pilgrims, those precursors of the modern tourist.

Bayreuth

This pilgrimage shrine is more pagan. First stop in the town staging the annual festival of Richard Wagner's operas is his home, **Villa Wahnfried**, at Richard-Wagner-Strasse 48. Now a museum, it houses 60 model stage sets, costumes, his piano, manuscripts, musical scores, kitsch

*J*ohannes Anwander's *18th-century frescoes, gracing Bamberg's town hall on its island in the Pegnitz river, pay allegorical tribute to the bishop on one side and the virtuous citizenry on the other.*

and curiosities. He is buried in the garden with his wife Cosima, daughter of Franz Liszt. (The Hungarian composer died at the 1884 festival and is buried in the town cemetery, Erlanger Strasse 40.)

Totally subservient to the operas' needs, the **Festspielhaus** (festival opera house) north of the city centre is architecturally quite ugly. Much more charming is the 18th-century **Markgräfliches Opernhaus**, built for the Margrave of Bayreuth by Bologna theatre designers Giuseppe Galli-Bibiena and son Carlo. Behind the solemn façade is a dazzling baroque interior of wood and stucco, with three galleries. The centrepiece is the Hofloge (Royal Box) which looks more like a baroque altar (or does a baroque altar sometimes look like a theatre box?).

Princess Wilhelmine, the sister of Prussia's Frederick the Great and wife of the margrave, built the **Neues Schloss**, a cheerful rococo change from Wagnerian solemnity.

The town also has a fascinating **Typewriter Museum** (*Schreibmaschinen-Museum*), Nibelungenstrasse 47. It includes such venerable exhibits as an 1864 wooden machine by Peter Mitterhofer, the Calligraph of 1883, the Pittsburgh Visible of 1890 and a Japanese machine that types 2,380 characters.

Fränkische Schweiz

The region south-west of Bayreuth known as "Franconian Switzerland" is a nice miniaturized version of that country. Rather than dramatic mountains, ravines, torrents and lakes, the landscape offers gently rolling hills, streams meandering lazily through green valleys and just an occasional castle or rocky crag.

Returning west along the Bamberg road, take the Wonsees turn-off north to the bizarre **Sanspareil rock gardens.** They were created by Wilhelmine, Margravine of Bayreuth, at the foot of Zwernitz castle for literary picnics in artificial caves. One remains, along with an octagonal rococo banquet hall and *Naturtheater*, in stylized ruin.

Drive south, past the genuine ruin of Krögelstein castle, to where Franconia's "Switzerland" really begins, along the little Wiesent river. West of Hollfeld, you will pass the formidable towers of **Ober Aufsess**, medieval in appearance, but actually 17th century. **Plankenfels** is a baroque redoubt and the castle at **Waischenfeld** has become a farmhouse, near the effusively rococo Laurentius chapel. A long way from California, **Tal des Todes** (Death Valley) earns its name from the shadow of the dark pine trees beneath the crag crowned by Rabeneck castle. Stop at the old **Behringer mill** for the view across to the castle of Gössweinstein. Dolomite rocks perched precariously on strange pinnacles threaten to topple into the little Püttlach stream below. This is the view that inspired traveller Joseph Heller in 1829 to invent the name of Fränkische Schweiz. Gössweinstein is renowned for its **Heiligste Dreifaltigkeit** (Holy Trinity) pilgrimage church, built by Balthasar Neumann. The twin-towered yellow sandstone edifice stands out impressively against the white and grey dolomite stone houses around it.

On your way west to the Bamberg–Nuremberg Autobahn at the Forchheim entrance, seek out the pagan **Walpurgiskapelle** (just south of Kirchehrenbach). Also known as "Walberla", it still attracts pilgrims to dance and carouse, especially on the first Sunday in May at the shrine of Freya, the goddess of fertility, love and war who rode in a chariot drawn by cats.

Nuremberg (*Nürnberg*)

This illustrious and handsome city is still valiantly recovering from the curse of Hitler's favour. It is also reminding the world that it was the home of Germany's greatest painter, Albrecht Dürer; before him, home of the Tannhäuser minstrels; and for all time a centre of great craftsmen, inventors of the clarinet and pocket watch and makers of marvellous mechanical toys. A toy fair is held every February and an inventor's exhibition every September. But it was precisely because of its fine traditions that Hitler chose it for his party rallies, seeking to associate the Nazis with Nuremberg's great national reputation. To wipe out that symbol, Allied bombs wreaked terrible destruction here. The city has made a courageous recovery and the meticulous reconstruction is slowly taking on a patina that recaptures at least something of the old grandeur. Much of the artwork has been preserved and, not to be ignored, the unique little Nuremberg sausages, grilled or boiled, are as delicious as ever.

Kaiserburg

To recall the glory of the past, start up at the Imperial Castle, reserved for the emperor's visits from the 11th to the 15th century. The Gothic-Renaissance Imperial Hall, with its black and gold ceiling, is more sober, more businesslike than the extravagant residences of Würzburg and

Nuremberg financiers were once the creditors of Europe's monarchs. Today's market in the shadow of the Frauenkirche is a more modest home-grown affair.

Bamberg. The 24 coats of arms on the walls encompass the world empire of Charles V, from Austria to Sicily and Spain, as well as Jerusalem, Corsica, Gibraltar and the Americas. The castle chapel is divided into two, the Romanesque Kaiserkapelle for the imperial family and below it the crypt-like Margarethenkapelle for commoners. The east terrace affords a good view of the city; for the best panorama of the surrounding countryside climb to the top of the round 12th-century tower, the Sinwellturm.

The Old Town

South-west of the castle, opposite the Tiergärtner Gate, the late-Gothic gabled **Dürerhaus** was bought by Albrecht Dürer in 1509. He lived there until his death in 1528. Furnished with authentic period pieces, the little museum displays memorabilia of the artist and scenes from his life. His paintings are exhibited at the Germanisches Nationalmuseum (*see* page 155).

The **Fembohaus** (1591), Burgstrasse 15, is a good example of the town's Renaissance mansions, its wood-panelled living rooms and kitchen now housing a museum of Nuremberg history.

On Rathausplatz stands the imposing 13th-century church of **St Sebald**. The majestic west chancel presents a sober Romanesque façade while the east chancel is in more elaborate Gothic style. The town's patron saint is buried in the east choir in a monumental bronze tomb by Peter Vischer. On the high altar is a *Crucifixion* by Veit Stoss (1520). In the east chancel is a fine painting by Hans von Kulmbach of Mary enthroned between St Catherine and St Barbara. In a side altar at the west end of the nave, sculptor Adam Krafft portrays Christ carrying the Cross.

THE DARK SIDE OF THE CITY

Without overdoing it, Nuremberg does not turn a blind eye to its role in the Third Reich. The tourist office (headquarters in the Rathaus) publishes a brochure "Nuremberg 1933–1945" on the major part that the city played in Nazi party activities. It organizes guided tours of the sites where the party rallies took place. From 1933 to 1938, week-long mass meetings were held late summer in the city's south-east outskirts. More than 250,000 people marched beneath searchlights that created what Albert Speer, Hitler's architect designing the ceremonies, called a "cathedral of light" in the sky. Most buildings erected for the rallies were destroyed in the war, but some remain as grim reminders.

Münchner Strasse takes you out to the Luitpoldhain, the parade ground for troops of the SS. It is now a pleasure park. At the nearby Zeppelinfeld, where Hitler reviewed units of the army for the rally's climactic *Tag der Wehrmacht*, the 350m- (1,150ft-) long grandstand and the Führer's rostrum are still there. The parade ground is used for car races and as a sports arena for the US Army. The Kongressbau was meant to recall Rome's Colosseum but of course more colossal. Never completed, it remains as a relic of the Nazi taste for gigantism. Behind the Zeppelinfeld, you will see a pretty pond, the Dutzendteich, in fact the foundations—filled with rain and ground-water—for the biggest project of them all, the Deutsche Stadion. The groundstone was laid in 1937 for a stadium that would have held 450,000 spectators.

The Renaissance **town hall** (1616) in solid Italian palazzo style asserts Nuremberg's self-confidence. The west façade has three impressive baroque porches. Inside the town hall, the 85m- (280ft) long Grosser Saal (1340) has played host to numerous imperial assemblies, most notably a peace banquet for 600 princes and other dignitaries at the end of the Thirty Years' War.

In Rathausgasse, the merry little bronze fountain, **Gänsemännchen-Brunnen** (1550), with a man carrying two geese, continues a tradition of Nuremberg humour in high art well implanted by Dürer and sculptor Adam Krafft. A far loftier fountain, the **Schöner Brunnen,** stands in the north-west corner of the market-place. It portrays princes and heroes both pagan and biblical, culminating in Moses and seven prophets.

Dominating the market is the step-gabled façade of the rebuilt 14th-century **Frauenkirche**. Set in the top of its projecting two-storey porch is a clock from which seven prince-electors and their emperor Charles IV emerge every day at noon. Inside, against the east wall in the north aisle, see the superb 15th-century Tucher altarpiece. The *Crucifixion* flanked by the *Annunciation* and *Resurrection* is painted by an unknown master regarded as the most gifted of Dürer's Nuremberg predecessors.

Stop on the Museum Bridge to view to the east the handsome **Heiliggeistspital** (Hospital of the Holy Ghost, 1416, now a restaurant) standing on arches over the Pegnitz river. South of the river, the Nassauerhaus, Karolinenstrasse 2, is an old watchtower house with graceful octagonal corner turrets and a corbelled oriel window that served as a private chapel. You can dine in its 13th-century arcaded cellars.

Lorenzkirche is a fine example of the city's painstaking restoration. The 15th-century Gothic church with its soaring steeples and splendid rose window is already nicely weathered (pollution, in small doses, has its advantages). Inside, the stained-glass windows in the chancel survived not by miracle but by prudent storage. Adam Krafft's elegant Sakramenthaus (ciborium) is a masterpiece of Gothic stone carving. Notice, too, hanging from the chancel vault, the *Annunciation* by Veit Stoss (1519).

On Hallplatz, the massive **Mauthalle** originally built in 1502 is a reconstruction of what was in turn the corn hall and customs house. Six rows of dormer windows lighten the gigantic roof.

Germanisches Nationalmuseum

On Kornmarkt, a disused Carthusian monastery has been extended eastwards by starkly modern buildings to house the vast collections of this magnificent museum. Covering the whole range of German culture, it has 100,000 coins and medals, a print collection of 300,000 pieces, and a library of over 400,000 books and manuscripts (with a major focus on artists' private papers). You can also see the armour of Emperor Maximilian I, weapons, a Gothic kitchen and Renaissance apothecary, and musical and scientific instruments, including Martin Behaim's globe of the earth completed in 1492 while Christopher Columbus was still trying to prove the world was round. The museum's proudest treasures, however, are its paintings by Albrecht Dürer, notably his *Beweinung Christi* (Lamentation of Christ, 1500) and portraits of Emperor Sigismund (1512) and Emperor Maximilian I (1519). Other important artists here include Tilman Riemenschneider, Lucas Cranach, Albrecht Altdorfer, Konrad Witz and Hans Baldung Grien.

Toy Museum

The Spielzeugmuseum, Karlstrasse 13, celebrates Nuremberg's time-honoured devotion to toy manufacturing. Bavaria, Thuringia and Eastern Europe are also honoured with a vast array of musical toys, building boxes, peep shows and optical toys. The marionette theatre stages plays.

A collection of 17th-century doll's houses and kitchens provide an authentic guide to the living styles of the grown-ups. No nonsense about the doll's china; it is of genuine alabaster, faience, earthenware, porcelain and crystal. The local speciality, mechanical toys, includes steam engines, toy-size but with functioning internal combustion engines, and an elaborate railway of model electric trains.

Eastern Bavaria

Bavaria's wilder and largely unspoiled eastern region is dominated by vast tracts of forest. The Bayrischer Wald and Oberpfälzer Wald are protected for the most part as nature reserves. Amberg, Regensburg and Passau serve as good bases for exploring the area.

Oberpfalz (Upper Palatine), with Regensburg as its capital, traces its name back to the 14th century when it was acquired by the Rhineland Counts of Palatinate.

Amberg

The town retains considerable charm inside the oval of its ramparts with their pyramidal-roofed watchtowers and gates. Start at the southern end of town where the old **Stadtbrille** ("town-spectacles") bridge spans the Vils river forming two perfect circles with the reflection of its arches. Once part of the city wall, the bridge links a Renaissance palace, now the municipal tax office—take a look at its handsome inner courtyard—to the Arsenal. North along the river, by an old roofed bridge, visit the tall gabled 14th-century **Eichenforst,** a mansion housing a museum of local history.

Across the bridge, you see the Gothic church of **St Martin**. Take a look at a notable painting attributed to Jan Polack, *Kreuzauffindung der Heiligen Helena* (St Helen and the Discovery of the Cross) on the north wall of the chancel. The 16th-century **town hall** is remarkably graceful with its finely carved spiral staircase on a façade of amber sandstone and white granite.

Regensburg

The Danube river reaches its northernmost point here before turning south towards Austria. The Romans chose the site as a garrison town—*Castra Regina* under Emperor Marcus Aurelius in AD 179—to guard the river, the empire's natural frontier, against barbarian invaders. The German city built its prosperity on trade with those eastern barbarians. It has been untouched by war since 1809 when the invasion came from the west, in the shape of Napoleon.

Start north-east of the cathedral at **Porta Praetoria**, the remains of a Roman gate on Unter den Schwibbogen. The archway and round tower with five windows were constructed without mortar.

The twin spires of **St Peter's Cathedral** give it a grandiose silhouette. Begun

Regensburg's Wurst-küche claims to be the oldest sausage restaurant in Germany. They have been serving sausages like this for over eight centuries.

in the late 13th century on the French model, it was completed six centuries later. The Flamboyant Gothic canopied porch of 1410 projects from the façade in a striking triangular form, with a statue of Peter on the centre pillar. Inside, see the choir's fine 14th-century stained-glass windows.

Walk over to the Danube and discover a vital monument of German cultural history, the 12th-century **Wurstküche**, the country's oldest known hot-dog stand. It served sausages to builders of the nearby **Steinerne Brücke** (Stone Bridge, 1146). With 16 arches (the 16th is now filled in), this was a triumph of medieval engineering. On the gatehouse guarding the bridge entrance to the town, next to the seated figures of King Philipp of Swabia and his wife, is a sculpture of Oswald, patron saint of travellers. Continue on past the old fish market to the Gothic and baroque **town hall** on Neue Waaggasse. While the aldermen were dancing at balls in the Reichssaal upstairs, less cheerful goings-on were going on in the ground-floor Wachtkammer (guard room). Here was the torture chamber known politely as the Fragstatt (questioning room). You will also see an executioner's sword and a rod broken as symbol of the death sentence.

The **municipal museum** on Dachauplatz is housed in a former Minorite monastery. The museum traces the town's prehistoric and Roman past and displays the region's medieval church sculpture and paintings from the 14th to the 19th century. The highlight is the work of Regensburg's best known artist (and former mayor) Albrecht Altdorfer (1480–1538). Besides his paintings, notice two etchings of Regensburg synagogue, which he made just before executing a municipal order to raze it.

Passau

Germany's border crossing with Austria stands at the junction of three rivers, the Danube, the Inn and the little Ilz. To enjoy the unique setting amid wooded hills and cliffs, take the Ferd-Wagner Strasse north of town to the fortress, **Veste Oberhaus**. The castle's museum exhibits regional art and craftwork, with special emphasis on Danube shipping and the art of German Bohemia.

The main part of town is built on a hilly ridge rising between the Danube and Inn and topped by the **cathedral of St Stephan**. With its three onion-domes and Flamboyant Gothic chancel, this massive church has an overpowering baroque interior (over 1,000 sculpted figures were inventoried during renovation). The cathedral claims to possess the world's largest church organ, with over 17,000 pipes. It is played every day during the summer, from May to September, promptly at noon. Tickets are sold in Domplatz.

East of the cathedral, Residenzplatz is framed by the baroque buildings of the **bishop's palace**, the dominant style of the old town's dwellings. After two fires in the 17th century devastated the medieval town, the new baroque houses adopted distinctive fire-resistant ridge-roofing. Most attractive in the formidable **town hall** are its arcaded inner courtyards.

A major attraction of Passau is its **Danube cruises** west to Regensburg or east to Vienna (departures from the Fritz-Schäffer-Promenade). At the east end of the Promenade, stand on the **Dreiflusseck**, junction of the three rivers. You can tell the waters of the Danube from the others by its unmistakable brownness, dismissing once and for all that Strauss nonsense about its being blue.

ART AND ARCHITECTURE

Germany often found it easier to assert a distinctive national style in its painting, sculpture and architecture than to achieve political unity. Regional variations have always existed, between Catholic Bavaria and Protestant Prussia, or between the Rhineland close to French influences and the north with its affinities to Dutch and Flemish art. But at all times, the Germans have put their own stamp on their art, whether it be a vigorous sense of realism or an occasional softer penchant for sentimentality.

Carolingian and Ottonian Art

It was Charlemagne's idea of empire rather than any aesthetic consideration that dictated German art forms from the mid-8th to the mid-10th centuries. To cement his alliance with the pope, he built churches and abbeys all across Germany. At Aachen, his imperial capital, the vaulted octagonal Palatine Chapel deliberately recalled Emperor Justinian's church of San Vitale. Charlemagne brought sculpture from Rome as models for his court artists, and ancient technique is visible in the chapel's bronze doors and gallery railings.

Little painting has survived from this period, but the Trier Landesmuseum has some expressive 9th-century frescoes from the church of St Maximin. The procession of four martyrs and Crucifixion show a certain Italian influence. The Carolingian encouragement of the arts is most exquisitely illustrated in the illuminated manuscripts. In the cathedral treasury at Aachen is a beautifully decorative version of the *Gospels* with full page portraits of the Evangelists. You will find other fine examples of the art in Munich: Charles the Bald's *Book of Hours* at the Residenzmuseum and the *Codex Aureus* in the Bavarian State Library.

After the coronation of Otto I in 936, the Byzantine and Roman prototypes in architecture and sculpture took on a more specifically German character. Churches were built with a clear geometric structure, of which St Pantaleon in Cologne and the Münsterkirche in Essen are admirable examples. Sculpture was more tense and otherworldly. Notable examples are the Essen *Madonna*, the *Gero Cross* in Cologne Cathedral, and two bronzes in Hildesheim—*Bernward's doors* in St Michael's and the *Easter Column* in the cathedral. Painting becomes more forceful, even monumental in the Oberzell frescoes at Lake Constance.

Romanesque

The sturdy Romanesque churches of the Rhineland were a cheerful expression of the German Empire's confidence in the early Middle Ages. With its double chancels crowned by twin towers east and west, Speyer Cathedral (1060) was the prototype for the imperial churches at Mainz and Worms built after 1100. Walls were now treated more sculpturally, with relief-like surfaces of projecting rounded forms. The ribless groin-vaulting of Speyer Cathedral's nave was the first of its kind in Germany. The abbey church at Maria Laach provided the model for the smaller Rhenish churches, while Cologne's St Aposteln pioneered the characteristic Rhenish ornament of blind arcades and dwarf galleries. In the north, Lübeck's cathedral was the country's first major church in brick.

With the exception of the goldsmith's art, design from the 11th to mid-13th centuries tends to be static and rigid. In Cologne Cathedral, Niklaus of Verdun's *Shrine of the Three Magi* is a masterpiece of concentrated energy. Of the painting, a rare survivor is Hildesheim's heavily restored biblical scenes on the ceiling of St Michael's, interesting for their tapestry-like effect. Representative sculpture includes the Brunswick Lion and Henry the Lion's tomb in Brunswick Cathedral, the *Sonnenburg Crucifixion* in the Schnütgen Museum, Cologne, and a pulpit from Alpirsbach abbey now in Freudenstadt parish church.

The Gothic Builders

Eying the bold experiments of the great French cathedrals, Germany's church builders at first made only tentative sorties into the new realm of Gothic architecture. Trier's Liebfrauenkirche (1243) with its central ground-plan makes elegant use of Gothic forms in its sculpture and vaulting but does not attempt the soaring spaciousness of its models across the border in the Champagne country.

In Marburg, the Elisabethkirche built 40 years later is High Gothic in style but has no ambulatory or side chapels around its choir and retains the classic German hall-church form with nave and aisles of the same height.

German Gothic became more adventurous in the 14th century. Whatever blood and tears have been spilled in the perennial Franco-German tug-of-war for Alsace, Strasbourg Cathedral must be considered a supreme achievement of German architecture. Certainly there was nothing very Gallic about its builders Erwin von Steinbach, Ulrich von Ensingen and Johannes Holz. At any rate, it inspired the indisputably German masterpiece of grace and dignity that is Freiburg Cathedral, completed with its majestic openwork tower in 1350. Sometimes the architects were more ambitious than budgets would permit. Cologne's mighty cathedral was consecrated some 30 years before Freiburg's, but had to wait six centuries for its two steeples to be completed. In the 15th century, similar, if less gigantic civic ambition was expressed in other south-German parish churches: Nördlingen, Dinkelsbühl and Amberg.

The bourgeoisie's new self-assertiveness became apparent in their tall step-gabled houses with elegant projecting bay windows and loggias, and most of all in the town halls, built like secular cathedrals or merchants' palaces. In Frankfurt's Römer, we can judge that pride only from a modern replica. Most bastions of city government in the north, notably Lübeck and Stralsund, were built of brick. The aristocracy was changing, too. In Meissen's Albrechtsburg and Bamberg's Alte Hofhaltung, you can see the nobles' castles evolving from feudal fortresses to more comfortable palaces.

The Gothic Sculptors

Among workers of wood, stone and bronze, there was a veritable explosion of talent. The reputation of the anonymous Saxon Masters of Naumburg won them commissions in Metz and Noyon as well as Hildesheim and Mainz (fragments of a rood screen exhibited in the cathedral museum). In the west choir of Naumburg Cathedral, their statues of 12 nobles and scenes of Christ's Passion on the rood screen (1249–70) form one of the most harmonious achievements of the Middle Ages.

The statues of Mary and St Elizabeth in Bamberg Cathedral followed the example of the *Visitation* in Reims, but with greater solemnity. The 13th-century equestrian *Bamberger Reiter* expresses an ideal of German chivalry. But in the next century, the statuary was gentler, less monumental, as can be seen in the pillar statues in the choir of Cologne Cathedral or on the high altar of Marburg's Elisabethkirche. By the 1390s this had developed into the "soft style" *("weicher Stil")* of the anonymous Master of the Beautiful Madonnas, whose influence can be seen throughout the Rhineland and southern Germany. Nuremberg offers examples in its Sebalduskirche and the Germanisches Nationalmuseum. The *Darsow Altar* in Lübeck's Marienkirche is a cooler northern variant. Ulm's Hans Multscher (1400–

Christ's arrest, Naumburg cathedral

67) marks the end of the "soft style" with his more severe *Schmerzensmann* (Man of Sorrows) in the cathedral and the royal figures on the town hall.

Jörg Syrlin affirms this austere, spiritually expressive manner with his choir stalls for Ulm Cathedral, while Erasmus Grasser brings a Bavarian exuberance to his Morris dancers for the Munich town hall (1480, Stadtmuseum). In the north, Bernt Notke (1430–1509) achieved his realism and sense of the extraordinary with stunning technique in his *Triumphal Cross* for Lübeck Cathedral.

Three master sculptors emerged in Nuremberg: wood-carver Veit Stoss (1447–1533) brings intense emotion without undue pathos to his *Crucifixion* in the Sebalduskirche, *Annunciation* in St Lorenz and a *Marienaltar* in neighbouring Bamberg. Working in stone, Adam Krafft (1455–1509) is more quiet and contemplative, notably in his tabernacle for St Lorenz. Peter Vischer (1460–1529) was the leading member of a bronze-casting family, who collaborated on his great Sebaldus shrine. He combined late-Gothic vigour with the new tastes and architectural forms of the Italian Renaissance.

The true genius of Germany's transition from Gothic to Renaissance sculpture was Tilman Riemenschneider (1460–1531), who also found time to be mayor of Würzburg. He came from the Harz mountains. While remaining quiet and reserved in form, his work expresses fervent emotion in his biblical scenes. By renouncing the colour that had been customary for altar frames, the sculptural impact is more immediate. His masterpieces include the *Holy Blood Altar* in Rothenburg's Jakobikirche, *Adam* and *Eve* in Würzburg's Mainfränkisches Museum, and the tomb of Heinrich II and Cunegund in Bamberg Cathedral.

Painting in the 14th and 15th Centuries
High Gothic religious painting evoked the spiritual fervour of the times with emphatic gesture and intense expression. See from Cologne Cathedral's choir enclosure the *Virgin Enthroned* and a *Crucifixion* (1320, Gemäldegalerie, Berlin-Dahlem). Master Bertram demonstrates a powerful narrative style in his *Grabow Altar* (1380, Kunsthalle, Hamburg). Konrad von Soest (active 1394–1420) depicts a more refined, idealized world in his altar for the Bad Wildungen parish church.

At this time, the "soft style" dominates Rhenish painting, most notably in Cologne (Wallraf-Richartz Museum). Stephan Lochner (1410–52), however, enhances it with a special grace and serenity.

A new vigour is apparent with the rise of the middle class and the emergence of book-printing to spread the fame of graphic artists. Swabian-born but more active in Basel than in Germany, Konrad Witz (1400–56) developed a powerful and highly personal realism closer to Masaccio than his fellow Germans—see his *Queen of Sheba* (Gemäldegalerie, Berlin-Dahlem). In Ulm, Hans Multscher's painting shows a certain force, but the energetic German style is best reasserted by Martin Schongauer (1450–91) in his *Last Judgment* fresco for Breisach Cathedral.

Augsburg's Hans Holbein the Elder (1460–1524), stately portraitist and superb colourist, was "court painter" to the south-German merchant class. His religious painting has a solemn but very human beauty, notably altar paintings for Augsburg Cathedral and the *Kaisheimer Altar* in Munich's Alte Pinakothek.

The Renaissance
Affirming their ascendancy in the 16th century, the merchants built themselves bigger and better town halls and guildhalls, culminating in Elias Holl's Augsburg town hall. Rothenburg's grand arcaded town hall is another classic example of this civic pride, and the step-gabled mansions of Dinkelsbühl proclaim the bourgeoisie's new prosperity.

Flemish rather than Italian decoration marked German Renaissance architecture. The Italianate portico on Cologne's town hall is an exception, and the Archbishop of Mainz's grand palace at Aschaffenburg is unabashedly French. More typical are Heidelberg's Haus zum Ritter and the castle's Ottheinrichsbau. In the north, Bremen's elegant scrolled step-gabling decorated with pinnacles or statuary became known as Weser Renaissance. Wolfenbüttel's Heinrichstadt quarter is a fine piece of restrained Renaissance urban planning, but further development in the 17th century was halted by the devastating Thirty Years' War.

The painting of the period was decidedly ambivalent. Besides the new self-confidence and humanism, it expressed the spiritual crisis of the Lutheran Reformation and the social unrest of the Peasants' War. Three men stand in the forefront: Albrecht Dürer, Matthias Grünewald and Lucas Cranach.

Travelling constantly between his native Nuremberg and Venice, Dürer (1471–1528) produced a unique synthesis of the Italian Renaissance and the vivid, highly sculptural art of the Rhineland and the Netherlands. From his goldsmith father he acquired the meticulous precision apparent in his drawings and engravings, his *Apocalypse* being a magnificent early example. In Dresden, see in the *Wittenberg Altar* (1495–97) his simple rendition of a profound inner psychology. His famous *Self-Portrait* at 29 in Munich's Alte Pinakothek shows him imbued with a mystical pride. The Berlin-Dahlem *Virgin with Weasel* (1506) shows the light and colour he had more than mastered from Giovanni Bellini. His mysticism grew after an encounter with Philipp Melanchthon and the Reformation, for which the eloquent *Four Apostles* (1526, Alte Pinakothek) can be said to be his personal testament.

Just as Germany's greatest Gothic church is in France—Strasbourg—so Matthias Grünewald's masterpiece, the *Issenheim Altar,* is in Colmar, also in Alsace. Grünewald was probably Würzburg-born around 1480, but more probably called Mathis Nithardt or Gothardt. Together with the Colmar painting, his works inside Germany justify his reputation as a rival to Dürer. He is more emotional, intensely subjective rather than analytical, as can be judged from his *Mocking of Christ* (Alte Pinakothek, Munich, see p. 86), *St Cyriakus* (Städelsches Kunstinstitut, Frankfurt) and the panels of the *Maria Schnee Altar* (Mary of the Snows) in Stuppach and Freiburg's Augustiner Museum.

No mystery about the prolific Lucas Cranach (1472–1553). This very public man epitomized the prosperity of the Renaissance merchant class, with considerable talent to boot. He was court painter to Duke Friedrich of Saxony, intimate of Martin Luther and, not unuseful for his business affairs, mayor of Wittenberg. He showed a piercing intelligence in portraiture, especially of Luther and family (Wartburg Castle and Weimar's Staatliche Kunstsammlung). His taste for sensuality sometimes shocked Brother Martin, with an *Adam* and *Eve* in almost every major German collection. See, too, the delightful *Fountain of Youth* (Berlin-Dahlem). But he was also capable of deep introspection in his religious painting, notably the Munich *Crucifixion* (Alte Pinakothek).

Less pious than his father, Hans Holbein the Younger (1497–1543) was a liberal, worldly fellow, friend of Erasmus and Thomas More, court painter to Henry VIII. He learned from his elder the techniques of the Italian Renaissance and surpassed him in incisive portraiture. See his Hanseatic merchant *Georg Gisze* (Gemäldegalerie, Berlin-Dahlem) or, from the London period after 1526, *Thomas Godsalve and Son* (Gemälderie, Dresden). He brought similar psychological insights to religious themes for the *Oberried Altar* (1521) in Freiburg Cathedral.

Dürer's Dürer

Augsburg painter Hans Burgkmair (1473–1551) developed a serene Venetian style which you can see in three colourful altar-paintings in the Alte Pinakothek and a *Madonna* in Nuremberg's Germanisches Nationalmuseum. Albrecht Altdorfer (1480–1538), Regensburg alderman and town architect, carved a niche for himself as one of Germany's greatest landscape artists. His penchant for canvases teeming with human figures, trees and plants reached cosmic proportions with his monumental *Battle of Alexander* (Alte Pinakothek). Hans Baldung Grien (1484–1545) was a faithful disciple of Dürer's ideals of beauty, but tinged with a certain morbidity—*Sebastian Altar* (Germanisches Nationalmuseum, Nuremberg) and *Adoration of the Magi* (Berlin-Dahlem).

Golden Baroque

Baroque art's initial creative impulse, like its political and religious motivation in the Counter-Reformation, came from Italy. In Munich, the pioneering church of St Michael was inspired by the Jesuit Gesù church in Rome (but the emperors and Wittelsbach dukes on the façade are unmistakably German). Agostino Barelli and Enrico Zuccalli were brought in to work on Theatinerkirche and the palaces of Nymphenburg and Schleissheim.

But by 1700, German architects, delighting in the new decorative possibilities of Baroque monumental building, were taking over. Matthäus Daniel Pöppelmann (1662–1736) needed no *Gastarbeiter* to help him with the magnificent Zwinger Palace in Dresden, and Andreas Schlüter (1660–1714) was just as masterly in Berlin, though only his Zeughaus remains for us to judge today. In Franconia, Johann Leonhard Dientzenhofer (1665–1707) built the abbey at Ebrach and the Bishop of Bamberg's splendid Residenz.

In Munich, Belgian-born François de Cuvilliés took his cue from French Rococo for his work on the Residenz, especially the exquisite theatre. Frederick the Great also turned to France for inspiration in building his Sanssouci Palace at Potsdam. His long-suffering architect Georg von Knobelsdorff (1699–1753) was given a freer hand with the east wing of Schloss Charlottenburg.

Indisputed master of German Baroque was Balthasar Neumann (1687–1753). His bold, imaginative vision can be seen to its full advantage in the episcopal palace at Würzburg and Vierzehnheiligen pilgrimage church. Two close rivals to this last masterpiece are Johann Michael Fischer's Ottobeuren abbey church and Dominikus Zimmermann's Wieskirche.

Like the architects, Italian sculptors and stuccowork craftsmen flooded into southern Germany, but native artists soon replaced them. The leading sculptor in the transition from Renaissance to Baroque was Jorg Zürn

Ottobeuren abbey church

(1583–1635), active around Lake Constance (relatively untouched by the Thirty Years' War). He indulged a taste for theatrical illusion in the monumental high altar for Überlingen's Nikolaus Münster, reserving his more naturalistic style for the choir stalls. In Dresden, the jewel-like quality of the Zwinger Palace is unimaginable without the sculpture of Balthasar Permoser (1651–1732).

As the Hohenzollerns' court sculptor, Andreas Schlüter absorbed Italian and French influences and proved energetic in his equestrian statue of the Great Elector at Schloss Charlottenburg, poignant in his keystone masks of fallen soldiers in the Zeughaus (Arsenal).

But the sunniest Baroque sculpture is in southern Germany. The work of Johann Baptist Straub (1704–84) is dreamily sentimental in the abbey churches of Ettal and Diessen on the Ammersee. In the Swabian Feuchtmayer family of woodcarvers and stucco sculptors, Josef Anton (1669–1770) let his cherubs run riot through Birnau, Meersburg, Überlingen and Weingarten. Johann Michael (1709–1772) made a separate name for himself with masterly work at Ottobeuren and Vierzehnheiligen. In Munich, before turning to his own Asamkirche, Egid Quirin Asam (1694–1750) worked together with Johann Georg Greiff and Austrian Andreas Faistenberger on the sumptuous high altar of St Peter's.

Some of these sculptors tried their hand at Rococo porcelain, but the great masters were Johann Joachim Kändler (1706–75) in Meissen and Swiss-born Franz Anton Bustelli (1723–63) at Munich's Nymphenburg.

The Baroque painters were bright and airy masters of trompe-l'oeil frescoes opening up church and palace ceilings to heaven, but as such, inevitably subordinate to the architects. Many participated on a family basis. Johann Baptist Zimmermann (1680–1758) worked with architect brother Dominikus on Wieskirche. He also decorated Schloss Nymphenburg and Amalienburg. Similarly, Cosmas Damian Asam (1686–1739) joined his sculptor-architect brother Egid Quirin on the Asamkirche. On his own account, he also painted frescoes for Munich's Dreifältigkeitskirche, Weingarten abbey and Schleissheim palace.

Neoclassicism and the 19th Century

With the inventiveness of Baroque and Rococo exhausted, historicism took over. Archaeological expeditions after 1750 awoke a new interest in the monuments of ancient Greece and Rome. Among the neoclassical architects it spawned, Karl Friedrich Schinkel (1781–1841) allied elegance with monumentality. His best buildings are in Berlin—the Neue Wache, the Schauspielhaus and the Altes Museum. In Bavaria, the more conventional Leo von Klenze (1784–1864) gave Ludwig I, obsessed with antiquity, a lofty Glyptothek for his ancient sculpture and, near Regensburg, a Parthenon-like "Walhalla" for Germany's heroes.

But the Grecian Revival petered out by the 1830s and the new German nationalism turned to the country's medieval roots. Neo-Gothic became the order of the day, thrusting pinnacled belfries on town halls all over the country and at long last topping off Cologne and Ulm cathedrals with their gigantic steeples. Schinkel, elegant as ever, added his own neo-Gothic note with an openwork canopy for the Luther monument in Wittenberg.

In Dresden, Gottfried Semper (1803–79) preferred neo-Renaissance in the Italian style for his graceful Opera House and the Gemäldegalerie wing of the Zwinger Palace.

The sculptural pendant to the neoclassical architecture was provided in Berlin by Gottfried Schadow's formidable Quadriga for the Brandenburg Gate and Christian Daniel Rauch's military heroes on Unter den Linden. Subsequent nationalistic bombast was expressed with such gigantic monuments as Berlin's Siegessäule (Victory Column) and the

Germania statue overlooking the Rhine at Niederwald.

Neoclassical painting—Anton Graff and Anton Mengs—tended to be rigid and formal in its portraiture of the Great Men. An agreeable exception is Goethe in der Römischen Campagna in which Johann Heinrich Tischbein (1751–1829) depicts the writer as timeless hero amid the noble ruins of antiquity (Städelsches Kunstinstitut, Frankfurt).

The Romantic reaction came with the new, almost childlike, naturalism and sentiment of Philipp Otto Runge (1777–1810), well represented in Berlin's Galerie der Romantik, Dresden's Gemäldegalerie and Hamburg's Kunsthalle. But the outstanding Romantic is Caspar David Friedrich (1774–1840), creating a disturbing ambiance of lyrical, mystical melancholy in meticulously realistic sea- and landscapes—Monk By the Sea (Berlin), Cross on the Mountain (Dresden) and Sea of Ice (Hamburg).

In contrast, the vast canvases of Adolph Menzel (1815–1905), a trained engineer, show a stark sense of social realities: Iron Foundry (Nationalgalerie, Eastern Berlin) and Berlin-Potsdam Railway (Nationalgalerie, Western Berlin). The prevailing philistinism of Biedermeier Germany was depicted by Carl Spitzweg (1808–85): Der arme Poet (Neue Pinakothek, Munich).

Dresden: Semper's Opera House

Inside Stuttgart's Neue Staatsgalerie

Caspar David Friedrich: Man and woman looking at the moon

Three Berlin painters, Max Liebermann (1847–1935), Max Slevogt (1868–1932) and Lovis Corinth (1852–1925), present in all the major national collections, provided the link with the 20th century. They absorbed the lessons of Impressionism from France, adding a tougher emotional content that heralded home-grown Expressionism.

Architecture in the 20th Century

Spectacular industrial progress and the accompanying growth in population called for a parallel revolution in architectural design. In the Darmstadt neighbourhood of Mathilden-höhe, artists of the decorative Jugendstil movement showed the ornate forms used in furniture, porcelain and glassware could also work for factories and housing.

In Berlin, Peter Behrens (1868–1940) set the tone in allying function with strong forms. He employed two of the founders of the Bauhaus movement, Walter Gropius (1883–1969) and Ludwig Mies van der Rohe (1887–1969). The clarity of what became known as the International style can be seen in Gropius's building for the Bauhaus school in Dessau and Mies van der Rohe's Nationalgalerie in the Berlin Tiergarten. More voluntarily dramatic were the Expressionist experiments of Erich Mendelssohn's fanciful Einstein Tower just outside Potsdam and Fritz Höger's soaring ship's-prow Chilehaus in Hamburg.

Nazi architecture was a throwback to historicism, on a massive scale befitting its totalitarian ideology. Among the survivors are Munich's Haus der Kunst, a giant fragment of Nuremberg's Congressbau and the Olympic Stadium in Berlin. After the war, East Germany's Stalinist architecture was similarly bleak.

In the west, hasty post-war construction was strictly functional, typified by Frankfurt's skyscrapers and Stuttgart's endless rows of steel and glass blocks. Things improved by the 60s. Eclipsed by the Bauhaus in the 20s, Hans Scharoun was at last able to indulge his taste for free-form structures like the Philharmonie and Staatsbibliothek in the Berlin Kulturforum. Günter Behnisch constructed an exciting tent-like Olympic Stadium for Munich. Foreign designers were also active, Finland's Alvar Aalto for the Essen Opera House and Britain's James Stirling for the postmodern Neue Staatsgalerie in Stuttgart and the Berlin Science Centre.

Otto Dix: The Artist's Family

George Grosz: Pillars of Society

German Expressionists and After

German Expressionist painting was an emotional revolt against the prevailing stuffy academic naturalism. Objective reality was subordinated to intense visual statements of anguish, joy and social protest. The pioneering group known as *Die Brücke* (The Bridge) was created in Dresden in 1905. Ernst Ludwig Kirchner (1880–1938), Karl Schmidt-Rottluff (1884–1976), Erich Heckel (1883–1970) and Max Pechstein (1881–1955) worked together in one studio but with no fixed programme other than a shared taste for violent colour and distorted forms. Their work is grouped in Berlin's Die Brücke museum, but shown also in Erfurt's Angermuseum and Dresden's Gemäldegalerie.

The *Blauer Reiter* (Blue Rider) group formed in Munich in 1912 moved quickly from figurative to abstract art. This cosmopolitan group included Russians Vasili Kandinsky (1866–1944) and Alexei von Jawlensky (1867–1941) and the Swiss Paul Klee (1879–1940) along with Franz Marc (1880–1916) and August Macke (1887–1914). One of the best collections of their work is at Munich's Städtische Galerie. Klee and Kandinsky took their Abstract Expressionism to the Bauhaus, where another visionary, Oscar Schlemmer (1888–1943), was painting robot-like creatures in a not so brave new world (Neue Staatsgalerie, Stuttgart).

A man apart, Emil Nolde (1867–1956) had joined Die Brücke briefly, but left to pursue—brilliantly—his preoccupations with Nordic mysticism and the soil. If you cannot get up to Seebüll to see his personal collection, look for his works in Hamburg Kunsthalle, Darmstadt Hessisches Landesmuseum and Dresden Gemäldegalerie. A similar, if somewhat less impassioned attachment to the soil and northern landscapes was shown by the artist's colony at Worpswede, near Bremen, most notably Paula Becker-Modersohn and Jugendstil adept Heinrich Vogeler.

In the fateful 1920s, Expressionism became a weapon for social justice. Max Beckmann (1884–1950) was a master of penetrating psychological portraits. George Grosz (1893–1959) poured vitriol on decadent capitalism. With photo-montagist John Heartfield (originally Helmut Herzfelde), Grosz led the Berlin branch of the anarchic Dada movement. But the most gifted, most ferocious of these socially involved artists was Otto Dix (1891–1969). His assaults on war were uncompromising, but studies of his family and self-

portraits were equally merciless. See his work at the Wallraf-Richartz Museum, Cologne, Gemäldegalerie, Dresden, and National-galerie, Berlin.

After 1945, German art at first picked up the threads of Surrealism and Abstract Expressionism. In the 60s, Group Zero dabbled in mathematical problems in Düsseldorf. Kassel staged international happenings at its *documenta* art fair. Cologne, Darmstadt and Berlin were major focuses for avant-garde talent, Georg Baselitz and Joseph Beuys among the principal figures. Beuys (1921–86) in particular attracted attention for his conceptual art and political involvement—bomber pilot turned pacifist and ecologist. The major collection of his free-wheeling collages of found objects is in Darmstadt's Hessisches Landesmuseum. One of his best-known artistic "actions" (Düsseldorf, 1965) asked the key cultural question: *"How Do You Explain Paintings to a Dead Hare?"*

Emil Nolde: Slovenians

Where the Danube and Neckar Begin, Poets Find Their Inspiration

The marriage of the two ancient duchies of Baden and Württemberg in 1952 has provided a region rich in outdoor pleasures and cultural delights. Ramble and relax around the Black Forest and Lake Constance. Enjoy a romantic adventure in the Danube and Neckar valleys. You will find the university towns of Heidelberg and Tübingen exuberant, both in and out of term time. Ulm proclaims its historic grandeur with its soaring Gothic spire, while the Stuttgart of Mercedes and Porsche chooses a strictly modern option.

Although part of Swabia was hived off to Bavaria during the Napoleonic Wars, its heartland between the Danube and the Alps remains in Baden-Württemberg. Less bumptious than Bavarians—"less arrogant", they would say—the Swabians are a reflective, mild-mannered people, witty rather than boisterous, curious and polite with strangers, but not cold. They are highly reputed craftsmen—of which those cars in Stuttgart are the natural 20th-century culmination. The Swabian mountains, *Schwäbische Alb* to the Germans, are a geological outcrop cut off from the French Jura and Swiss Alps by the Rhine Valley and Lake Constance. Although relatively modest in altitude, rarely rising above 900m (3,000ft), their peaks provided valuable redoubts for the mighty Hohenstaufen and Hohenzollern barons.

Be ready to vary your mode of transport as you travel. A delightful train threads its way through the Black Forest from Offenburg south-east to St Georgen. The most restful way to visit the main sights of Lake Constance is by boat, starting out from Lindau, Friedrichshafen or Constance. Boat cruises also explore the Neckar Valley either between Heidelberg and Heilbronn or north from the Stuttgart suburb of Bad Cannstatt.

Scholarship at Tübingen can be both idyllic and inspiring when you have Romantic poet Friedrich Hölderlin's tower in the background.

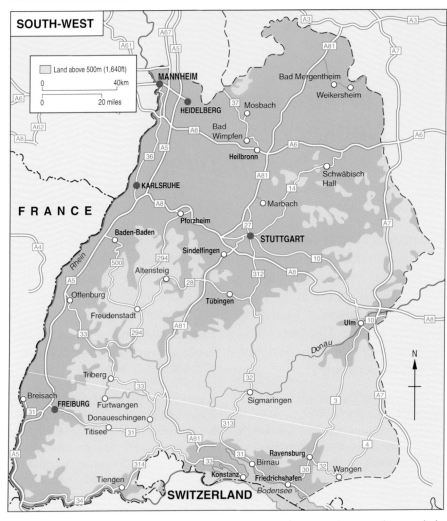

SOUTH-WEST

Land above 500m (1,640ft)

One of the good reasons to abandon your car occasionally is the excellent choice of local wines. You will find them robust in the Neckar Valley, and mellower west of the Black Forest and around Lake Constance.

Unlike the neighbouring regions of Bavaria and the Rhineland, much of Baden-Württemberg has traditionally been a Protestant stronghold. As a result, you will see a good many more Gothic and even Romanesque buildings spared the baroquification that was characteristic of the Catholic Counter-Reformation.

Heidelberg

The contagious verve of its ancient university has made this town one of the most enjoyable in the whole country. The scholars here have always drunk a lot, duelled a little and, when necessary, done an amazing amount of serious academic work. Beautifully situated in the Neckar Valley, it has been a poet's delight, a cradle of the German Romantic movement. The former capital of the Palatinate (shifted to Mannheim in 1720) has survived its strife-ridden history to offer visitors a haven of pure pleasure. Americans have long had a special affinity for the town. In the 1920s, alumni of the university donated funds for new buildings. Some of them must also have been high-ups in bomber command in 1945 when the city was spared, having already been singled out as headquarters for the US Army at the end of the war. The ruin of the castle was the work of troops of Louis XIV back in 1689 and 1693.

To take in the panorama of the old city at the foot of the castle, illuminated at night, start out on the opposite bank of the river with a stroll along the **Philosophen-weg** (Philosophers' Path). The sign-posted walk begins in the Neuenheim suburb from Ladenburger Strasse and climbs through pretty gardens—one dedicated to the poet Hölderlin—up to the Heiligenberg with ruins of a Celtic refuge near the top. The winding Schlangenweg leads you back down to the old bridge, **Karl-Theodor-Brücke**, with statues of the 18th-century Palatine prince and allegorical figures representing the rivers of his realm and the virtues of his reign. The **Marktplatz** retains something of the city centre's 17th-century atmosphere. Little shops and market stalls still cling to the **Heiliggeistkirche** (Church of the Holy Ghost). After the Protestant iconoclasm had deprived the late Gothic church of almost all its sculptural and other ornament, French looters in 1693 left in the chancel only the 15th-century carved tombstone of Prince Ruprecht and Princess Elisabeth.

Opposite, at Hauptstrasse 178, is the superb Renaissance **Haus zum Ritter** (House of the Knight—St George guarding the gable), the only private house to survive the French fires. Its Huguenot owner, the merchant Charles Bélier, was apparently a broad-minded fellow. To the pious gable inscription, *Soli Deo Gloria* ("Glory is God's Alone") he added, lower down, *Persta In Invicta Venus* ("May Venus Endure Unconquered").

Take the funicular railway (*Bergbahn*) up to the **castle**, more attractive as a ruin than many of the too-perfectly restored palaces you may see elsewhere. From the entrance, turn left through the Stückgarten, the emplacement for the castle's heavy artillery pieces originally mounted on the Rondell, a semicircular tower affording a fine view of the Neckar valley. At the far end of the garden are remains of the Fat Tower (*Dicker Turm*), originally 40m (130ft) tall with walls 7m (23ft) thick, blown in half by French cannons.

Double back via the Elisabethentor (1615), a triumphal arch built for Elizabeth Stuart, daughter of England's King James I and wife of Palatine prince Friedrich V. Notice directly across the moat the prison-dungeon ominously named *Seltenleer*, "Seldom Empty".

Skirt the moat and cross the bridge with its domed tower-gate leading to the main castle. In the summer, concerts and a theatre festival are held in the castle courtyard. On your right, the ticket-office and a restaurant are located in the Soldatenbau (guards' quarters) with a projecting well-house in front.

To the left is the **Ruprechtsbau**, built from 1398 to 1545. On the upper left of the façade, notice the prince's stone eagle holding in its claws the Palatine lion, and the Bavarian lozenge pattern. Inside, in the

Knights' Hall (*Rittersaal*), is a fine Renaissance sandstone fireplace.

Diagonally opposite stands the castle's most important building, the **Ottheinrichsbau**. This landmark of German Renaissance architecture was built by Prince Otto Heinrich in 1559. It lost its gables in the French invasion, but the façade retains its decorative elegance with rich statuary around the windows and triumphal arch doorway. Among the biblical and mythological heroes, look out for Joshua with helmet, Samson with ass's jawbone, Hercules with cudgel and David with sword and Goliath's head.

On the north side of the courtyard, the more baroque façade of the **Friedrichsbau** (1607, restored in the 19th century) presents an ancestral gallery of rulers from Charlemagne in the upper left corner to the building's patron, Prince Friedrich IV. A ramp leads down to the **Fassbau** (Barrel Wing), specially constructed to hold two gigantic wine barrels. The 1751 barrel holds 221,726 litres (48,780 gallons), that of 1662 a mere 45,000 litres (9,900 gallons). The guardian of the barrels was a dwarf named Perkeo, ex-jester to the Medici court in Florence. He was said to have drunk 10–12 litres (2.2–2.4 gallons) of wine a day and lived to the age of 83—dying after drinking a glass of water.

Visit, too, the **Apothecary Museum** (*Deutsches Apothekenmuseum*)—the entrance is beneath the staircase of the Ottheinrichsbau. Ten rooms trace the history of pharmacy and medical instruments. Hypochondriacs have a field day among the herbal chests, porcelain and crystal medicine jars, mortars, pestles, balances and retorts.

The regional **Kurpfälzisches Museum**, Hauptstrasse 97, boasts among its collections of Gothic and Renaissance painting and sculpture a magnificent group carved by Tilman Riemenschneider, the *Windsheimer Zwölfbotenaltar* (altarpiece of the Twelve Apostles). Among 19th- and 20th-century paintings are works of the Heidelberg Romantics, Max Slevogt, and German Expressionists Karl Schmidt-Rottluff and Emil Nolde.

Founded in 1386, the **university** on Universitätsplatz and Augustinergasse is the oldest in Germany. (In the German-speaking world, only Prague's German-language university founded in 1348 and Vienna's in 1365 are older.) Its great scholars have included sociologist Max Weber, physiologist Hermann von Helmholtz, physicist Robert Kirchhoff and his colleague Robert Bunsen, famous for his burner used in laboratories, and existential philosopher Karl Jaspers.

The burned-out shell of Heidelberg's castle was left by the armies of Louis XIV in 1689; remarkably little damage was done to the city in World War II.

POETS AND THINKERS

Baden-Württemberg is a land fertile in poets and great scholars. Friedrich Hölderlin and Friedrich Schiller will be the most familiar, but Swabia is equally proud of Ludwig Uhland and Eduard Mörike. Born in Marbach in 1759, Friedrich Schiller studied medicine in Stuttgart. Thanks to an enlightened lecturer who taught psychology with Shakespeare texts, Germany lost a doctor but gained a poet. Ludwig Uhland (1787–1862) gave up law studies at Tübingen to devote himself to Romantic poetry, making generations weep with his "Ich hatt' einen Kameraden".

Dr Faustus was not a figment of Goethe's or Marlowe's imagination but a real, live 16th-century scholar (or charlatan) who turned up at the monastery of Maulbronn and the taverns of Schwäbisch Hall before being fetched away by the Devil in Breisgau. Absorbed in his pursuit of the Absolute Idea, the philosopher Georg Wilhelm Friedrich Hegel was less frivolous, though as an undergraduate at Tübingen he did do time in the student jail. His crime is not known, but he is thought to have just needed a quiet place in which to disentangle his first thoughts on the phenomenology he was to teach at Heidelberg. In our century, Martin Heidegger blotted his philosophical copybook lecturing at the university of Freiburg with too many approving remarks about the Nazis.

Ulm, on the other hand, gave birth not only to the tallest church spire in the world, but also to Albert Einstein.

Heavy 19th-century Biedermeier furniture, highly priced in antique shops all around Germany, took its name from a creation of Heidelberg scholars. The "great Philistine poet" Gottlieb Biedermeier was a total invention, imagined by two university satirists to pillory the insensitive materialism of the times. For lesser crimes, students were jailed in the **Karzer** (Latin *carcer*), open to visitors at Augustinergasse 2. This displays the rascals' black silhouette portraits and their insolent graffiti.

Across the river, the university's **Museum of Geology and Palaeontology**, Im Neuenheimer Feld 234, reconstitutes 2 billion years of earth history from the Big Bang to today's whimper. The highlight is the smiling lower jaw of *Homo heidelbergensis*, 600,000 years old.

Neckar Valley

The Neckar river snakes across the southern edge of the Odenwald forest, its dark green foliage broken here and there by the red sandstone of ruined castles. While still in Heidelberg, you can get a superb view of the valley up on **Königstuhl** hill, a 5km (3-mile) walk from the castle or by the funicular railway (*Bergbahn*).

Take the river road 37 east to **Neckarsteinach** where the Swallow's Nest (*Schwalbennest*) up on a precipice tops the town's four castles. Opposite at **Dilsberg**, via Neckargemünd on the left bank, you can climb the castle tower (97 steps) for a grand view of the river. **Hirschhorn** offers the comfort of a bar from which to see the river looping around three sides of the renovated Renaissance castle-hotel.

Further east, past the little spa resort of Eberbach, the valley narrows dramatically. Above the road, the russet turrets of **Zwingenberg** castle loom out of the forest. Britain's Prince Philip is a frequent guest of the Margrave of Baden to hunt stag and boar. West of the river, you pass the three-storeyed Gothic ruin of **Minneburg** where three knights somehow managed to live together married to three sisters chattering to each other out of the three distinctive oriel bay windows.

Approaching the confluence of the Elz river, the forest gives way to open fields and orchards. Turn off briefly to **Mosbach** to see its pretty half-timbered houses and 16th-century town hall.

Back on the Neckar road, **Burg Hornberg** stands amid vineyards whose full-bodied product you can sample in a tavern in the converted stables (*Marstall*). In the castle, the great 16th-century knight Götz von Berlichingen (*see* page 177) spent his last days writing the memoirs that inspired one of Goethe's most popular plays. His armour is displayed in the Treppenturm.

Further south, the castle of **Guttenberg** put up stout resistance to invading armies over the centuries and has held on to its Gothic and Renaissance furnishings. Its museum collections include a Bible dating from 1430 and a botanist's strange 18th-century **Holzbibliothek**, book-shaped wooden boxes, each devoted to a different tree. Bound in the tree's bark, each contains samples of twigs, leaves, seeds, dried fruit, moss and tree-bugs.

Bad Wimpfen

Its medieval allure makes the old imperial town one of the most charming stops along the Neckar. In the lower town, Wimpfen im Tal, can be seen vestiges of an old Roman garrison that guarded this stretch of the imperial frontier. The rough-hewn **abbey-church** is in part 11th-century Romanesque with an interesting narrow porch on its French Gothic south side. Notice inside the finely carved choir stalls (1298). Built against the transept, the cloisters display pure early Gothic on the east side (1300), with column capitals carved with birds, frogs and strawberries,

but the delicacy disappears from the two later arcades.

The upper town, Bad Wimpfen am Berg, was the residence of the Hohenstaufen dynasty in the 13th century. It has an imposing medieval **Imperial Palace** (*Kaiserpfalz*)—Friedrich Barbarossa was here in 1182 to oversee its building. On the square Blue Tower (*Blauer Turm*) at the western end, the battlements and turrets are a 19th-century addition. To the east, the red sandstone Roter Turm is notable for its toilet bay projecting out over the ramparts. The arcaded gallery between the two towers has handsome sculpted pillars in its windows. The 12th-century **Steinhaus** with a stepped gable added 400 years later now houses the town museum.

Salzgasse, with the gables of its half-timbered houses leaning tipsily over, leads to a Renaissance fountain, the **Adlerbrunnen** (1576). Among the many noteworthy houses on Hauptstrasse, take a peek into the inner courtyard of the old hospital at No. 281.

Neckarsulm

This is a town for motorbike enthusiasts. NSU has its factory here, and the **Deutsches Zweirad Museum**, Urbanstrasse 11, exhibits two-wheel contraptions from an 1817 penny farthing to the most modern easy and not-so-easy riders.

Heilbronn

Much of the old town was destroyed by 1944 bombings, but the church of **St Kilian** survived. Its pride and glory is the ornate tower (*Kiliansturm*) of 1528, the first large-scale Renaissance construction in Germany. The famous gargoyles were carved in 1525 at the height of the Peasants' War, not to frighten off demons but to express the people's anger at the

OLD IRON HAND

Götz von Berlichingen lost his right hand in battle but carried on swashbuckling with an iron substitute. He fought feuds all around the country from Cologne to Nuremberg and Bamberg. For four weeks in the Peasants' War of 1525, he led the peasants' Odenwald militia, but more to moderate their ardour than lead them to victory. He died in his bed at the ripe old age of 82 and was buried in Schöntal Abbey west of Hornberg. The soldier's fans steam out there on the old Jagsttal railway from Möckmühl to pay respects at his tomb. The sculpted monument shows him to bear an uncanny resemblance to another old warrior, Ernest Hemingway.

The sculpted memorial to Götz von Berlichingen.

clergy of the time. They show a monkey in monk's habit, a nun and monk with bird's bodies and a bishop with his mistress. Inside the church, the wood sculpture of the **high altar** by Hans Seyfer (1498) matches in intensity the work of Tilman Riemenschneider and Veit Stoss. Look, too, for the fine 15th-century chancel and canopied ciborium by Austrian sculptor Anton Pilgram (who portrays himself supporting the ciborium's spiral staircase).

The 16th-century **town hall** with its astronomical clock has been lovingly restored, as well as the gabled **Käthchenhaus** of the sleepwalking lass who inspired Heinrich von Kleist's play, *Käthchen von Heilbronn.*

Heilbronn's town hall clock counts the days and months, and before each hour, an angel toots twice on his trumpet. In addition, a cock crows at 4, 8 and 12 o'clock, day and night.

Make a quick side-trip east to the vineyards of **Weinsberg**. Sample the wine at the foot of the ruined **Weibertreu castle**. The castle was attacked in 1140 by King Konrad III, but not before he told the women they could leave with whatever they could carry. They earned the ruin its immortal name "Castle of True-Hearted Women" by coming out with their husbands on their backs.

Schwäbisch Hall and the Tauber Valley

This excursion takes you through the unspoiled country of the Swabian Forest to a stretch of the Romantic Route (*see* page 142) where the Tauber river meanders across the north-east corner of Baden-Württemberg.

The old imperial city of Hall ("Schwäbisch" only since 1934) climbs the slopes of the narrow Kocher valley, its medieval charm blessedly intact. The pretty little river is spanned by tile-roofed wooden bridges. They afford a fine view of the tiered ochre, lemon and dove-grey façades of the town's handsome gabled mansions. Hall owed its prosperity to salt springs, used by the Celts back in 600 BC and now only for health-baths. The town's silver mint produced the Heller, a standard coin of the old Reich.

The sloping **Marktplatz** makes a dramatic focus for town life—and open-air theatre productions in summer. The monumental **Fischbrunnen** (1509), a fountain with statues of Samson, St George and St Michael, stands at the foot of a broad stairway (53 steps), leading to the church of **St Michael**. The archangel's statue is at the centre of the church's porch. Inside the 15th-century Gothic basilica is an impressive **high altar** (1470) with scenes of Christ's Passion sculpted and painted by anonymous Dutch artists. The *Crucifixion* is by a local Swabian artist, Michael Erhart.

Opposite the church, the restrained baroque architecture of the **town hall** (1730) with its stately lantern tower adds a quiet dignity to the square. Leading away to the south, Renaissance half-timbering with balconies and terraces strike the predominant note of the fine houses on **Obere** and **Untere Herrengasse.** Taverns here claim the dubious patronage of Dr Faustus and diabolical sidekick Mephistopheles. The town's **history museum** is housed in the Keckenburg in Untere Herrengasse, a ten-storey Romanesque tower, once inhabited. Towering over the south side of town is the **Grosses Büchsenhaus** (1527), variously arsenal and granary until a troupe of English players came there in 1604 to perform Shakespeare's *Romeo and Juliet*— only nine years after it was written. It has served as a theatre ever since.

About 3km (2 miles) south-east of town is the fortified Benedictine **Comburg Abbey.** Although extensively baroquified,

the abbey retains important works of the 12th century. Past the baroque and Renaissance gates, look for the superb Romanesque **Klostertor** with its twin towers and graceful arcade. The abbey-church has three Romanesque towers. Inside is a grandiose wheel-shaped chandelier of gilded copper and iron (1130) ornamented with Old Testament patriarchs and prophets. At the entrance to the choir, a decorative altar frontal (*antependium*), also of gilded copper from the same period, shows Christ with the Apostles.

Bad Mergentheim

Highway 19 north of Schwäbisch Hall joins the Romantic Route at this quiet spa resort with a Renaissance-baroque palace. On the way, stop off at **Stuppach** where a chapel shelters one of Germany's great art treasures. In 1812, the parish church acquired the central panel of Grünewald's **Maria Schnee Altar**, originally painted for the abbey-church of Aschaffenburg— a wing of the altar is in Freiburg (*see* page 183). Many art scholars rate Grünewald second only to Dürer. With just a handful of his works surviving, this portrait of a warmly maternal Mary painted in 1519 attracts pilgrims scarcely less fervent than those seeking out the relics of saints.

The waters of Bad Mergentheim, good for drinking and bathing, work marvels for liver and intestinal ailments—useful if you have gone overboard on the rich Swabian cuisine. Then make for the 16th-century **Deutschordensschloss**, the castle of the Teutonic Knights. This sprawling residence was built for knights remaining Catholic after their leader Albrecht von Zollern-Brandenburg followed Luther's urging in 1525 to turn the Teutonic Order's Prussian lands into a secular state. A museum traces the knights' history

178

from the carnage of the Crusades to today's more charitable institution. The brightly lit castle church is a baroque creation of François de Cuvilliés, its ceiling frescoes celebrating the Triumph of the Cross. In the gardens, the knights indulged their nostalgia for the Crusades by building a little Turkish mosque.

Weikersheim

Built for the lords of Hohenlohe, the town's refined 18th-century **palace** is baroque but without excessive ornament. Only in the Knights' Hall (*Rittersaal*) with its monumental fireplace is there a touch of folly in the painted stucco elephant, lion and boar on the walls. Unspoiled by war and plunder, the original furnishings of the royal apartments have survived, including the porcelain, Venetian crystal, silk tapestries and ancestral paintings.

Among the statues in the formal gardens are caricatures of court figures, notably pot-bellied dwarfs, precursors of a widespread German taste for garden dwarfery. At the end of the gardens, the Orangery, an elegant semi-circular Ionic colonnade, frames a pretty view of the Tauber valley.

Creglingen

A miraculous communion wafer brought pilgrims to the 14th-century Chapel of Our Lord (*Herrgottskapelle*). Today it is Tilman Riemenschneider's magnificently carved **Assumption of Mary Altar** (1505). Surrounding the sovereign Mary, each Apostle figure is charged with emotion: Bartholomew awe-struck, Thomas astonished, Matthew sceptical, Peter and Andrew imbued with faith. On the predella (altar base), Riemenschneider has carved a suffering self-portrait: the second of the three scribes.

The Black Forest

Without a doubt, this is one of the most attractive holiday regions, not just in Germany but in the whole of Europe. Besides the forest itself, the region embraces spa resorts offering mountain air cures as well as potent mineral waters, vineyards, orchards and a wealth of cultural monuments.

The forest grows on a mountain plateau. With only a couple of peaks, Belchen and Feldberg in the south, standing out enough to give you a bird's-eye view, you can plunge here into the depths of *Waldeinsamkeit*, the "forest-loneliness" beloved of German Romantics. It is 160km (100 miles) long from north to south and 60km (37 miles) at its widest point. For the northern half, Karlsruhe and Pforzheim are worth a visit, but the resort of Baden-Baden makes a more convenient base for excursions. It is the north, dense with conifers that, without ever being forbidding, most readily evokes the dark mysteries of the forest's name.

The cathedral city of Freiburg is ideal for exploring the south. Gradually the forest opens up, pine groves alternating with cow pastures and flowery meadows. Approaching the Alps, the forest grows denser again and is distinguished by its fast flowing streams and, to the east, the resort lakes of Titisee and Schluchsee.

Karlsruhe

The duchy of Baden's old capital, home now of Germany's supreme law courts, makes a good stop for travellers coming to the Black Forest from Frankfurt and the Rhineland. After the French burned the ruler's residence at Durlach, the town was built in 1715, fanning out geometrically from the new baroque palace. This has

Many small farms in the Black Forest region are run part-time by people who have a job in the nearby town as well.

been restored from its World War II ruins to house the art and regional folklore collections of the **Badisches Landes-museum**. The exhibits include Phoenician ivories and Egyptian, Greek, Etruscan and Roman ceramics and sculpture. Besides the German medieval sculpture and Renaissance furniture and textiles, Black Forest costumes and cuckoo clocks, look out for the exotic Turkish war booty (*Türkenbeute*) of weapons, carpets, flags and jewellery.

Artistically more important are the collections of European painting at the **Staatliche Kunsthalle**, Hans-Thoma-Strasse 2. They include major German works of Cranach, Grien, Grünewald,

Dürer and Holbein. Among Dutch and Flemish painters are Lucas van Leyden, Rembrandt, Ruisdael, Rubens and Jordaens. A fine French collection includes Poussin, Delacroix, Courbet, Monet, Cézanne and Gauguin. The adjacent **Orangerie** is devoted to 20th-century art: Nolde, Kandinsky, Klee, Kokoschka, Max Ernst, Juan Gris and Henry Moore.

The red sandstone **Pyramid** on Markt-platz is the mausoleum of the city's founder, Margrave Karl Wilhelm.

Baden-Baden

There is plenty of warmth left in the afterglow from this golden spa resort's 19th-century heyday. An old watering-hole of the crowned heads of Europe and other scoundrels, it still extends a gracious welcome with its mellow microclimate in the sheltered Oos valley on the western edge of the Black Forest.

The centre of the resort's social life is the gleaming white neoclassical **Kurhaus**, with café, restaurant, ballroom and casino (roulette, baccarat and blackjack). The waters in the **Kurgarten** are reputedly good for royal gout or democratic rheumatism. Respiratory problems are treated at the hot springs (58–69°C/ 136–156°F) of the **Friedrichsbad** near the castle. Further east, the **Caracalla-Therme** combines hot-spring pool and ultra-modern gymnasium. Between the two, on Römerplatz, you can see remains of the **Roman baths** where Emperor Caracalla

---

FANCY DRESS AND RUSSIAN ROULETTE

In the middle of the 19th century, anybody who mattered in London, Paris, Berlin and St Petersburg took a summer holiday in Baden-Baden. On the Lichtentaler Allee, Bismarck meditated on the unification of Germany. In 1861, a German student shot at Prussia's Wilhelm I for not doing it fast enough. The Prince of Wales rode to a fancy dress ball disguised as a ghost. His mother Victoria also came to town, but did not go to the ball. Party or no party, Napoleon III and wife Eugénie dressed up as Emperor and Empress.

The French set the tone. Jacques Bénazet and son Edouard opened the casino—and closed it again in 1872 after the Franco-Prussian war. Berlioz opened the opera house, and the Paris Jockey Club organized the horse races out at Iffezheim (still a summer fixture). It was here, at the Badhotel zum Hirsch, that Balzac took his long-suffering mistress-by-correspondence, Countess Hanska. Hiding out from arch-enemy Napoleon III, Victor Hugo checked in as a "Belgian".

Prominent among the Russian colony were writers Nikolai Gogol and Ivan Turgenev. Signing in as a lieutenant of the Imperial Russian Army, Dostoevsky gambled away his fortune. The casino features in his novel *The Idiot* as the symbol of hell. Russians returned in 1943, to Baden-Baden's prisoner-of-war camp.

(211–217) came with his soldiers to ease their war-weary limbs.

The main attraction, however, is the **Lichtentaler Allee,** still one of Europe's most elegant promenades. Stroll along the swift-flowing Oosbach in the shade of stately tulip trees with greenish-yellow blossom, Japanese ginkgo and maple, white poplar, and crimson and yellow azalea and magnolia.

The Renaissance Neues Schloss houses a **museum** of the town's history. Another, devoted more specifically to amusing paraphernalia of the spa and casino, is located in the **Gasthof zum Baldreit,** Küferstrasse 3. In the southern suburb of Lichtental is a **Johannes Brahms museum,** Maximilianstrasse 85, where the composer lived with Clara Schumann.

The vineyards west of town make a popular excursion along the **wine route**, signposted *Badische Weinstrasse* around Varnhalt, Neuweier and Umweg.

The Northern Forest

A scenic route along the crest of the forest's mountain plateau, Highway 500 south of Baden-Baden, is signposted as the *Schwarzwälder Hochstrasse.* On sideroads off to the west, you will find several charming mountain resorts such as **Sasbachwalden**, a good base for forest hikes. The scenic route winds up above the **Bühlertal**, with vantage points marked for viewing waterfalls and mountain streams along the way. Picnic or siesta at **Mummelsee**.

Then make a detour west at Ruhestein to visit the **Buttensteiner waterfall** cascading over the haunting ruin of the 13th-century Gothic **Allerheiligen** abbey-church. It was destroyed by fires and the subsequent rapacity of building merchants, but surviving vaults and columns still point to noble antecedents of Strasbourg cathedral and Paris's St-Denis.

After World War II bombardment, **Freudenstadt** made a heroic reconstruction of its old city centre around the Marktplatz. The parish church (1608) has preserved several fine pieces of art. Notable are the Romanesque baptismal font and lectern supported by the four Evangelists, both 12th-century, and a wooden *Crucifixion* (1500).

North-east from Freudenstadt, Highway 28 is signposted *Schwarzwald Bäderstrasse* (Black Forest Spa Route) for the many resorts offering cures of bracing mountain air and mineral waters along the way. At **Altensteig**, the spotless white and russet 16th-century timbered houses hug the hillside in tiers, nestling up against the parish church and medieval castle. On the Nagold river, **Calw** is the birthplace of writer Hermann Hesse (1877–1962). A

small museum is devoted to this cult figure of 1960s flower-children in the stately 18th-century Vischersche Haus, Bischofstrasse 48, and includes some of his watercolours. Leading to the town centre, the **Nikolauskapelle** (1400), distinguished by some fine Gothic rib vaulting, is built directly on a bridge over the river. Admire, too, the handsome timbered houses on Marktstrasse.

Hirsau presents the romantic ruin of its Benedictine **abbey** in a beautiful setting of wooded hills. This bastion of the powerful Cluny empire was destroyed by the French in 1693 during their attack on the nearby ducal castle. Its gutted walls and turrets loom beyond the abbey's fine Romanesque Eulenturm (Tower of Owls, 1120) and Flamboyant Gothic cloister (1494). Notice the lovely elm tree growing out of the castle's ruins. Two churches, the Aureliuskirche and Marienkapelle have been restored, the latter as a museum for the monastery's sculpture.

Pforzheim and Maulbronn

On the northern outskirts of the forest, Pforzheim was almost totally levelled in 1945. But the traditional centre of goldsmiths, jewellers and watchmakers that earned it the name of *Goldstadt* has been resurrected. A very good **Jewellery Museum** (*Schmuckmuseum*), Jahnstrasse 42, presents a 4,000-year history of the art from Egyptians and Etruscans via the Renaissance to Pop, Op and kinetic design.

Drive 20km (12 miles) north-east to Maulbronn's **Cistercian monastery**

Geroldsauer Falls in the Black Forest. The beauties of the area are hidden from the roads.

founded in 1147. The Protestant Reformation retained the buildings' Romanesque and Gothic forms. (The Duke of Württemberg's Renaissance mansion, now a school, was added in 1588. Prominent students at the abbey school included astronomer Johannes Kepler and writers Friedrich Hölderlin and Hermann Hesse.) From the south-west entrance, you see to the left the monastery's old hostel, bakery, granary, forge and stable. Straight ahead is the abbey-church with its elegant Gothic porch, known as *Paradies*. The simple Romanesque interior received its Gothic fan-vaulting in the 15th century. A rood screen preceded by a huge stone *Crucifixion* divides the laymen's church from the monk's choir. The oak choir stalls are carved with Old Testament scenes such as the sacrifice of Isaac, and Moses with the burning bush. Left of the Paradies porch, the cloisters are notable for their ornately carved column capitals. From the cloister garden, see the monumental 14th-century Fountain Chapel (*Brunnenkapelle*).

In the south-east corner of the monastery grounds is the **Faust Tower**, referring to a visit by Dr Faustus in 1516. Faust fans can visit his birthplace in nearby **Knittlingen** where a little museum has been installed in the town hall.

Freiburg

This university city on the edge of the forest has a distinctive light-hearted atmosphere, the legacy of more than 400 years of Habsburg rule ended by Napoleon in 1808. Summer daytime heat is cooled by pleasant evening breezes blowing in from nearby hills, encouraging a Mediterranean-style stroll around **Münsterplatz**, centre by day of a lively fruit and vegetable market.

BLACK FOREST RAILWAY

The *Schwarzwaldbahn* winds its way diagonally across the southern half of the forest between Offenburg and St Georgen. The best stretch is between Hausach and Triberg when it twists and turns through 36 tunnels.

The **cathedral** (*Münster Unserer Lieben Frau*) is one of the glories of German Gothic architecture. One of the rare examples in Germany to be completed in the Middle Ages (1350), the main tower, 115m (377ft), is at once powerful and ethereally light. From a buttressed square base embracing the cathedral's majestic porch, it rises to a graceful octagon supporting the lace-like openwork spire. Over the transept, the twin Cock Towers (*Hahnentürme*) have Romanesque mullioned windows, but openwork Gothic lanterns and spires match the main tower.

Access to the porch interior or narthex is inside the church. A veritable gallery of 14th-century sculpture depicts sin and temptation (colour added 500 years later). Notice the splendid tympanum tracing Christ's life from Nativity in the lower field via the Passion to the central Crucifixion, beneath the Day of Judgement—the blessed waiting patiently on Christ's right and the damned in chains on his left. On the west wall facing the nave is a fine French-style *Madonna* (1290). The nave's 14th-century stained glass was donated by the guilds, each showing an emblem—for instance, the bakers' pretzel. For the high altar, Hans Baldung Grien has painted a vividly colourful *Coronation of Mary* (1516) and on the rear side a *Crucifixion*. In the University Chapel to the right of the high altar, see Hans Holbein the Younger's *Oberried Altar* of Christ's birth and the *Adoration of the Magi*.

The cathedral is complemented by three handsome buildings on the south side of Münsterplatz. With its steep roof, pointed turrets and Renaissance arcade, most striking of the trio is the merchants' **Kaufhaus**. The façade statues are of Habsburg princes. The baroque **Archbishop's Palace** (*Erzbischöfliches Palais*) shows admirable restraint. The patrician

Haus zum Schönen Eck, also 18th century, now houses the music academy.

Explore the picturesque medieval quarter of fishermen and artisans along the **Gewerbekanal** (Tanner's Canal) between the massive city gates Schwabentor and Martinstor. Housed in the former monastery church, the **Augustinermuseum**, Salzstrasse 32, exhibits Gothic sculpture

On the north portal of the chancel at Freiburg cathedral, the 14th-century tympanum tells the story of Adam and Eve.

reputedly warmest climate to produce some of the best vineyards in southern Germany. On the **wine route** around Burkheim and Kiechlingsbergen, try the Ruländer whites and rosés.

For centuries, the hilltop town of **Breisach** was a fiercely contested bastion on the Rhine. It was destroyed in 1793 by the French and in 1945 by Allied bombs. The triumphal arch (*Rheintor*, 1670) is a relic of fortifications built by Louis XIV. In the reconstructed Romanesque-Gothic **church**, rid of its 19th-century additions, notice at the high altar a late Gothic painting of Jesus crowning a bemused Mary, with God looking on, strangely troubled. Martin Schongauer's frescoes of the *Resurrection* and *Day of Judgement* show their war damage.

The Central Forest

Highway 294 north-east of Freiburg follows the Elz river to **Waldkirch**. The forest church of the town's name is the pretty baroque **St Margaretha**, with a fine rococo pulpit. To find it, set in a cluster of 18th-century houses, turn off on the road winding south up to the **Kandel** mountain (chair-lift to the top, 1,242m/4,075ft). Further south, the smart little resort of **St Peter** boasts an elegant 18th-century abbey-church built for the old Benedictine monastery by Peter Thumb, the architect of the great Birnau church on Lake Constance (*see* page 199). The rococo sculpture is by Josef Anton Feuchtmayer.

from the Rhine region as well as important works by Hans Baldung Grien and Grünewald—including a panel of the Maria Schnee Altar from Aschaffenburg.

Kaiserstuhl and Breisach

The "Emperor's Throne" (*Kaiserstuhl*) west of Freiburg is a prehistoric volcano whose soil combines with the country's

Furtwangen is *the* place to get your Black Forest cuckoo clock. Shops abound, but the craziest clocks are found in the **Clock Museum** (*Uhrenmuseum*), Gerwigstrasse 11. Besides tracing the very serious 600-year history of chronometers from iron Gothic to modern quartz and atomic, it displays enough astounding birdsong clocks to drive a cuckoo human.

Triberg is a resort popular for the spectacular nearby waterfall, cascading a total of 160m (535ft) through the forest in seven stages. The town's **folklore museum**, Wallfahrtsstrasse 4, is devoted to Black Forest mining, musical instruments and clocks.

Gutach (by train, get off at Hausach) has a superb **open-air museum** (*Freilichtmuseum "Vogtsbauernhof"*) devoted to the great farmhouses of the Black Forest, reconstructed here in a lovely setting of meadow and woodland. You will see not just simple peasant cottages but monumental rustic mansions. The typical *Eindachhof* ("One-Roof Farm") came with cattle-trough, workshops, bakery, granary and living quarters all under one huge thatched roof.

The Southern Forest

Start out from Freiburg again, south-east on Highway 31. **Höllental** (Hell Valley) is more idyllic than infernal, though some get a little shiver in the dark narrow gorge of **Ravennaschlucht**. Up on the precipice, a bronze stag marks the spot from which a hunter and dog leapt across in pursuit of their prey. **Hinterzarten** is a health resort much appreciated by insomniacs for its restful climate. Those who have no such problems come just for the rambles in summer and cross-country skiing in winter around the handsome old farmhouses. In nearby Höllsteig, visit the little

Oswaldkapelle (1148), one of the oldest churches in the forest.

The resort town of **Titisee** is almost invariably crowded, but the lake itself is a delight. Drive around to the more peaceful western shore for a picnic beneath the fir trees. Take the chair-lift up the **Feldberg** for the panorama from the highest point in the forest, 1,493m (4,900ft). You will find there another statue of Bismarck, honoured, it seems, wherever an extensive view gives you a sense of the country he unified.

Schluchsee is an artificial lake formed by a hydraulic dam, but nonetheless popular for sailing and windsurfing. Continue south on Highway 500 to **St Blasien** to visit a quite astonishing Benedictine **abbey-church,** a gigantic neoclassical pile (1783) rising from the valley of the Alb river. A Doric-columned portico flanked by two massive square towers leads back to an enormous dome, the whole making broad hints at Athens's Propylaeum on the Acropolis, the Pantheons of Paris and Rome, and even St Peter's. (Successive fires have destroyed much of the interior's original baroque decoration.)

Bernau has some grand Black Forest farmhouses, the most handsome being the Resenhof, preserved in its 18th-century form to demonstrate the *Eindachhof* principle of all under one roof. In the town hall of his birthplace, the **Hans-Thoma-Museum** is devoted to the painter (1839–1924) who epitomizes the old sentimental view of Germany's rural life. Drive west over to the steep dome-shaped **Belchen** mountain, 1,414m (4,639ft) for a view of the Alps and across the Rhine to the Vosges in Alsace.

A winding road leads north down through the lovely **Münstertal**, prospering of old from its silver mines. The disused **Devil's Mine** (*Grube Teufels-grund*) is open to visitors. The local honey is a great delicacy, and in Obermünstertal town hall there is a fine **Beekeeping Museum** (*Bienenkunde-Museum*), the biggest of its kind in Europe. Exhibits include fossilized bees 20 million years old and medieval beehives. Much is made of local hero Wilhelm Wankler, the father of queen bee breeding (1855–1929). The onion-domed church of **St Trudpert** has a sober baroque interior with a noteworthy 17th-century *Crucifixion* by Christoph Daniel Schenk on the north wall. In the sacristy is a precious ceremonial cross in gold and silver (1175).

Staufen makes a cheerful last stop with its stately patrician houses along Hauptstrasse and exuberant Renaissance town hall and 17th-century fountain on the Marktplatz. It was here in the Gasthof zum Löwen, Room 5 on the 3rd floor, that Dr Faustus is said to have died. According to

one story, he was an alchemist, killed in an explosion when one of his attempts to turn lead into gold failed. In Goethe's version, a band of angels saved the doctor's soul in the nick of time, but a plaque at the inn tells what really happened:

"In the year 1539, Doctor Faustus, a wondrous necromancer, came to The Lion at Staufen and died a miserable death. And the story tells how one of the supreme devils, Mephistopheles whom in his lifetime he just called his brother-in-law, did, after the pact of 24 years had run out, break his neck and deliver his poor soul to eternal damnation."

Lake Titisee in the Black Forest can be overrun with visitors at summer weekends, but you will escape a lot of them if you hire a rowing boat.

Stuttgart

*G*et out for a moment from the dense pine trees to take in the panorama from the Belchen, one of the Black Forest's few peaks with a view.

This is the modern German city *par excellence*. After the devastation of World War II, the authorities rebuilt a few symbolic historic monuments but otherwise chose to play the card of modernity. Beyond its world-famous Daimler-Benz and Porsche car factories, the city is the

home of avant-garde ballet, theatre and an internationally admired orchestra and opera company. Faithful to the spirit of architectural innovation in the 1920s Weissenhof housing development (still intact), the new state art gallery is a major achievement of post-modern architecture.

A magnificent natural setting in a basin is enhanced by the greenery of parks and gardens. For a good first view from its southern ridge, take the Degerloch exit from the Karlsruhe–Munich Autobahn. On the south-east corner of town, you can stop off at the **Fernsehturm**, the prototype (1956) for television towers all over the world. The concrete and steel needle is 217m (712ft) high with a restaurant in the "basket" at 152m (498ft) for a panoramic

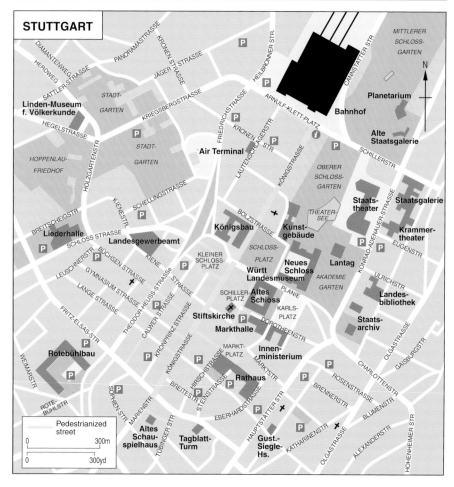

STUTTGART

view of the city and the Swabian mountains to the south-east.

The centre of city life is the pedestrian zone around Königstrasse. It borders the little cluster of monuments preserved and restored around Schillerplatz. More than a church, the **Stiftskirche** offers, with its solid Renaissance clock tower and slender Romanesque steeple, an emblem of the city's lost past. Over the modern bronze door in the porch are medieval sculptures, salvaged from the World War II bombardment. On the south wall of the chancel is a 14th-century tympanum of the Cruci-

fixion. Nearby, the somewhat forbidding turreted fortress exterior of the 16th-century **Altes Schloss** conceals an elegant Renaissance palace. It is now home of the **Württembergisches Landesmuseum**, exhibiting works of Tilman Riemenschneider and Hans Multscher among its church sculpture, and costumes, crystal, porcelain, clocks and musical instruments.

To the north, you can stroll in the delightful **palace gardens** (*Schlossgarten*) past the French classical Neues Schloss, rebuilt after the war to house state ministries. Opposite the Staatstheater, on

Konrad-Adenauer-Strasse, is the neoclassical **Alte Staatsgalerie**. Its excellent collection of European art includes German works by Cranach, Strigel and Holbein; Flemish and Dutch works of Memling, Rubens, Ruisdael, Rembrandt and Hals; Italian art of the 14th century, the Venetian Renaissance and baroque; and French paintings by Courbet, Manet, Monet, Cézanne, Gauguin and Renoir. German Expressionists are exhibited as a transition to the modern museum next door.

The **Neue Staatsgalerie**, designed in 1984 by British architect James Stirling, is itself a controversial masterpiece, a self-contained piece of urban landscape. The variation of stone, glass and colour gives it no clearly defined façade. A long ramp leads to a "hamlet" of galleries and halls built around an outdoor sculpture court. In addition to one of Germany's largest Picasso collections, 20th-century European artists here include Klee, Dix, Kokoschka and Schlemmer (Stuttgart-born) and sculpture by Rodin, Maillol, Giacometti and Beuyst. Among the Americans are Warhol, Pollock, Rauschenberg and Newman.

Time for a picnic—head for the beautiful **Killesberg** park up on the heights north-west of the city centre. A miniature railway chugs around the flower beds, and an observation tower overlooks the city. Across Stresemannstrasse, the nearby **Weissenhof-Siedlung** is a landmark development by leading European architects of the 1920s. Prototypes for mass-produced housing include Bauhaus master Ludwig Mies van der Rohe's apartment block, Am Weissenhof 14; terraced housing by Holland's Mart Stam (No. 24); semi-detached house by the Swiss Le Corbusier and French Pierre Jeanneret, Rathenaustrasse 1; and an "organic" house

---

KINGS OF THE ROAD

Karl Benz (1844–1929) and Gottlieb Daimler (1834–1900) never met. Benz worked in Mannheim, less interested in cars than in a general-purpose motor. In Stuttgart, Daimler manufactured tin cans before turning to motor vehicles. Police raided his workshop, suspecting an illegal mint. The Benz and Daimler companies amalgamated in 1926 and named their most famous car after Mercedes Jellinek, the 12-year-old daughter of the French distributor.

Austrian-born Ferdinand Porsche (1875–1951) worked with Daimler-Benz before Hitler called on him in 1934 to create a cheap popular car to rival the American Ford. The Volkswagen, in whose design Hitler himself eagerly participated, did not go into production until after the war. Porsche preferred to move upmarket.

---

by Berliner Hans Scharoun. A small museum of the project is contained in the building designed by the father of modern German architecture, Peter Behrens (Am Weissenhof 30).

The **Daimler-Benz Museum**, Mercedes Strasse 137a, is out in the eastern suburb of Untertürkheim. It displays 160 cars and motors, including the great engineers' first babies, the *Daimler-Motorkutsche* and *Benz-Patent-Motorwagen*, invented in 1886. Racing cars dating back to 1899 include the *Blitzen Benz* (Benz Flash) and the *Silberpfeil* (Silver Arrow).

In the northern suburb of Zuffenhausen, the **Porsche Museum**, Porschestrasse 42, has 35 historic examples of the great sports car, first produced in 1948 by the man who also designed the Volkswagen for Hitler.

North to Marbach

The Neckar river north of Stuttgart makes a pleasant day trip, either by boat from the

spa town of Bad Cannstatt or on Highway 27. First stop is **Schloss Ludwigsburg**, a huge baroque residence that Duke Eberhard Ludwig of Württemberg built in 1704 for his mistress Wilhelmine to keep her away from his wife in Stuttgart. An extravagant example of the Versailles craze obsessing the princes and paupering their tax payers, it has geometric French gardens to the south and a more romantically landscaped English park to the north.

The birthplace of Friedrich Schiller (1759–1805), **Marbach** is an attractive town of half-timbered houses hugging a slope above the Neckar river. The poet's manuscripts are collected in the **Schiller-Nationalmuseum** (Schillerhöhe 8), also devoted to other German writers from Hölderlin to Günter Grass. More folksy memorabilia are collected in Schiller's bedroom and kitchen at the family home, Niklastorstrasse 31.

Further downriver, explore the charming wine country around Besigheim and Hessigheim. Try the sweeter wines with a piece of the local onion pie.

Tübingen

Contemplative types in this university town of Hegel, Hölderlin and astronomer Johannes Kepler escape its bustle to meditate down on the Neckar river. Stroll along the delightful **Platanenallee**, a long shady garden-island of plane trees stretching west along the middle of the river

On show at Stuttgart's Daimler-Benz Museum, this Mercedes Type 500 lent a little class to a limp comedy entitled Die Drei von der Tankstelle (*The Filling Station Trio*).

from the Eberhard Bridge. There are punts and rowing boats for hire opposite the east end of the garden. Romantics pay homage to poet Friedrich Hölderlin at the house where he spent the last, mentally disturbed years of his life, in the **Hölderlinturm**, Bursagasse 6.

Locals come into town in their regional costumes to sell their wares on the market square beside the town hall and its Renaissance fountain of Neptune. On Holzmarkt, visit the 15th-century church of **St Georg**. Besides an admirable late-Gothic triple-arched rood screen and sculpted pulpit, the church's most impressive monuments are the rows of Renaissance tombs of the Württemberg dukes in the chancel. Here lies Eberhard the Bearded, the founder of the university.

The rampart terraces of the largely 16th-century **castle** offer fine views of the town and river. Carved on the ornate triumphal arch of the outer gate is England's Order of the Garter with the royal motto *Hon(i) Soit Qui Mal Y Pense* bestowed by Elizabeth I on the Duke of Württemberg in 1597.

The university's **Dental Museum** (*Zahnärztliches Museum*), Osianderstrasse 2, is a sado-masochistic joy. Drills, clamps, probes, extraction forceps, root elevators, and bone-chisels ancient and modern; you are spared nothing. Of one instrument, it is noted: "When manipulating without due care, whole pieces of jaw were pulled out."

Hohenzollern

A short drive south of Tübingen on Highway 27, the Hohenzollerns' **castle** crowns a thickly wooded outcrop of the Swabian mountains. Entirely reconstructed in 1867, this neo-Gothic pile was less a residence than a self-congratulatory

monument to the Hohenzollern dynasty's conquest of Germany. The highly stylized fortress, with the kind of turrets and battlements favoured by jigsaw puzzles or construction-kits, makes a very popular family outing. A shuttle-bus takes you from the car park to the top, offering a splendid view over the Neckar valley. A rare relic of the castle's medieval origins is the 15th-century Gothic chapel of **St Michael**. The tomb of the Prussian king Frederick the Great was kept in the castle's modern Protestant chapel after World War II, but has now been returned to Potsdam.

Haigerloch

This sleepy town enjoys an absolutely enchanting location on the banks of a double loop in the little Eyach river, a tributary of the Neckar. On the north bank, you can visit the 18th-century **castle church**, built on the promontory rock. Sixty carved figures decorate the monumental Renaissance altar. (The castle is now a hotel.) On the south bank, make your way up to the Upper Town (*Oberstadt*) to the chestnut-shaded terrace of the church of **St Anna** for an exquisite view over the river. The church has a fine rococo interior by Johann Michael Feuchtmayer. At the top of the Upper Town is the **Roman Tower** (*Römerturm*), which is in fact medieval in origin.

This sculpture is part of the late-Gothic choir stalls in Tübingen's 15th-century church of St Georg, built by Duke Eberhard V of Württemberg, founder of Tübingen University.

Danube Valley

Follow the great Danube (*Donau*) river—Europe's second longest after the Volga—from the cathedral city of Ulm back to its source outside Donaueschingen. Narrower and progressively more picturesque west of Sigmaringen, the valley cuts through the Swabian mountain plateau—Schwäbische Alb—a northern geological extension of the Swiss Alps.

Ulm

The city has done a superb job of restoring at least a small part of its historic centre. Go down to the riverside gardens to view the skyline of steeple and gabled houses.

Follow the canal branching off the river to explore the **Fischerviertel** of old fishermen's and artisans' houses with dormer windows in the steeply gabled roofs. Notice in particular the half-timbered 16th-century **Schiefes Haus** (Crooked House) leaning tipsily over the paved street and the **Schwörhaus** (Oath House), from which the mayor traditionally reads the oath of city freedoms.

The Gothic **cathedral** was never more than a parish church, but in 1377 the city elders decided to go for broke with a church for 29,000 worshippers in a town of 12,000 inhabitants. Broke indeed, because Ulm could not complete the spire—at 161m (528ft) the tallest in the world—until 1890. Brave souls who make it up the 768 steps to the top are rewarded with a view of the Alps and along the Danube, it would seem, all the way to Hungary. On the triple-arcaded main porch stands a noble **Schmerzensmann** (Suffering Christ). Hans Multscher's original sculpture of 1429 is now safe from corrosive pollution inside on the choir arch

to the right. The interior has a finely carved pulpit and tall stone canopied ciborium, but most of the 15th-century decoration was destroyed in the iconoclasm of the Protestant Reformation. Miraculously the masterly **choir stalls** escaped unscathed. Over the 98 seats, Jörg Syrlin portrayed Apostles, saints and martyrs above Old Testament prophets and heroes in half-relief. On seat arms are figures of classical antiquity: Pythagoras as a musician, Ptolemy with a globe, and Seneca slashing his wrist with a hook—a rare case of a suicide portrayed in church. Syrlin also sculpted the **Fischkasten fountain** south of the cathedral on Marktplatz by the colourful Renaissance town hall with its astronomical clock.

The **Ulmer Museum**, Neue Strasse 92, has an outstanding collection of work by the great artists living in Ulm in the 15th and 16th centuries: painters Bartholomäus Zeitblom, Martin Schaffner and Bernhard Strigel; and sculptors Jörg Syrlin, Hans Multscher and Daniel Mauch. Besides a model of the cathedral as it was before the 19th-century steeple, the original foundation stone of 1377 makes an intriguing exhibit: on one side is a sculpted relief of the mayor offering Mary a model of the church, on the other a Hebrew inscription revealing that this was the gravestone of Rabbi Moses, the son of Rabbi Eleasor.

*T*he Danube starts *as two Black Forest streams which join just outside Donaueschingen. For the sake of neatness, the town fathers built this pond and called it the Donauquelle—"Source of the Danube".*

In a country where the bread is so deliciously varied, Ulm's **German Bread Museum** (*Deutsches Brotmuseum*), Fürsteneckerstrasse 17, deserves a visit. From corn to oven to bakery, it traces 5,000 years of the history of bread, but also devotes a special section to hunger.

The southern suburb of **Wiblingen** boasts a splendid Benedictine **monastery**. Its baroque abbey-church of Johann Michael Fischer (the architect of Ottobeuren) with frescoes by Januarius Zick makes magnificent use of light and colour, but surely the rococo library, with its dazzling blues, pinks and golds, is too beautiful to work in.

Sigmaringen

For the Hohenzollerns, its strategic position guarding the upper Danube made it an ideal site for a citadel. The **castle**, rebuilt since its destruction by the Swedes in the Thirty Years' War, rises from a crag directly above the river. Flemish tapestries, Renaissance armour and weapons are highlights of the guided tour. In 1944 the Germans kept their French puppet, Marshal Pétain, here until he returned to France to stand trial for collaboration. Some handsome 17th- and 18th-century houses grace Fürst-Wilhelm-Strasse.

From here, the river meanders beneath spectacular pinnacles and overhanging rocks, many of them crowned by ruined castles. Stop at **Inzigkofen** for a look at the 18th-century abbey-church and a walk beyond the gardens to the forest. The path rises to the arched cliff-top **Teufelsbrücke** spanning a deep gorge and giving a dramatic view of the Danube. If you continue west, you'll see **Werenwag castle** rising from the forest on the north bank, then opposite, further upriver, the massive bastions and towers of 16th-century **Wildenstein**.

The sprawling abbey at **Beuron** is closed to the public except for its rococo church, renowned for the Gregorian chant at mass.

Mühlheim is a pretty market town with half-timbered houses built into its medieval fortifications along a mountain ridge. In the lower town, the 12th-century church of **St Gallus** has Gothic wall-paintings in the choir.

Donaueschingen

The town makes two liquid boasts, one more authentic than the other. Its beer is indeed among the best in Germany, but the well that it presents as the source of the Danube, *"Donauquelle"*, is in fact just a neat piece of chamber-of-commerce puffery. The monumental balustraded fountain in the castle park was built in the 19th century. The great Danube's real beginning, the confluence of the Breg and Brigach rivers, is much less romantically situated, south of town under the viaduct of Highway 27 as it approaches the Autobahn.

A more serious reason for coming here (besides the beer) is the Fürstenberg family's superb collection of Gothic and Renaissance art, the **Fürstenberg-Sammlungen**, Karlsplatz 7. The highlight is Hans Holbein's 12-panelled *Graue Passionsaltar*, but look out for other important works by Lucas Cranach, Bernhard Strigel and Bartholomäus Zeitblom. In October, the town holds a major festival of modern music featuring such composers as Stockhausen, Boulez and Hindemith.

*T*oo *beautiful to work in, the baroque library of the Abbey of Wiblingen near Ulm was designed by Johann Michael Fischer, architect of Ottobeuren.*

Lake Constance

The lake, Bodensee to the Germans, was originally a basin formed by the Rhine glacier flowing in from the south-east. At the town of Constance it divides into two arms, and the Rhine continues out along the Swiss–German border at Stein. This is the closest Germany gets to an inland sea, 76km (47 miles) long and 14.5km (9 miles) at its widest point. The resorts' beaches and first-class sailing facilities and the good local wine create a German version of the Italian lakes. In spring, the Alpine cool quickly gives way to a mellow climate encouraging not only orchards and vineyards but even, in parts, gardens of tropical flora.

Constance (*Konstanz*)

The quiet city on the Swiss border makes a pleasant base for exploring the lake. Regular ferries serve the north shore and boat cruises leave from the downtown harbour. From 1414–18, the town hosted an important council to try to end the Great Schism of the Catholic Church. Cardinals met in conclave at the harbourside **Konzilgebäude**, a merchants' warehouse now used for conferences and concerts. The council also tried and executed Jan Hus, Czech reformer and precursor to Martin Luther. The **Hus-Haus** where he was imprisoned (on Hussenstrasse) is now a museum of Hussite memorabilia and Czech art. Protestants make pilgrimages to the **Hussenstein** where he was burned at the stake, west on the road to Gottlieben.

The town **basilica (Münster Unserer Lieben Frau)** suffers from the 19th-century neo-Gothic spire stuck unharmoniously in the centre, but the interior has some fine 15th-century choir stalls and an imposing organ loft on the west wall.

North of the church are the cloisters and 14th-century Mauritius chapel housing the Gothic **Heiliges Grab** (1280), shrine of the Holy Grave, with carved figures of Jesus's childhood and the Apostles and topped by a baroque statue of Isaiah.

The town hall has a graceful Renaissance arcaded courtyard. Housed in the 15th-century Butchers' Guild Hall, the **Rosgartenmuseum**, Rosgartenstrasse 3, displays regional sculpture and painting, in addition to some interesting artefacts of prehistoric lake dwellers.

Mainau Island

A short boat cruise takes you over to this lovely garden of tropical plants in the grounds of an 18th-century castle, owned by the Swedish count Bernadotte. From the terraces of orange, lemon and banana trees, magnolias and hibiscus, you get a superb view of the lake. A place to dream.

Reichenau

Connected to the mainland by a causeway, the long island of Reichenau was famous for the great scholars and church poets of its Benedictine monastery founded in the 8th century. The monks' herb gardens have given way to thriving commercial market gardens and vineyards. The monastery's three churches are rare Romanesque monuments. At **Oberzell**, visit the hilltop Carolingian church of St Georg. Red-tiled and whitewashed, the simple three-aisled basilica with a tower over the transept-crossing has wall-paintings of Christ's miracles dating from the 10th century. The *Day of Judgement* on the west wall is 11th century.

At **Mittelzell**, the island's principal settlement, a tall Gothic choir (1447) completes the Romanesque transepts and tower of the abbey-church (*Münster*). Inside, a splendid sandstone *Madonna* (1310) stands at the high altar. In the sacristy are five precious Gothic reliquaries.

Tucked away in *Niederzell* on the northwest corner of the island, the 12th-century basilica of Peter and Paul was baroquified in 1756. An 11th-century fresco of the *Pantocrator* (Christ Omnipotent) was recently uncovered in the apse.

The North Shore

A modern resort in a medieval setting, **Überlingen** offers good tennis and sailing facilities along with its cold-water cures. The late-Gothic **Minster of St Nikolaus** has a monumental high altar (1616) teeming with figures sculpted by Jörg Zürn. He also carved the attractive choir stalls and sandstone canopied ciborium.

The **town hall** (1490) was the first public edifice north of the Alps with the rough-hewn masonry characteristic of the Italian Renaissance. Inside, visit the wood-panelled council chamber. Its carved doors present a splendid gallery of 15th-century aristocratic and municipal life.

In a patrician mansion of rough-hewn stone like the town hall, the **town museum**, Krummenbergstrasse 30, has a collection of Gothic, Renaissance and baroque sculpture, including some charming Christmas cribs. The house's terraced garden affords a fine view of the town and lake.

Birnau

The Cistercian monks' grand baroque **pilgrimage church** (*Marienwallfahrts kirche*) enjoys an idyllic setting amid vineyards and meadows overlooking the lake. It was designed by the Austrian architect Peter Thumb and consecrated in 1750. The dignity of the palace-like façade gives way to the festive ambiance of the rococo interior. Sculptor Josef Anton Feuchtmayer's cherubim play everywhere, plucking harps, cuddling sheep, licking honey, even lightening the tone of Christ's Calvary. The prodigious ceiling frescoes around the theme of the Assumption are by Gottfried Bernhard Göz.

Unteruhldingen

From the sublime to the Stone Age, the town's lakeside open-air museum is a **prehistoric village** built on stilts (*Pfahlenbaudorf*). A boardwalk leads out into the lake among wooden dwellings of the kind used by hunters and fishermen around 2200 BC. The reconstructions group findings from Stone and Bronze Age excavations around the lake and in Upper Swabia.

Meersburg

This popular resort has colourful flowerbedecked half-timbered houses along Steigstrasse. Concerts are performed on the terrace of the 18th-century bishop's residence (*Neues Schloss*), offering a fine view across the lake to the Alps. The nearby **Altes Schloss** is an old stepgabled, turreted castle keep full of dungeons and medieval armour.

Friedrichshafen

This port town was the home of Count Ferdinand von Zeppelin (1838–1917). He developed here his famous airships, gigantic "balloons" of latticework aluminium which achieved their apocalyptic finale in 1937 when the *Hindenburg* burned in New Jersey, USA. The **Bodensee-Museum** in the town hall on Adenauerplatz has a large scale-model of the *Hindenburg*, as well as Dornier flying boats that were tested on the lake. The

---

THE MAN WHO MADE AIRSHIPS

Ferdinand Graf von Zeppelin first went up in a balloon in 1861 when he was acting as an observer during the American Civil War. The limitations of a floppy gasbag as a means of travel were as obvious then as they are today. Balloons only go where the wind takes them: attempts to drive or steer them are useless. Zeppelin realized that a rigid, streamlined structure was required to hold the gas, with motors and propellors slung beneath it and rudders to steer by. He waited until he retired from the army in 1891 before beginning development, and it was not until 1900 that the first of his cigar-shaped "Zeppelins" flew from a floating hangar at Friedrichshafen on Lake Constance.

Hundreds were eventually built: during World War I they flew ocean patrols and bombing missions over England, and afterwards went into service carrying passengers. The famous *Graf Zeppelin* made 144 transatlantic crossings long before any airliner had the necessary range. The *Hindenburg* disaster, which left 36 people dead, put an end to the use of hydrogen-filled passenger-carrying airships.

---

ground-floor art collection includes some good Gothic and baroque sculpture, as well as 20th-century paintings, notably by Otto Dix.

The town was badly hit in World War II, but spare time for a stroll along the **promenade**, one of the most attractive on the lake.

Lindau

Just inside the Bavarian border, this charming medieval town is without doubt the lake's most popular resort and a major port of call for the cruise ships. Its island is joined to the mainland by railway and road. Ships pass between a lighthouse and the monumental Lion of Bavaria to dock in the harbour near the 13th-century **Mangturm**, also once a lighthouse and part of the medieval ramparts. Coming in by road, you pass the casino and municipal park with its view over to the mountains of Liechtenstein. Maximilianstrasse, the main thoroughfare, is bordered with nicely preserved Gothic, Renaissance and baroque houses, and the **Altes Rathaus** (Old Town Hall, 1578) on Bismarckplatz is notable for its brightly frescoed façade. The promenade facing the harbour is lined by hotels and enticing restaurants, and is also often thronged with people out for a stroll. To escape the crowds, wander around the ramparts to the **Pulverturm** (Gunpowder Tower) at the west end of the island.

The Allgäu

The hinterland of Lake Constance to the Bavarian border is a fertile region reputed for its asparagus and beer-hops. In spring, blossoming orchards make a glorious sight against the Alpine backdrop.

Wangen

With its gilded wrought-iron inn signs and ornamental fountains, the town retains a timeless atmosphere, particularly around the picturesque **Marktplatz**. Colourful baroque façades have been added to the 15th-century town hall and city gate of the adjoining **Pfaffenturm**. Fine Gothic and Renaissance houses line Paradiesstrasse on its way west to the **Lindauer Tor**, a brightly painted gate with wrought-iron gargoyles. Germany is everywhere proud of its poets, and here the **Eichendorff-Museum**, Atzenberg 31, pays tribute to Joseph Freiherr von Eichendorff, one of

the most popular Romantics, and his Silesian homeland (now part of Poland).

Ravensburg

On the east side of town, castle ruins bear witness to what was a major stronghold of the Welf barons whose great 12th-century leader Henry the Lion (*see* page 54) was born here. Climb the round, white **Mehlsack** (Flour Sack) tower, nearly 50m (164ft) high, for a good view of the town and across to Weingarten Abbey. A lively market is held on the elongated **Marienplatz.** It is dominated by the 16th-century **Blaserturm** (Trumpeter's Tower) with its octagonal look-out from which the town watchman blew his horn in time of danger. Opposite is the step-gabled town hall with two handsome council chambers.

Weingarten

The Benedictine abbey's massive **basilica** is, with Bavaria's Ottobeuren, Germany's largest baroque church—102m (335ft) long and 44m (144ft) wide at the transepts. Its curving gabled façade has two elegant towers, and the lantern-crowned dome beyond recalls St Peter's in Rome. The vast interior is masterfully lightened by the succession of arches with vault frescoes by Munich's Cosmas Damian Asam. The superb carving and intarsia marquetry of the choir stalls is by Josef Anton Feuchtmayer. Notice, too, the gilded wrought-iron choir screen with its *trompe-l'oeil* perspective and grand organ loft.

*L*indau's town hall dates from the 15th century when the town was the prosperous purveyor of mail, money and goods across the Alps from Germany to Milan.

Fels

v. Seutter

v. Pfister

v. Ruepprecht

Gruber

Heider

Rader

Varnbüler

Furtenbach

Pappus

SOLI D

ALTES RATHAUS
AN STELLE EINES REBGARTENS
ERBAUT 1422-1436

Sip a Cool White Riesling and Succumb to the Lorelei's Charms

In the mists and towering rocks, terraced vineyards and avenues of poplars, Gothic churches and ruined castles, the Rhineland assembles every poetic image dear to the German soul. Yet coal barges and power plants remind us that Rhinelanders indulge their dreams only after a hard day's work. On the other hand, if Frankfurt's stock exchange measures the profits from that work, the town's most famous son, Goethe, broke his heart and found his lyrical touch in Hesse's valley of the Lahn.

The Rhine flows through six countries—Switzerland, Liechtenstein, Austria, France, Germany and the Netherlands—starting high in the Swiss Alps and running down to the North Sea at Rotterdam. However, it is in the stretch from Mainz to Cologne that the river's vigorous productive energy is tempered for a while by a more contemplative mood. This was perhaps just what West Germany—and the world—needed when it came to choosing

The Lorelei has come down from her rock overlooking the Rhine and donned traditional costume to lure unsuspecting lads to an enjoyable fate at the local festival.

that most unlikely town of Bonn as the post-war capital. Besides avoiding socialist strongholds like Hamburg or Frankfurt, the future Chancellor, Konrad Adenauer, himself a Rhinelander, could also continue to look after his beloved rose garden at nearby Rhöndorf.

Encompassing the core of the Rhineland, the Palatinate, the Mosel valley to the west and Hesse to the east, this central region of Germany has long been at the heart of national affairs. Mainz was the Romans' capital for Upper Germania and subsequently Germany's most powerful archdiocese. Worms was the venue for the crucial imperial assembly at which Luther defended and launched the Protestant Reformation. German emperors were crowned in Charlemagne's capital at Aachen and later in Frankfurt, which became the seat of

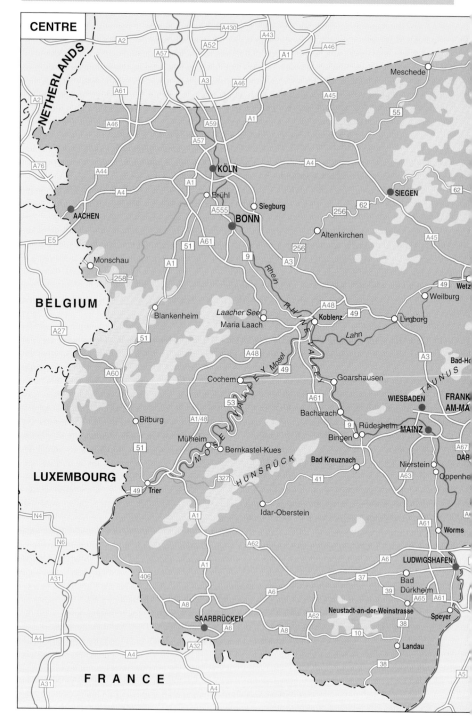

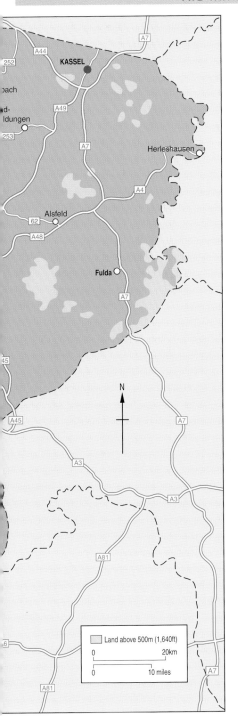

Germany's first national parliament. The completion of Cologne cathedral symbolized the national reawakening.

There is also a less solemn side to life. When Cologne and Mainz vie for the title of Germany's craziest carnival (*see* page 38), wives put away their wedding rings and husbands are not home to complain.

The Rhineland

Our itinerary goes "against the current" between the two great cathedral towns of Cologne and Mainz, with plenty of romantic castles and the superb Rheingau vineyards in between. For a really thorough exploration of the valley, take a river cruise one way, double back by train (no extra charge on most rail passes) and pick up your car to visit the towns—and wineries—that interest you most.

Cologne (*Köln*)

The mighty twin-steepled **cathedral** that is the symbol of the city occupies a position

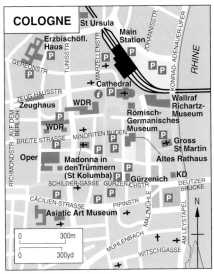

*A*n outstanding feature
of the Rhine is the Cologne
skyline dominated by the
great Gothic cathedral and
the Romanesque church
of Gross St Martin.

that has been sacred since Roman times.
In AD 50, when the town was known as
Colonia Claudia Ara Agrippinensis, it was
the site of the Temple of Mercurius Augustus. The first Christian church was
built there in the 4th century by Bishop
Maternus. Progressively expanded over
the next few centuries, the church began
to burst at its seams in the 13th century

when pilgrims flocked in their thousands to view a shrine containing the relics of the Three Kings. In 1248 the new cathedral was conceived on a gigantic Gothic plan. Work went on for 300 years, but funds ran out before the steeples could be built. Three more centuries passed and, at the urging of German Romantics and nationalists, the steeples were topped off in 1842 and construction completed in 1880. The church survived the devastating bombardments of World War II, and today, amid Cologne's shining rebuilt prosperity, it soars above its terrace like a somewhat haughty dignitary.

At 157m (515ft), the steeples make an undeniably grandiose silhouette. However, those who feel that the 19th-century architects followed too slavishly the 600-year-old plans rediscovered in Darmstadt and Paris consider the exterior's effect is rather frigid, too symmetrical. (You can climb to the base of the spires—not up them.) Inside, the cathedral's real glory is its chancel, a magnificent example of 13th-century Gothic intensity, its slim lines achieving a miracle of delicacy in such a massive edifice. Inspired by the French cathedrals of Amiens and Rheims, it provided a workshop for the masonry craft of Gothic churches throughout Germany. Notice the natural elegance of the statues of Christ and Mary flanked by the Apostles. Sacred and profane meet in the richly carved oak choir stalls where biblical figures mix with mythical animals, musicians, dancers, lovers and warriors.

The cathedral's most cherished treasure, looking itself like a basilica, is the gold **Shrine of the Three Kings** (*Dreikönigenschrein*) behind the high altar. The Three Kings' bones were brought from Milan in the 12th century by Friedrich Barbarossa's chancellor, Reinald von Dassel. Designed by Nikolaus of Verdun in 1181, this masterpiece of the goldsmith's art took 40 years to complete. The solid gold figures include kings and prophets of the Old Testament surrounding scenes of Christ's baptism and the Adoration of the Kings. Each of the three skeletons lacks a finger; these were donated to Hildesheim (near Hanover) where Dassel had been dean.

Cologne cathedral's 12th-century Shrine of the Three Kings is the biggest gold sarcophagus in Europe, made for the supposed bones of the Magi who visited the infant Jesus.

In a chapel south of the choir, see Stephan Lochner's splendid **Dombild** (1440), a triptych celebrating the town's patron saints, Ursula and Gereon, and the Three Kings.

The Museums

Cologne always happily marries the pagan and Christian. Next door to the cathedral, in the **Römisch-Germanisches Museum**, is a joyful Roman tribute to Bacchanalian pleasure, the **Dionysus Mosaic**. One of the few nice things to have happened in Cologne during World War II was the discovery of this marvellously well-preserved work in the course of digging an air-raid shelter. The museum is built

around the mosaic's original site, the floor of a prosperous 3rd-century Roman wheat merchant's dining-room. The Greek god Dionysus—also known as Bacchus to the Romans—leans tipsily on an obliging satyr while around him other satyrs and nymphs cavort and make music. Anyone who has witnessed the Cologne Carnival knows that the tradition continues today.

The museum itself presents the city's Roman origins in a remarkably unstuffy manner, the everyday life of the Romans of Colonia and their Germanic neighbours shown through the artefacts of their homes and workshops.

Over towards the river, the **Wallraf-Richartz-Museum**, the Rhineland's most important art gallery, is housed in a new building that includes the Cologne Philharmonic orchestra hall in the basement and the modern Museum Ludwig on the top floor. Based originally on the private collection of Ferdinand Wallraf (1748–1824), the main museum offers a unique view of the great Cologne School that flourished from the 14th to 16th centuries, culminating in the exquisite masterpieces of Stephan Lochner (1405–51). His monumental *Jüngstes Gericht* (Day of Judgment) and the delicate *Muttergottes in der Rosenlaube* (Virgin and Child in the Rose Bower) epitomize the Rhenish artists' sensitive use of colour and serenity of form. Works of the German Renaissance include Albrecht Dürer's cheerful *Pfeifer und Trommler* (Piper and Drummer), Lucas Cranach's ornate study of Mary Magdalen, and Hans Burgkmair's disturbing portrait of the Schellenbergs. In the Flemish and Dutch rooms are fine works by Rubens (masterful self-portrait), Rembrandt and Frans Hals. Among the Italians, see Tintoretto's *Entombment of Christ*. The French Impressionists include

> ## RIVERBOAT SHUFFLE
>
> Forget the car or train for a while and take a boat. From spring to autumn, cruise the Rhine, Mosel, Main and Lahn rivers.
>
> It was the British who first took a steamboat up the Rhine in 1816 from the North Sea to Cologne. The Germans liked the idea and soon set up a company with a name almost as long as the river—the Preussisch-Rheinische Dampfschiff-fahrts-Gesellschaft Köln. It was the precursor of today's Köln–Düsseldorfer, known in these more hurried times as the KD. The modern fleet is almost entirely motor-powered, with only a few steam-driven paddleboats for nostalgia's sake.
>
> With a certain effort of imagination, the trip through the heart of the Rhine Valley shows you the river as sailors of the Middle Ages saw it. In the shadow of towering cliffs, they navigated uncertainly through the rocks at the mercy of pirates, robber-barons or any petty prince who cared to claim a toll from them at the point of a sword. About the only risk you run today as you pass the treacherous Lorelei is not being able to keep up with the words of the song as it comes over the ship's loudspeakers. If your German is rusty, console yourself with the song's first line: "*Ich weiss nicht, was soll es bedeuten ...*" ("I don't know what it is supposed to mean ...").

Renoir, Cézanne and Monet, along with Van Gogh's *Bridge at Arles*.

The 20th-century **Museum Ludwig** on the top floors has a superb American collection, notably Jasper Johns, Rauschenberg, Oldenburg and Wesselmann. Outstanding among the German Expressionists are Kirchner, Dix, Beckmann and Macke. Among the Russian artists here are Malevitch, Jawlensky, Chagall and Kandinsky. The **Photography Museum** presents exhibitions of modern masters.

The restful way to see the Rhine valley—a leisurely cruise with stops for visits to some of the towns and castles.

The **Schnütgen Museum** in the converted church of St Cecilia, Cäcilienstrasse 29, is devoted to the Romanesque and Gothic art of Cologne's medieval heyday. The museum lovingly assembles sculpture and altar paintings rescued from the city's

bombed churches, as well as masterpieces of Rhenish gold, enamel and ivory.

The Old Town

If wars and revolutions—but also 19th- and 20th-century building speculation—obliterated much of Cologne's golden past, vestiges of the tiny Altstadt can be found down by the river. Explore the streets between the church Gross St Martin and the Deutzer bridge. There around the old Fischmarkt, along the Salzgasse and across the Eisenmarkt (Ironware Market), you can find miracles of survival and restoration. Houses dating back to the 13th and 14th centuries form the core of a thriving neighbourhood of restaurants, antique shops, art galleries and apartments with attractive gardens.

On the west side of the Alter Markt (notice in passing the statue of a fellow baring his bottom to no one in particular—typical local humour) is the proud **Altes Rathaus** (Old Town Hall). The Flemish-style belfry is reconstructed, but the Renaissance loggia survived the war

---

THAT'S A LOT OF VIRGINS

Ursula is a legendary British princess who, in the 4th century, led a pilgrimage of 11,000 virgins to Rome, all of whom were massacred by the Huns at Cologne on their way home. To add bones, if not flesh, to the legend, some 300 skulls of various origin are arranged ornamentally in a bizarre baroque golden chamber (*Goldene Kammer*) in the church of St Ursula, north-west of the Hauptbahnhof.

---

intact, its elegance shaming the forbidding Spanischer Bau of the new municipal offices. The old town hall was built over the Jewish ghetto, destroyed in a pogrom during the plague of 1348. The 12th-century Romanesque structure of the Jewish women's **Mikvah**, or ritual bath (*Judenbad*), was rediscovered in recent excavations—the entrance is across from the loggia and the keys are kept at the Rathaus car-park.

The Judengasse takes you from the town hall to the **Gürzenich** (1447), the home of historic merriment. Cologne's most important civic Gothic building served as a dance hall for the city government and its honoured guests, including the occasional Habsburg or Hohenzollern. It is still the most prestigious venue for Carnival balls, banquets and concerts, a perfect secular complement to the cathedral.

Three Churches

Of this archbishopric's myriad churches rescued from wartime ruin, three at least are worth a look. The 13th-century **St Aposteln**, west of the Neumarkt on Mittelstrasse, is one of the most handsome Romanesque edifices in the Rhineland. From the north-east, view the chancel's finely modulated apses with elegant dwarf arcades circling the domes. In the Protestant **Antoniterkirche**, Ernst Barlach's bronze *Trauernder Engel* (Mourning Angel, 1927) takes fellow artist Käthe Kollwitz as its model. For many, the most poignant of Cologne's churches is the **Madonna in den Trümmern** (Madonna in the Ruins), a modern chapel built out of the rubble of the Gothic St Kolumba church on Brückenstrasse. The church owes its name to a statue of the Virgin Mary that escaped unscathed from bombs

that otherwise left standing only the stump of a tower and part of one outer wall. Gottfried Böhm's design in the 1950s artfully integrates modern simplicity with the Gothic remains, a monument to the city's pain and recovery.

Brühl

A short trip south, the grand baroque palace known as **Augustusburg** takes you back to the opulent world of an 18th-century prince of the church, Cologne's archbishop, Clemens August. The Wittelsbach prince-elector called on his family's Bavarian court architect François de Cuvilliés to design a Versailles-style château and a hunting-lodge, Falkenlust. The centrepiece of the palace, a magnificent ceremonial staircase, was the work of baroque master Balthasar Neumann, who also designed the high altar in the palace church. The formal gardens were landscaped by Frenchman Dominique Girard.

Bonn

It was always difficult to take the town seriously as the capital of West Germany. Now, with many of the functions of government soon to move in due course to Berlin, Bonn continues to go about its affairs of state with a quiet serenity. The town's modest charm has been rather a nice surprise as the seat of government for such a busy, purposeful nation. The departure—when it comes—of the diplomats and many of the civil servants will be greeted with mixed feelings.

Government offices stand between the Rhine and Adenauerallee, appropriately named after the chancellor who imposed his choice of Bonn as the post-war capital. Rising above the river is the brand-new building originally intended to be the Bundeshaus (the parliament). Nearby are

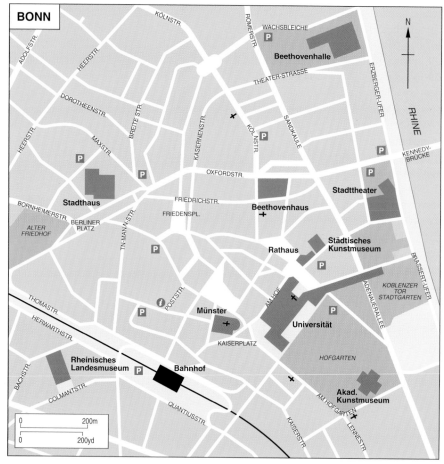

the neo-Renaissance **Palais Schaumburg**, where the chancellor has traditionally entertained his international guests, and the **Villa Hammerschmidt**—until 1990 the official home of the federal president. The 30th-floor public restaurant of the Deputies' Building (*Abgeordnetenhochhaus*) has a fine view across the Rhine.

At the other end of Adenauerallee, take a peaceful stroll around the old trees of the **Hofgarten.** This was the garden of the prince-archbishop of Cologne's residence, and is now part of Bonn University. In the private chapel (now destroyed), a bright 16-year-old schoolboy named Ludwig van

Beethoven performed his first music. The long **Poppelsdorfer Allee** offers a fine walk beyond the railway along a handsome avenue of chestnut trees to the remains of the Poppelsdorfer Schloss in the university's botanical gardens.

With Berlin to take over again, in due course, as the national capital, politics in Bonn may well centre on the charming town hall once more.

214

LUDWIG VAN BEETHOVEN (1770–1827)

Beethoven's musical genius needed no verbal support to express his powerful personal philosophy. Even the last choral movement of his grandiose Ninth Symphony serves less to declaim Schiller's poetry of joy than to raise the human voice to the level of a symphonic instrument. Musically, he was rooted in the Classical tradition of Haydn and Mozart, but his works also embraced the humanism of his contemporaries, Goethe and Schiller, and the French Revolution's ideals of liberty and individual dignity, much prized in his native Rhineland.

Beginnings in Bonn

He was born on December 17, 1770, in Bonn, the eldest surviving child of Johann and Maria Magdalena van Beethoven, of Flemish farming stock. Like any other craft in the 18th century, music was a family affair. Grandfather Louis rose from singer in the Archbishop of Cologne's palace choir in Bonn to *Kapellmeister*. Father Johann, who also sang in the palace choir, sought to emulate Leopold Mozart by trying to turn young Ludwig into a prodigy at the piano. But he was too strict and erratic and ultimately ruined by alcoholism. Ludwig had to leave school at 11 and become the family breadwinner at 18.

Playing the organ at the court chapel, Beethoven had attracted the attention of Archbishop Maximilian-Franz, the enlightened liberal brother of the Austrian emperor, Joseph II. In 1787, he sent the boy to study in Vienna where he is believed to have met and impressed Mozart, court composer at the time. His mother's death brought him home again after just two months, but the attraction of what was then the musical capital of Europe proved too strong to resist for long. During his five last years in Bonn, he played the viola in the court orchestra and supported his family by coaching the children of wealthy courtiers. He was encouraged to compose by Count Ferdinand von Waldstein, and when Haydn passed through Bonn on his way to London, he offered to take him on as a pupil back in Vienna. After Mozart's death, Waldstein predicted: "With the help of unremitting labour," he wrote, "you will receive Mozart's spirit from Haydn's hands."

His early piano music was heavily influenced by the florid Mannheim school, laced with torrential arpeggios running up and down the scale over several octaves, a feature known as "Mannheim rockets". As he left for Vienna in 1792, other explosives rained down on the Rhineland with the invasion of the armies of the French Revolution.

The Vienna Years

Emotion was always a vital element in Beethoven's music, showing his affinity for the *Sturm und Drang,* literally the "Storm and Stress" of the drama and poetry of Goethe and Schiller. But he balanced this with a strong sense of form that kept him closer to the Classical composers than the Romantics who followed him. In Vienna, he found an enlightened aristocracy devoted to music rather than get involved in the reactionary politics of the new emperor, Franz II. In that hypersensitive age, they were frequently moved to tears at Beethoven's recitals, where he earned the reputation of being an even greater piano improviser than Mozart. He outgrew his tutor, Haydn, and turned to other Viennese masters, notably court composer Antonio Salieri, to expand his repertoire.

He gave his first major Vienna concert in 1795, presenting his Piano Concerto No. 2. Over the next three years he produced three Trios for piano, violin and cello, numerous sonatas and the first of his symphonies. He toured Prague, Nuremberg, Dresden and Berlin, where he performed his new cello sonatas for Friedrich Wilhelm II.

But his days as a virtuoso soloist were numbered. He suffered from his first serious ear ailments in 1796, and by 1800 he realized he was going deaf. His life was further complicated by the burden of having to support his two brothers and a beloved but highly neurotic and ultimately suicidal nephew. He remained a bachelor but had several women in his life, notably Therese of Brunswick and Countess Giulietta Guicciardi, a piano pupil to whom he dedicated the *Moonlight Sonata*—"a dear sweet girl who loves me and whom I love", but who left him for another. His griefs found expression in his music, but without eliminating the positive sides of his personal philosophy.

In 1802, in deep depression from his growing deafness, he wrote his famous *Heiligenstadt Testament,* named after the hillside village on the Vienna outskirts where he had a house. To those who found him "malevolent, stubborn or misanthropic," he explained: "I was ever eager to accomplish great deeds but reflect now that for six years I have been in a hopeless case, made worse by ignorant doctors." He admitted to thoughts of suicide, "but only Art held me back. It seemed unthinkable for me to leave the world forever before I had produced all that I felt called upon to produce." Nonetheless he ended on a grim note: "As the leaves of autumn wither and fall, so has my own life become barren."

He found his own splendid antidote two years later in the *Eroica* Symphony, a major landmark in composition and a triumph of will and courage over the despair of Heiligenstadt. He had written it in honour of Napoleon as a champion of liberty, but when the Frenchman made himself emperor, Beethoven ripped out the dedication page and wrote instead: "For the memory of a great man." After his victory at Austerlitz in 1805, Napoleon spoiled the première of Beethoven's only opera, *Fidelio,* by sending his troops into Vienna and scaring audiences away.

"Utterly Untamed"

But he continued to make a comfortable living from the sale of his works, tutoring Archduke Rudolf and becoming the first composer to be paid a salary to compose whatever and whenever he liked.

In 1812, he met Goethe and found him "too fond of the atmosphere of the courts, more so than is becoming in a poet." Beethoven told him: "Aristocrats must make room for us, not we for them." For his part, Goethe wrote: "I am

His birthplace

astonished by his talent, but he is an utterly untamed personality who is not altogether in the wrong in holding the world to be detestable, but surely does not make it any more enjoyable either for himself or for others by his attitude."

By 1819, Beethoven was totally deaf. He communicated with friends in "conversation books" in which they wrote their questions and comments. He composed on country walks around Vienna, writing in sketchbooks (exhibited in the Bonn museum) which show him to be as meticulous in composition as he had been volatile in improvisation. Mere mortals are reassured to see how banal were the first ideas that developed into the magnificent themes of the *Emperor* Concerto or *Kreutzer* Sonata.

He conducted the première of his sublime Ninth Symphony in 1824 and died three years later from a cirrhosis of the liver after a long bout of pneumonia. Among the 20,000 attending his funeral, Franz Schubert was one of the torch bearers.

*T*he Bundestag chamber
in Bonn. What use will be found
for it now that the parliament is
moving to Berlin?

Bonn's sunny rococo style can be appreciated in the festive **town hall** with its balustraded outer staircase. From the Markt, Remigiusstrasse leads to the **Münster**. In its transitional style between Rhenish Romanesque and Gothic, the church exterior's sober elegance has survived heavy 19th-century restoration. The eastern view of the chancel is especially attractive with its dwarf-galleried apse flanked by slender steepled towers. The interior is baroque. The lovely cloister south of the church is an oasis of peace.

Beethoven was born in Bonn in 1770 and his birthplace, the **Beethovenhaus** at Bonngasse 20, is preserved as a museum of the composer's memorabilia. It includes one of his grand pianos, a viola, scores and manuscripts, and acoustical instruments he used to fight his deafness. Beethoven left for Vienna at 22 to flee his alcoholic father. An introduction to the elector-prince's court, where his father was a tenor in the chapel choir, had at least prepared him for the high society of the Habsburgs.

Two museums claim attention. The **Rheinisches Landesmuseum**, Colmant-strasse 14, is famous for its anthropological section exhibiting the Neanderthal Man and a Cro-Magnon couple. Old Neanderthal—50,000 years old, in fact—was found by railway workmen in a quarry near Düsseldorf in 1856. Remains include the top of his skull and 16 other bones, enough to determine he was 163cm (5ft 4in) tall and 60 years old when he died. He hunted animals like the mammoth displayed nearby. The Cro-Magnon man and woman (10,000 BC) were found entombed in Bonn-Oberkassel with bone figures symbolic of animals they were accustomed to eat—probably intended to provide ritual food for the afterlife.

The municipal art museum, **Städtisches Kunstmuseum**, Rathaus-gasse 7, is devoted to 20th-century art, from August Macke, Rhenish painter of the Blaue Reiter school, to eclectic sculptor and performance artist Joseph Beuys.

Laacher See

On the way south to Koblenz, stop off to visit this fascinating volcanic crater lake, typical formation of the sprawling Eifel plateau (*see* page 234). The lake, 8km (5 miles) in circumference, is surrounded by the cones of four extinct volcanoes. In an idyllic green setting at the south end of the lake is the fine 11th- and 12th-century Benedictine abbey of **Maria Laach**, built largely of local lava stone. The graceful six-towered church stands squarely in the Rhenish Romanesque tradition of Mainz, Worms and Speyer, but the massive impact of these ecclesiastic fortresses is lightened by the exquisite cloistered atrium, **Paradies**, added to the western apse.

Koblenz

Taking its name from the Latin *confluentes*, the town has also profited from its strategic position at the confluence of the Mosel and Rhine rivers. Besides serving as a centre for the wines of the Mosel and the Rhine, Koblenz levied tolls on merchant boats passing from one river to the other. Archbishops of Trier preferred to live here to keep an eye on both Rhine and Mosel. Though over 80 per cent of the town was destroyed in World War II, it still offers an attractive glimpse of its past, plus a foretaste of the pleasures of wine sampling off to the west and south.

Rheinanlagen

Start with a walk along this delightful airy river-promenade lined with maples and willows. The brainchild of a French prefect during the Napoleonic occupation of the Rhineland, the riverside park was laid out in its present form by Augusta, the wife of Kaiser Wilhelm I.

Thirsty strollers stop at the popular taverns of the **Weindorf** (wine village), a relic of the 1925 wine fair. North of the Pfaffendorfer Bridge, pass the **Kurfürstliches Schloss** (Prince-Elector's Palace), an imposing neoclassical structure deprived of its opulent interior by the bombs of 1944.

Beyond the Schloss, the Rhine quay continues to the well-proportioned Romanesque church of **St Kastor**. Its interior has two monumental Gothic tombs of Trier archbishops Kuno von Falkenstein and Werner von Königstein. North of the church, open-air operas and concerts are performed in the striking setting of the **Blumenhof**, courtyard of the Deutschherrenhaus (House of the Teutonic Knights).

The Rhine promenade ends at the **Deutsches Eck**, where a formidable stone monument was erected for Kaiser Wilhelm I in 1897 and dedicated to German unity. A direct hit on the Kaiser's equestrian statue in World War II reduced the stone pile to its huge pedestal with the motto: "Never will the Reich be destroyed if you are unified and loyal." Plans are afoot to restore the old statue. Meanwhile, you can climb the 107 steps of the pedestal for a good view of the old town along the Mosel and the more modern construction along the Rhine.

The Old Town

Begin your tour of the Altstadt at the splendid **Balduinbrücke**, the bridge built across the Mosel in 1343 by powerful Archbishop Balduin, the brother of Emperor Heinrich VII. The bridge withstood all war and revolution until, in 1945, a bomb knocked out three of its 14 arches. Near the bridge, a castle-lodge (now the municipal library) is all that survives of the **Alte Burg**, the victim of Louis XIV's troops in 1689. On Münzplatz is the **Metternich-Hof**, birthplace of wily chancellor of Austria, Klemens von Metternich (1773–1859). In the absence of a unified German nation, it was more natural for his old Catholic Rhineland family to turn to Vienna for a diplomatic career than to Protestant Prussian Berlin. Napoleon turned Metternich's house into a law school for the application of the Napoleonic Code to the Rhineland. Münzplatz now has a lively flower, fruit and vegetable market.

Hunt down the few old houses that miraculously survived the war. The oldest (1300) is at Kastorstrasse 2. The charming 17th-century **Vier Türme**, at the corner of Am Plan and Löhrstrasse, has four projecting oriel bays, a feature of the 18th-century guild halls, the grocers' (*Krämer*) on Kornpfortstrasse and cobblers' (*Schuhmacher*) on Görgenstrasse. These houses would have no special impact in a well-preserved old town, but in war-battered Koblenz they stand out like jewels.

Ehrenbreitstein Castle

As an *apéritif* to the fortresses further south, cross the Rhine to this medieval stronghold. (Drive across Pfaffendorfer Bridge or take the ferry from Rheinstrasse and a chair-lift to the castle.) In the year 1000, it was the redoubt of a knight named Heribert. The archbishops of Trier claimed it for the German empire, the French blew it up in 1801, the Prussians rebuilt it and the Versailles treaty of 1918 forbade it to be used for military purposes. So today it is a youth hostel, restaurant and museum. It also offers a superb panoramic view of the Mosel and Rhine valleys.

The Rhine Valley

Geographically, the whole Rhine from the Swiss Alps to the North Sea constitutes its "valley", but the Rhine Valley of popular

*T*he elegant Vier Türme, *House of Four Towers (actually four oriel bay windows), was built in 1691 and stands at the entrance to Koblenz's wine merchants' quarter.*

fantasy is the part between Koblenz and Mainz. Here the mountain plateau of the Hunsrück to the west and the Taunus and Rheingau-Gebirge to the east meet at the river to form a narrow valley of steeply terraced vineyards and pine forests guarded by castles and towering rocks. Myth and history mingle inextricably with the saga of the Nibelungs, medieval feuds and piracy, and the idylls of the Romantic poets.

The Left Bank

The idyll begins 6km (4 miles) south of Koblenz on Highway 9, high above the river at **Stolzenfels castle**. From the ruins of a 14th-century fortress sacked by the French in 1689, Prussia's Friedrich Wilhelm IV built his medieval dream at the height of the German Romantic movement when the nation was lovingly reconstructing its past. His Koblenz architects gave it the full treatment—turrets and crenellated battlements, funny little arches, giddy external staircases leading nowhere in particular, half-hidden rose windows under knobby minarets—all integrated into a "natural" setting of paths winding past gurgling brooks among pine trees, and shrubbery to break the fall of anyone accidentally cast into the dry moat.

From this Romantic pastiche, plunge into the real Middle Ages at **Rhens** with its old imperial traditions and authentic Gothic half-timbered houses. The best of these are the **town hall** and **Deutschherrenhaus** (House of the Teutonic Knights) directly overlooking the Rhine. Rhens stands at the junction of the fiefdoms of Cologne, Trier, Mainz and the Palatinate—ruled by four of the seven prince-electors who chose the German emperor. As such, it was ideal for the conclave that elected the new emperor in the

13th and 14th centuries. North of town is Friedrich Wilhelm IV's replica of the monumental **Königsstuhl** (King's Throne) on its raised platform. Napoleon destroyed the original when dismantling the German empire.

From Rhens, the vineyards extend their invitation to the smiling town of **Boppard**. Suddenly industry and government are a million miles away as you walk along the tree-lined Rheinallee. Stop off at the **Karmeliterkirche** to admire the interior's Renaissance decoration, particularly the choir stalls.

As you continue to St Goar, spare a kind thought for the little Burg Thurnberg on the right bank. Better known as **Burg Maus** (Mouse), it is coupled in the popular imagination with **Burg Katz** (Cat) further south, directly opposite St Goar. Katz was built at the end of the 14th century by Count Johann von Katzenelnbogen (his name means "cat's elbow") to snatch away the river-tolls that previously went to Maus. St Goar itself has a splendid castle ruin, **Burg Rheinfels**,built by an earlier, equally rapacious Katzenelnbogen in 1245. French troops reduced it in 1797 to the picturesque ruin you see today. The best vantage point is the clock tower, from which you can see the extent of this once enormous fortress and the valley it commanded below.

The pretty little town of **Oberwesel** owes much of its charm to its "red" and "white" churches and the nicely preserved remains of ivy-covered turreted ramparts. The red sandstone **Liebfrauenkirche** has a fine Gothic rood screen and a 14th-century high altar with superbly carved biblical figures from Adam to Jesus. Gothic altar-triptychs grace the "white"

Brass bands, jazz bands, street musicians and symphony orchestras—you'll have music wherever you go in the land of Beethoven.

OF MICE AND MEN

Archbishop Hatto of Mainz (850–913) showed little compassion for his starving flock. He locked up the most importunate of the begging multitude in a barn and set fire to it. "Listen to the squeals of my little mice," he said as he walked back to his palace. The fire killed the beggars but also drove out thousands of mice from the hay and into the archbishop's palace. Hatto fled to the tower in the middle of the river, but the mice swam after him and gobbled him up.

Martinskirche. The 12th-century Schönburg castle is now a hotel.

Opposite Kaub, in the middle of the river, is **Pfalzgrafenstein castle**, built on an island in 1327 by Ludwig of Bavaria to enforce his right to collect tolls from passing merchant ships. The pentagonal central tower is Ludwig's, the turreted hexagonal outer wall is late Gothic.

A 13th-century German scholar suggested that **Bacharach** derived its name from the Latin *Bacchi ara*, "altar of Bacchus". Modern etymologists may balk at this, but visitors to this enchanting wine village are soon convinced the old sage was right. The place has an unassailable air of peace and joy with its flower-bedecked houses, especially attractive around the market-place. Bacharach has earned this peace after a long history of trouble. Not that the community was always innocent, as attested by the Gothic **Wernerkapelle**, now an elegant ruin on a slope above the town. The chapel commemorates the death of a boy named Werner in 1287 when superstitious bigotry encouraged the belief that he had been ritually murdered by the Jews, justifying their massacre and the confiscation of their property. A French army, landslides and

even an earthquake have turned the chapel into a romantic windowless shell overgrown with wild flowers and shrubbery.

The Bingen road takes you past fanciful 19th-century reconstructions of old medieval castles at **Sooneck**, once the redoubt of 13th-century robber-baron Reichenstein (now a hotel), and **Rheinstein**, notable for its collection of weapons and armour. As the Rhine bends east at Bingerbrück, look out at the old customs-post, the garish yellow **Mäuseturm** (Mouse Tower). It is notorious for its gruesome legend surrounding the end of a prince of the church (*see* sidebar left).

The best thing about **Bingen** is its vineyards sloping back behind the town. Try the local wine before boarding the ferry across to Rüdesheim to explore the Rhine's opposite bank.

The Right Bank

Before continuing east to Mainz or Wiesbaden, complete your Rhine Valley itinerary by doubling back north from Rüdesheim at least as far as St Goarshausen. The slopes on this side are wilder and steeper, less touched by man and his architecture, and you will have a panoramic view of the castles and churches you saw up close on the left bank.

Rüdesheim is perhaps the best known of the Rhineland's wine-villages. Certainly its Drosselgasse has the liveliest collection of taverns and wine-cellars in the region. Here try the Rheingau's famous

The quintessence of the Rhine Valley's romance, Stahleck Castle (overleaf) looms between Bacharach's vineyards and the river.

Rieslings, sparkling *Sekt* and locally distilled brandies. Find out how it is all done in the **Rheingauer wine museum** at the Brömserburg castle. Most of the original old timber-framed houses were bombed in World War II, but the reconstructed replicas are weathering nicely. In the Obergasse, the **Brömserhof** has kept its Gothic and Renaissance buildings intact.

Take a side-trip to Niederwald to see the **Germania monument**. The 10.5m (35ft) statue of a Teutonic woman brandishing the imperial crown inspires awe in some, wry amusement in others. The monument was erected in 1883 to celebrate the unification of Germany following the defeat of France in the war of 1870–71. The terrace is a nice place for a picnic.

Continue on down to **Assmannshausen**, where you can sample one of the Rhineland's few good red wines. People also come for the warm lithium bromide waters at the Kurhaus to cure their rheumatism or lumbago.

UNHAPPY HEINRICH

Ich weiss nicht, was soll es bedeuten,
Dass ich so traurig bin;
Ein Märchen aus alten Zeiten,
Das kommt mir nicht aus dem Sinn.
He was 26 when he wrote his poem of the Lorelei legend—26 and hopelessly in love. Jilted by cousin Amalia, he fell for her sister Therese, with equal lack of success. The **Lorelei** was one of dozens of poems into which he poured his despair: half-suicidal, half-ironic. No question that the beautiful siren with the golden hair, golden comb and golden necklace was his cruel, beloved Therese. And the poor woeful sailor in his little boat, blindly entranced by her song and dashed to death on the rocks below, was Heinnch Heine.

NASTY NIBELUNGS

The murky legend of the Nibelung which inspired Richard Wagner's four-day "Ring" cycle comes to us from the Rhineland's Darkest Ages. The Nibelungs are evil dwarfs, keepers of a magic hoard of gold with a curse on it.

Siegfried, a brave prince from the north, wins the treasure away from them and goes on to the royal palace at Worms to woo Kriemhild, sister of King Gunther. For his part, Gunther hankers after the fierce Icelandic queen, Brunhild, and Siegfried offers to go and get her. It takes a lot of brute force and treachery to bring back Brunhild to marry Gunther. When she finds she is not getting Siegfried himself, she has him killed by Gunther's henchman, Hagen.

Poor widowed Kriemhild hopes at least to hold onto the Nibelung treasure, only to see even that snatched away by Hagen and dumped into the Rhine. To get her revenge, she finds just the right fellow, Attila, marries him and gets his Huns to punish Brunhild, Hagen and company in one of their usual bloodbaths. German cultural historians say that the Germans are drawn to these tales by the themes of fate and loyalty.

En route for Lorch, look across the Rhine at those reconstructed castles of Rheinstein, Reichstein and Sooneck; they appear much more romantic at this distance. In **Lorch**, visit the Gothic church of **St Martin**, notable for its 15th-century high altar, carved choir stalls and a *Crucifixion* from the 13th century.

The Rhine Valley nears its romantic climax north of Kaub. Vineyard-covered slopes give way to ever steeper cliffs. Make this stretch of the journey in late afternoon when a low sun casts the appropriately romantic shadows, and dream your way back to the mysteries of the Rhine's golden past. As the river turns east towards St Goarshausen, begin the climb towards the rugged tree-covered cliff of the **Lorelei**. Leave the river road and take the winding route up to the myth-laden rock of the siren that inspired Heinrich Heine's celebrated poem. Good timing should bring you up to her ledge in the evening sunshine described by Heine. Enjoy the grand view across to Oberwesel and Schönburg castle and down the crag from which the lady lured sailors to their doom in those swiftly flowing waters. Do not despair if it is misty or even raining. The melancholy effect that a drizzle spreads across the valley is worth yet another poem.

The Rheingau

Back at Rüdesheim, start in earnest your journey through the region's greatest wine country with a visit to **Johannisberg**, to taste the excellent wines in the castle's cellars. Following the Congress of Vienna that partitioned Napoleon's empire in 1815, the castle was handed over to the Habsburgs who gave it to Metternich for his efforts on behalf of the old monarchies. With a little proviso: the Habsburgs were to receive each year part of the revenues from the wine harvest. The castle still belongs to the Metternich family, and the Habsburgs still get their share of the wine profits.

The riverside villages of **Geisenheim**, **Oestrich-Winkel** and **Eltville** are delightful places to stroll through, both for their charming old, and not so old, timber-frame houses and venerable, and not so venerable, wine cellars. The jewel of the Rheingau, however, is the former **Kloster Eberbach**, one of the best-preserved monasteries in Germany, set back in a valley at the southern end of the Taunus. The intriguing paradox of Eberbach was the ability of the Cistercian monks to combine the strictest spiritual asceticism with a mastery of the most refined techniques of wine growing. After the Romans had introduced the grape, it was the Eberbach monks who were the veritable founders of the modern wine industry in Germany. Though long since secularized, the abbey still produces some of the Rheingau's best wines. The 12th-century abbey-church has an austere splendour, emphatically Romanesque in spirit despite the Gothic and baroque additions of later centuries. Its interior is at once bright and cool, with only a few Gothic tombstones for decoration. The cloister and long double-aisled dormitory still convey a feeling of monastic tranquillity. Visit the wine cellars and refectory to see the marvellous collection of decorative winepresses, a gentle smile amid the abbey's prevailing sobriety.

Mainz

If the Rhineland has a reputation for being cheerful, Mainz must take much of the credit. Over the centuries, it has been a key part of the Roman empire's northern defences, an indispensable element in the Vatican's control of Catholic Europe, a major trade centre in the Middle Ages, the home of printing pioneer Johannes Gutenberg and a focus of intellectual ferment in Germany's rise to national unity. Not always a lot of laughs there, but the city known as Golden Mainz has always been good for a chuckle, madly merry during the Carnival, managing a grin even in the face of countless invasions and wars. None was more destructive than the last, World War II, which spared only one out of every five buildings. After a slow and painful reconstruction, the town today is once more prosperous, lively and cheerful.

The **cathedral** epitomizes the character of the town and its people—plump, ruddy-complexioned and, despite its massive proportions, somehow cosy and intimate. Get an overall view from the old cemetery (*Leichhof*), south-west of the church. Typically for the Rhineland, the Romanesque basilica has chancels at either end, each with a majestic tower: on the east the austerely simple construction of the 12th century and on the west a more ornate synthesis of Romanesque, Gothic and baroque. This is the tower visible at a great distance if you approach Mainz from the east along the Main valley.

Fires, wars and even rapacious building speculators removing the masonry have stripped the interior of much of its old riches, but reconstruction has been heroic, and some splendid works of art have survived. Enter by the 13th-century Market Porch (*Marktportal*) with its thousand-year-old bronze doors. Of 45 archbishops buried in the cathedral, 29 have magnificent monumental tombs. The most important, at the west end of the nave, are three 16th-century sculptures by Hans Backoffen of archbishops Uriel von Gemmingen, Jakob von Liebenstein and Berthold von Henneberg. Note the elegant rococo choir stalls in the west chancel. The St Magnus chapel left of the east high altar has a superb 15th-century sculpture group of the **Burial of Christ** (*Grablegung*).

With a cathedral that has suffered as much as this, its **museum** is worth a visit to see the statuary salvaged over the centuries. Notice in particular fragments of the 13th-century rood screen. One of the statues is of the architect, plainly groaning from an aching back from having to serve as a pillar for a doorway.

North of the cathedral on the lively market square is the oldest Renaissance fountain in Germany, the splendid **Marktbrunnen** of 1526 commemorating Charles V's victory over the French at Pavia.

The **Gutenberg Museum** on Liebfrauenplatz is a modern building incorporating the old 17th-century inn, Zum Römischen Kaiser. Since 1962, it claims the grand title of World Museum of the Art of Printing (*Weltmuseum der Druckkunst*). It traces the history of men's efforts to communicate by writing, from primitive stone and papyrus via a Gutenberg Bible to the most modern sophisticated technology. Homage is paid to the Koreans who developed printing techniques before Gutenberg, while the Mainz master's workshop is imaginatively reconstructed in the basement.

Get a feel for the old town of Mainz by exploring the triangle leading from the cathedral along Ludwigstrasse and around to the river on the Grosse Bleiche. Among the fine baroque residences in this area are **Dalberger Hof** on Klarastrasse, now police headquarters, **Bassenheimer Hof** on Schillerplatz and the **Erthaler Hof**, Schillerstrasse 44.

Mainz is a major centre for the wine trade, and the town holds a wine fair at the end of the summer. You can sample a variety of wines from all over Germany at the **Haus des Deutschen Weines** on Gutenbergplatz.

The Mosel

In contrast to the Rhine Valley, which mixes its charms with a faint air of melancholy and perhaps even a hint of menace, the Mosel offers nothing but light and good cheer. In this carefree winding valley, a mean old Nibelung would be chased away with happy laughter. The river itself is narrow and much more amenable than

One green bottle, painted on a wall ... proclaims the distinctive character of the Mosel Valley's wines. Rhine wines come in brown bottles.

the Rhine, the countryside here gentler and less dramatic. Mosel wines stand proudly beside those of the Rhine, and indeed there are many French wine connoisseurs who are happier with the Mosel wines because of their affinity with the wines of Alsace.

Starting from Koblenz, follow the river road 416 to Moselkern for the turn-off to **Burg Eltz**, a fairy-tale castle piled piece upon piece between the 12th and 16th centuries in an enchanting conglomeration of all the fantasies anyone ever had about castles—towers, soaring granite walls, turrets, half-timbered gables and look-outs tucked away where you would least expect them. Perched on a hill above the

babbling Eltzbach stream, this fortress cannot fail to make you smile rather than shiver—the very essence of the Mosel's good nature.

At **Cochem**, a popular wine-tasting centre, you can take the chair-lift up the Pinnerkreuz hill for a view of the sleepy little town with its restored castle. The valley winds lazily round to **Beilstein**, which has some handsome half-timbered houses of the 16th century. Metternich was the last owner of the castle ruins here, left by the French forces of 1689 with scarcely more than the pentagonal belfry and an arched doorway left standing. On the left bank as you approach Zell is the graceful ruin of the 12th-century **Marienburg** convent, closed in the 16th century because the Archbishop of Trier disapproved of the nuns' unseemly behaviour. It was destroyed in the Thirty Years' War in successive occupations by the Bavarians, Swedes and French. The French came back in 1792 to finish it off. The convent commands a lovely view of the valley and rolling vineyards.

Bernkastel-Kues

The vintages of this picture-book wine village—actually twin villages on either side of the river—are justly famous. There are some splendid half-timbered houses on Römerstrasse, but if the taverns seem almost too cute, head for the wine cellars for more serious tasting. The **Markt** on the Bernkastel side of the river is the popular focus of town life. Notice the old pillory with its iron chain still standing in the north-west corner. The fine Renaissance **town hall** overlooks an octagonal fountain (1606) graced by the town's patron saint Michael. Most bizarre of the half-timbered houses, just off the market place, is the top-heavy **Spitzhaus** (Pointed House) built in 1583, a triumph of will-power over structural stability.

The Hunsrück

The side-trip from Bernkastel-Kues up to the densely wooded Hunsrück mountain ridge is popular with hunters and anglers. The southern slope descends to the Nahe valley where trout fishing (with permit) is highly prized, and the vineyards produce some excellent whites to go with the catch.

Join the beautiful panoramic **Hunsrück Höhenstrasse** ridge road (Highway 327) at Morbach and head west. At Thalfang, cut back east into the Idarwald forest, rich in deer and wild boar. Stop at the Hunsrück's highest point, the **Erbeskopf**, 818m (2,684ft), for the magnificent view and a walk through the meadows and woods—grand cross-country skiing in winter.

The town of **Idar-Oberstein** is situated in part at the bottom of a dramatic gorge cut by the Nahe river through volcanic rock. Set into the cliff 60m (197ft) up, the 15th-century Gothic **Felsenkirche** (Church of the Rocks) is reached by 214 steps from Oberstein's Marktplatz. It has a fine altar painting of *Christ's Passion* (1420). Idar is the centre of the town's renowned jewellery manufacture. The 22-storey Diamond Exchange, Mainzerstrasse 34, houses the dazzling **German Precious Stone Museum** (*Deutsches Edelstein-Museum*) displaying every imaginable precious and semi-precious rock. Visit, too, the **Gem Cutting Centre** (*Weiherschleife*) at Tiefensteiner Strasse to see the stones cut and polished in a traditional grinding mill.

Following the Nahe river east, pass the horseshoe-shaped castle ruin at Dhaun on the way to the wine village of **Monzingen**, where the grape was introduced by the Romans. It has handsome half-timbered houses dating back to the 16th century and a noble Gothic parish church. At **Sponheim**, see the solid Romanesque abbey-church of the Benedictines.

The wines of **Bad Kreuznach,** most notably the Schloss Böckelheim, make it an obligatory stop for connoisseurs. The festive atmosphere is enhanced with a genuine medieval meal at the Kautzenburg inn. The centre of the spa's social life is **Badewörth Island**, reached by a venerable old bridge bowed down by its 15th-century half-timbered houses. The park is appreciated for its nightingales and roses.

Dr Faustus seems to turn up wherever you go in Germany. Lodging at Magister-Faust-Gasse 47, the old scholar or charlatan was rector of the high school until driven out for pederasty.

Trier

Not content with being Germany's oldest city, Trier proudly proclaims it is even older than Rome. A house on the market place bears the inscription *Ante Romam Treveris stetit annis mille trecentis* ("Trier was standing 1,300 years before Rome"). But the claim that Trier was founded by Trebeta, son-in-law of the Assyrian queen Semiramis, was a legend invented to boost the town's image in the early Middle Ages. Already a major settlement of the Celtic Treveri in 15 BC when Augustus made it a provincial capital, *Augusta Treverorum*, it was a favourite home from home for many Roman emperors in the 3rd and 4th centuries. Constantine, the first Christian emperor, spent the early years of his reign here. With a bishop installed in 315, Trier became Germany's earliest Christian centre and has been a Catholic stronghold ever since.

There is definitely something sunny and Mediterranean about Trier, sitting comfortably in the Mosel valley plain. Nowadays the town provides an easy-going centre for the Mosel wine trade and enjoys unspectacular but satisfactory prosperity by not encouraging heavy—dirty—industry. The light-hearted ambience is greatly enhanced by the presence of 2,500 university students.

The town's Roman origins are still visible, and the basic urban ground-plan unchanged for more than 2,000 years. Access to the town centre is still through the massive **Porta Nigra** (Black Gate), more fortress than gate. Standing at the north end of town, it faces the road to the Rhine as a formidable bastion against the Germanic hordes. Dating from the 2nd century AD, its sandstone blocks were joined not by mortar but by iron clamps. "Porta Nigra" is a post-Roman reference to the pollution of the ages, but at the base you can see that the gate was once pale pink.

In 1028, the Syrian monk Simeon came to Trier on a pilgrimage from Jerusalem and shut himself up to die in a cell inside the gate. The Archbishop of Trier honoured him by transforming part of the structure into a church, the **Simeonsstift**. Its superb two-storey cloister now houses the **municipal museum** (and tourist information centre). The ground-floor archways are a beautiful combination of white limestone and red sandstone. The museum has an important collection of church sculpture and monastic furniture.

South on Simeonstrasse, notice on the left (No. 19) the rather garishly renovated but still graceful 13th-century **Dreikönigenhaus** (House of the Three Kings). In the old days the front door was on the second storey, reached by a staircase that could be removed in case of danger.

The **Hauptmarkt** is in every sense the heart of Trier, a lively centre for cheerful vendors around the **Petrusbrunnen** (St Peter's Fountain, 1595) that proclaims the cardinal virtues of Wisdom, Justice, Moderation and Strength. These are the qualities that speak from the stones of Renaissance and baroque houses surrounding the square, lovingly reconstructed since their wartime damage. South of the square rises the sturdy tower of the 15th-century St Gangolf church, approached through a fine baroque archway between the houses.

Trier's **cathedral** is massive and fortress-like, a powerful Romanesque edifice symbolizing the town's ancient function as a citadel of the Roman empire—pagan and holy. The basic limestone structure is 11th century, but reddish sandstone masonry dates back to the 4th century, and makes it the earliest church building in Germany. Inside, on the south side, notice the pulpit (1572) and All Saints' Altar (*Allerheiligenaltar*, 1614), both

sculpted by Hans Ruprecht Hoffmann. The cathedral is particularly rich in supposed holy relics: Christ's robe, two links of the chain that bound St Peter, St Anne's arms, one of St Andrew's feet and one of the 34 nails used in the Crucifixion. The adjoining 13th-century **Liebfrauenkirche**, pioneer among German Gothic churches, is built on a central Greek cross plan. The interior, with its floor forming a 12-petal rose, the mystic flower-symbol of the Virgin Mary, has an appealing dignity.

The **Rheinisches Landesmuseum**, Ostallee 44, offers a lucid introduction to the region's life under the Romans. Among the wall paintings, mosaics and sculptures, the outstanding exhibit is the stone carving of a Roman wine ship (AD 200), loaded up with barrels and a grinning sailor looking as if he has been sampling the merchandise. The **Kaiserthermen** (Imperial Baths) date from the early 4th century AD. At the eastern end is the wonderfully preserved *caldarium*, the hot bath-house. To the west was a domed *tepidarium* and a *frigidarium* with five swimming pools, next to a dressing room, massage parlour and steam bath. At the other end of Kaiserstrasse, turn left on Friedrich-Wilhelm-Strasse to the cosier **Barbarathermen**, 200 years older than the Imperial Baths. The ruin is nicely overgrown with moss, grass, ivy and wild flowers. At the Mosel, see the Roman Bridge (*Römerbrücke*) with its 18th-century arches on 2nd-century pillars.

*T*he fat lady strikes a bizarre baroque note in the Romanesque cathedral of Trier where the country's first bishopric was founded in the year 314.

From the bridge, Karl-Marx-Strasse takes you directly to Brückenstrasse 10, birthplace of this Catholic town's most famous and most uncatholic son. Surrounded by sex shops and strip-joints, the **Karl-Marx-Haus** has a fascinating collection of memorabilia of the founding father of the Communist movement—though some may now find this of archaeological, rather than historic, interest. Besides private and public letters, his most famous text, *Das Kapital*, is here in manuscript form, along with photos of the young Marx with all the great revolutionaries of his day. Like most good revolutionaries, he had a nice bourgeois home.

Aachen

Charlemagne's ancient imperial capital is now an industrial town in a coal mining area along the Belgian border. Although a major target of World War II bombardments, it is still worth a visit for its relics of the great emperor who set Germany on the path to nationhood (*see* page 53). Thirty German kings were crowned here from the 9th to the 16th centuries.

The core of the **cathedral** was built as the palace chapel in 800 (hence the town's French name of Aix-la-Chapelle). Charlemagne's octagonal basilica is best seen from Münsterplatz. Topped by a 17th-century baroque copper dome, it is now crowded in by other chapels and a Gothic chancel added in the 14th century.

The interior with its ambulatory aisle gives a better sense of the Carolingian chapel's Byzantine inspiration. It is a more elaborate version of Ravenna's San Vitale—affirming Charlemagne as successor to the first Christian emperors whose capital was Ravenna. Hanging in the centre is a monumental 12th-century gilded copper chandelier whose turrets symbolize the celestial Jerusalem. In the Gothic choir extending to the east, the plain stone table that served as the basilica's high altar in 800 is adorned with a resplendent 11th-century **Pala d'Oro**, a golden altarpiece. It has a relief of Christ enthroned and scenes from the Passion. Notice, too, the gilded pulpit of the same period. At the far end of the choir, **Charlemagne's shrine** (*Karlsschrein*) contains the emperor's bones. His simple marble throne is up in the western gallery.

Make a quantum leap into the modern world with a visit to the **Neue Galerie**, Komphausbadstrasse 19. Its fine collection pursues post-war avant-garde painting from Pop Art and American Expressionism through photorealism and conceptual art to New York graffiti. Roy Liechtenstein, Robert Rauschenberg, Duane Hanson and Georg Baselitz are among the artists represented.

Pontstrasse pays a double homage to journalism. At No. 13, the **International Newspaper Museum** (*Internationales Zeitungsmuseum*) covers the press from the 17th century to the present day in a collection of 100,000 issues from all over the world, including first and last editions and special numbers. At No. 117, a plaque marks the **Reuterhaus** (1737), the home of Paul Julius Reuter, who founded the now London-based international news agency. He started his career here in 1885 with carrier pigeons flying stock market prices from his rooftop loft to Brussels. The birds provided the missing link in telegraph communications between Berlin and Paris. The Aachen method was used again in 1944 when Reuter correspondent Monty Taylor used a pigeon to carry news back to London of the D-Day landings in Normandy.

The Eifel

This sprawling plateau of rolling hills, woods and volcanic lakes is a quiet, uncrowded place for some rambling and

contemplative fishing. Start on Highway 258 south of Aachen, at the Eifel's western edge in the almost absurdly pretty 18th-century town of **Monschau**—the best view is up at the cemetery. The slate-roofed, half-timbered houses are built on the steep slopes of the Rur river gorge. Along narrow streets, balconies are bedecked with flowers, carved oak doorways kept immaculately polished. The finest of the mansions is the **Rotes Haus** (1762), Laufenstrasse 10, preserving as a museum its interior around a splendid rococo stairway.

The meandering Rur offers some breakneck canoeing over its dam, or more sedate boating and fishing on the **Rurstausee** reservoir. Further east at **Mechernich-Kommern** is an open-air museum of Eifel rural life with windmills, water mill, workshops, stables and a miniature village school.

At **Bad Münstereifel**, imposing medieval ramparts with four Gothic-arched gates span the Erft river. The parish church has a noble 11th-century Romanesque façade.

A group of volcanic lakes are to be found west of the Koblenz–Trier Autobahn between the spa town of Daun and Manderscheid, dominated by two ruined castles. The half-dozen volcanic lakes or *Maare*—**Pulver Maar** is the prettiest—are craters formed by eruptions of gas that did not produce lava but left a circular ridge of cinders in which water collected.

Ancient volcanic activity formed the Eifel, a land of lakes, rushing streams, wooded hills and charming villages. It's a favourite with local hikers.

The Palatinate

The region of the Pfalz bordering on the confluence of the Neckar and Rhine rivers constituted the domains of the Palatine princes, historically the highest nobles in the German empire. Slopes of vineyards rise from the Rhine to a plateau of red limestone used in many of the region's churches. Ramblers head west to the dense woodland of the Pfälzer Wald nature reserve. Palatine wines are harvested late, producing some robust, fruity reds as well as Rieslings, heady and full-bodied, to be discovered along the signposted wine-route.

Worms

The city has been a veritable crossroads of the three spiritual persuasions that have marked Germany's history—Catholic, Protestant and Jewish.

In characteristic Rhenish fashion, the largely Romanesque **cathedral** has apses east and west. They extend beyond twin towers flanking the broader octagonal towers over the transept crossings. The massive structure is lightened by dwarf-galleries around each of the towers. Inside the Gothic south porch, notice the fine 12th-century sculpture of Christ enthroned. The grand baroque altar is by Balthasar Neumann.

Jews made their home in Worms in the 10th century and built their house of worship in 1034. The oldest stone-built **synagogue** in Europe stands on the north side of the city centre in the Hintere Judengasse. Destroyed over and over again by the local citizenry, it was rebuilt most recently in the 1960s, with much of the original masonry, over the still-intact Mikvah, the women's ritual bath. Next door is a small museum, the **Raschi-Haus** named

*T*he tumbled old gravestones of the Jewish cemetery at Worms serve as a reminder that the city was once a major centre of Jewish culture.

acronymically after the great Talmudic scholar Rabbi Schlomo ben Itzhak who taught in Worms in the 11th century, when Jews constituted 30 per cent of the city's population. The house was once the ghetto's dance hall. The **Jewish cemetery** (*Judenfriedhof*) with several hundred Hebrew-inscribed tombstones is over on the south-west corner of town off the Andreasring.

The Protestants' place in Worms is assured with the **Luther Monument** (*Lutherdenkmal*) celebrating the Reformation leader's defiant confrontation with the Catholic Church at the Diet of Worms in 1521. The 19th-century monument north of the cathedral shows Luther surrounded by other heroic rebels of the Church, including England's John Wycliffe, Czechoslovakia's Jan Hus and Italy's Girolamo Savonarola.

The town also pays a little homage to paganism on the **Nibelungenbrücke**, where a statue of Hagen is shown throwing the Nibelungs' treasure into the Rhine (*see* page 226). Wagner's opera cycle is set in part in Worms, where the Huns overthrew Burgundian king Gunther in 436. Weapons and jewellery from this era are displayed in the **municipal museum** (*Städtisches Museum*), Weckerlingplatz 7.

If you are wondering where the Rhineland's best-known wine, Liebfraumilch, got its name, it is the 15th-century Liebfrauenkirche on the north side of town, still surrounded by its vineyards.

The Wine Route

The Palatine's officially signposted *Deutsche Weinstrasse* (German Wine Route), on Highway 271 west of Worms, extends from Bockenheim down to the French border. Serious wine enthusiasts, however, prefer first to go north on Highway 9 to the venerable vineyards of

DIET OF WORMS, NO HUMBLE PIE

The Imperial Diet (or assembly) took place in Worms three months after Luther was excommunicated for refusing to retract his attacks on the Church (*see* page 57). The papal nuncio did all he could to keep Luther away from Worms, foreseeing an enormous propaganda success for the Reformation cause if he came. An emissary rode out to warn Luther his enemies would kill him if he dared to enter town. Luther replied: "Tell your master that if there were as many devils at Worms as tiles on its roofs, I would still come in." Safely inside Worms, where he encountered more supporters than devils, Luther refused to recant "because to act against one's conscience is neither safe nor salutary, so help me God". If ever he did say his famous: "Here I stand, I can do no other," it was drowned out in the tumult, because no eyewitness recalled it, and it only entered the Luther legend many years later.

Nierstein and **Oppenheim**, considered part of the Rhenish rather than Palatine wine region. Oppenheim is also worth a visit for its 14th-century Gothic **Katharinakirche**, noted for the south façade's splendidly carved stonework around gabled windows.

On the Deutsche Weinstrasse itself, the cheerful spa resort of **Bad Dürkheim** makes a good first stop. It boasts the world's biggest wine barrel, the **Dürkheimer Riesenfass**. It would hold 1,700,000 litres (374,000 gallons), enough to fill 2,266,666 bottles, nearly eight times the size of the famous barrel at Heidelberg Castle. It serves as a tavern for 55 customers on the **Wurstmarkt**, the site of an equally gigantic wine festival every September. The local climate is so mild that you will find almond and fig trees in the **Kurgarten** (spa park).

Connoisseurs accord pride of place to the vineyards of **Wachenheim** as the best in the Palatinate. The wine growers' patrician houses bespeak the town's prosperity. But **Forst** and **Deidesheim** are also prestigious, the latter distinguished by a main square of grand medieval allure.

Neustadt an der Weinstrasse (to distinguish it from all the other Neustadts in Germany) is a major distribution centre for the region's wines and holds a big harvest festival, **Deutsches Weinlese-Fest**, in October. Notice the handsome Renaissance town hall. South of town, the ruin of **Hambacher castle** is something of a national shrine, since it was here that Germany's black, red and yellow flag was raised for the first time in 1832.

In Schweigen at the southern end of the Wine Route, a formidable **Wine Gate** (*Weintor*) seems to suggest to people travelling north from France that *this* is where the serious wine country begins.

Speyer

Dominating the Rhine plain, the imposing silhouette of the cathedral proclaims Speyer's importance as an imperial town. The church was a pantheon for German emperors, and diets were convened here throughout the 16th century for the princes to debate the empire's response to the Reformation. It was here in 1529 that a Protestation of Lutheran princes launched the name of Protestants.

As at Worms, the **cathedral** (1060) has twin steeples flanking broader domed towers with chancels extending east and west. Notice the galleries which provided an upper passage all around the intricate pattern of exterior walls. The tiered arcades suggest the influence of Roman aqueducts. Beneath the southern transept and chancel, the great crypt is a masterly organization of space around the massive Romanesque pillars. At the entrance to the **Imperial mausoleum** (*Kaisergruft*) is a monumental tombstone of Rudolf von Habsburg. Buried here are eight emperors and kings, three empresses and a princess, and five bishops. As you leave, notice near the main entrance the 15th-century **Domnapf**, a giant sandstone bowl. It is traditionally filled with the local wine for the citizenry to toast imperial or other illustrious visitors—recently Pope John Paul II. People used to help themselves from the 1,580-litre (350-gallon) wine-bowl free of charge with their own huge wooden tankards. Now it is ladled out at ten marks a quarter litre (.05 gallon) (donated to church funds).

The **Palatine Museum** (*Historisches Museum der Pfalz*), Grosse Pfaffengasse 10, exhibits artefacts of the region's Roman origins and has a fine collection of Frankenthal porcelain and treasure from the imperial tombs. The main attraction, however, is its **Wine Museum**, one of the biggest in Europe. Among the wine-presses, ancient barrels and wine-growers' tools, look out for the oldest known wine in Germany, a 3rd-century Roman vintage, still liquid, preserved by the bottle's sealing wax turned to stone-hard resin.

Hesse

The region was founded as a federal state after World War II. *Hessen* in German, it extends from the Rhine eastwards to Thuringia and from the Odenwald forest in the south to the industrial town of Kassel in the north. At its heart is Germany's business capital, Frankfurt. The bankers unwind in the forests of the Taunus and Westerwald or perhaps at spa resorts like Wiesbaden and Bad Homburg, and tears well up in their eyes when they contemplate the romantic Lahn Valley.

Frankfurt

Unrivalled concrete symbol of German economic power, the city is reasserting its historic cultural role, as the town of books as well as banks. Hoping to make it the political capital of West Germany, Frankfurters rebuilt their bombed-out city on the Main river as rapidly as possible. That meant purely functional skyscrapers to replace the elegant but impractical Renaissance and Gothic buildings that graced the city before 1945. The political plum went to Bonn, but big business made itself comfortable in steel and glass towers that gained the city the nickname of "Mainhattan". Nostalgics had to be content with perfect replicas of Goethe's house and the old municipal buildings around the Römerberg. The cathedral, where emperors were crowned for over two centuries, survives intact.

Now, theatres have sprouted up all over town. The old opera house has been reconstructed for concerts, while opera has moved into new premises. A happy marriage of money and good taste has produced a group of museums along the south bank of the Main river of awe-inspiring range and quality.

The highlights of the trade fairs are the Automobile Show (every two years) in September and the annual International Book Fair, the biggest in the world, held in October.

The Old Town

The valiant effort to restore the Römerberg square around the graceful 15th-century city hall (Romer) has produced a historical document in stone rather than a

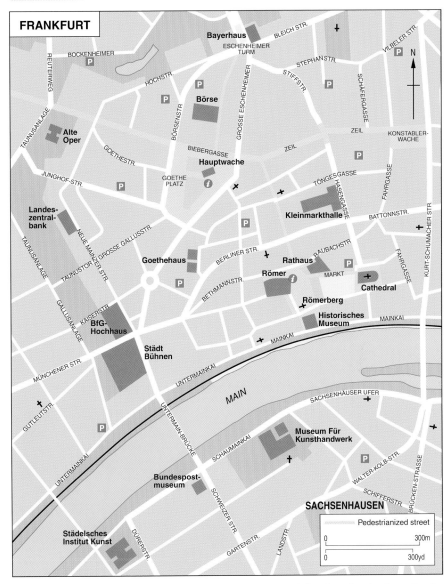

FRANKFURT

living set of buildings. Behind the **city hall**'s balconied façade of triple step-gables, visit a gleaming replica of the **Imperial Banquet Hall** where the emperor's coronation was celebrated from 1562 to 1792. The portraits present a complete set of 52 Holy Roman Emperors from Charlemagne to Franz II, whom Napoleon obliged to be the last. In the middle of the square, the 17th-century **Justice Fountain** is the real thing, except that it used to gush wine on coronation days. To the south is the slender Gothic **Nikolaikirche**, and on the north-east side of the square are patrician houses from the 15th to 18th centuries.

The soaring 15th-century Gothic steeple of the red sandstone **cathedral** provides a dignified retort to the bumptious bankers' towers looming on the skyline. Inside the tower hall is a splendid sandstone sculpture group of the *Crucifixion* by Mainz artist Hans Backoffen. The church's austere interior has some finely carved 14th-century choir stalls. To the right of the choir is the simple **Wahlkapelle** (Election Chapel) where the prince-electors met in conclave. In front of the cathedral, a **Historical Garden** reveals excavations of the town's Roman settlement and foundations of a Carolingian castle.

The **Goethe House** is handsomely reproduced at Grosser Hirschgraben 23. The furnishings of his study are authentic, as are the Blue Baroque dining room, the copper pots in the kitchen and the absence of electricity. The imposing bourgeois residence was built in 1590 and received Johann Wolfgang into its bosom on 28 August 1749. In old age, the Great Man recalled his home as bright and cheerful, and that is how it seems today, but in his prime he wrote: "The old nooks and crannies and the gloomy disposition of the house in many places was apt to awaken shudders and fear in a childish mind."

The Museums

Most of the museums are over on the left bank of the river, but a couple are within easy walking distance of the Römerberg. In a town so drastically transformed, the

*B*anks soar high into the Frankfurt sky to watch over the country's economy and remind us that the name of this city's game is money.

Historisches Museum, Saalgasse 19, is a good place to start, to get a feel for what the old days were like. A scale model of the city shows what the war destroyed. Exhibits of life from the 15th century to the modern day include an artisan's kitchen and the imperial banquet table, set for the coronation feast.

The **Jewish Museum** (*Jüdisches Museum*), Untermainkai 14, is in the restored neoclassical Rothschild-Palais (1821), the home of the banking family that sent its sons all over Europe to build a great financial empire. The museum traces the history of Jews in Frankfurt, reproducing parts of the old ghetto.

Amid the pleasant greenery of Museumufer (river bank of museums) along the Schaumainkai, a group of neoclassical patrician houses provides a handsome setting for the city's great art collections. Most prestigious is the **Städelsches Kunstinstitut**, Schaumainkai 63. Created in 1816 from the collection of Frankfurt banker Johann Friedrich Städel—rather than the treasures amassed by a royal family—the characteristic art works are more personal than stately or monumental. At the entrance to the galleries containing European art from the 14th century to the present day is Johann Heinrich Tischbein's famous portrait of Goethe in a classical Italian landscape, *Goethe in der römischen Campagna*. The Italian works include Fra Angelico's *Madonna Enthroned*, Verrocchio's sculptural *Madonna and Child,* and two strikingly contrasting portraits of women: Botticelli's gently sensuous *Simonetta Vespucci* and Pontormo's cool *Aristocratic Lady*. Among the Dutch and Flemish masters are Vermeer's magnificent *Geographer*, a brutal *Blinding of Samson* by Rembrandt and an elegant *Madonna* by Van Eyck. Highlights of the

German collection are Grünewald's massive rustic *St Cyriakus*, Holbein's *Abendmahl* (Last Supper) and Dürer's *Verspottung Hiobs* (Mocking of Job). German Expressionists include Dix, Beckmann and Kirchner. The French are well represented by Courbet, Monet, Degas and Matisse.

The **Architekturmuseum**, Schaumainkai 43, displays with models and master drawings the whole world of architecture from the Italian Renaissance of Bramante and Michelangelo to the most recent innovations of Tokyo, Paris and Chicago. It explores the design of shopping centres and pedestrian zones as well as the baroque or Classical palaces of Fischer von Erlach and Mansart.

New York architect Richard Meier's design for the **Applied Arts Museum** (*Museum für Kunsthandwerk*), Schaumainkai 17, incorporates the neoclassical Villa Metzler into a gleaming modern structure of white enamel and glass. There are superb collections of Persian and Chinese ceramics, Meissen, Nymphenburg and Sèvres porcelain, Venetian and modern American crystal and Art Deco book binding.

The **Film Museum**, Schaumainkai 41, is great fun. The cinemathèque shows three or four classics daily, often accompanied by a 1926 Wurlitzer organ. Film lovers can trace the machinery from the 17th-century magic lantern and Victorian peep-shows to the Lumière brothers' cinematograph. It also reconstitutes the studio of Georges Méliès and a modern special-effects lab.

The **Liebieghaus**, Schaumainkai 71, assembles an impressive collection of sculpture from Sumer and Egypt to Europe's neoclassical era, with special emphasis on German Gothic and baroque.

The Modern City

Behind the museums on Schau-mainkai, the left-bank district of **Sachsenhausen** is the centre for bars and discos. More charming are the taverns serving bottomless jugs of the local cider variously known as *Apfel-wein, Äppelwoi* or *Ebbelwei* as the quantity broadens the dialect.

Back on the right bank, a bustling shopping centre spreads out along a broad pedestrian street, the **Zeil**, leading to the landmark clock tower of the baroque **Hauptwache,** once the police station, now housing a café. Grosse Bockenheimerstrasse is "restaurant row", popularly known as *Fressgass'*, lined with Mediterranean-style outdoor bistros and cafés. It leads over to the neoclassical **Alte Oper**, renovated for concerts and operetta now that the opera has moved to the **Städtische Bühnen** on Theaterplatz down near the river. At the **Stock Exchange** on Börsenplatz, a visitors' gallery is open during morning business hours.

The Taunus

The Taunus mountain ridge stretches in a wide arc north of Frankfurt from Bad Nauheim over to the Rheingau wine country. Spa resorts benefit from its mild climate and rich mineral springs, and ramblers enjoy the forests of oak, beech and pine, now protected nature parks.

Within easy reach of Frankfurt on Autobahn 5, **Bad Nauheim** is renowned

*A*fter World War II, *Frankfurt was rebuilt in modern style, but the charming façades of the Römerberg, 15th-century home of municipal government were reproduced.*

for its exquisite *Jugendstil* architecture (1905). The great Darmstadt school (*see* below) has designed everything from the spa buildings to bathroom fittings. A highlight is the **Sprudelhof** with its four-leaf clover of basins. Even if you do not take the waters, have a stroll in the lovely gardens of the Kurpark.

Drive south-west via Usingen to the excavated Roman garrison of **Saalburg**, part of the ancient *Limes*, or frontier fortifications. The patron, emperor Wilhelm II, commissioned a bronze of his Roman predecessor, Antonius Pius, at the entrance. The crenellated battlements on the reconstructed walls are a 19th-century fantasy, but there are interesting weapons and utensils from the 2nd century AD in the museum. Notice the leather shoes found miraculously preserved in the garrison wells.

The nearby **Freilichtmuseum Hessenpark** is an open-air museum of a more recent era, displaying houses and crafts of rural communities of the 18th and 19th centuries.

The tranquil spa resort of **Bad Homburg** has several claims to fame. The castle, 17th-century home of dramatist Heinrich von Kleist's hero Prince Friedrich of Homburg, was honoured with Germany's first water closet, imported by the English-born Countess of Hesse in 1835. Another odd attraction is the prince's silver leg, which is in fact wooden with silver joints. The spa's casino was Europe's first, established in 1841 by François Blanc who went on to "make" Monte Carlo. Visiting in the 1890s, the Prince of Wales took his felt hat, dented the crown, turned up the brim at the sides and invented the Homburg. The **Hat Museum**, Louisenstrasse 120, displays Chancellor Konrad Adenauer's version, along with US President Lyndon Johnson's cowboy hat and other illustrious headgear.

For a view over the region drive up to the **Grosser Feldberg**, 878m (2,880ft). Then continue to the medieval and baroque castle of **Königstein** which has a fine rococo altar in the little Marienkirche.

The biggest of the Taunus spas is **Wiesbaden**, the capital of Hesse and an elegant resort with fashionable boutiques along Wilhelmstrasse. The **municipal museum** (*Städtisches Museum*) has some good German art—Lucas Cranach, Bartel Bruyn, Max Beckmann, Lovis Corinth and Max Liebermann—as well as the Russian Alexey Jawlensky. In the **Kurpark**, snooze among the flowers and shrubs at one of the many open-air concerts, or stroll off for half an hour into the pretty **Rambach valley**.

Darmstadt

The old capital of the duchy of Hesse remains an important town for science and technology, particularly in electronics, but also for the arts. Designers continue the traditions of the Bauhaus and the innovations begun when Grand Duke Ernst Ludwig brought leading European architects to Darmstadt at the end of the 19th century. They included Peter Behrens from Berlin and Josef Maria Olbrich from Vienna, and you can see their *Jugendstil* houses and studios at the **Mathildenhöhe**, an artists' colony on the east side of town. Outstanding are Olbrich's **Exhibition Hall** (*Ausstellungsgebäude*) with its delightful terrace of lime trees and the "five-fingered" **Hochzeitsturm** (Marriage Tower) celebrating the Grand Duke's wedding.

His ancestor Ludwig I is honoured in the centre of town on Luisenplatz with

Langer Ludwig, a landmark bronze statue on top of a 33m (108ft) column. It looks down at the 18th-century palace which has a collection of ornate carriages even more extravagant than those of Bavaria's King Ludwig II. On Friedensplatz, the **Hessisches Landsmuseum** has superb paintings by Stephan Lochner and Lucas Cranach, as well as Brueghel, Rubens and Rembrandt. Among 20th-century artists, Nolde, Feininger and Macke are well represented, and the museum boasts Germany's most important collection of the works of Joseph Beuys. Take a walk in the English park of the Herrengarten, behind the museum.

Lahn Valley

Meandering between the forests of the Taunus and the Westerwald, the Lahn river creates a romantic atmosphere with more serenity, and on a more intimate scale, than the Rhine. Wander quietly along avenues of maple trees or make your way up to the dramatic vantage points of castle ruins.

The bridge at **Lahnstein** and the restored **Lahneck castle** both afford good views of the confluence of the Lahn and Rhine.

Bad Ems is a sleepy little spa good for nose and throat ailments and river cruises. The **Benedetti Stone**, dated 13 July 1870, marks the spot where Wilhelm I and French ambassador Vincent Benedetti had the fateful conversation which Bismarck exploited to launch the Franco-Prussian War (*see* page 67).

At **Nassau**, only a ruin remains of the castle where the counts of Laurenburg, the ancestors of the House of Orange, had their home. On a rocky pinnacle south of the river is the Romanesque-Gothic **Arnstein Abbey**. The barons and Archbishop of Trier vied for control of the river with castles—now in ruin at Balduinstein and Laurenburg or reconstructed at Schaumburg.

In the town of Diez, the 17th-century baroque **Oranienburg castle** traces the history of the House of Nassau and Orange with the family's paintings, sculpture and furniture. The garden is a pleasant place from which to contemplate the river.

Limburg has a fine 13th-century cathedral, built on a rock high above the river. It combines a Rhenish Romanesque exterior with French Gothic groin vaulting inside. The southern transept towers are a 19th-century addition. There are some lovely tall half-timbered houses in the old town, including one 14th-century dwelling on the steps leading to the cathedral that is thought to be the oldest in Germany.

Runkel is a pretty riverside village best viewed from the old bridge (1440). A classic medieval fortress towers above in the ruin left by Count Wallenstein's Croatian troops in the Thirty Years' War. Climb its tower for a super panorama of the Taunus, Westerwald and Lahn valley.

Weilburg

Around the market square and its Neptunbrunnen, the town has kept intact much of the Renaissance and baroque elegance of its days as residence of the counts of Nassau. In their 16th-century **palace**, summer concerts find an exquisite setting in the Renaissance courtyard with handsome arcaded gallery and wrought-iron-balconied clock tower. Inside the palace is some first-class baroque and Biedermeier furniture. The terraced gardens lead down from the market place to the river. On the middle terrace is a baroque Orangery, now housing a restaurant.

The **Folklore and Mining Museum** (*Heimat- und Bergbaumuseum*) on

Schlossplatz has an interesting display of regional mining for potash, roofing slate and ceramic clay.

Wetzlar

The town unites romance and industry. In the 18th century, sessions of the imperial court were held here, attracting young lawyers like Johann Wolfgang von Goethe. It was here in 1772 that he fell in love with Charlotte Buff, the Lotte who drove the hero to suicide in Goethe's most famous work, *Die Leiden des jungen Werthers* (The Sorrows of Young Werther). The 18th-century Buff family home, **Lottehaus**, part of the Teutonic Knights' buildings on Lottestrasse, is now a museum of Goethe and Werther memorabilia.

The town is also where Europe's most famous camera, the Leica, is manufactured. The Ernst Leitz company **museum** in Ernst-Leitz-Strasse traces the firm's evolution from the first microscopes (1849) via the original Leica, *Urleica* (1913) to the latest models.

The **cathedral** is a strange hodgepodge of styles, from the dark grey limestone Romanesque northern tower, graceful Flamboyant Gothic southern tower in red limestone and buff-coloured basilica and chancel. Protestants and Catholics share the interior.

Marburg

The town owes much of its cheerful atmosphere to the students of the venerable university, founded in 1527 during the first struggles of the Reformation. The peasants from the Lahn valley also add their touch of colour coming into town on market days (Wednesday and Saturday.)

Start near a branch in the Lahn river at the noble church of **St Elisabeth**. Elisabeth of Hungary, the wife of the Landgrave of Hesse, was made a saint after sacrificing her life for plague victims in a Marburg hospital. Consecrated in 1283, St Elisabeth's is the pioneer of Germany's flat-vaulted Gothic hall-churches. The church is richly endowed with works of art. At the end of the nave, notice the superb carving of the openwork rood screen, with a modern *Crucifixion* by Ernst Barlach on the altar. To the left of the chancel is Elisabeth's statue (1470). Her tomb is in the northern transept, with a 14th-century bas-relief on the sarcophagus depicting her burial in the presence of Christ. Notice also, to the left, a poignant *pietà* at the base of the Madonna Altar. Elisabeth's Shrine, a masterful gold reliquary, is in the sacristy in the north-east corner of the church. Philip of Hesse, the Protestants' champion and the saint's direct descendant, had her relics removed to discourage unseemly idolatry. The southern transept or Landgraves' Chancel houses the

---

FAREWELL TO ARMS

When Goethe fell for her, Lotte was engaged to his friend Johann Christian Kestner. Aged 23, Goethe toyed with the idea of suicide, but decided instead, without saying goodbye, to leave on a walking-tour of the Lahn valley. The next month, he learned that another Wetzlar friend, Carl Wilhelm Jerusalem, had shot himself for the love of a married woman. Two years later, after another of those hopeless love affairs that were stock in trade for any self-respecting Romantic, Jerusalem and Goethe were amalgamated in the fateful character of Werther. The book became a worldwide bestseller, translated into 30 languages. In the Napoleonic Wars, it was bedside reading on both sides, and many a sentimental soldier who did not fall in battle decided to end it all anyway after finishing the book.

AGREEING TO DIFFER

Philip of Hesse made Marburg University a centre of Protestant theology after bringing in Martin Luther, Philipp Melanchthon and Ulrich Zwingli to debate Reformation doctrine. They hammered out 14 points on which they could all agree, but for the 15th, the Swiss Zwingli could not accept Luther's insistence that at the moment of communion, Christ's flesh and blood were present in the bread and wine. It was a point they never resolved.

monumental tombs of the Landgraves of Hesse. The last, an alabaster sculpture of Wilhelm II (1516), follows the gruesome French fashion of showing, beneath the ruler in his prime, his corpse being devoured by worms.

At the top of Marburg's hill, the **castle** belongs now to the university. It is worth the climb both for the view of the Lahn and for the **Cultural History Museum** (*Museum für Kulturgeschichte*) devoted to the region's life from prehistoric to modern times. The tour of the castle's apartments and chapel includes the study where Philip of Hesse received Martin Luther and his Protestant brethren and rivals in 1529.

Kassel

Once the illustrious residence of the Hesse nobility, the city was practically wiped out in World War II because it was also—and is once more—a major centre for manufacturing railway equipment. Today it counterbalances its industry and commerce with a lively arts policy.

About 14km (8 miles) west of the city centre, the palace and park at **Wilhelmshöhe** are still a wonderful attraction. For a superb view, make for the huge **Hercules Monument**, 70m (230ft) tall, reproducing at the top of a pyramid the

Greek statue by Lysippus (4th century BC, shown in Naples as the Farnese Hercules). Try to get here in the afternoon (check with the tourist office for exact days and times) to observe what is perhaps Europe's most spectacular **fountain show** (*Wasserkünste*). Water cascades from below the Hercules Monument down to the **Neptune Basin**. From here you can follow the play of water, springs and cascades past the Devil's Bridge and the ruins of the Roman aqueduct all the way down to the **Great Fountain** behind the palace.

The palace's **Picture Gallery** (*Gemäldegalerie*) comprises one of Germany's major collections. The German painters include Altdorfer, Dürer, Cranach and Grien, the Flemish and Dutch Rubens, Rembrandt, Van Dyck and Ruisdael; Titian, Ribera, Murillo and Poussin are also represented.

Every five years (1997 next) Kassel's **documenta** exhibition attracts the élite of the world's avant-garde art community. Meanwhile, the **Neue Galerie**, Schöne Aussicht 1, offers a fine collection of 20th-century art, American and European.

Next door, the **Grimm Museum** is devoted to the compilers of the world's best-known book of fairy tales. As court librarians here, Jakob and Wilhelm Grimm published "*Kinder- und Hausmärchen*" in 1815. Besides the personal affairs of these indefatigable researchers, contemporary pictures of the Hesse landscape show the local settings for many of the tales.

The town is also a good base for excursions into the pretty Waldeck region and rambles in the Kellerwald forest. At the spa resort of **Bad Wildungen,** be sure to visit the 14th-century parish church to see Konrad Soest's magnificent *Wildungen-Altar* (1403).

Seaports and Steel Mills, High Fashion and Bare Beaches

This is where the hard work is done—from the Hanseatic trading cities of Hamburg, Bremen and Lübeck to the Ruhr's great steel belt. But the region boasts popular resorts on North Sea and Baltic beaches and the Frisian islands too. Industrial wealth has assembled some of Europe's best art collections, and Düsseldorf, the Ruhr's administrative capital, is also the national fashion centre. Romantics can wander away from it all into the mysterious Harz mountains.

The north coast has always been Germany's natural gateway to the world. The sober, dignified image that Hamburg likes to cultivate is not the one the sailors remember in erotic fantasies on faraway oceans. The naval port of Kiel has abandoned the Kaiser's dreams of empire for the more pacific pleasures of international regattas. The heyday of transatlantic liners has gone, but Bremerhaven and Cuxhaven attract a prosperous cruise traffic. Preferring to forget Thomas Mann's

*T*he best way to see Hamburg is from the water. Dozens of ferries and water buses ply the network of canals, rivers and lakes.

often cruel insights into its conservative materialism, Lübeck looks to the Baltic trading opportunities it has regained since the Eastern European revolutions.

Visitors to Schleswig-Holstein are struck by the subtle play of northern light, nuancing the colours on the dunes and heath that entranced the province's great Expressionist painter Emil Nolde. Other artists—Fritz Mackensen, Bernard Hoetger, Paula Becker-Modersohn—were attracted to the luminous skies over the moorland north of Bremen, founding the colony of Worpswede, still active today.

More conventional folk are happy to expose their skins and breathe the bracing air of the Frisian island of Sylt or other thriving resorts like Travemünde or the Timmendorfer Strand. There are fine

249

facilities for sailing and other water sports all along the coast. Even when the weather is not so hot, holiday-makers enjoy the therapy of seawater swimming pools with the restful effects of artificial waves—guaranteed unpolluted.

Hamburg

This ancient Hanseatic port is, like Berlin and Bremen, a city-state with a regional government enjoying the same autonomy as, say, Bavaria or Baden-Württemberg.

NORTH-WEST

Its great prosperity derives not only from trading activities, but from aircraft and ship building, printing, publishing, oil refineries and chemical industry.

Visitors arriving by sea might be overwhelmed by the bustle of the gigantic port and its industrial facilities. Conversely, newcomers driving into the city are struck by its greenery, extensive parkland and handsome gardens, and the charm of its inland waterways. Hamburg is situated on the Elbe estuary some 110km (68 miles) from the North Sea. It is served by two other rivers, the little Bille tributary from the east and the Alster from the north forming two delightful lake-like basins in the city centre, the Binnen- and Aussenalster.

Devastated by fire in 1842 and again by the bombs of World War II, the city is predominantly modern in aspect. A traditional taste for gracious living is still evident in the turn-of-the-century patrician villas bordering the Alster and along the Elbe west of the harbour. Even the tall redbrick warehouses impose a certain elegance on the docks.

The good people of Hamburg are also reputed to speak the most elegantly accented German—pure vowels, superb umlauts, and *st* and *sp* pronounced in the "English" manner, not the *scht* and *schp* you hear elsewhere.

Binnen- and Aussenalster

The town's fashionable promenade remains the **Jungfernstieg** along the waterfront of the Binnenalster basin. The most popular rendezvous here is the terrace of the **Alsterpavillon** café, an institution

*H*amburg's imposing *Rathaus (Town Hall) in the Renaissance style was built in the late 19th century.*

The City Centre

Towering over the market square is the rebuilt 19th-century neo-Renaissance **town hall**, at the centre of the popular shopping district. The square, **Rathausmarkt**, is the focus for beer and wine festivals in the summer months.

Burchardplatz is the centre of the **counting house quarter** (*Kontorhausviertel*) where the great Hamburg merchant community counts its money behind grand brown clinker-brick façades. The best known is Fritz Höger's **Chilehaus**, a masterpiece of Expressionist architecture shaped like a ship's prow which was built in right the middle of Germany's 1923 economic crisis.

Fire and war spared none of the city's churches. Of Sir George Gilbert Scott's majestic neo-Gothic **Nikolaikirche** (1863), only the soaring 147m (482ft)

since 1799. Down on the quayside, take an hour's boat cruise on the *Weisse Flotte* around the Aussenalster. (Enquire also about canal and twilight cruises beginning here.) The Alster cruise is quite the most enjoyable way to take in the skyline of lovingly reconstructed church steeples and town hall belfry. On the Ballindamm along the east quay are the head offices of the famous Hamburg–America shipping line—now Hapag-Lloyd—the biggest in the world, until 1914. Beyond the Lombard and Kennedy bridges on the west shore you cruise past the chic residential area of **Pöseldorf**, worth a visit later for its boutiques and art galleries. As the basin narrows to the river at **Harvestehude**, you will see some of the town's finest villas, neoclassical and *Jugendstil*, gleaming white with immaculate gardens right down to weeping willows at the water's edge.

*I*n the booming 1880s, *Hamburg's merchants declared that their new Speicherstadt (Warehouse Town) was their "treasure chest" and ought to look the part.*

spire survives. Among the best restored is the 15th-century Gothic **St Jacobi**, worth a visit for the sculpted triptych of its Trinity Altar (1510) and splendid baroque organ. The baroque **St Michaelis** (1762) is airy and bright, beloved locally for its handsome brick tower popularly known as the *Michel*, offering a grand view of the city and port from the top of its 449 stairs.

The Old Town

St Michaelis is at the heart of what remains of the old town between the Zollkanal and Nikolaifleet waterways. Nearby at Krayenkamp 10–11 is an alley of quaint brick and timber **almshouses** (*Krameramtswohnungen*) of 1670, converted now to art galleries and restaurants.

Along the **Deichstrasse**, where the great fire broke out in 1842, are some grander merchant houses of the 17th and 18th centuries and warehouses served by barges along the canal. You get a nice overall view from the **Hohe Brücke** bridging the narrow Nikolaifleet.

The Port

Harbour cruises leave from the St-Pauli-Landungsbrücken on the Elbe river. Founded in 1189, Germany's biggest port now has 60 dock basins covering 87km^2 (33 square miles). It handles 16,000 ocean-going vessels a year. You will see close-up huge oil tankers from the Persian Gulf, rusty freighters from South America and Russia, and immaculate luxury yachts. The tour takes the customs canal (*Zollkanal*) past the formidable 19th-century **Speicherstadt** (Warehouse Town) of monumental eight-storey brick edifices with ornate turrets, cornices and gables—an appropriately exotic design for their fragrant stores of Oriental spices and silk, and Caribbean rum, coffee and tobacco.

Come early on Sundays for the busy **St Pauli fish market**, from 6–10 a.m. In the old days, people used to come here directly from a sleepless night on St Pauli's notorious **Reeperbahn**. The sex shops, strip-shows and prostitutes are still there, but disease and drugs have taken most of the fun out of the sin. Among the myriad discotheques is one cultural monument: Reeperbahn 136 is where the Beatles started their career.

The Museums

The city's major art museum is the **Kunsthalle** on Glockengiesserwall east of the Lombard bridge. It boasts one of the finest collections of paintings in Germany, from the 14th century to modern times. The highlight of its medieval collection is the 1379 *Grabower Altar* by Meister Bertram for St Peter's church. Flemish and Dutch painters represented here include Rembrandt, van Goyen, Ruisdael and Pieter Hooch. Among the German Romantics are Philip Otto Runge and Caspar David Friedrich—note his dramatic *Eismeer* (Sea of Ice). Together with paintings by Max Liebermann, a fine Expressionist collection presents Edvard Munch, Lovis Corinth, Ernst Ludwig Kirchner, Emil Nolde, Franz Marc, Otto Dix and Oskar Schlemmer. French Impressionists here include Manet, Renoir, Pissarro, Gauguin and Cézanne. Prominent among the Moderns are Britain's Francis Bacon and David Hockney.

At the **Museum für Kunst und Gewerbe** (Arts and Crafts), Steintorplatz, the outstanding exhibit is the jewellery collection from antiquity, Byzantium, Asia and Europe, including modern *Jugendstil* and Bauhaus. See, too, the magnificent Renaissance furniture, 18th-century porcelain and the section of Japanese art.

The **Museum für Hamburgische Geschichte** (city history museum, Holstenwall 24) will fascinate kids and adults alike with its model railway shunting yards and 18th-century model ships including a "floating baroque palace". To show it did not pay to interfere with Hamburg shipping, the museum exhibits the skulls of two beheaded pirates.

For history buffs, the **Bismarck Museum** involves a short excursion out of town—30km (18 miles) east to the Witzhave exit on the Berlin Autobahn. It is housed on **Friedrichsruh**, the country estate to which the Iron Chancellor retired in 1891 and where he spent the last seven years of his life. Besides paintings of the Great Man and his Kaisers, you can see his letters, boots, pistols and floppy hat.

Schleswig-Holstein

The country's northernmost state links Germany to the Danish peninsula and was administered jointly with the Danes until 1866. Off the windswept dunes of the North Sea coast to the west are the island resorts of Sylt, Föhr, Amrum and the Halligen archipelago. The Baltic coast to the east is commanded by the naval port city of Kiel—the state capital, and the old Hanseatic trading centre of Lübeck via its harbour at Travemünde, now a seaside resort. In the rural interior, green heathland and cattle pastures are dotted with windmills and thatched cottages. The fish stews and cottage hams are justly famous.

Lübeck

The town was built up by Henry the Lion in the 12th century as a centre for Baltic trade and launching pad for eastern colonization. Today, German unification and the Baltic republics' independence are bringing back the source of Lübeck's old prosperity. Viewed from the west along the Trave canal linking the Elbe to the Baltic, the steepled skyline evokes the quiet dignity of the town's ancient role as headquarters of the Hanseatic league.

Skirt the town's medieval fortifications, for which the canal serves as a moat, and come in from the north through the sturdy but elegant brick **Burgtor**, a bastion built in 1444 and topped off by a baroque cupola. In the old days, this was the only way into town. Down Grosse Burgstrasse, tall redbrick façades make an imposing

*L*übeck's Holstentor gatehouse stands guard near the canal which since the 14th century has served the town as a protective moat.

impression. On the left, the **Heiligen-Geist-Hospital** (Holy Ghost hospital) is a fine Gothic edifice completed in the 14th century, its three redbrick gables separated by slim pointed turrets. It now serves as a home for the aged.

Opposite, over on Breite Strasse, is the equally venerable seamen's tavern, **Haus der Schiffergesellschaft**. Characters right out of a novel by Joseph Conrad drown their sorrows at long dark wooden tables and benches beneath brass lanterns of uncertain age hanging from the beams.

In the little Gothic **Jakobikirche**, take a look at the splendidly carved wooden organ lofts dating from the 16th and 17th centuries.

THOSE TERRIBLE MANN BOYS

There was no love lost between the Mann brothers and Lübeck. They disliked the city's mercantile atmosphere in general and their father's warehouse business in particular. Heinrich, four years older than Thomas, fled the "stink of millions" first to Dresden and then to Berlin where he achieved fame as the author of *The Blue Angel*. The novel's ridiculed hero, Professor Unrat—Emil Jannings in the film, falling for showgirl Marlene Dietrich—was modelled on Heinrich's Latin teacher in Lübeck. At high school, Thomas was noted only "satisfactory" in his German classes, "defective" in gym. A schoolmate joyfully recalls the future Nobel prizewinner's contempt for the parallel bars. Family and town alike were deeply insulted by *Buddenbrooks*. Uncle Friedrich, depicted in the novel as hypochondriac, Christian Buddenbrooks, took out an advertisement in a Lübeck newspaper to protest. "It is a sad bird that fouls his own nest," Uncle declared. When Thomas returned 50 years later to receive the Freedom of the City, half the council walked out.

South on Königstrasse, at No. 11, the handsome **Behnhaus** (1777) is one of the town's rare neoclassical edifices, now a museum of 19th- and 20th-century art including: Romantics Caspar David Friedrich, and Expressionists Edvard Munch, Erich Heckel, Oskar Kokoschka, August Macke and Max Beckmann. In the adjoining **Drägerhaus** are neoclassical works of local painter Friedrich Overbeck and, almost reluctantly, busts and a few memorabilia of the town's most famous sons, novelists Heinrich and Thomas Mann.

The 14th-century **Katharinenkirche** has also been converted into a museum, devoted to religious art. In niches on the western façade are three Ernst Barlach sculptures (1930–32), part of a cycle stopped by the Nazis and completed in 1945 by Gerhard Marcks. A highlight inside is Tintoretto's *Awakening of Lazarus* (1576).

Turn down the Glockengiesser-strasse to a baroque sandstone archway at No. 23. Beyond is a collection of charming old houses set in a peaceful flower-bedecked courtyard, **Füchtingshof**. These, and similar homes at No. 49, the **Glandorpshof** (and Domeshof over at Schumacherstrasse 15), were gifts to the poor by Lübeck's prosperous merchants of the 17th century.

Cut over to Breite Strasse to the superb 14th-century twin-steepled **Marienkirche**,

The beach baskets at Travemünde offer shelter from wind or flying sand, and privacy even on a crowded day. If you want the sun, just pull back the lid.

built by the town's patricians as a defiant response to the cathedral. It is a masterly translation into local brick of the style set by the great Gothic cathedrals of northern France. It in turn set the pattern for Gothic churches throughout the Baltic region. The church holds Buxtehude organ concerts in honour of the Danish composer who worked here in the 17th century.

Facing the north side at Mengstrasse 4 is the white baroque-gabled **Buddenbrooks House** where Thomas Mann was born in 1875 and set the family saga of his brilliant first novel, completed at the age of 25. The house is now a bank.

The **town hall** is a model of civic pride. The ornate façade of dark glazed brick has gables pierced with round windows under blind Gothic arches, topped by a parade of pointed turrets. A Renaissance staircase was added in 1594 on the Breite Strasse.

West of the town hall is the monumental gatehouse, **Holstentor**, with two massive pepperpot towers. It houses the town history museum, notably displaying a model of the city in the 17th century, weapons, ship models and some rather nice instruments of torture.

On the south side of town, the **cathedral** is Romanesque with a huge Gothic chancel added in the 14th century. Dominating the choir is Bernt Notke's magnificent *Triumphal Cross* (1477). The *Crucifixion*, with 24 smaller Old Testament figures surrounding Jesus on the Cross, is flanked by statues of Adam,

Mary and Mary Magdalen to the left, and the Bishop of Lübeck, Apostle John and Eve to the right. Beyond the Triumphal Cross is a 17th-century rood screen and clock on sandstone pillars.

Nearby at St-Annen-Strasse 15, the **St Anna convent** serves now as a museum for the richest treasures salvaged from Lübeck's war-damaged churches. The highlight is Hans Memling's grandiose *Passion Altar* (1491) from the cathedral.

Travemünde

At the mouth of the Trave river, as its name suggests, the town is Lübeck's seaside resort, 16km (10 miles) to the east. At once chic and provincial, it has fine sandy beaches and a choice of old-fashioned spa hotels and casino or ultra-modern sports-oriented facilities. In the yachting harbour, Sunday sailors love the **Passat**, a 56m (185ft) four-master that now serves as a training ship and nautical museum. Car ferries sail from Travemünde for Scandinavian ports.

Kiel

From a sleepy fishing port under the Holstein dukes, Kaiser Wilhelm I turned the capital of Schleswig-Holstein into a home for the Reich's new navy. As the chief base for the Third Reich's naval operations, it was comprehensively bombed and has been rebuilt as a modern city. In June, the colourful international Kiel Week regatta attracts 3,000 sailing boats.

Stroll alongside the ships on the airy **Hindenburgufer**, a 3km (1.5-mile) sea promenade, or take a cruise out into the **Kieler Förde** (Kiel Fjord) to visit on the west shore the sailing harbour of Schilksee and beach resort of Strande. At the east shore resort of **Heikendorf**, a World War

The ancient craft of thatching with straw or reeds, common throughout Schleswig-Holstein, keeps houses warm in winter and cool in summer.

II submarine (*U-Boot*) stands as a monument on the beach. **Laboe** has a mighty Naval Memorial and a tower shaped like a ship's stern, 87m (285ft) tall, erected in 1936. The observation platform gives you a good view of the fjord. At the base of the monument is a **nautical museum** (*Historische Halle*), tracing the region's maritime past from the Vikings to the merchant and colonial shipping of the 19th century and the warships of World War II. The U-995 submarine stands outside.

The best place to see the Kiel Canal linking the North Sea to the Baltic is the **Holtenau lock** (*Schleuse*). Over 50,000 ships pass through each year, making it the busiest in the world.

Schleswig

It can claim to be the oldest town in the Baltic region, growing out of the ancient Viking capital of Haithabu on the Schlei inlet. (Excavations of the south shore settlement can be visited off Highway 76.) The **archaeological museum** (*Archäologisches Landes-museum*) in the baroque Schloss Gottorf displays artefacts of the Viking era such as fish-nets, gold bowls and dishes. The prize exhibit is the 23m (75ft) **Nydam-Schiff**, a 4th-century oak boat for 36 oarsmen, miraculously preserved in the Nydam marshes across the Danish border, along with a corpse, clothes, shoes, axes and spearheads. The palace's original treasures were removed to Copenhagen in the 18th century, but the **art and cultural history museum** has decorated and furnished its halls in authentic Gothic, Renaissance and baroque style. Notice the splendid inlaid panelling of the duke's private chapel.

In the Gothic brick **cathedral**, see Hans Brüggemann's sensual, richly carved Bordesholm altar (1521) in the chancel.

Denmark's King Frederick I (1551–55) is buried here. Rest a while in the 14th-century cloisters and admire the floral motifs on the vaults.

In the old town around Friedhofplatz, you will see an attractive fishermen's quarter of squat little gabled houses festooned with climbing roses.

Seebüll

On your way to or from the island of Sylt (*see* page 261), be sure to visit the **Emil Nolde Museum** in *Haus Seebüll*, the home the great Expressionist painter, designed on a hillock rising from the marshes. From the Niebüll car-train station for Sylt, the house is a 12km (7-mile) drive north via Neukirchen, signposted *Nolde-Museum*. The display consists of some 220 paintings, watercolours and drawings of the master (1867–1956). His studio is reserved for his religious works, including the brutal, almost demonic series of nine paintings devoted to the life of Christ. A poignant feature of the museum is the collection of 1,300 "Unpainted Pictures" (*Ungemalte Bilder*), miniature watercolours executed from 1941 to 1945 when the Nazis had forbidden him to paint. The irony of Nolde's condemnation as a painter of "Degenerate Art" (*see* page 123) is that he was a vehement racist and had been an early adherent of the Nazi Party.

North Sea Islands

People do not have to be health fiends to enjoy the islands off Schleswig-Holstein and scattered along the coast north-west of Bremerhaven, but they may come back converted. The bracing sea air and exhilarating walks along the cliffs and dunes encourage them to throw their chests out and do knee-bends and press-ups they never dreamed of back home. If the surf is too rough for swimming, they can enjoy the controlled waves of the resorts' sea-water swimming pools or squelch barefoot across the islands' leeward mud flats—great for the ankles.

These North and East Frisian islands (the West Frisians are Dutch) are part of the Friesland region whose inhabitants are the butt of many malicious German jokes. Anglo-Saxons will be more respectful, for they share a common ancestry.

For Sylt, take the car-train over the causeway from Niebüll. The other North Frisian islands are served by boat from Sylt's southern port of Hörnum. East Frisian islands are served by ferry from Emden or Norddeich.

Sylt

This long sliver of dune and heath is the biggest and most popular of the North Frisian islands. Its west coast is one long 40km (25-mile) beach of fine white sand and spectacular breakers out to sea. The east coast has rippled mud flats (*Wattenmeer*) with a fascinating play of light and changing tides. At the crowded modern resort of *Westerland*, you will find smart boutiques and a casino. It boasts the island's best-equipped sea-wave swimming pool (*Wellenbad*), which is great in winter when the water is still 24°C (75°F). The aquarium is next door.

Just to the north, **Wenningstedt** is a quieter resort centred around a village pond, home to swans, ducks and gulls. Nothing much has happened here since Anglo-Saxons Hengist and Horsa left in 449 to conquer south-east England. North of the pond is the **Denghoog** burial chamber dated 2200 BC—12 giant blocks

supporting three even bigger roof slabs and believed to have been brought from Sweden, but nobody knows how.

Hike over to the **Rotes Kliff** and notice the water below turning red as it erodes the foot of the cliff. Behind the cliffs, the **Uwe Dune**, 53m (174ft) high, is a good vantage point from which to take in both the North Sea to the west and the mud flats to the east. Nature-lovers head north of Kampen to the **Vogelkoje** bird sanctuary. This old lair for duck-hunters is now a nature reserve protecting Sylt's rare woods of alder, poplar, honeysuckle and elder, and has a pond to watch for warblers, snipe and wild duck.

Sylt's most charming village is **Keitum**, on the east coast, to which Danish, Dutch and German sailors retired in the 19th century. With lovely oak-shaded gardens, some of their white-washed, thatch-roofed cottages and mansions have been converted into hotels or serve as homes for weavers, potters and other craftsmen (there is a big "green" vote here). The village's **folklore museum** (*Sylter Heimatmuseum* on Museumsweg) exhibits their predecessors' arts and crafts, costumes and nautical instruments. Next door, you can visit a fine brick-and-thatch 18th-century Frisian house with a beautiful wood-panelling interior.

Föhr

Neither fashionable nor crowded, Föhr is popular with writers, artists, musicians and those who seek the quiet life. People rent bicycles or walk everywhere, especially on 15 August (Assumption Day) when everyone joins in a hike all around the island. Locals often dress in traditional Frisian costume and favour a dialect close to old Anglo-Saxon. The main town is **Wyk**, appreciated for its mud-baths and the old fortified fishing port area where you can buy fresh prawns right off the boats. The **Frisian folklore museum** occupies a 17th-century farmhouse. The most attractive village is **Nieblum**, most jealously attached to its traditions. Known locally as the *Friesendom* (Frisian Cathedral), its 13th-century church of **St Johannis** boasts an altar carved and painted by Lübeck's Bernt Notke.

One moral imperative on any stay is the guided **mud-flat ramble** from Dunsum Deich in a 3km (1.5-mile) crescent across to the bird sanctuary on the neighbouring island of Amrum. Tides rarely permit a return trip on foot, so come back by ferry.

Amrum

Half of this small but pretty island is dunes, some of them up to 32m (100ft) high, and surrounded by pine groves. Very much a place to bike and hike. Visit the old weaving establishments at **Nebel** in the middle of the island or the **Odde bird sanctuary** at its northern tip, but avoid the tourist trap of Wittdün port.

Halligen

This archipelago of ten windswept islets, sand-spits and mere hillocks rising from the sea really gets you away from it *all*. For a moment of simple, austere solitude, make for **Hooge**, 550 hectares (1,360 acres) of dune. No cars—just cattle, sheep, seals and fisherfolk. Old whalers' houses perch in tiny clusters each on an artificial mound (*Warft*), the ultimate sandcastle. On the biggest, *Hanswarft*, one dwelling is grandly known as *Königshaus* (King's House) to honour Denmark's Frederick VI, who stayed there in 1826. You can see the splendidly sculpted Frisian tile-stove that warmed him up.

Heligoland (*Helgoland*)

Some 50km (30 miles) west of the Schleswig-Holstein coast (but accessible by boat from Cuxhaven or Hamburg), this old British possession was swapped for Zanzibar in 1890, used as a German military base in World War II and blown up by the British Army in 1947. (A lone, duly commemorated mulberry tree survived.) The island has been rebuilt as one big duty-free shop in a delightful natural setting of red cliffs and greenery. After they have stocked up with whisky and brandy, visitors take a bracing walk along the cliffs. See the **Oberland bird sanctuary** and take in the spectacular view from the towering *Lange Anna cliff*, 60m (200ft). The neighbouring Düne islet has some pleasant beaches.

East Frisians

The islands serve as a breakwater strung out along the mainland coast. Quiet little **Borkum** has good beaches on its north coast and mud-flats to the south. With its splendid dune walks, **Norderney** is Germany's oldest North Sea resort, founded in 1797, and has a certain panache. Its sea-wave swimming pool was Germany's first. The **Fischerhaus Museum** offers a good insight into Frisian traditions. The sandy beaches and charming fishing village on tiny **Baltrum**, just 6.5 km^2 (2 square miles), make it popular with families.

Bremen

Real style and pride exude from this great Hanseatic city-state with its port on the Weser river. Besides its heavy industry—steel, oil, electronics and textiles—it roasts most of the coffee for Germany's divine pastry shops.

The "Bremen Town Musicians": figures of a donkey, dog, cat and cockerel from a Grimms' fairy tale have become a symbol of the city.

Marktplatz

To feel the town's civic spirit, just stand on this superb market square, one of the finest urban ensembles in the country. Its façades vary from plain Gothic gables to the ornate scrolled step-gabling with pinnacles and statuary that created the style known as "Weser Renaissance".

The early 15th-century **town hall** is a magnificent brick edifice with steeply pitched roof and graceful arcades to which a Renaissance gabled façade was added in 1612. Facing the square, between the lofty windows, are statues of Charlemagne and the prince-electors—the originals are in the Focke Museum (*see* page 265)—with Old Testament prophets and ancient philosophers around the sides. Inside, a spiral staircase leads to the grand **Obere Halle** with Bartholomäus Bruyn's painting of *Solomon's Judgment* (1532), counselling wisdom to the city elders. The ceiling of ornate roof-beams is hung with monumental models of sailing ships from Bremen's maritime heyday—from the 16th to the 18th centuries. Along the wall facing the Marktplatz is the opulent **Güldenkammer**, the council chamber, in Heinrich Vogeler's renewed *Jugendstil* design with inlaid panelling and gold leather wall-hangings. Even the basement **Ratskeller** is no ordinary tavern. More properly known as *Rates Weinkeller* (the council's wine cellar), it serves beneath its hallowed vaults (1408) no beer but "only" 600 different German wines, the best selection in Germany. See the 18th-century wine barrels, but don't be tempted to sample the oldest wine, a 1653 Rüdesheimer—it costs a couple of thousand marks a sip and, according to the *sommelier*, tastes awful.

Under a Gothic canopy in front of the town hall stands a much revered but faintly comical 15th-century **statue of Roland**, Charlemagne's loyal knight. He is protected by the imperial double-headed eagle, with a modesty belt across his tights.

On the square's south-west side is the handsome Renaissance merchant's guildhall, the **Schütting**, designed by Lüder von Bentheim to match the façade he had put on the town hall. To the east, **St Petri Dom** is a noble twin-steepled cathedral, rebuilt in the 16th and 19th centuries, but still Romanesque and Gothic in its interior, with fine fan vaulting. The 16th-century organ loft has sculptures of Charlemagne and Bremen's first bishop. Notice, too, the finely carved 17th-century pulpit.

Down to the Weser

Behind the Schütting, **Böttcherstrasse**, a street of distinctively designed art galleries, boutiques, taverns, theatre and museums, leads from the Marktplatz to the river. It was a 1920s brainchild of industrialist Ludwig Roselius, who made a fortune decaffeinating coffee. On the street's west side are traditional redbrick and stone gabled houses facing more complex sculptural forms by Expressionist artist Bernard Hoetger. **Roselius House**, No. 6, rebuilt from a merchant's mansion of the 16th century, is a museum for the industrialist's private collection of German Gothic and Renaissance art. Outstanding are works by Lucas Cranach and Tilman Riemenschneider. A Gothic room includes 15th-century wood sculpture from Wienhausen Abbey. The **Paula Becker-Modersohn House** next door is largely devoted to the sober Expressionistic paintings of this exceptional member of of the Worpswede artists' colony (*see* page 266).

To the east, between Kolpingstrasse and the river, the **Schnoor** is a quaint old fishermen's quarter of gaily repainted cottages from the 15th to 17th century. Not all the restaurants, craftware shops and galleries are tourist traps. Trust your instinct.

The Port

Two out of every five adults in Bremen are employed in the port, which handles

*B*remen's reconstructed 17th-century Gewerbehaus (guildhall) served originally as a banquet hall. Its scrolled gables and lattice windows offer a fine example of Weser Renaissance architecture.

cotton, wool, coffee, wood, copper and ore. **Boat tours** leave from the Martinskirche landing stage for three main harbours, Übersee-, Europa- and Neustädter Hafen.

Museums

The city's prosperity is reflected in the wealth of its museum collections. At the **Kunsthalle** art gallery, Am Wall 207, be sure to see Albrecht Altdorfer's *Geburt Christi* (Birth of Christ, 1507), and the *Himmelfahrt Mariae* (The Assumption, 1752) by Franz Anton Maulpertsch, the most brilliant of Germany's baroque painters. Other major German artists represented here are Lucas Cranach, Caspar David Friedrich, Max Beckmann, Lovis Corinth, and the Worpswede group, led by Paula Becker-Modersohn. Besides baroque works by Solimena and Tiepolo, a masterpiece in the Italian collection is a *Madonna* (1423) by Masolini da Panicale, Masaccio's collaborator at the Brancacci Chapel. The Dutch and Flemish include van Dyck, van Goyen, Rubens and Rembrandt. Among the French here are Delacroix, Simone Vouet, Courbet, and Manet, Monet, Cézanne and Pissarro.

The **Überseemuseum** (Overseas Museum), Bahnhofplatz 13, emphasizes Bremen's maritime link through trade to remote continents. Attractively displayed cultural and anthropological exhibits of Africa and Asia include a reconstructed Papuan village, Chinese house and Japanese Shinto temple in a traditional garden.

In a pleasant park (with restaurant), the **Focke Museum**, Schwachhauser Heerstrasse 240, houses a splendid collection of art and cultural history. The town hall's Gothic statues are here, along with a colourful display of costumes, china and furnishings from the Renaissance and baroque homes of Bremen patricians. Shipping history is traced from prehistoric vessels via Roman and early Saxon craft to the whalers and ocean liners of modern times. The nearby **Riensberg House** presents an authentic 18th-century farmhouse with rustic costume, furniture and toys.

Worpswede

Just 25km (16 miles) to the north, this intriguing artists' colony is signposted from Bremen city centre. The sleepy farming village, once surrounded by a peat bog, was "discovered" in 1884 by Düsseldorf art student Fritz Mackensen. Fellow artists Heinrich Vogeler, Bernard Hoetger, and Otto Modersohn and his wife Paula Becker-Modersohn were also attracted by the surrounding moorland, mild climate and, above all, the striking luminosity of the sky at all seasons. The poet Rainer Maria Rilke was a frequent visitor. They formed no school of painting wedded to a "Worpswede" style, but a group of independent artists happy to work near each other in congenial surroundings, exhibiting with success in Munich, Bremen and Berlin.

Today, the play of colour remains bewitching—a sky infused with mauves and reds, meadows a bright green, fields of brilliant yellow colza set off by strips of deep black soil. Painters, sculptors, weavers and potters once again work in the studios. The original group's homes, often of their own design, are now museums and galleries. In a park adjoining the fanciful Café Worpswede, designed in 1925 by sculptor-architect Bernard Hoetger, the main museum of the original group is the **Grosse Kunstschau**, Lindenallee 3. Vogeler's house, *Barkenhof*, at Osterdorfer Strasse 10, is now a handsome museum and home for foreign artists. His own work, including his *Jugendstil* furniture and paintings from his Soviet exile, is exhibited at the **Haus im Schluh**, Im Schluh 35. In the town cemetery, visit the **tomb of Paula Becker-Modersohn**, with its poignant sculpture by Bernard Hoetger.

Bremerhaven

Bremen's sea port was founded in 1827 for transatlantic liners and still serves cruise ships and ferries, but its **fishing port** is the main attraction, especially for the weekday auctions at 7 a.m.

In the Old Port (*Alter Hafen*), visit the splendid **German Maritime Museum** (*Deutsches Schiffahrtsmuseum*), Van-Ronzelen-Strasse. This open-air museum has its own port for 80 vessels and 500 models which you can steer yourself. The oldest boat-relic dates from the end of the Ice Age. A single-sail Hanseatic cog boat (*Hanse-Kogge*) of 1380 was found in the port in 1962. From a luxury liner, the museum has salvaged a cabin, deck, bridge and bell.

Cuxhaven

Autobahn 27 from Bremen continues north to this major fishing and ferry port commanding the mouth of the Elbe. Transatlantic liners dock here, as do ferries for Heligoland and the North Frisian islands. The best vantage point to observe the port traffic is the *Alte Liebe* pier, its name distorting that of the good ship *Olivia* wrecked here in 1732.

The emblem of Cuxhaven is a large beacon, the *Kugelbake*, at the end of a breakwater, marking the geographical mouth of the Elbe.

The town also boasts a unique **Shipwreck Museum** (*Wrackmuseum*), Dorfstrasse 80. Centuries of fascinating ship relics have been dredged up from the Elbe and Weser estuaries and off the North Sea coast—giant anchors, prows, cannons, figureheads, even a complete pocket-size submarine.

Walsrode

This magnificent **bird sanctuary** (*Vogelpark*) lies 56km (35 miles) southeast of Bremen, just off the Hanover Autobahn. Ornithologists count 900 species among the 5,000 birds, the large majority wandering free—among them, penguins, emus, ostriches, pelicans, cranes, herons and pink flamingoes. Visit the parrot house (*Papageienhaus*) and tropical bird hall (*Paradieshalle*). Botanical attractions in this beautifully laid out park covering 22 hectares (54 acres) include Rhododendron Valley and an exquisite rose garden.

Lower Saxony

Farming and cattle raising are the state's chief occupations. At the centre of the heath and moorland, an industrial belt stretches from Osnabrück in the west via the capital, Hanover, to Wolfsburg, home of the Volkswagen. The dukes have gone, but their palaces in Celle, Brunswick and Wolfenbüttel are reminders of a golden past. Hildesheim has done a heroic job of restoring its exemplary Romanesque churches. The region's fairy-tale world lives on with the ghost of the Pied Piper of Hamlin and the witches of the Harz mountains.

Celle

Its heyday as a ducal residence has left an elegant mark on this garrison town for British and German troops at the southern

---

SAUCE FOR THE GOOSE

Princess Sophie Dorothea, born in the Ducal Palace at Celle in 1666, seemed to have it all. Her sophisticated French Huguenot mother Eléonore had given her a taste for the good things in life. She was beautiful and spirited. If the cousin she married, England's future King George I, was a boor, she did at least fulfil her dynastic obligations, providing an heir for the English throne and a queen for Prussia's Soldier King, Friedrich Wilhelm I. While George pursued his many mistresses, Sophie fell for her childhood chum, Count Philipp Königsmarck. When he discovered their love letters, George had the count murdered and Sophie banished for life to the isolated Ahlden Castle.

---

edge of Lüneburg Heath. The Hanoverian dukes held court here from 1378 to 1705—before taking over the English throne. The stud-farm founded by King George II in 1732 still provides a splendid stallion parade every autumn.

The **Ducal Palace** reflects the styles of those three centuries. Its superb chapel has Gothic vaulting, opulent Renaissance organ loft and pulpit, and an altar painting of the *Crucifixion* (1569) by Flemish artist Martin de Vos. The baroque court theatre (1674) is the oldest still in use today in Germany.

Opposite the palace, the **Bomann Museum**, Schlossplatz 7, is devoted to Hanoverian folklore, including a reconstructed 16th-century farmhouse. The old town rectangle east of the palace displays the Weser Renaissance style of scrolled step-gables and pinnacles. The pale yellow 16th-century **town hall** is a fine example, with its slender oriel projecting from the roof. See also the **Hoppener House** (1532), Poststrasse 8, and the 17th-century **Stechinelli House**, Am Grossen Plan 14.

South of the old town, in the French Garden (*Französischer Garten*), is a very informative **Beekeeping Museum,** Wehlstrasse 4a, honey being a major product of the Lüneburg Heath.

Bergen-Belsen

Some 25km (16 miles) north-west on Highway 3, the **Concentration Camp Memorial** (*Gedenkstätte*) is a simple obelisk with a tribute in 13 languages to the victims of the Nazi terror. Mounds mark the common graves, including that of Dutch schoolgirl Anne Frank. The camp installations have been razed.

Hanover (*Hannover*)

The capital of Lower Saxony, now largely industrial, and devoted to rubber, records and car manufacture, has proud cultural traditions. Philosopher Gottfried Leibniz was the court librarian and Georg Händel the court composer—both in Hanover and, after the duke became King George I, in London.

The royal palace was destroyed in World War II, but its baroque **Herrenhausen Gardens** on the north-west side of

---

RETURN TICKET, HANOVER–LONDON

The Hanoverian claim to the British throne arose from the marriage of Duke Ernst August to Sophia, grand-daughter of James I. Their son became George I of Great Britain in 1714, though he could not speak a word of English. Since Hanoverian dynastic tradition accepted only male rulers, all future claim to the throne was renounced when Victoria became queen in 1837. The arch-conservative Duke of Cumberland, Victoria's uncle, went off in a huff to become King of Hanover.

---

town continue the musical tradition with opera, ballet and symphonic concerts throughout the summer—and delightful walks all year round. Surrounded by a Dutch moat, the **Grosser Garten** is laid out in French style with geometrical flower beds, classical statuary, a maze, open-air theatre and, between them, a fountain soaring over 80m (nearly 270ft) into the air. **Berggarten** is a botanical garden rich in orchids and cacti.

Badly bombed, the city is now resolutely modern, but one of its best 20th-century buildings is pre-war, Fritz Hoeger's *Anzeiger-Hochhaus* (1928). It can also claim some of north Germany's finest art museums. The **Niedersächsische Landesgalerie**, Am Maschpark 5, has a first-class collection of Flemish and Dutch art, French Impressionists, German Romantics, early Expressionists and the Worpswede group. At the **Sprengel Museum**, Kurt-Schwitters-Platz, highlights of its 20th-century collection are collages by Hanover-born Schwitters and a strong group of Blauer Reiter works by Kandinsky, Marc, Macke and Klee. A Calder stabile rises from the lake. An attractive curiosity is the **Bahlsen Biscuit Museum**, Podbielski-strasse 11, housed in the company's *Jugendstil* offices and showrooms, with biscuit tins and advertising posters designed by major artists—Heinrich Vogeler, Bernhard Hoetger and Peter Behrens.

*H*anover's 19th-century town hall mixes Gothic, Renaissance and baroque, but when architect Heinrich Tramm resisted the city fathers' request for a little Jugendstil too, he was fired.

Hildesheim

Only islands of old half-timbered houses have survived from the grand medieval city destroyed in World War II, but the major churches which made it one of Europe's most important cities of Romanesque architecture have been lovingly reconstructed.

The majestic buff sandstone **cathedral** (1035) has recovered its original simplicity. The Gothic side chapels remain, but it has been stripped of all baroque modifications except the elegant lantern dome over the transept. Kept safe in the war, Bishop Bernward's 11th-century bronze doors stand once more in the west narthex with beautifully wrought scenes of Adam and Eve and Christ's Passion. Other treasures include a giant chandelier (1060) over the transept crossing, symbolizing celestial Jerusalem, and at the end of the north aisle a 13th-century stone baptismal font supported by allegorical figures of the Apocalypse. In the cloister off the south transept, the "thousand-year" rose bush which Emperor Ludwig is said to have planted here, miraculously blooming again in 1945, may well be 500 years old.

Reconstruction has also recaptured the noble quality of the fortress-like **St Michael's church**, originally part of a Benedictine abbey. This jewel among Hildesheim's Romanesque churches has apses east and west, and round towers flanking a massive square tower, a veritable castle-keep, over the transept crossing. Stored away during the war, the biblical scenes of the 13th-century painted wooden ceiling are back in place. Notice, too, the carved reliefs of the choir enclosure.

The ancient Egyptian collections in the **Pelizaeus Museum**, Am Steine 1, are second in Germany only to Berlin's. A highlight is the life-size seated statue of Hemi-iunu, the vizier who built the great pyramid for Cheops in the 3rd millennium BC.

Brunswick

Braunschweig, largely industrial now, was the Welf capital of Henry the Lion in the 12th century. The most handsome vestiges of its historic centre surround the **Altstadtmarkt**, notably the step-gabled 15th-century town hall—its two wings built at right angles to each other. In the 14th-century **Pfarrkirche St Martini**, see a sculpture of St Martin at the base of the pulpit and, in the south aisle, the Annenkapelle with its sculptural groups of the Virgin Mary and Ann, and Joachim and the three Magi. The **Gewandhaus**, Guildhall of the Textile Merchants, has a sober Gothic west façade with more decorative Renaissance gables on the east side.

The **Herzog-Anton-Ulrich-Museum,** Museumstrasse 1, houses the Duke of Brunswick's magnificent collection of Flemish, Dutch and Italian masters— Rubens, Rembrandt and Vermeer, Giorgione, Palma Vecchio and Veronese.

In front of **Burg Dankwarderode**, a 19th-century neo-Romanesque reconstruction of the ducal castle, bearing an uncanny resemblance to an American Ivy League college, stands Henry's Lion monument. The original (1166), the earliest of such heraldic bronzes in Germany, is with other historic memorabilia in the **Landesmuseum**, two adjacent half-timbered 16th-century houses on Burgplatz.

The late Gothic **cathedral** of St Blasius has a rather ponderous façade of twin octagonal towers joined by a gabled belfry, but is notable for the spindled columns of its interior and the tomb of Henry and his English wife Mathilda in the nave.

Wolfenbüttel

The elegant, airy town has preserved the impressive Renaissance urban planning of the dukes of Brunswick. In the **Heinrichstadt** quarter, east of the palace, the squares have been laid out in strict rectangles, and the streets are so straight that an exception is named Krumme Strasse, "Bent Street". Take a look at the the court officials' fine half-timbered houses with ornate oriel bay windows on Kanzlei-, Reichs- and Harz streets. On the Stadtmarkt, the brick-and-beam **town hall** is formed by two adjoining 17th-century mansions.

With the Oker river serving as a moat, the medieval **palace** was baroquified by the dukes of the 18th-century Enlightenment. Duke August's **library** has amassed 600,000 books and manuscripts that make it a centre of international research, especially in the field of music and cartography. The handsome Renaissance building on the north side of the palace square is the **arsenal** (*Zeughaus*), housing part of the library. The playwright Gottfried Ephraim Lessing was court librarian from 1770 to 1781. In his graceful home, **Lessinghaus** (now a museum), he wrote *Nathan der Weise*, inspired by his friend, the Jewish thinker Mosel Mendelssohn.

On the west side of the city centre, the classical ochre and white façade of **Trinitätskirche** (1719), incorporating two towers of the old city gate, has the charming look of an orangery. The characteristic Weser Renaissance scrolled gable and statuary verge on the rococo, an impression emphasized by the theatre-like rich golden interior. In this Protestant church, a decorative pulpit has taken the place of a high altar.

The late-Gothic **Marienkirche** on the Kornmarkt, with its slender lantern tower, has also acquired an ornate Renaissance façade, festooned with some 250 angels and masks. Statues of the 12 Apostles stand on the buttresses, Peter and Paul on the west façade.

Harz Mountains

The mountain barrier to winds sweeping across the north German plain from Poland gathers a romantic misty melancholy about its pine forests with their woodmen's huts and hints of dark fairies and Hänsel and Gretel.

A driving tour should start out from the attractive mining town of **Goslar**—silver giving way to lead and zinc in the nearby Rammelsberg mines. Its old town is among the best preserved in northern Germany. The 15th-century **town hall** has a dignified Chamber of Homage (*Huldigungssaal*), with the German emperors portrayed on the walls and Life of Christ on the ceiling. Craftsmen and merchants here were proud people, and it is hard to decide which is more imposing, the **Cloth-Cutters' Guildhall** (*Haus Kaiserworth*, now a restaurant) on Marktplatz, the **Bakers' Guildhall**, Marktstrasse 45, or the magistrate's towering **Haus Brusttuch**, now the chamber of commerce, Hoher Weg, all built in the 16th century. Hans Siemens, founder of the great industrial dynasty, was a Goslar brewer living in a fine 17th-century house at Siemensstrasse 12.

Follow the Oker river south as it babbles between granite cliffs to a **waterfall** near the Romkerhalle power station. Beyond is the pretty **Oker-Stausee** reservoir.

The popular winter sports resort **Braunlage** is also a good summer base for rambles into its surrounding parks and forests. Cut back west via **St Andreasberg**, where you can visit the disused

Samson silver mine. The winding Harz Hochstrasse, Highway 242, offers some spectacular mountain views on its way over to Clausthal-Zellerfeld which, with Goslar, is the major mining centre of the Harz. The **Oberharzer Bergwerk-museum**, Bornhardstrasse 16, gives you a fascinating insight into old mining methods. Visit, too, the Holy Ghost parish church (1642), built entirely of wood.

Hamlin (*Hameln*)

On the Weser river, the town of the Pied Piper flourished in the Middle Ages as a member of the Hanseatic League. Today, happily calling itself the *Rattenfängerstadt* (Rat-Catcher Town), it makes a fortune from the legend of the fellow who piped away first the rats and then the kids—providing weekly Pied Piper parades, marzipan rats and other associated paraphernalia. The town is, in any case, worth a visit for its houses—built in the handsome Weser Renaissance style of scrolled gables and pinnacles long after the piper left.

Osterstrasse is the centre of the old town. The **Hochzeitshaus** (Wedding House), now the town hall, is where the Pied Piper plays not a flute but a clarinet, every Sunday at noon, joined by kids dressed up as rats—two birds with one stone? An ornamental clock enacts the tale at 1 and 5.30 p.m. The town's two finest houses, **Leisthaus** and **Stiftsherrenhaus**, at Osterstrasse 8 and 9, have been combined as a museum giving the Pied Piper legend the full treatment, both as folklore and history. A grand added attraction is the array of 11,000 tin soldiers at the 1866 Battle of Langensalza between the Hanoverian and Prussian armies. Other superb Renaissance houses are at Osterstrasse 28 and Bäckerstrasse 16, both restaurants.

"YOU DIRTY RATS!"

So this is the story: in 1284, a stranger wearing a brightly coloured tunic and tights promised the mayor and aldermen to rid the town of its plague of rats—for suitable remuneration. The city fathers agreed, but after he had lured the rats away with his flute and led them to drown in the river, they refused to cough up the reward. The Pied Piper bided his time till Sunday, 26 June, when the adults were in church, and then enticed the children out of their houses with his magic flute. They all disappeared, leaving just two behind, one blind who heard the flute and one deaf and dumb who saw them all go and did not know why.

Scholars offer a historical explanation: the "children" were in fact citizens of Hamlin, adults and children alike, who had been press-ganged into colonizing Germany's eastern territories.

Hämelschenburg

At the edge of the Weser valley just 11km (7 miles) south of Hamlin, this 16th-century castle makes a pleasant excursion both for its masterly expression of Weser Renaissance architecture and a walk in the surrounding woods. The owners have built a pyramid there as the family mausoleum.

Göttingen

The town, as Heinrich Heine said after being thrown out for duelling, "is famous for its sausage and university". Indeed, with Heidelberg, Marburg and Tübingen, it makes up Germany's quartet of great university towns, where students have long enjoyed a special status similar to that of Oxford and Cambridge. In the old days, students wandered regularly from one to the other like journeymen weavers, masons or other craftsmen. Today, the **Marktplatz** is the main meeting place for the students, gathering around the *Jugendstil* **Gänseliesel fountain** (1901), and drinking coffee in the outdoor cafés in summer or beer in the **Ratskeller** in winter. By tradition, everyone awarded a doctorate by the university must kiss the "Goose Girl", whose statue tops the fountain. Among the fine old half-timbered houses, the most decorative is the 16th-century **Junkernschänke inn**, Barfüsserstrasse 5, richly ornamented with medallions of Old Testament figures and the house owners at the corner. Some of the oldest houses stand on Rote Strasse—13th-century at No. 25, 14th-century at No. 40.

Münden

Founded where the Fulda and Werra rivers flow together to form the Weser, the town enjoys a beautiful setting in a basin surrounded by dense forest. Home of Göttingen University's forestry department, it offers a superb nature reserve for ramblers. In the old town, stroll around the picturesque houses on Burgstrasse, the **Haus zur Windmühle** on Ziegelstrasse, and Lange Strasse leading over to the venerable 14th-century **Werra Bridge**. In the late-Gothic parish church of **St Blasius**, see the sandstone pulpit supported by men riding dragons which are themselves riding lions. Opposite is the imposing 17th-century **town hall**.

Ruhr District

In the state of North Rhineland-Westphalia, the Ruhr epitomizes German economic and industrial might—a vast concentration of coal, iron, steel, machinery and textile production served by an intense railway and autobahn network. Fortunately for the visitor, the region's great cities have enormous energy but also an obsession to maintain a cultural counterbalance to that heavy industry.

Essen

Since the war, the home of Krupp has moved its steel works out of town to replace them by machine manufacture. The town is pleasantly and strikingly *green*, making full use of the **Gruga Park** on the south-west side, 70 hectares (173 acres) of botanical gardens, aquariums, fountains and charming restaurants. The **Grugabahn** is a miniature railway to take you around it.

On Burgplatz, the **Münsterkirche**, one of the oldest churches in Germany, has been rebuilt and boasts two magnificent treasures from the original 10th-century edifice: the *Golden Madonna* (980) in the north chapel and a huge, seven-branch bronze candelabra with geometric patterns (990) in the nave.

Essen gives high priority to its cultural life, led by the Folkwang-Hochschule for music, theatre and dance. The striking new **Opera House** by Finnish architect Alvar Aalto is worth a look even if you are unable to get a ticket. The **Folkwang Museum**, Goethestrasse 41, displays an outstanding collection of French and German painting and sculpture of the 19th and 20th centuries, but also has an impressive section devoted to the American avant-garde.

*E*urope's biggest brewer, Dortmund, also considers itself to be the best. There is a museum of brewing here, tracing the history of the industry which began here in the Middle Ages.

For shopping, fashionable boutiques on **Ketwiger** and **Limberger Strasse** compare with the best in Germany.

The town's working life is well handled at two museums on Kennedy-platz. **Haus Industrieform** is devoted to modern industrial design. The **Ruhrland Museum** deals with the living and labour conditions of German workers in the 19th and 20th centuries.

Dortmund

This formidable steel centre also has an old trading tradition as a member of the Hanseatic league and is still active in the wheat and sugar trade. Connoisseurs consider the beer of its six breweries the best in Germany.

North-east of the market, two important churches have been rebuilt. Romanesque-Gothic **Marienkirche** deserves a visit to see Conrad von Soest's splendid altar painting of the *Virgin* (1420). In the Gothic **Reinoldikirche**, with its 104m (340ft) tower, see the 14th-century statues of Charlemagne and St Reinold in the chancel.

The **Museum am Ostwall**, Ostwall 7, puts the emphasis on German Expressionists: August Macke, Max Beckmann, Paula Becker-Modersohn, Emil Nolde and Karl Schmidt-Rottluff, but there is also a first-rate collection of American and European avant-garde.

The **Brewery Museum**, Märkische Strasse 85, traces 700 years of local beer history and shows how the ale is made.

South of the city centre, as if to prove air pollution can be beaten, **Westphalia Park** has a superb Rose Garden with over 3,000 varieties.

Düsseldorf

Banker and clerk for the Ruhr's industrial magnates, the capital of North Rhineland-Westphalia brings a little chic and sophistication to the factory belt. The town is a major centre for fashion designers.

The girls walk along its famous **Königsallee** with a spring in their step and a sparkle in their eye to match any on the Champs-Elysées or Fifth Avenue. The wide, long, straight avenue, known simply as the "Kö", is a masterpiece of urban elegance. It has a fountain and waterway running down the middle, with swans swimming through the reflection of the overhanging chestnut trees. Its west side is rather sombre, lined with banks and insurance companies, while the east side catches the afternoon sun and is known as the *Schokoladenseite*. This is where you sit on the café-terraces, buy pastries and chocolates in the dainty shops and *haute couture* in the boutiques.

The prize exhibit at the regional art museum, **Kunstsammlung Nordrhein-West-falen**, Grabbeplatz 5, is a donation of 88 works by Paul Klee, shown in rotation. His contemporaries Kokoschka, Macke, Marc and Nolde are also well represented. Look out, too, for Picasso, Braque and Juan Gris, the Dada and Surrealist collection and American works— Pollock, Kline and Rauschenberg.

The **Municipal Art Museum** (Städtisches Kunstmuseum), Ehrenhof 5, has a magnificent collection of glass: 5,000 pieces from antiquity to the present day, with special emphasis on *Jugendstil*. It is also strong in modern textiles, furniture and industrial design since the 1920s.

West of the Kö on Schwanenmarkt is a striking modern **Heinrich Heine monument** by Bernd Gerresheim. This

---

"... WOULD SMELL AS SWEET"

Built where Napoleon razed old fortifications, Düsseldorf's prized thoroughfare was named Kastanienallee (Chestnut Avenue) until Prussia's Friedrich Wilhelm IV paid a visit in the turbulent year of 1848. Radicals pelted him with horse manure ("horse apples" in the delicate German term) and city fathers sought to make amends by renaming the street Königsallee (King's Avenue).

Vexiergesicht, a face disintegrated like a puzzle, conjures up the complexities of Germany's greatest poet after Goethe— some hesitate to say "after". Heine (1797–1856) was born in Düsseldorf during the French occupation. He converted to Protestantism in the hope of overcoming anti-semitic discrimination in the university world, and then pursued his taste for French culture to Paris as an antidote to Germany's repressive intellectual atmosphere in 1830. But he kept his melancholy-ironic, German-Jewish view of the world.

On Marktplatz in the old town, notice the fine **equestrian statue** of another Francophile, 18th-century Prince-Elector Jan Willem, a popular local hero, and ponder Heine's comment:

"As a boy, I heard the tale that the artist who cast this statue noticed during the casting that he did not have enough metal. The citizens came running up with their silver spoons to complete the casting. And I stood for hours in front of the statue wondering how many silver spoons were in it and how many apple tarts you could get for all that silver. Apple pies, you see, were my passion then—now it is love, truth, freedom and crab soup."

The Heart-Warming City Where The Cold War Began— and Ended

Is there a city on earth more emotionally charged than Berlin? In little more than a century since it first became Germany's capital, it has excited pride for its strength, admiration for its culture, hatred as the centre of Hitler's tyranny, compassion as a bastion of post-war freedom, fear as a focus of Cold War conflict and now immense hope as a symbol of European unity. It is also a place of enthusiasm and fun. If Germany has a sense of humour, its headquarters is Berlin.

For the source of each emotion which the name Berlin evokes, the city has an appropriate symbol. Royal monuments on Unter den Linden honour the formidable Prussian past, and the Brandenburg Gate proclaims the city's regained unity. The Reichstag recalls Germany's attempts at parliamentary democracy in the 1920s, while the gigantic Olympic Stadium expresses the bombast of Hitler's dictatorship. The chaos and destruction he

*S*he has wheeled this hurdy-gurdy from Berlin to Stuttgart and back to her pitch on Unter den Linden. Behind her, the German flag flies on the Reichstag.

wreaked have a quite deliberate reminder in the bombed-out shell of the Kaiser Wilhelm Memorial Church.

Boosted by the fall of the Wall, the city is more vibrant and forward-looking than ever in its artistic, intellectual and economic activity. The Cultural Forum in the Tiergarten park is expanding its concert halls and art galleries. Western Berlin's Schiller Theatre and Schaubühne now form with the Berliner Ensemble and Deutsches Theater in the east one of the world's most prestigious theatre establishments. The city has three major symphony orchestras, three opera- and comic opera-houses. Cinema, with the Berlin Film Festival as its flagship, is resuming the activity of its great creative period in the 1920s. Well over 100,000 students, professors and other academic personnel

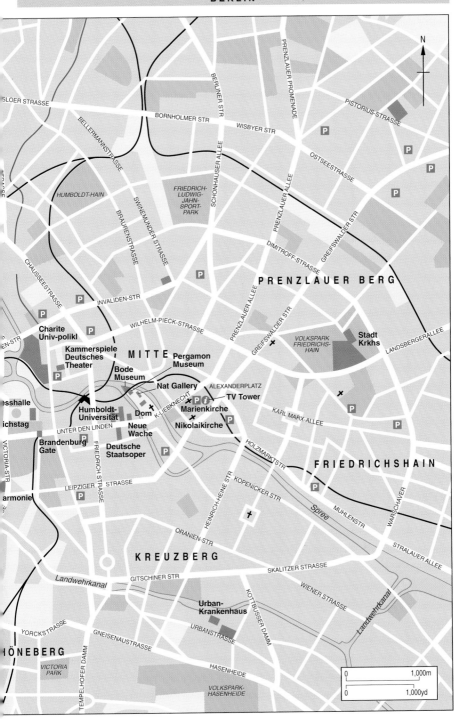

BERLIN'S CRAZIEST DECADE

The turbulent 1920s gave Berlin a place apart in the world's popular imagination. Before democracy died in 1933, the city experienced a charmed life of exciting and disturbing creativity that left its stamp on the whole of European culture.

Defeat in World War I had shattered the rigid certainties of Berlin's "Prussianness" and left the town open to radical, often wildly eccentric ideas—adventures in social and artistic expression almost unimaginable in the older cultural capitals of Vienna, London and Paris. Artists of the avant-garde Dada movement called for state prayers to be replaced by simultaneous poetry, progressive unemployment by immediate mechanization of all physical labour, and regulation of sexual intercourse through a Central Dada Sex Office. Long before the New York "happenings" of the 1960s, Berlin Dadaists organized races between a sewing machine and a typewriter, with artist George Grosz and writer Walter Mehring as jockeys.

The hilariously absurd and the deadly serious went hand in hand. Nightclubs on the Tauentzienstrasse combined strip-tease and fierce political satire. Heavy drinking, hashish and sexual licence accompanied acute analysis of the world scene. The painting of Grosz, Otto Dix and Max Beckmann was brutally realist. The spectacular productions of Max Reinhardt, theatrical equivalents of Hollywood film extravaganzas, yielded to the politically committed revolutionary theatre of Erwin Piscator and Berthold Brecht, with the acerbic music of Kurt Weill. The dissonance of the times was aptly symbolized by the atonal music composed in Berlin by Arnold Schönberg and his pupil Alban Berg. Such was the creativity of this period that Berlin hosted the first performances of no less than 12 new operas from 1919 to 1932, with Erich Kleiber and Otto Klemperer as conductors. Wilhelm Furtwängler led the Berlin Philharmonic and Bruno Walter the Städtische Oper.

The conservative establishment watched helplessly as the Prussian Writers' Academy made Heinrich Mann its president. Author of such masterful novels as *Der Untertan* (English title: *The Man of Straw*) and *Professor Unrat*, Thomas Mann's elder brother was a violent critic of the German bourgeoisie and supporter of the Communist Party. *Professor Unrat* was made into Josef von Sternberg's film *The Blue Angel*, famous for revealing the vocal talents (and thighs) of Marlene Dietrich.

work in a new buoyant atmosphere in the three universities and numerous research institutes. Adding to the considerable investment in textiles, chemicals, engineering and electrical equipment, many more major companies—German, Japanese and American—have set up new operations.

The eastern districts of the city are essentially the old, densely populated centre whose *Mietskasernen* (tenements, literally "rental barracks") inspired the 1920s proletarian theatre of Erwin Piscator and Berthold Brecht. If post-war Berlin had to be divided it was appropriate that the Soviet sector, devoted to the communist experiment, should cover most of the working-class neighbourhoods, while West Berlin had as its centre the eminently bourgeois neighbourhood of Charlottenburg.

Beyond the stone, steel and glass, Berlin is the greenest metropolis in Europe. If a city had to be walled off from its hinterland, few were geographically better suited for survival than West Berlin when it came to breathing space. Of its 480km^2 (185 square miles), a full one-third is parkland, woods and water. Besides the Tiergarten and River Spree in

*I*n the tradition of the 1920s, cabaret and satire kept spirits up on both sides of the Wall during the long years of Berlin's division.

the centre, there are forests, rivers and lakes to the west; to all this, Eastern Berlin can now add its Müggel lake and the woods and parkland around Treptow and Köpenick. Small garden colonies abound and even some little farming communities flourish within the city limits.

The total area, 883km² (340 square miles), is more than *eight* times the size of Paris, but you can get around on the excellent underground (U-Bahn) and overhead (S-Bahn) railway or the delightful double-decker buses. However, we recommend renting a car to reach conveniently the outlying areas, especially the Dahlem museums and the recreation parks and lakes. To get your bearings, it is a

good idea to start with an organized sightseeing tour—buses at the east end of the Kurfürstendamm, or at the Radisson Plaza (Karl-Liebknecht-Strasse) or Alexanderplatz.

Even with the Wall dismantled, a division of 45 years has left the city in two distinct halves and it will take some time for, in Willy Brandt's now immortal words, "what belongs together to grow together". To respect the undeniable visual distinction, our tour of the city retains the geographical division.

Western Berlin

The hub of what was Berlin's western sector is known to the Berliners themselves as the *City*. The roughly triangular precinct is bounded by Leibnizstrasse, Hardenbergstrasse, Lietzenburger Strasse and Tauentzienstrasse. Here are most of the major shops, restaurants, cafés, cinemas, theatres and art galleries. You will find that racy combination of elegance,

281

prosperity and cheerful impudence that distinguishes Berlin from all the other German cities.

Around Kurfürstendamm

Literally the "Prince-Elector's Embankment", the city's main thoroughfare is known to all as the Ku'damm. It is perhaps the liveliest avenue in all of Germany, pulsating with traffic late into the night. Impressed by the prolongation of the Champs-Elysées in Paris to the Bois de Boulogne, Bismarck wanted to extend the Ku'damm out to the Grunewald forest, but the imperial pretensions were never realized, and the avenue ultimately linked Kaiser Wilhelm Memorial Church to nothing grander than the Halensee railway station.

Sooner or later, everyone comes to promenade on the Ku'damm, and a place to watch them is the **Café Kranzler**, a venerable Berlin institution at the corner of Joachimstaler Strasse. Decidedly bourgeois now, the original Kranzler in the east was a hotbed of radical intellectuals in 1848.

The avenue's *Jugendstil* architecture of its Wilhelminian heyday was almost completely destroyed in World War II, but a vestige can be seen in the elegant **Café Möhring** across the road (next to Wertheim department store). Note, too, the façade of No. 52, an elegant Art Deco apartment building. Otherwise the street is resolutely modern, gleaming glass, steel and an occasional touch of marble, but still a magnet for elegant shopping.

Off the avenue at Fasanenstrasse 79 is the **Jewish Community Centre** (*Jüdisches Gemeindehaus*) serving as a cultural centre for the few hundred Jews still living in Berlin—there were 173,000 in 1933, one-third of all Jews in Germany. Framing the entrance is the domed portal

from the synagogue burned to the ground in the fateful *Kristallnacht* of 1938. A new Jewish Museum is being built to adjoin the Berlin Museum in the Kreuzberg district (*see* page 298). From here, take Kantstrasse to fashionable **Savigny-platz**, centre of art bookshops and galleries, outdoor cafés, bistros and bars, particularly along Grolmannstrasse.

Back on the Ku'damm, head east to **Breitscheidplatz**, a popular gathering place to watch street-theatre troupes around Joachim Schmettau's monumental granite fountain (1983). Events have happily weakened the split globe's symbolism of the East–West division of which Berlin was the centre. Soaring above it is another pregnant symbol, the sombre **Kaiser-Wilhelm-Gedächtniskirche** (Memorial Church). The war-scarred tower has been preserved as a ruin to recall the city's suffering from bombardment. Flanking it, a modern octagonal church to the east and a chapel and hectagonal tower to the west represent the city's post-war rebirth. Modern stained glass made in Chartres set in walls of moulded concrete glows over the Ku'damm at night.

The remains of the neo-Romanesque church built to honour Wilhelm I still celebrate the Hohenzollerns' pious monarchism. A mosaic of *Christ the King* is set above friezes and reliefs of Prussian monarchs. On one wall, Wilhelm I confers with Chancellor Bismarck and field marshals Moltke and Roon. On the hour, the tower's clock chimes out a melody written by Prince Louis Ferdinand, the Kaiser's great-great-grandson. With their taste for irreverent nicknames, Berliners have deflated the monuments' various imperial or pacifist intentions by dubbing the original church the "broken tooth" and the two main additions the "lipstick" and "powder compact".

Beyond the church is the 22-storey **Europa-Center** extending from Tauentzienstrasse to Budapester Strasse. There are scores of boutiques, an excellent 60-minute "multi-vision" show on Berlin (with an English-soundtrack version), a casino, the famous *Stachelschweine* political cabaret, discotheques, pubs and a rooftop café with a splendid view across the city. The Berlin Tourist Office is on the building's Budapester Strasse side.

Ka-De-We on Tauentzientrasse is more than just a department store. Founded in 1906, long before the Wall, it was not conceived, as its name *Kaufhaus des Westens* (The West's Department Store) might suggest, as some Cold War provocation ostentatiously proclaiming western prosperity, but that is what its sheer abundance made it look like after 1945. In the weeks following the opening of the Wall, it was a major target for East Germans making their first assault on Western consumerism. The food department is phenomenal, with stand-up counters for the gourmet globe-trotter—Chinese, Japanese, Italian, Russian and Swiss snacks, with properly chilled French champagne.

As zoos go—and many would like to see them go—the **Zoo**, entrance on Budapester Strasse, has one of the most varied collections of animals in Europe. Beyond the colourful pagoda-arched Elephant Gate are 35 hectares (86 acres) of parkland where you can compare Indian and African elephants, giant pandas from China and rare, single-horned rhinoceroses from India. Besides the killer sharks and carnivorous piranhas, the **aquarium** has some nice boa constrictors, tarantulas and scorpions.

Tiergarten Area

Despite its name, the **Tiergarten** (Animal Garden) is not another zoo. For the Hohenzollern princes, it was a forest for hunting deer and wild boar. After Frederick the Great cleared away the woods to create a formal French garden for his brother August Ferdinand, it was replanted with trees in the 19th century and transformed into a more natural English-style landscaped park. In World War II, Berliners stripped away the trees again—for fuel. Everything you see today has been planted since 1950, among pleasant boating ponds, cafés and monuments

*L*ily pads grow as big as tea-trays in the year-round tropical heat of the Botanical Gardens' glasshouses.

to German writers and composers, and Soviet soldiers. Dedicated to these last, the **Sowjetisches Ehrenmal**, Strasse des 17 Juni, flanked by two T-34 tanks which led the 1945 invasion of Berlin, was built of marble from Hitler's Chancellery.

The **Englischer Garten** beside Altonaer Strasse, financed by British donations, was laid out by the Shropshire Horticultural Society. It is part of the grounds of **Schloss Bellevue**, a neoclassical palace reconstructed as a residence for the German president.

On the north-west side of the Tiergarten is the **Hansa-Viertel**, a chic residential neighbourhood rebuilt in 1957 by architects from all over the world, notably Bauhaus founder Walter Gropius (Händelallee 1–9) and Finland's Alvar Aalto (Klopstock-strasse 30). The Arts Academy (*Akademie der Künste*), Hanseatenweg 10, holds concerts, plays and exhibitions of avant-garde art.

At the centre of the park, on the circle of the Grosser Stern, the soaring **Siegessäule** (Victory Column) is a monument to Prussian militarism. It was completed in 1873—two years after victory over the French, but also celebrates successes against Denmark in 1864 and Austria in 1866. The bronze reliefs were fashioned from melted-down cannons and other spoils of war. In 1945, the French insisted they be removed, but let them be restored in 1987 for the city's 750th anniversary—Germans were beginning to complain about equally bellicose reliefs of Napoleon's victories over the Germans on the Arc de Triomphe in Paris. In a hall at the column's base, mosaics depict more pacific events leading to Germany's 19th-century unification. A climb of 285 steps takes you to the top of the column for a magnificent city view from beneath the gilded bronze statue of Winged Victory. On the north side of the Grosser Stern are monuments to the architects of that first unification, Chancellor Bismarck and field marshals Moltke and Roon.

Directly south of the Siegessäule on Landwehr Canal is the museum of the **Bauhaus-Archiv** (*see* page 293), designed by Walter Gropius, the founder of Germany's hugely influential Bauhaus school of art, architecture and design. It makes an appropriate start to a tour, east along the canal, of some major monuments of 20th-century architecture. On the corner of Stauffenbergstrasse, notice Emil

*T*he 1873 Victory column was built to proclaim the Prussian triumphs which led to German unity.

Fahrenkamp's elegantly curved travertine-clad **Bewag building** (Berlin gas and electric company, 1932). A striking rose and pastel blue sandstone façade dominates British architect James Stirling's postmodern **Wissenschaftzentrum** (Science Centre, 1989), Reichpietschufer 48. At the corner of Potsdamer Strasse, Gropius' Bauhaus colleague Mies van der Rohe's design for the **Nationalgalerie** of 19th- and 20th-century art (*see* page 292) is a square, glass-wall structure with a vast black steel roof supported by eight massive steel columns. This work of characteristic elegant simplicity was completed in 1968, a year before the master's death. It stands on a raised granite platform that serves as a **sculpture court** for such huge outdoor pieces as Alexander Calder's *Heads and Tail* and Henry Moore's *Archer*, and as a playground for skateboarders. Mies would not have minded.

What counted for him was the purity of a building's form. Function was secondary—the museum's design derives from an idea he originally had for the offices of a Cuban sugar factory. (In dignified isolation beyond the gallery is the slender-steepled neo-Romanesque church of St Matthäus, the only pre-war building here to survive demolition by Hitler's architect, Albert Speer, or the bombs that followed.)

Kulturforum

The Nationalgalerie is part of the city's Cultural Forum for music and fine arts.

*M*ies van der Rohe, *prominent in the Bauhaus movement in the 1920s, designed Berlin's Nationalgalerie.*

(Eventually the European paintings and sculpture in the Dahlem museums will have a new home here.) Architect Hans Scharoun, the mastermind of the complex of museums, libraries and concert halls, designed the **Staatsbibliothek** (State Library), Potsdamerstrasse 33, opposite the Nationalgalerie. Despite the library's formidable dimensions, it is a model of peace and harmony, open to the public and well worth a visit. An ingenious network of staircases lead smoothly to multi-level reading rooms and easily accessible stacks. The library holds photographic and documentary exhibitions and concerts.

Scharoun also built the intriguing ochre and gold **Philharmonie** (1963), Matthäikirche-Strasse 1, which owes its tent-like shape to the demands of the concert hall's acoustics and sight-lines. The home of the renowned Berlin Philharmonic Orchestra was designed from the inside out, from the orchestra outwards to the walls and roof. A white-façaded **chamber music hall** (*Kammermusiksaal*) has been added to the rear. From across Tiergarten-strasse, the nearby **Musical Instruments Museum** is reminiscent of an open card-index file.

The **Arts and Crafts Museum** (*Kunstgewerbemuseum*), Tiergarten-strasse 6, is a rather confusing labyrinth of red brick and white granite but worth a visit for its superb collection of medieval jewellery.

The Reichstag

The august parliamentary home of imperial and Weimar Germany still bears the proud dedication *Dem deutschen Volke* ("To the German People"). This appeal to democracy on the pediment above its six Corinthian columns has outlasted the burning in 1933 (*see* page 71) and the bombs

of World War II. In 1954 its dome, with the imperial crown, was blown up, and the building served as an assembly for West Berlin's members of the Federal German parliament. It also houses a permanent exhibit, "German History Under Question" (*Fragen an die deutsche Geschichte*). This frank examination of Germany's social and political history from 1800 to the present includes an interesting section on the post-war history of Berlin itself. See how good was John F. Kennedy's command of German in his famous speech in 1963 when he proclaimed, from phonetically written notes: "Ish been ahn Bairleener".

Schloss Charlottenburg

The carefully restored palace is an exemplary piece of Prussian baroque and rococo architecture and decoration. Since the war-damaged Stadtschloss (town palace) in East Berlin was razed in 1951 and replaced by the Communist régime's ultra-modern Palast der Republik, Schloss Charlottenburg is the city's only surviving major Hohenzollern residence. (For a description of the palace's Gallery of Romantic Art and the nearby Egyptian and Classical Antiquity museums, *see* page 296.)

It was conceived as a summer retreat for the future Queen Sophie Charlotte in the 1690s, when the site beside the Spree river west of the Tiergarten lay well outside the city limits. It was a *little* palace—

Escape from city bustle to the gardens of Schloss Charlottenburg. Across the carp pond, the Belvedere tea house is the home of a museum of Berlin porcelain.

LAST TRAIN TO SAFETY

If you drive over to Eastern Berlin via Friedrichstrasse, spare a moment as you pass Askanischer Platz to look at the poignant arcaded ruin of Anhalter Bahnhof. This elegant neo-Renaissance façade is all that remains of what was once Berlin's most glamorous railway station linking the city to Europe's other great capitals. The westbound platform at Anhalter Bahnhof also staged the tragic last act of the Weimar Republic. Soon after Hitler became Chancellor, Berlin's most gifted artists and intellectuals, Heinrich Mann, Bertold Brecht, Kurt Weill, George Grosz, Albert Einstein and other Jewish and left-wing luminaries left town, their bags packed for exile.

scarcely one-fifth of the huge structure you see today. Only with the addition of a majestic domed tower with the goddess Fortune as its weather-vane, the Orangerie to the west and a new east wing did it become big enough for Frederick the Great. If he had to leave his beloved Potsdam, this was where he came.

In the palace courtyard is a splendid **equestrian statue** (1697) of the Great Elector Friedrich Wilhelm, designed by Andreas Schlüter. One of many art works lost in World War II, it was recovered in 1949 from Tegel harbour, where it had sunk with the barge that was taking it to safety. It originally stood beside the ill-fated Stadtschloss (also designed by Schlüter).

To recapture the interior's gracious rococo atmosphere, furnishings and decoration from other 18th-century Prussian palaces have replaced what was irretrievably destroyed here during the war. You are free to roam at will through the ornate world of the Hohenzollerns, except for Friedrich I's and Sophie Charlotte's apartments in the central building and west wing, for which there are regular guided tours.

In the **Gobelinzimmer**, notice the fine 18th-century tapestries by Charles Vigne, and in the **Rotes Tressenzimmer** two exquisite blue and white Meissen vases. The rays of sunlight on the ceiling of the **Audienzzimmer** (reception room) and dazzling yellow damask walls in the **royal bedroom** (*Schlafzimmer*) imitate the obsessive motif of the Prussian rulers' hero, Louis XIV, the Sun King. Chinoiserie dominates the opulent **Porzellankabinett**, filled with hundreds of pieces of Chinese and Japanese porcelain, including life-size figures of mandarins. The relatively sober **Japanische Kammer** has beautiful lacquered cabinets and tables and tapestries depicting, despite the chamber's name, landscapes of China. Chamber music recitals are held in the **Oak Gallery** (*Eichengalerie*) and the **chapel** (*Eosander-Kapelle*), with an extravagant rococo décor that makes it more theatre than place of worship.

TEUFELSBERG, DEVIL'S MOUNTAIN

At the beginning of the Grunewald, in the middle of the flat northern European plain that stretches from Warsaw to the Netherlands, is a mountain. Aptly named Teufelsberg (Devil's Mountain), it is small—only 115m (380ft) high—but a mountain nonetheless, created by a pile of rubble from World War II bombardments.

In summer, the hill is grassed over for toddler mountain climbers to scramble on or hang-gliders to jump from. In winter, snow makes it an excellent toboggan run, a good nursery slope for skiers and even two bone-rattling ski jumps.

The **east wing**, designed for Frederick the Great by Georg von Knobelsdorff, his favourite architect, subtly combines dignified late baroque façades with exuberant rococo interiors. Part of the ground floor is at present given over to the Gallery of Romantic Art (*Galerie der Romantik*)—to be housed later in the Tiergarten's Kulturforum. Leading to Frederick the Great's state apartments, the **Treppenhaus** (ceremonial staircase) has an abstract modern ceiling fresco by Hann Trier in place of the original rococo décor destroyed by fire. Trier also painted the ceiling of the **Weisse Saal** (throne room and banquet hall). Knobelsdorff's finest achievement at Charlottenburg is the spacious **Goldene Galerie** in gilt and green marble. It leads to the two rooms boasting a remarkable group of eight **Watteau paintings**. Frederick the Great enjoyed his *Enseigne du Gersaint*, a shop sign for art dealer Gersaint in which a portrait of Louis XIV is being unceremoniously packed away. Other superb works include *Quiet Love, The Shepherds* and *Embarkation for Cythera*.

Formal French **gardens** juxtapose English landscaping. Among the many buildings in the grounds, nearest to the palace is the elegant little 19th-century neoclassical **Schinkel-Pavillon** designed by Karl Friedrich Schinkel. See upstairs an amusing panorama of 1830s Berlin by Eduard Gaertner. North of the carp pond, the baroque Belvedere tea-house is now a **Berlin Porcelain Museum**. A Doric temple provides a mausoleum for Hohenzollerns of the 19th century.

Olympic Stadium and Congress Centre

Two monstrous buildings command our attention west of Charlottenburg. Hitler's **Olympic Stadium**, built for the Games of 1936, was spared bombardment to serve

*B*erlin's futuristic *Internationales Congress Centrum looks like a space station out of* Star Trek.

as headquarters for the British Army. The structure's bombast is eloquent testimony to the Führer's architectural taste. From the main Olympic Gate, it looks remarkably "low slung" until you see inside that the field itself has been sunk 12m (40ft) below ground level. Still used for sporting events and open daily to the public, the stadium was built originally for 120,000 spectators—the whole Olympic complex conceived for half a million.

On Masurenallee, south-east of the stadium, another colossus, the ICC (*Internationales Congress Centrum*) presents German technological know-how and commercial power wrapped in a gigantic aluminium skin. The complex has 80 conference halls and meeting rooms for 400 congresses each year. A guided tour reveals the building's ingenuity and formidable efficiency. **Hall 1**, the biggest, seats 5,000, but **Hall 2** is the most fun. At the press of a button, a convention hall with tiered seating rises and disappears into the ceiling to reveal within minutes a banquet room for 4,000 diners. Conference delegates are each equipped with individual microphones—press a button and one pops up from the arm of your seat—as well as built-in facilities for simultaneous translation in any of eight languages. It comes almost as a disappointment that there are no seat belts and it does not fly.

Amidst all this gigantism, the **Funkturm** (Radio Tower) on the neighbouring exhibition grounds (*Messegelände*) seems positively tiny—150m (492ft) to the tip of its antenna, half the size of the TV Tower in Eastern Berlin. But for the view, take the lift to the restaurant, 55m (180ft) up, or the observation platform at the top. Look south-west down the stretch of Autobahn known as the **Avus**, acronym of the Automobil-, Verkehrs-

---

TEDDY BEARS' PICNIC

If you go down to the Ku'damm today, you'd better go in disguise. For every bear that ever there was is gathered there for certain: Kurfürstendamm 206 has a terrific Teddy Bear Museum. See the earliest Teddy (1900) on iron wheels, pulled by a chain. Thereafter, the bears are liberated—Paddington, Winnie the Pooh and Rupert are all there, along with Germany's wide-eyed Steiff, the Rolls-Royce of stuffed bears.

---

und Übungsstrasse (Automobile, Traffic and Training Road). Built in 1921, it was Germany's first racetrack, a simple 8km (5-mile) two-way straight with a loop at either end. The record speed was Rudolf Caracciola's 396kph (248mph) in a Mercedes. No longer used for racing, it now links the city centre to the westbound autobahn.

Grunewald and Wannsee

The pre-war dense pine forest, largely stripped for fuel in 1945, has been replanted, adding to the 18 million pines some 6 million chestnut, linden, beech, birch and oak trees. The wooded areas form a reserve for deer, wild boar, marten, foxes and myriad rabbits, but there are plenty of green meadows for picnics.

Buses and trains serve the forest and lakes. Drivers take the Avus and turn off on the Hüttenweg to **Grunewaldsee**, a lake offering good swimming off sandy beaches. On the east shore, in a pretty lakeside setting of beech trees, the **Jagdschloss Grunewald** was a hunting-lodge built in 1542 for Prince Elector Joachim II and later baroquified. A good collection of German and Dutch paintings includes works by Lucas Cranach, Jordaens, Rubens and Bruyn. The portrait of Prince Joachim is by Cranach's son.

B erliners can find beaches and plenty of room for sailing on the Wannsee lakes.

On the Grunewald's west side, via Havelchaussee, ferry stations offer boat rides on the **Havel river** and forest lakes. The east bank of the Havel is lined with pleasant sandy beaches all the way down to the Wann lakes. **Strandbad Wannsee** is Berlin's biggest beach. With its promenades, restaurants and hooded wicker beach shelters (*Strandkörbe*), Wannsee is comparable in atmosphere to elegant resorts on Germany's North Sea coast. The sailing here is first class.

West of the Grosser Wannsee, Königsstrasse crosses Berliner Forst, an extension of the Grunewald to **Kleinglienicke Park**. Its whimsical landscaping of little hills and dells, bridges and ponds was the work of Peter Josef Lenné in the early 19th

century. The **palace** (1828) is a rather austere neoclassical edifice by Karl Friedrich Schinkel, but the nearby cloister, villa and garden houses add a more romantic touch.

A ferry service links **Pfaueninsel** (Peacock Island), a delightfully tranquil nature reserve in the Havel, to the northern edge of Berliner Forst. Venerable oaks and giant Californian lodgepole pines remain from an arboretum created in the 18th century. The island menagerie served to stock Berlin Zoo, but as a bird sanctuary it still has much to offer the nature lover, including, of course, peacocks. At the south tip, half-hidden in the trees, is Schinkel's Swiss Cottage, but the island's major curiosity is the fake ruin **Schloss Pfaueninsel**. It was built in 1797 as a hideaway for Friedrich Wilhelm II and his mistress, Countess Wilhelmine von Lichtenau. The white wooden façade imitates granite blocks and the sweet little turrets are linked at the top by a pretty, but rather flimsy-looking bridge. The façade's arched gateway seems to lead to an idyllic landscape, but it is just a painted niche—more make-believe. Take a look inside the palace at Anton Graff's portrait of Friedrich Wilhelm—it's hard to imagine this gloomy fellow being so playful.

Königsstrasse extends to an illustrious relic of the Cold War, **Glienicker Bridge**, once a highly restricted border crossing between West Berlin and East Germany where the KGB and CIA exchanged their spies.

Spandau

With a history longer than Berlin's, the borough of Spandau remains fiercely independent-minded. It was the most reluctant of the townships to be annexed by the metropolis in 1920, and residents still ask taxi drivers to take them "to Berlin" when going to the city centre.

The **old town** at the confluence of the Havel and Spree rivers was less hurt by bombardment than the rest of Berlin and retains much of its charm. You will see a few gabled houses, Renaissance façades and even traces of the 14th-century town wall along Hoher Weg, east of Falkenseer Platz. Spandauers claim that **St Nikolai** church on Reformationsplatz is where Prince Joachim II converted to the Protestant faith. The much-restored brick Gothic structure has a fine Renaissance altar.

The 16th-century **citadel** in the Havel river was the scene of heavy fighting during the Napoleonic Wars. Its walls enclose the old **Juliusturm**, a castle keep from prior medieval fortifications. It was the repository for gold coins paid by the French as reparations after the Franco-Prussian War and returned as part payment for reparations after World War I.

Following the death of its last inmate, Rudolf Hess, in 1987, the Spandau prison for Nazi war criminals was razed to make way for a community centre.

North of the borough, **Spandauer Forst** is half the size of the Grunewald, but just as beautiful. The forest incorporates important nature reserves where rare plants are protected in their wild state. **Teufelsbruch**, regularly recording Berlin's coldest winter temperatures, harbours shrubs and flowers from the sub-Arctic tundra. Just east of Teufelsbruch, summer bathing and camping are popular at **Bürgerablage beach** on the Havel river.

Museums

Like everything else in Germany, Berlin's museum scene is in a state of flux. With expansion of the Kulturforum (*see* page 285) and changes brought about by German unification, Berlin is reorganizing its art collections. After 1945, many works originally in the eastern half of the city or Potsdam found a new home in the west. As the museums of Eastern Berlin are renovated, some paintings and sculptures may move again, in both directions. Pending final decisions, our descriptions keep the best possible account of the flux.

Tiergarten Area

Nationalgalerie, Potsdamer Strasse 50. The ground floor is used for temporary exhibitions, with the permanent collections of 19th- and 20th-century art on the lower level. After the catastrophic Nazi confiscation of "Degenerate Art", the gallery is gradually rebuilding its modern collection. (The Galerie der Romantik, presently in Schloss Charlottenberg, is to be incorporated in an annex.)

German painting: Adolph Menzel depicts the rise of 19th-century Germany with his *Berlin–Potsdam Railway* (1847) and *Wilhelm I's Departure for the Army* (1871). Lovis Corinth has a tenderly observed *Donna Gravida* (1909), Max Slevogt a striking *Still Life with Lemons* (1921) and Max Liebermann a splendid self-portrait (1925). Outstanding among the Expressionists: Norwegian-born Edvard Munch's *Life Frieze* (1906); Max Beckmann's *Woman's Bath* (1919); the Otto Dix portrait of art dealer *Alfred Flechtheim* (1926); and George Grosz's *Pillars of Society* (1926).

French painting: three Courbet landscapes, notably *The Cliffs of Etretat* (1870). Among the Impressionists, Monet's *St-Germain l'Auxerrois* (1866), Manet's *In the Winter Garden* (1879); also van Gogh's *Moulin de la Galette* (1886) and works by Renoir and Bonnard.

American painting: important works by Jackson Pollock, Mark Rothko, Barnett Newman and Frank Stella.

Bauhaus-Archiv,
Klingelhöferstrasse 13.
The museum documents the achievements of Europe's most progressive 20th-century school of architecture and design. It was established in Weimar in 1919, transferred to Dessau and, briefly, to Berlin before Hitler drove it into exile in 1933, where it regrouped in Chicago and Cambridge, Massachusetts. Architects Walter Gropius, Mies van der Rohe and Marcel Breuer, and artists Paul Klee, Vasili Kandinsky, Oskar Schlemmer, Lyonel Feininger and Laszlo Moholy-Nagy sought to integrate the arts, crafts and architecture into 20th-century mass industrial society.

On view is a selection of objects they created: tubular steel chairs, desks, tables, teapots, cups and saucers, new weaves for carpets, chess pieces and children's building blocks. There were also pioneering designs for factories, schools, housing projects, and even newspaper kiosks. One of the most beautiful architectural models is Mies van der Rohe's 30-storey round skyscraper made entirely of glass. The 1921 project was never realized, but a variation was built recently in Chicago by one of Mies's pupils, emphasizing the enduring modernity of Bauhaus ideas.

Musikinstrumenten-Museum,
Tiergartenstrasse 1.
Among the museum's many historical musical instruments are a 1703 Stradivarius violin and the 1810 piano of composer Carl Maria von Weber, as well as a monumental Wurlitzer cinema organ from New York, 1929.

Kunstgewerbemuseum
(Arts and Crafts), Tiergartenstrasse 6.
Outstanding in the museum's astounding collection of jewellery is the Welfs' treasure (*Welfenschatz*). These examples of the goldsmith's art from the 11th century—richly bejewelled crosses, reliquaries and portable altars—were presented to St Blasius Cathedral in Brunswick by succeeding generations of Welf dukes. Other prized exhibits include glazed Italian majolica and an exquisite array of porcelain—Chinese, Meissen

*B*erlin by night: *Kurfürstendamm curves to the left, Hardenbergstrasse to the right. Between them, Kantstrasse heads for the horizon through the café and restaurant district (overleaf).*

Frankenthaler, Nymphenburger and Berlin's own Königliche Porzellan Manufaktur (the royal KPM).

In and Opposite Charlottenburg

Ägyptisches Museum,
Schloss-Strasse 70.
The museum boasts one of the greatest collections of Egyptian art outside Egypt itself. Covering 3,000 years, it displays sculpture, pyramid fragments and hieroglyph tablets. Among recent major acquisitions is the monumental Kalabsha Gate (20 BC), saved from the waters of the Aswan Dam in the 1960s. The carved relief shows Roman Emperor Augustus as an Egyptian Pharaoh.

The most famous piece is undoubtedly the beautiful head of Queen Nefertiti (1340 BC), consort of Akhenaton. The Germans acquired it by pure luck. It was found in the ancient capital of Tel-el-Amarna just before the outbreak of war in 1914. French archaeologists sharing the dig with the Germans showed no interest in what they called "a very mediocre plaster block". Back in Berlin, the plaster was chipped away to reveal the exquisite features of Nefertiti, a name meaning "the beautiful woman has arrived".

Egyptologists believe the reason she has only one eye is that the head was merely a working model abandoned when Tutankhamen, successor to Akhenaton, moved his capital to Thebes.

Look out, too, for the many smaller gems in the collection, notably a charming Married Couple (2400 BC) and the meticulously carved wooden Ship of Mentuhotep (1900 BC).

Antikenmuseum, Schloss-Strasse 1.
This twin museum to the Egyptian houses Greek and Roman antiquities. Highlights are fine Minoan figurines from Crete; bronzes from Sparta, Samos and Dodona; red-figured Attic vases; and an important collection of Greek and Etruscan gold ornaments.

Galerie der Romantik,
Schloss Charlottenburg, East Wing.
The superb collection of German Romantics is ultimately to be reincorporated in the Nationalgalerie. Meanwhile, the palace provides an admirable setting for major works by Philipp Otto Runge, Friedrich Overbeck, Carl Blechen and Carl Spitzweg. However, the gallery boasts, above all, Germany's most comprehensive collection of works by Caspar David Friedrich. Among his mystic land- and seascapes, notice *Abbey in the Woods* (1809), *The Monk by the Sea* (1810) and *The Lonely Tree* (1822).

Dahlem

The museums of the Prussian State art collections, notably European painting and sculpture, are located between Arnimallee

---

COMING IN FROM THE COLD

Spy exchanges are usually done in secret, but one cold dawn in 1962, the international press had been alerted: the American U-2 pilot Gary Powers was being traded for ace Soviet spy Colonel Rudolf Abel. Big black cars rolled up on opposite sides of the Glienicker Bridge. The Americans took Abel to the middle of the bridge, where the Russians examined him to make sure the merchandise was genuine and in good condition. At the same time, the Americans checked Powers. Everything was fine and the deal was completed. Meanwhile, under the bridge, the swans swam back and forth from east to west, with nobody checking.

and Lansstrasse near the Dahlem Dorf U-Bahn station. Dahlem also groups the museums of Indian, Oriental and Islamic Art and the ethnographic museum, noted for its pre-Columbian collection. These will take over the entire Dahlem installations when the European collections are moved to the Tiergarten's Kulturforum and, in part, to the Museuminsel in Eastern Berlin.

Gemäldegalerie (Picture Gallery), Arnimallee 23.
The collection of European art from the 13th to the 18th centuries ranks among the most important in the world. We present some highlights.
Italian: Giotto *Death of Mary* (1310); Simone Martini *Entombment of Christ* (1340); Pollaiuolo *Portrait of a Young Woman* (1465); Botticelli *Mary Enthroned* (1484); Giovanni Bellini *Christ Dead, Supported by Two Angels* (1485); Giorgione *Portrait of a Young Man* (1506); Caravaggio *Amor Vincit Omnia* (1602).
German: Konrad Witz *Queen of Sheba* (1437); Martin Schongauer *Birth of Christ* (1480); Albrecht Altdorfer *Resting on the Flight to Egypt* (1510); Hans Baldung Grien *Crucifixion* (1512); Dürer *Hieronymus Holschuher* (1526); Lucas Cranach *Fountain of Youth* (1546).
Dutch and Flemish: Jan van Eyck *Mary in the Church* (1425); Rogier van der Weyden *St John Altar* (1450); Hugo van der Goes *Adratin of the Magi* (1470); Pieter Brueghel *Netherlandish Proverbs* (1559); Rubens *St Sebastian* (1618); van Dyck *Genoese Couple* (1626); Rembrandt *Parable of the Rich Man* (1627); Vermeer *Young Lady with Pearl Necklace* (1665).
French: Georges de la Tour *Peasant Couple Eating* (1620); Poussin *St Matthew* (1640); Watteau *French Comedy and Italian Comedy* (1716).

Spanish: Velázquez *Portrait of a Lady* (1633); Zurbarán *Don Alonso Verdugo* (1635); Murillo *Baptism of Christ* (1655).
English: Joshua Reynolds *George Clive and his Family* (1766); Thomas Gainsborough *The Marsham Children* (1787).

Drawings and prints in the excellent **Engravings Department** (*Kupferstichkabinett*) range from illuminated manuscripts of the 14th century to modern woodcuts by Expressionist Erich Heckel and lithographs by Willem de Kooning. There are outstanding works by Botticelli, Dürer and Rembrandt.

Sculpture Gallery, also Arnimallee 23. The gallery has a magnificent collection of Romanesque and Gothic sculpture from Saxony, Bavaria and the Rhineland, and major pieces by Tilman Riemenschneider and Martin Zürn. Italian sculptors represented here include Donatello, Cosimo Tura and Sansovino.

Brücke Museum, Bussardsteig 9.
The museum was created in 1967 thanks to a legacy of Karl Schmidt-Rottluff, a member of the Expressionist group Die Brücke (The Bridge). His own bold paintings hang beside the searing works of Erich Heckel, Ernst Ludwig Kirchner, Max Pechstein and Emil Nolde, who worked together in Dresden from 1905 to 1913. Inspired in part by van Gogh, Gauguin and Cézanne, the canvases are a robust reaction to the aesthetic delicacies of *Jugendstil*.

Kreuzberg
Berlin Museum, Lindenstrasse 14.
The municipal museum is housed in the cheerful baroque building of the former Kammergericht (Supreme Court), nicely

restored. Models of the old city show how Berlin has grown over the eight centuries since its founding. Authentically furnished rooms illustrate the material life of the bourgeoisie from the elegant age of neo-classical architect Karl Friedrich Schinkel (late 18th century to 1840), the solid Biedermeier days of the mid-19th century, the ponderous Gründerzeit (era of Germany's first unification), the lighter *Jugendstil* period and the years leading up to World War I. The fashion of these periods is especially well treated and there is a charming collection of toys.

Jewish Museum,
Stresemannstrasse 110.
Awaiting a new building adjoining the Berlin Museum, memorabilia of the city's once-flourishing Jewish community are presented in the Martin-Gropius-Bau, a handsome 1881 building designed by a great-uncle of Bauhaus master Walter Gropius. Without ignoring the community's tragic end, the museum emphasizes its positive social, cultural, and even sporting role in the local and national life. Exhibits include paintings and sculptures of prominent Jewish figures in Berlin's artistic and social life, documents of the literary salons, photos and ritual artefacts from the synagogues.

Berlinische Galerie,
Stresemannstrasse 110.
Also in the Martin-Gropius-Bau, the gallery illustrates Berlin life from 1870 to the present day through the eyes of the city's major artists. Beginning solemnly with Hohenzollern court painter Anton von Werner, the collection presents a razor-sharp view of the city, from Impressionists Max Liebermann and Lovis Corinth, Expressionists Otto Dix and

Conrad Felixmüller, the great social critics of the 1920s George Grosz and John Heartfield, to the abstracts and photorealists of the contemporary era, including foreign Berlin residents like American Ed Kienholz and Hungarian Laszlo Lakner.

Eastern Berlin

Since the momentous changes of November 1989, what was once the capital of the German Democratic Republic has become an object of curiosity. Besides the Communist regime's rather pompous

The city's symbol since 1791, the Brandenburg Gate was cordoned off from both east and west during the years of division.

governmental buildings and the Stalinist residential architecture of Karl-Marx-Allee, it also offers proudly refurbished monuments from the more stylish Prussian era on and around Unter den Linden avenue. Churches and many of the museums are undergoing painstaking restoration, but the Pergamon, the Bode and Märkisches museums are worthy partners to those in the western half of the city.

The charm of the old popular neighbourhoods is being only slowly discovered in Mitte, Prenzlauer Berg, Pankow and Friedrichshain. Meanwhile the Nikolai district is presented as something of a showcase. (Be prepared for changes in street names as Communist luminaries make way for Prussian predecessors or more recent heroes.)

When you talk with the people, remember that Eastern Berlin did not turn overnight into a solid bastion of anti-Communism. Even though the conservatives won the municipal elections in December 1990, the successor-party to the Communists did exceptionally well here, and the town still has a strong left-wing base.

Brandenburg Gate

The grand symbol of the united city seems at last to be realizing the vision of the man who crowned it with the **Quadriga**, the copper statue of Winged Victory in her four-horse chariot. Johann Gottfried Schadow wanted the monument, completed in 1793, to be known as *Friedenstor*, the Gate of Peace. He had titled his sculpted relief beneath the chariot "Procession of Peace". This fitted in with the propaganda of the East Germans for whom the Brandenburg Gate was the centrepiece of their Anti-Fascist Protective Wall (*Anti-Faschistischer Schutz-wall*).

They removed a bellicose Prussian eagle and Iron Cross added to the Quadriga in 1814.

The Gate itself was designed by Carl Gottfried Langhans with Athens's Propylaeum gatehouse as his inspiration. Two rows of six Doric columns form the gateway proper. Part of the city wall, even then, it was intended by the pragmatic Prussians not as a triumphal arch so much as an imposing toll gate for collecting duties and a control post to stop desertions from the Prussian Army. Until recently, desertions here were still frowned upon.

Unter den Linden

Sweeping east from the gate, the avenue literally "beneath the linden trees" was Berlin's grandest. Frederick the Great saw it as the centre of his royal capital, and for the aristocracy and wealthy bourgeoisie it became the best address in town. Some of its baroque and neoclassical splendour fell victim to 19th-century building speculation, but the avenue remained fashionable until the bombs of World War II reduced it almost all to rubble. Now the linden trees have been replanted and the major monumental buildings restored or rebuilt.

Its western end has traditionally been embassy row, dominated on the right as you come from the Brandenburg Gate by the former Soviet Embassy to the German Democratic Republic. East of Charlottenstrasse, beyond the State Library

*I*mage of two dinosaurs: mirrored in the windows of what was the parliament building of the German Democratic Republic is the dome of Kaiser Wilhelm II's cathedral.

(*Staatsbibliothek*), is Frederick the Great's "Forum Fridericianum", renamed by the East Germans **Lindenforum**. On the avenue's centre strip is the king's imposing **equestrian statue** (1851) by Christian Daniel Rauch. Frederick commissioned an opera-house, Royal Academy and a palace occupied by his brother, Prince Heinrich. Only the opera-house was built in Frederick's lifetime, the rest completing a splendid classical architectural testament, admirably restored. Heinrich's palace is now part of **Humboldt University**. The institution founded in 1810 counted among its professors and students the Grimm brothers, Hegel, Engels, Marx and Einstein. Opposite its rather severe classicism is the gently curving baroque façade of the **Alte Bibliothek** (Old Library), based on a design of Vienna's Fischer von Erlach. Across Bebelplatz is Knobelsdorff's grand Palladian-style **Deutsche Staatsoper** (German State Opera). The **Opera Café** is housed in the baroque town house of the Prussian princesses (*Prinzessinnenpalais*). Since unification, its open-air terrace has become one of the most popular rendezvous in Eastern Berlin.

Notice Christian Daniel Rauch's 19th-century statues of military heroes of Germany's battles against Napoleon. The East Germans resurrected them to reaffirm the Prussian military tradition. Beside the university is **Neue Wache**, the Prussian army guardhouse. This Doric-porticoed building was Karl Friedrich Schinkel's first important neoclassical design, completed in 1818. Next door, the elegant late 17th-century baroque **Zeughaus** (Arsenal) houses part of the reunited city's German History Museum (*Museum für Deutsche Geschichte*). In the inner courtyard are poignant sculpted masks by Andreas Schlüter of dying warriors (1696).

South of the Staatsoper is **St Hedwig's Cathedral**, built in the 18th century for the Catholics incorporated into Protestant Prussia by Frederick's conquest of Polish Silesia. The massive domed structure is inspired by Rome's Pantheon.

The celebrated Gendarmenmarkt architectural ensemble, now Platz der Akademie, is being meticulously restored. Schinkel's **Schauspielhaus** (Playhouse), now serving as a concert hall, has a noble Ionic portico. The edifice provides a harmonious link between the **Französischer Dom** (French Cathedral) to the north, built for Berlin's immigrant Huguenots, and the **Deutscher Dom** (German Cathedral) to the south, both early 18th century. The twin domes were added in 1785.

Karl-Liebknecht-Strasse

Schloss-Brücke (Marx-Engels-Brücke under the East German régime), designed by Schinkel, links Unter den Linden to Karl-Liebknecht-Strasse. On the bridge, look over to the left at the monumental Museumsinsel, site of Eastern Berlin's great museums (*see* pages 292–98). Beyond the bridge, **Marx-Engels-Platz** was laid out as the equivalent of Red Square, the focus for the Communists' May Day military parades and mass rallies. It was the site of the Hohenzollern's war-damaged 17th-century Stadtschloss (City Palace), razed rather than rebuilt. (The northern part of the square has regained its old name of Lustgarten.)

The palace where Spartacist leader Karl Liebknecht proclaimed his abortive "Socialist Republic" was replaced by the vast **Palast der Republik**. It houses an assembly hall originally used by the East German Volkskammer (Parliament) and a 5,000-seat conference hall where the

*T*he Rotes Rathaus (Red Town Hall) in the former East Berlin took its name from the colour of the bricks, not from any Marxist connections.

Communists held their party congresses. Conceived as a "house for the people", it also contains restaurants, cafés, a discotheque and a bowling alley. The white marble structure's extravagant populism is countered across the street by the imperial pomposity of Kaiser Wilhelm II's monstrous **Dom** (cathedral). Prussian

Berlin was full of cathedrals. This one has a crypt for 95 Hohenzollern sarcophagi.

Continue along Karl-Liebknecht-Strasse to the 13th-century **St-Marien-Kirche** on Neuer Markt, a haven of sober Gothic simplicity. Inside, see Andreas Schlüter's grand baroque marble pulpit (1703) and a late-Gothic fresco of the Dance of Death (1484) in the tower-hall.

The neo-Renaissance **Rotes Rathaus** (Red Town Hall) owes its name to its red clinker masonry, not its ideology. Built in 1869, it expresses with a certain style the city's pride when Prussia was top-of-the-world, a pride revived now that it is once more the seat of the reunited municipal government.

Beyond the huge Neptune Fountain—not that you could miss it—is the **Fernsehturm** (Television Tower, with Information Centre on the ground floor). Built in 1969, at 365m (1,197ft) it tops the Eiffel Tower by 65m (213ft) and absolutely dwarfs Western Berlin's Funkturm, which was the object of the exercise. It looks like a billiard cue that has miraculously skewered one of the balls. The **observation deck** and café are in the ball, 207m (679ft) up. The view is great and the café revolves.

Nikolaiviertel

Around Molkenmarkt south of the Rotes Rathaus, the Nikolai neighbourhood was restored for the city's 750th anniversary celebrations in 1987 as a rather "clean" example of Old Berlin. It clusters around the city's oldest parish church, the twin-steepled Gothic **Nikolaikirche**, put up in 1230 and consecrated as Berlin's first Protestant church in 1559. It now serves as part of the Märkisches Museum (*see* page 307) devoted to the city's history. Among typical buildings of the 1900s resurrected here is the **Gaststätte Zum Nussbaum**, favourite tavern of famed cartoonist Heinrich Zille. More stately is the reconstructed **Palais Ephraim**, Poststrasse 16, rococo mansion of Friedrich II's Jewish financier Veitel Heine Ephraim and also devoted now to exhibitions of Berlin history.

Alexanderplatz

"Alex", as the huge square is known, was once the undisputed heart of Berlin, and somehow retains the magic spirit of the city despite relentless post-war modernization. Now a bustling pedestrian area of cafés, hotels, department stores and apartment blocks, Alex has always been the hub of night and day life, celebrated in Alfred Döblin's great 1929 novel *Berlin Alexanderplatz*. On the south side of the square, two buildings survive from that era, the **Berolinahaus** municipal offices and **Alexanderhaus** department store. They were designed by Peter Behrens, dynamic master builder whose pupils included Le Corbusier, Walter Gropius and Mies van der Rohe.

His lessons were not learned by the designers of the bleak apartments, hotels and shops along **Karl-Marx-Allee** leading south-east from Alex. Drive up and down it if only for the lesson of what soulless buildings Stalinist architecture could produce—until 1961 the street was named Stalinallee.

Köpenick

The borough of Köpenick, with its delightful **old town** of 18th- and 19th-century houses, lies on the outskirts south-east of Eastern Berlin's centre. Like Spandau in the west, Köpenick has a longer history than Berlin itself, having been a Slav settlement on an island in the Spree river from the 9th century. It has a similarly independent-minded history. Socialist before the proclamation of the Weimar Republic, the town led the counter-assault which ended the right-wing Kapp Putsch of 1920 (*see* page 70). Local workers' resistance to Hitler in May 1933 led to the *Köpenicker Blutwoche* (Köpenick Bloodbath) in which storm-troopers killed 91 workers.

The sturdy 17th-century **Schloss Köpenick** occupies its own little island in the Dahme river. It houses an **Arts and Crafts Museum** (*Kunstgewerbemuseum*), noted for an excellent collection of medieval gold jewellery, Meissen porcelain, Venetian glass and 18th-century rococo furniture.

From Köpenick, a branch of the Spree leads to the **Grosser Müggelsee**, Berlin's largest lake, which is very pleasant for boat cruises or picnics on the shore. On the east side of the lake is the charming old fishing village of **Rahnsdorf** where single-storey stucco-façaded houses line the tranquil Dorfstrasse.

South of the lake, up in the wooded Müggel hills, the **Müggelturm,** a tower 30m (98ft) high, offers a good view beyond the city borders.

Museums

Eastern Berlin groups most of its art collections on **Museumsinsel** (Museum Island), just across from Marx-Engels-Platz in a fork of the Spree.

Pergamon Museum

Kupfergraben.

Housing many magnificent works of classical antiquity, the Near East, the Islamic world and the Orient, the museum is named after its most prized possession: the gigantic **Pergamon Altar** (2nd century BC). This masterpiece of Hellenistic art comes from what is now Bergama, near the west coast of Turkey. The great colonnaded altar dedicated to Zeus and Athena has been re-assembled to fill one great hall of the museum. A frieze more than 2m (7ft) high extends along the altar's base, relating the tortured struggle of the Greek gods with the giants.

Equally impressive is the **Babylonian Processional Street** (604–562 BC), built

Prize exhibits of the Pergamon Museum, Babylon's Processional Street and Ishtar Gate were excavated by German archaeologists in the 19th century.

during the reign of Nebuchadnezzar II. Lions sculpted in relief stride along the street's blue- and ochre-tiled walls towards Ishtar Gate. Bulls and dragons decorate the gate, also in blue and ochre tile. The museum's scale model shows how the processional street continued through the gate, on the edge of Babylon, to a house set aside for New Year festivities.

A third great treasure is the Roman **market gate of Miletus**, from Greek Asia Minor (AD 165). Its mundane name belies the elaborately pedimented monument—both gateway and shopping complex.

The **Islamic Museum** in the Pergamon's south wing exhibits the splendid façade of the 8th-century desert **Palace of Mshatta** (from modern Jordan). It is embellished with intricately incised or

perforated animal or plant motifs. A German art historian rescued this *tour de force* of early Islamic decoration at the beginning of the 20th century by dissuading the Sultan of Turkey from using it as building material for a railway to Mecca. The collection also includes an exquisite 14th-century Spanish synagogue carpet decorated with the sacred scrolls of the Hebrew Torah.

Bode Museum

Kupfergraben/Monbijou-Brücke.

The museum groups Egyptian, Early Christian, Byzantine and European art. The **Egyptian** collection includes an unfinished sandstone head of a queen (14th century BC). She is probably Nefertiti, bringing a complement of delicate grace and serenity to the beauty of the painted head in the Charlottenburg museum.

In the **Early Christian and Byzantine** department, look out for a 6th-century Ravenna mosaic from the church of San Michele, depicting Jesus as a young teacher and later, bearded, at the Day of Judgement.

Outstanding in the **sculpture** department are works by Luca and Giovanni della Robbia, Tilman Riemenschneider and Andreas Schlüter.

Because American troops retrieved those of Berlin's art treasures stored in Thuringia, most of the best ended up in Dahlem rather than on the Museuminsel.

*T*he great market gate built by the Romans at Miletus, Asia Minor, in 165 BC, reassembled by 19th-century German archaeologists at the Pergamon Museum.

But the Bode's **European paintings** do include notable works by Lucas Cranach, Adam Elsheimer, Jan van Goyen, Jakob van Ruisdael, Abraham Bloemaert and Nicolas Poussin.

Nationalgalerie

Bodestrasse 1.

Although its collection was depleted by Hitler's assault on "Degenerate Art" and the ravages of war, the museum has some interesting German works of the 19th and early 20th centuries: Carl Blechen, Max Slevogt and Max Liebermann (*The Flax Workers* and portraits of Wilhelm von Bode and Richard Strauss). Adolph von Menzel's *Iron Foundry* (1875) is a striking portrayal of industrial labour. Oscar Kokoschka's *Pariser Platz* (1926) recalls the bustle that once surrounded the Brandenburg Gate. The Brücke school is present, with works by Emil Nolde, Karl Schmidt-Rottluff, Erich Heckel and Ernst Ludwig Kirchner. A small international collection includes Goya, Courbet, Degas and Cézanne.

Märkisches Museum

Am Köllnischen Park 5.

The exhibits are generally an interesting proletarian antidote to the predominantly bourgeois displays of the Berlin Museum in Kreuzberg (*see* page 297). It has a nice collection of Berliniana: the first bicycles, sewing machines, telephones—and the 1881 telephone directory with all of 41 names in it—a 19th-century worker's kitchen, and a model of the infamous *Mietskasernen* (rental barracks) that nurtured unrest prior to the 1848 revolution. The museum's most beautiful item is one of the original sculpted horse's heads from the Quadriga on Brandenburg Gate. Which is where we came in.

FILM IN GERMANY

Scholars like to trace the origins of German cinema back to 1646, when archaeologist-mathematician **Athanasius Kircher** invented the magic lantern. Princes and dukes used it to entertain their palace guests with picture shows of erotic and mystical fantasies, enduringly popular themes with German film-makers of the modern day.

Around the time that the Lumière brothers were presenting their cinematograph in Paris in 1895, the Germans were coming out with their own fancifully named contraptions: Elektrotachyskop, Bioscop, Biophon and Seeberophone, the last two designed, unsuccessfully, to synchronize sound with picture. Although its technical quality was inferior to the French invention, **Max** and **Emil Skladanowsky's** Bioscop can claim Europe's first film-show at the Berlin Winter Garden (two months before Paris).

But the most important pioneer of German cinema was **Oskar Messter** (1866–1943) whose Berlin studio produced in 1897 the first feature films with scenario and artificial lighting. He showed Frederick the Great playing his flute at Sanssouci Palace, and an erotic treatment of *Salomé*, launching a fashion that found its audiences mainly in nightclubs.

The early 20th century's nationalism was reflected in the work of **Carl Froelich** (1875–1953). He specialized in historical biographies and military themes—*Pro Patria* (1910), vaunting Germany's first submarines, and *The Eagle of Flanders* (1918), portraying a heroic pilot convinced of Germany's victory in World War I.

The first stars of German cinema were Scandinavian, most notably **Asta Nielsen** (1881–1972). *Dance of Death* and *Little Angel* made her a pin-up in the war trenches on both sides. In Berlin, the Danish actress made her name in more serious roles—Strindberg's *Miss Julie* and Ibsen's *Hedda Gabler*. Her chief home-grown rival was **Henny Porten** (1890–1960) who at first incarnated the sexy promise of the girl next door and then became under Froelich's direction the symbol of German womanhood.

Created in 1918 as a national response to the invasion of the American and Scandinavian film industries, the **UFA** (Universum-Film Aktiengesellschaft) production company was financed by a consortium of banks and industrial magnates including

Murnau's Nosferatu

Krupp and Thyssen. Its production concentrated on mass-market entertainment, patriotic extravaganzas and sentimental comedies, in the face of suspicious artistic tendencies among Berlin film-makers.

Actor-writer **Paul Wegener** (1874–1948) began this dangerous trend in 1913 with the internationally successful *Student of Prague*, which drew on the German Romantic tradition of symbolism in nature and murky mixture of fantasy and reality. There was nothing Disney-like about his psycho-sexual treatment of fairy-tale characters like the giant *Rübezahl* and *The Pied Piper of Hamlin*.

Like many of the early creative talents of German cinema, he had begun in the theatre of **Max Reinhardt** (1873–1943). This magician of stage spectaculars was not himself very successful in the transition to the cinema (though he did create for Hollywood in 1935 a memorable *Midsummer Night's Dream* starring James Cagney and Mickey Rooney). But this master of dramatic lighting, monumental set composition, brilliant ensemble acting and crowd movement formed a whole generation of directors (Ernst Lubitsch, F.W. Murnau, Wilhelm Dieterle) and actors (Emil Jannings, Werner Krauss, Conrad Veidt, Elizabeth Bergner and, yes, Marlene Dietrich).

Ernst Lubitsch (1892–1947) shared Reinhardt's taste for royal parades, but this impudent scion of a Polish-Hungarian Jewish family of tailors had no respect for the aristocracy. His historical costume dramas were pure pastiche. *Madame Du Barry*, starring the smoky sex-symbol **Pola Negri** (originally a Polish dancer named Barbara Apolonia Chalupec) treated the French monarchy and revolution alike as bedroom farce. English history fared no better in *Anne Boleyn* with the great **Emil Jannings** as Henry VIII. The wit and precision of the celebrated "Lubitsch touch" that was to make his fortune in Hollywood were honed in light but acerbic comedies, often about bright and cheeky clerks marrying the boss's daughter—*Fräulein Seifenschaum* (Miss Soap Foam) and *The Pinkus Shoe Palace*. He reached the summit of his Berlin career with *The Oyster Princess* (1919) combining a satirical fairy-tale atmosphere with vulgar realism. Four years later, he left for California.

In the creative ferment of the Weimar Republic, Berlin was the capital of European cinema. The stark, highly charged emotions of Expressionist painting found their cinematic equivalent in *The Cabinet of Dr Caligari* of **Robert Wiene** (1880–1938), whose career was otherwise conventional. The story of a doctor in a lunatic asylum manipulating a sleepwalker to commit murders is played out in an atmosphere of dream and nightmare matched by grotesque décors, make-up and costumes and stylized acting. This landmark film reflects the age's social anarchy and preoccupation with psychoanalysis.

Friedrich Wilhelm Murnau (1888–1931) was more durably creative. The World War I fighter-pilot had learned his brilliant lighting technique from Reinhardt. With *Nosferatu*, he brought dramatic subtlety to the horror genre based on the Dracula theme. *The Last Man* is an acute psychological study of a chief porter in a grand hotel losing his splendid gold-braided uniform and self-respect when demoted to toilet attendant, while his *Faust* was an impressive in its use of ambitious special effects.

Georg Wilhelm Pabst (1885–1967) emphasized social realism. *Die Freudlose Gasse* (The Joyless Street) depicted the misery and and profiteering of the post-war years—and presented a new star named

Marlene Dietrich in Sternberg's Blue Angel

Fritz Lang's Metropolis

(Germany's equivalent of Hollywood or Cinecittà) to build fabulous landscapes for his two-part *Nibelungen* and an extravagant futuristic city for *Metropolis*.

The Nazi years saw an exodus of Germany's greatest talents, but a few opportunists and true believers stayed behind, like musical comedy star **Zara Leander,** actor **Werner Krauss** (who had played Dr Caligari and now performed the tour de force of five Jewish roles at once in the anti-Semitic film of *Jud Süss*) and producer-director Carl Froelich. One artist happy to serve the régime was **Leni Riefenstahl** (1902–). Trained as an "interpretative dancer", she had acted in sport and nature films in the 20s and was a symbol of the active, emancipated woman. Now she revealed a great talent as documentary director for Adolf Hitler in *Triumph of the Will*, a dramatically vivid portrayal of a Nazi Party rally at Nuremberg with its forest of flags and torch-lit processions. *Olympia* provided an equally brilliant account of the 1936 Berlin Olympics and set the standard for filmed sports coverage. Comparing the athletes' bodies to classical sculpture, it also glorified the Aryan superman.

The immediate post-1945 generation of film-makers was characterized by cheap sentimentality, with a few isolated exceptions like **Bernhard Wicki**, who tells in *The Bridge* a gripping story of 15-year-old boys enlisted in the German Army in the last days of World War II, sacrificing their lives in futile defence of a bridge. **Peter Lorre** returned from Hollywood to direct *The Lost Man,* a pathological scientist acquitted of murder by the Nazis because of his national importance and con-

Greta Garbo. But his great discovery for the German cinema was the American actress **Louise Brooks,** a luminous presence in *Diary of a Lost Girl* and as Lulu in *Pandora's Box*. His first sound film, *Westfront 1918*, was a striking pacifist document showing men as parts of an inhuman machine deprived of personal identity. But his *Threepenny Opera* was disowned by Brecht for avoiding the original's social criticism—at the insistence of its American financiers.

Even more to their liking was the film of **Josef von Sternberg** that revealed **Marlene Dietrich**: *The Blue Angel*, emblematic work of Berlin's decadent 20s showing a school-teacher befuddled by a flighty cabaret-singer.

In **Fritz Lang** (1890–1976), UFA found someone who could combine commercial and artistic values. His action thrillers, the *Dr Mabuse* series and most notably *M*, the story of a child-murderer starring the splendid **Peter Lorre** (1904–1964), showed men and women driven by their passions to tragic action against the dramatic social background of the times. This son of an architect and student at the Vienna graphic arts academy was also a master of the large-scale production. He used the resources of the Neubabelsberg studios

Peter Lorre as M

Solveig Dommartin in Wings of Desire

tinuing to kill. In East Germany, **Wolfgang Staudte** (1906–1984) also treated the Nazi theme, but his best film remains *Der Untertan*, from Heinrich Mann's novel of a nasty petty bourgeois in Wilhelminian Germany, *Man of Straw*.

In the 1960s, a new generation of creative directors emerged. Many were politically committed, like **Alexander Kluge** *(Farewell to Yesterday)* and **Peter Fleischmann** *(Hunting Scenes from Bavaria)*. There was a heavy literary emphasis in the work of **Volker Schlöndorff**, who turned for inspiration to novelists Robert Musil *(Young Törless)*, Heinrich Böll *(Lost Honour of Katharina Blum)* and Günter Grass for his Oscar-winning *Tin Drum*.

The prolific **Rainer Werner Fassbinder** (1946–82) brought a more personal vision to his work. His films avoid straightforward story-telling, keep the characters ambivalent and avoid moralizing. *The Bitter Tears of Petra von Kant* pays a sardonic tribute to Marlene Dietrich. *The Third Generation* depicts the disarray of political terrorists in the 1970s who no longer know what cause they are defend-ing, but his *Lili Marleen* is equally ambiguous about the Nazi period with its fascination for the pomp and uniforms. His best-known film is

The Marriage of Maria Braun, exposing the relentless materialism of West Germany's post-war "economic miracle".

Werner Herzog is obsessed by wild ec-centrics, using the astonishing **Klaus Kinski** to act out his fantasies as the title-role in *Aguirre, The Wrath of God*, a conquistador in the Peruvian jungle, or *Fitzcarraldo*, an Irish rubber magnate carrying a ship over a moun-tain to stage an opera, again in the South American jungle. A more intimate film is *The Enigma of Kaspar Hauser*, the disturbing but often witty story of a boy brought up in solitude, chained and fed like an animal and "tamed" in the bourgeois city of 19th-century Germany.

But the most creative of Germany's post-war directors remains **Wim Wenders.** He brings a European vision to the traditional American "road movie" in *Alice in the Cities* and *Paris, Texas*. The aesthetic is always more important than story. Even in a thriller like *The American Friend*, he is more interested in cre-ating a rich visual atmosphere than solving the crime. His *Wings of Desire*, made two years before the Wall came down, with the enigmatic **Bruno Ganz** as a fallen angel landing in Berlin, provides a perfect epitaph to the city's, indeed Germany's erstwhile schizophrenic existence.

Treasures of Potsdam and Dresden, the Romance of Goethe's Weimar

After the "quiet revolution" of 1989, the German Democratic Republic dissolved itself in a union with the Federal Republic and left a region of ancient tradition to lick its wounds, clean up its countryside, and restore its historic treasures. The gates are open again to retrace the footsteps of Luther, Bach, Goethe and Schiller, to see the baroque glories of Potsdam and Dresden, the delicate porcelain of Meissen, or explore the lakes of Mecklenburg and the wooded slopes of the Elbe Valley.

The historic *Länder* (states) of Brandenburg, Mecklenburg, Thuringia, Saxony and Saxony-Anhalt were, like their West German counterparts of Bavaria and Hesse, originally duchies or principalities—even kingdoms. Each had its own capital—its royal court—accumulating princely monuments and remarkable art collections. In Weimar, Potsdam and Dresden, these remain major attractions. For economic and also ideological reasons, churches and palaces were not always accorded a major priority in post-war reconstruction, but the artistic heritage is reclaiming its birthright, and you will find things in better shape than a few years ago.

When organizing your itinerary, remember that advance hotel reservations are an absolute necessity because good accommodation is still limited. For practical details *see* FACTS AND FIGURES, page 7.

Brandenburg

The state surrounding, but excluding, Berlin became the Hohenzollerns' power base in the 15th century, gradually incorporating the Prussian territories until being absorbed in the new kingdom of Prussia in 1701. The region east to Frankfurt-on-Oder at the Polish border is largely

Years of Communist rule did not abolish the taste for traditional costume, here sported with panache at Finsterbergen in Thuringia.

EASTERN GERMANY

Kieler Bucht

BALTIC SEA

Hiddensee
Sassnitz
Rügen
96

Fischland-Darss-Zingst
Stralsund
Mechlenburger Bucht
Warnemünde
105
ROSTOCK
Greifswald
109
111
Usedom
103
108
96

A1
105
Wismar
Schweriner See
Malchin
104
Neubrandenburg

A24
Schwerin
Müritz See
198
Prenzlau

N

POLAND

A7
Wittstock
96
Rheinsberg
E74
E14

103
Neuruppin
Kyritz
167
189
Oranienburg

Stendal
BERLIN
POTSDAM
E6
A2
189
Brandenburg
1
E74
E8
Frankfurt-an-der-Oder

E8
MAGDEBURG
SPREEWALD

A7
81
Halberstadt
E6
Wittenberg
E15
E22
Cottbus
Wernigerode
Quedlinburg
Dessau
187
Herzberg
E22
Elbe
81
6
E15
80
HALLE
101
Kamenz
Naumburg
6
Görlitz
Mühlhausen
87
LEIPZIG
Meissen
Mortizburg
Bautzen
6
84
ERFURT
Weimar
Jena
E63
DRESDEN
SÄCHSISCHE SCHWEIZ
Eisenach
E63
7
4
2
GERA
93
CHEMNITZ
THÜRINGER WALD
ZWICKAU
Oberhof
Ilmenau
E6
Schleiz
E62
19
Meiningen

CZECH REPUBLIC

Land above 500m (1,640ft)

0   50km
0   30 miles

A9
A7
A3

industrial, but pretty forests and lakes characterize the area west of Berlin around Potsdam, the royal capital, and the ancient bishopric of Brandenburg which gave the state its name.

Potsdam

In the eyes of Europe, Potsdam was Prussia, although many thousands of Protestant French Huguenots had made their home here, and brought their skills, after the Prince-Elector Friedrich Wilhelm's Edict of 1685 offered them sanctuary. It was his son, the self-proclaimed King Friedrich I who turned Potsdam into a pleasure dome where he could indulge in distinctly un-Prussian frivolity.

The soldier-king Friedrich Wilhelm I was made of sterner stuff than his father. He laid out parade grounds here for his beloved Prussian infantry to goose-step to the forefront of European armies. His son, Frederick the Great, refined the image by attracting to his Sanssouci Palace the cream of Europe's artists and intellectuals.

In 1933, Goebbels plumped for Potsdam's militarist tradition for the Führer's blessing by Field Marshal Hindenburg in the Garnisonskirche (Garrison Church). And Potsdam witnessed the end of it all when the victorious Allies met here in 1945 to carve up the Reich.

Today the area around the palaces is a green and pleasant place of spacious parks, and woodland and lakes, just beyond the south-western suburbs of Berlin. The nearby town of Potsdam suffered in World War II, and from subsequent neglect as well as from some ugly modern additions.

Frederick the Great's **Sanssouci Palace** was designed by Georg von Knobelsdorff in 1745 from the king's own sketches.

The Italian Renaissance Orangerie at Sanssouci was added by Friedrich Wilhelm IV to shelter his guests as well as his exotic plants.

A WISH FULFILLED

Sanssouci was Frederick the Great's favourite palace. Lonely and disillusioned in his later years, he declared that he wanted his final resting place to be in the gardens there beside his beloved greyhounds. But when he died in 1786, this was thought to be unseemly, and he was buried in the royal vault, later visited by Napoleon. At the end of World War II, his coffin was taken to the west. Only in 1991, in a moving ceremony, was it brought back and his will at last respected.

Frederick wanted a place where he could forget the affairs of state and pursue his passion for philosophy and the arts without worry—*sans souci*. The result is a charming rococo edifice perfectly integrated with its terraced gardens. In the palace's graceful interior, see the handsome cedarwood-panelled library in the east wing's rotunda. Next to the king's study and bedroom is a splendid Concert Room with paintings by Antoine Pesne. In the west wing is Voltaire's study, where the French writer served as writer-in-residence from 1750 to 1753.

East of the palace in the royal **Picture Gallery** (*Bildergalerie*) are works by Caravaggio, Guido Reni, Rubens and van Dyck. South-west of the terraced gardens and fountain, take a look at Frederick's **Chinese Pavilion** with

*A*t Potsdam,
Frederick the Great followed 18th-century taste for chinoiserie with this fanciful Chinese tea house in the Sanssouci Palace's former deer garden.

gilded palm trees for columns and a pagoda-style roof topped by a gilded mandarin. Some fine Chinese porcelain is displayed inside.

Beside the lake north of the city centre is a pleasant English-style park, **Neuer Garten**, landscaped in 1824 by Peter Joseph Lenné. It provides an apt setting for **Schloss Cecilienhof**, an ivy-covered, half-timbered pastiche of an English country manor. Built in 1916 for Crown Prince Wilhelm and his wife Cecilie, this architectural oddity is crowned with no fewer than 55 chimneys of which only three actually work. Unlike some real English country houses, it has excellent central heating. This was the only one of the Hohenzollern palaces in which the family was permitted to live after 1918, staying in fact until 1945.

Winston Churchill (and then Clement Attlee), Harry Truman and Joseph Stalin met here in July 1945 to draw up the Potsdam Agreement that fixed the division of Germany for the next 45 years. Since this provided the German Democratic

A LEMON AT THE COURT OF KING FREDERICK

Voltaire was employed as the king's chamberlain, hiring as secretary a promising young fellow named Gotthold Lessing, a future shining star of Germany's Enlightenment. Voltaire dined each night at the king's table with other leading men of letters and science, all French, but his relations with Frederick were tense. He resisted pressure to ghost-write the king's political testament and was upset by Frederick's note to a courtier that he regarded Voltaire as a "lemon to be squeezed and discarded". What he resented most of all was Frederick's miserliness, making him pay for his chocolate and candles.

The Cecilienhof at Potsdam was meant to look like an English country house. It was the site of the 1945 conference, in which the victorious Allies carved up Germany after World War II.

Republic's *raison d'être*, the conference room and delegation suites were preserved with the summit meeting's original tables, desks and national flags. One of the documents on show lists John F. Kennedy among the accredited press photographers. Part of the Cecilienhof now operates as a hotel and restaurant.

Outside the palace parks, the war spared little of old Potsdam, and the Communist régime allowed many of the surviving buildings to decay further, as well as adding some concrete boxes of their own. It's worth looking for the handsome 18th-century baroque **Accounting House** (*Oberrechnungskammer*), Yorkstrasse 19. Nearby is Karl Friedrich Schinkel's massive Palladian-style neoclassical **Nikolaikirche**. The elegant **Royal Stables** (*Marstall*) redesigned by Knobelsdorff in 1746 now house a Film Museum. The equestrian sculpture over the porticos is by Friedrich Christian Glume, who produced much of the statuary for Sanssouci.

Brandenburg Town

On the Havel river about 40km (25 miles) west of Potsdam on Highway 1, the town is a good base for visiting the surrounding lakes: Beetz See, known for its regattas and swimming facilities, Plauer See and Breitlingsee. The historic bishopric converted to Protestantism in 1567, but the Romanesque–Gothic **cathedral**, situated on an island in the river, has retained much of its interior ornament. Notice the 13th-century stained glass, some finely sculpted capitals and, above all, the beautifully painted *Coronation of Mary* for the 14th-century Bohemian altar.

South of the cathedral island, in the Neustadt district, visit the 15th-century **Katharinenkirche** to see the admirable Flamboyant Gothic gables and rose windows of the Corpus Christi chapel (*Fronleichnamskapelle*).

In the old town west of the cathedral, the dignified 15th-century step-gabled brick **town hall** has a lofty clock tower and Gothic porch with a tall, rather gloomy looking, statue of Charlemagne's worthy knight, Roland, in front.

Just off the Berlin–Hanover Autobahn, 20km (13 miles) south-east of town, is the largely 13th-century **Lehnin Monastery** (restored in 1877). The brick ensemble of church, granary, abbot's house and cloisters is a fine example of late-Romanesque and Gothic styles brought here by Cistercian monks from northern France.

Further Afield in Brandenburg

If you have your own transport, you'll be able to see more of the region which rings Berlin. You can use the capital as a base or find somewhere to stay in one of the pleasanter towns—there's some way to go, but standards are rising as hotels and restaurants open up.

North of Brandenburg town, **Neuruppin** was a base for the Prussian army and, in recent times, for the Soviet occupying forces. The lakeside setting, some fine old town houses and the 13th-century chapel of the Dominican monastery are the highlights. The chapel was restored by the leading architect of Neoclassicism, Karl Friedrich Schinkel, who was born in Neuruppin. A short drive west, the little town of **Kyritz** was once an important river port with access to the Elbe and the open sea. It was even a member of the Hanseatic league, and some of its medieval merchants' houses have been well restored. To the east, **Rheinsberg** was made famous by the humorous writer Kurt Tucholsky, whose memorial is in Rheinsberg castle (where Frederick the Great lived when he was Crown Prince).

South-east of Berlin, the low-lying **Spreewald** is criss-crossed by far more streams and canals than roads. City-dwellers discovered it over a century ago, taking gentle punting trips along the waterways. You can do the same today, propelled by local men and women of the

Slavic Sorb community dressed in their national costume (*see* page 329). The old fortified town of **Cottbus** was heavily damaged in World War II but part of the historic centre survived, around Old Market Square, and the 1907 Art Nouveau Stadttheater is unique.

Saxony

Historically, the duchy centred on the Elbe river was a bastion of the Reformation and Enlightenment and remains a force for independent-minded free thinking. Baroque Dresden has risen valiantly from its World War II ashes and the old trading city of Leipzig led East Germany's revolution of 1989. Meissen still produces some of the world's most exquisite porcelain. In the woodlands and cliffs of the Elbe valley you will find some of Eastern Germany's most beautiful country for rambling.

Dresden

The city's skyline of palace domes and church steeples on a bend in the Elbe river is one of the glories of European civilization. As it stands today, it is the result of three catastrophes. In 1685, fire ravaged the Renaissance city, and Saxony's scheming, ambitious prince Augustus the Strong (August der Starke) rebuilt it as a baroque residence for his court. Seventy years later, the Prussians wreaked new destruction in the Seven Years' War. Again Dresden rebuilt, adding a splendid neo-Renaissance opera-house in the 19th century. In 1945, from the night of 13 February to noon the next day, British and American fire-bombs rained down and practically razed the city centre.

Post-war reconstruction has been painful but resolute, and is still going on.

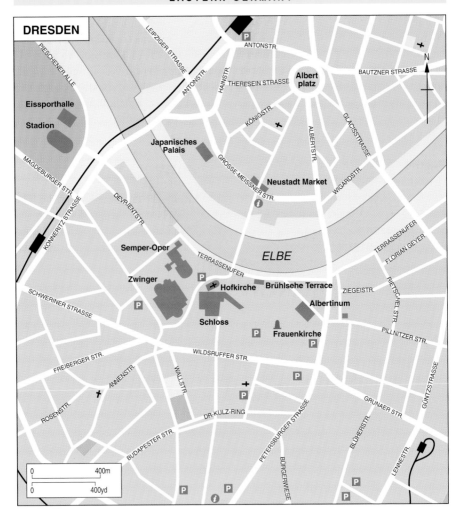

DRESDEN

If the city's modern architecture is uninspired and bleak, the old historic centre has recovered much of its charm. This, the cheerful spirit of the people and magnificent royal art collections, which happily escaped destruction, make Dresden the most popular of Eastern Germany's cities.

Zwinger Palace

Literally a barbican or outwork defending the entrance to a castle, the Zwinger was in fact a pleasure palace, not a fortification. Architect Matthäus Daniel Pöppelmann designed his rococo masterpiece (1709–32) as an extravagant grandstand for court festivities. It was to have been part of a larger palace that was never completed.

Enter from the south on Julian-Grimau-Allee through the exuberantly ornate **Kronentor**, its onion dome topped by Augustus the Strong's Polish crown. (Currying favour with the German emperor, Augustus had turned Catholic to become a prince elector in 1674 and king of Poland in 1697.)

There is a magnificent harmony to the single-storey sandstone galleries linking two-storey pavilions around a formal French-style garden courtyard. The roofs and balustrades are embellished by the sculpture of Pöppelmann's indispensable collaborator, Balthasar Permoser, and the whole evokes the delicacy of Meissen porcelain.

The Long Gallery (*Langgalerie*) to the right of the Kronentor houses Dresden's **Porcelain Museum** (*Porzellansammlung*)—entrance outside on Postplatz. With its windows looking out on the rococo palace, the gallery is the perfect setting for one of the world's most important collections of Meissen, Japanese and Chinese porcelain. The best of the Meissen sculptural pieces are by the 18th-century master, Johann Joachim Kändler—harlequins, monkeys, lions and a monumental equestrian statue. The galleries of the Zwinger's east wing curve inward to clasp the grand **Glockenspielpavillon** named after Kändler's porcelain carillon (which you can see in the Porcelain Museum). Opposite, with Balthasar Permoser's **Nymphenbad fountain** beyond the north-west gallery, the **Wallpavillon** houses a museum of mathematical and scientific instruments. More romantically, summer concerts (*Zwingerserenaden*) are held in its garden.

The north side of the palace was completed in 1854 in Italian Renaissance style by Gottfried Semper, the builder of the opera-house. It is the home of the world-famous **Dresden Picture Gallery** (*Gemäldegalerie*), temporarily housed in the Albertinum pending the prolonged restoration.

Theaterplatz

The square forms a handsome architectural ensemble around the proud **equestrian statue** (1883) of King Johann of Saxony. Behind him is Gottfried Semper's masterly state opera-house, better known as the **Semperoper** (1841, restored 1985). In the neo-Renaissance style the architect brought back from his travels through Italy, the opera-house makes an

THE END OF A CONTROVERSY?

With the proposed rebuilding of the Frauenkirche, the post-Communist municipality wants to stop the recriminations that arose from the 1945 bombardment. However, the historical debate remains: why was Dresden destroyed?

With no vital industries and enjoying the protective image of a "city of art", it escaped attack until the war neared its end. Churchill's memoirs refer to "a heavy raid on Dresden, then a centre of communications of Germany's Eastern Front". But British military historian Basil Liddell Hart says "Dresden was subjected to a devastating attack—with the deliberate intention of wreaking havoc among the civil population and refugees—striking at the city centre, not the factories or railways." (The presence of countless refugees from the east made it impossible to fix the number of dead, estimated at around 35,000.) Liddell Hart attributes the attack to Bomber Command's "revival of terrorisation as a prime aim ... largely to please the Russians."

The British saw it as retaliation for the Luftwaffe's destruction of Coventry and residential neighbourhoods of London. For East German Communist propaganda, forgetting Russian encouragement, it provided grounds for stigmatizing "Anglo-American imperialism". For old—and new—Nazis, it eased a bad conscience. The rebuilt church may reconcile Dresden with its past and future.

impact of sober elegance amid Dresden's predominantly baroque and rococo monuments. The statues on the façade portray Shakespeare beneath Sophocles, and Molière beneath Euripides. Flanking the entrance are Goethe and Schiller

On the west side of the square is the **Katholische Hofkirche** (1755), the Catholic court church (cathedral since 1980) in this heavily Protestant city. It forms an imposing silhouette with Gaetano Chiaveri's onion-bulb lantern tower and horseshoe-shaped basilica adorned by statues around the balustrades. Inside, see Balthasar Permoser's white rococo pulpit (1722) and, on the high altar, Anton Mengs' painting of *Christ's Ascension to Heaven* (1751).

The porcelain-tiled Princes' Procession on Dresden's Royal Palace.

long Renaissance wing leading to the royal stables (*Stallhof*) has a splendid Tuscan-style arcade.

Neumarkt and the Elbe

On Neumarkt square is the ruin of the baroque **Frauenkirche** (Church of Our Lady), once considered by many to be the most beautiful Protestant church in Germany. Today, only two gutted window bays still stand, facing each other across a mound of rubble and shrubbery. Since 14 February 1945, when the church collapsed just as the last fires were extinguished, the ruin was kept as a monumental reminder of what a bronze plaque called the Anglo-American "imperialist barbary". Now, the town is to rebuild in its original form the lofty dome surrounded by four small turrets over a majestic Greek-cross ground-plan shaped like a tortoise-shell.

Stroll over to the river for a walk in the 18th-century gardens of the **Brühlsche Terrasse**. Among the sculpture is Dresden's oldest surviving statue, the **Moritz monument** (1553), showing the fallen prince Moritz of Saxony handing his sword to his brother. *Weisse Flotte* **river cruises** start down on the quay below the terrace. Entrance to the Albertinum, presently housing the city's main museums (*see* page 324), is from the Brühlsche gardens.

Apart from the hotels and shopping, the one good reason for going to the **Neustadt** (New Town) district on the north bank of

Behind the church, most of the Royal Palace (*Residenzschloss*) remains a bombed-out shell. But on the Augustusstrasse, notice the 19th-century **Princes' Procession** (*Fürstenzug*), a frieze of 25,000 pieces of painted Meissen porcelain depicting 35 Saxon princes, artists and scientists on the façade of the **Langer Gang** (1591). Along its inner side, this

the Elbe is the view you get of the old town, best of all from the grassy river bank by the bridge known as Augustusbrücke. There is also one monument worth seeing: the gilded equestrian statue of Augustus the Strong as an armoured Roman emperor, the **Goldener Reiter** (1736).

Museums

Pending the restoration of the Zwinger's north wing, Dresden's principal art collections are kept together in the **Albertinum**, Brühlsche Terrasse. The building, incorporating the Renaissance arsenal, is named after Saxony's 19th-century King Albert.

Space there allows only a selection to be shown from the astonishingly rich collections of the **Gemäldegalerie**, divided into Old Masters and 19th and 20th Century (Alte and Neue Meister). Begin with Canaletto's views of Dresden's 18th-century heyday: notably the Frauenkirche on Neumarkt and a river view showing the Hofkirche covered, even then, in scaffolding.

Here are some of the other highlights. **Old Masters—Italian**: the museum's most celebrated painting, Raphael's *Sistine Madonna* (1513), shows a somewhat bewildered-looking Mary watched by the martyred Pope Sixtus. Giorgione's sensual, languorous *Slumbering Venus* (1510) was completed by Titian adding the landscape. Titian's *Tribute Money* (1516) depicts Jesus admonishing a Pharisee to "render unto Caesar ...". Trouble and anguish replace Botticelli's usual sweet serenity in his *St Zenobius*.

Flemish and Dutch: Van Eyck achieves an exquisite piety in his altar painting of *Mary Enthroned* (1437). Rubens' sumptuous *Bathsheba* (1635) looks as if she is wondering when David is going to notice her. Rembrandt's vivid *Samson at the Wedding Feast* (1638) has a cinematic movement to it. Vermeer's wonderful *Girl Reading a Letter* (1659) evokes a hint of romance blowing through the open window.

German: Dürer's great *Wittenberg* or *Dresdner Altar* (1496–97) is a synthesis of what he had learned from the grand Venetian Renaissance and more personal Flemish tradition. Lucas Cranach established his reputation as a major Renaissance artist with his grandiose *St Catherine Altar* (1506). Holbein the Younger's *Thomas Godsalve and Son* (1528) subtly captures the two men's family likeness and psychological differences.

Spanish: In Velázquez's portrait of *Hunting Master Juan Mateos* (1632), the regard is piercing, the hands unfinished. Zurbarán brings a gripping blend of mysticism and realism to his *St Bonaventura* (1629).

French: Poussin's *Adoration of the Magi* (1633) shows Christianity born in the ruins of a Roman temple. Joy and refinement triumph in Watteau's *Pleasures of Love* (1717) and *Country Festivities* (1720).

The collection of **19th- and 20th-century** paintings (*Neue Meister*) is predominantly German. Outstanding are Caspar David Friedrich's haunting *Two Men Watching the Moon* (1820), Adolph von Menzel's *Afternoon in the Tuileries Gardens* (1867), a subtle study in light and

*T*he quality of Meissen's centuries-old porcelain manufacturing process has been painstakingly preserved, with an emphasis on hand-painted decoration.

shade, and the monumental *War* triptych (1932) of Otto Dix. Lovis Corinth's *Walchensee* (1920) shows the enduring influence of Cézanne. Measure the impact of the French Impressionists on the Brücke group (founded here in Dresden) by comparing Karl Schmidt-Rottluff's *After the Bath* (1912) and Emil Nolde's *Sailing Boats on the Yellow Sea* (1914) with the gallery's works by Gauguin, van Gogh and, to a lesser extent, Degas and Manet.

Awaiting its relocation in the restored Royal Palace, the extravagant treasures that Augustus the Strong kept in his **Grünes Gewölbe** (Green Vault) are also exhibited in the Albertinum. Among the gold, silver and jewellery from the 14th to 18th centuries, the prize piece is the dazzling *Royal Court of Grand Mogul Aurangzeb* (1708). Goldsmith Johann Melchior Dinglinger fashioned the fabled Delhi court with 3,000 precious gems— diamonds, emeralds, rubies and pearls.

Pillnitz

One of the more pleasant boat cruises from the Brühlsche Terrasse takes you up-river (south-east) to **Schloss Pillnitz** (1724), another rococo creation of Matthäus Daniel Pöppelmann. The Saxon princes' summer residence has two main wings, the riverside **Wasserpalais** and the inland **Bergpalais**, separated by a formal French garden. More playful than the Zwinger, the palace has a faintly Chinese air with its pagoda-like roofs. The Bergpalais houses a nice little **arts and crafts museum** (*Museum für Kunsthandwerk*) displaying the region's furniture, musical instruments, porcelain, crystal and pewter. Take a stroll in the English-style landscaped park that stretches north and west of the palace.

Meissen

The home of Europe's first porcelain manufacture is also a wine-growing town of considerable architectural beauty, although rather run-down after decades of post-war neglect. At the confluence of the Elbe river and its Triebisch and Meisa tributaries, Meissen was founded in the 10th century as part of Germany's earliest eastward expansion.

Coming from Dresden past the vineyards on Highway 6, stop on the bridge for a first view of the **Albrechtsburg citadel** dominating the town. The triangle of castle, cathedral and episcopal buildings forms a splendid late-Gothic ensemble. The distinctive feature of the **castle's** western façade is the massive **Wendelstein**, a spiral staircase cut from one solid stone block. The fortress served as Meissen's porcelain factory until 1864.

In the twin-spired **cathedral** (1290), be sure to see the magnificent 13th-century statues by the renowned sculptors of Naumburg (*see* page 343). In the choir are Emperor Otto I, his smiling wife Adelheid, St John and St Donatus, and in the Octagonal Chapel, Mary and Child with John the Baptist and a church deacon. The Naumburg masters also carved the rood screen. Notice, too, on the high altar, a fine 16th-century *Adoration of the Magi* painted by a Netherlands artist. The *Crucifixion* (1526) on the lay altar in front of the rood screen is attributed to Lucas Cranach's workshop.

*A*lbrechtsburg, a citadel of cathedral, castle and episcopal buildings, dominates the Meissen skyline from its strategic position above the town.

*P*orcelain is still made by the traditional methods in the factory at Meissen. Whether it's to your taste is another matter.

The **Domherrenhöfe**, an attractive group of houses to the right of the cathedral, dates from the 15th to 18th centuries. The baroque decoration on No. 9 is probably the work of its 18th-century owner, Johann Joachim Kändler, master designer for Meissen porcelain.

Down by the market-place, the belfry of the 15th-century **Frauenkirche** boasts a porcelain bell, fashioned in 1929, with a leather-bound clapper. Nearby, admire the gables of the 16th-century Renaissance **Brewery** (*Brauhaus*) and visit the ivy-covered Vincenz Richter wine tavern.

The **Meissen Porcelain Factory** (*Staatliche Porzellanmanufaktur*) has its showrooms at Talstrasse (formerly Leninallee) 9. A guided tour explains the time-honoured manufacturing process with craftsmen at work. Locally quarried kaolin, fine white china clay, and russet-coloured feldspar are modelled on a potter's wheel that is still foot-propelled to control the speed for complicated forms. For Meissen's famous cobalt blue, the porous porcelain sucks up the paint, which is at first grey-green and then, after firing and glazing, achieves the distinctive hue.

Moritzburg

A short drive—or a narrow-gauge railway ride—north-west of Dresden, this ochre and white palace was a hunting-lodge and summer retreat for the royal court. Augustus the Strong had the present lake formed by merging smaller ones so that he could stage "sea battles" and regattas. Now, Moritzburg's spacious parks and wildlife reserve attract crowds from the city to swim, fish and camp, especially on summer weekends. The interior of the castle houses some fine furniture, porcelain and hunting paraphernalia.

Elbe Valley

The mountains along the Elbe river from Dresden to the Czech border have given the area the name of "Saxon Switzerland"—*Sächsische Schweiz*. They rarely rise more than 400m (1,300ft), but bizarre sandstone rock formations stand out from forests of oak, beech and lime, in addition to the usual pine and fir. Hundreds of miles of tracks and 1,000 registered climbs have made the mountains a popular destination for ramblers and rock climbers.

The spa resort of **Bad Schandau** near the Czech border makes a good base for exploring the area. The **Heimatmuseum**, Badallee 10, gives an interesting introduction to the region's distinctive geology. Notice in the **Johanniskirche** a 16th-century pulpit carved from a solid block of the local sandstone. Of the town's older houses, the 17th-century **Brewery** (*Brauhaus*), Marktplatz 12, is particularly noteworthy for its octagonal staircase tower and handsome porch. There are some fine half-timbered houses up in the old Ostrau and Postelwitz quarters above the town centre. Enquire at the tourist office in the Heimat-museum about **paddleboat cruises** on the Elbe.

For those averse to hiking, a little train chugs 8km (5 miles) east of town to the pretty **Kirnitzsch Valley** with its babbling stream and the **Lichtenhainer Waterfall**. Another little excursion, just 3km (2 miles), follows a footpath well marked with yellow triangles to the spectacular wall of sandstone pillars known as the **Schrammsteine**, 417m (1,368ft) high. The castle of **Königstein**, towering over the river near a dramatic sandstone outcrop of the same name has been at various times an impregnable fortress, pleasure palace, wine store and prison. (One of its inmates was Johann Friedrich Böttger, who discovered how to make porcelain and was locked up when suspected of trying to sell the formula.)

Oberlausitz

The region of Lusatia stretching east and north-east of Dresden to the Polish border is the home of one of Germany's oldest-established minorities, the Sorbs. Frequently persecuted in the past, now some 90,000 strong, they are mostly Catholic peasants of Slavonic stock. Old customs are still observed, both Christian and pagan. Bonfires are lit on Easter Sunday and, on the eve of 1 May, *Walpurgisabend,* witches are burned in effigy. Towns are signposted in both German and Sorb.

In **Kamenz**, the older generation can still be seen wearing traditional costume, particularly the women in dark headscarves or red bonnets, colourful embroidered blouses and blue skirts. At carnival time, the men deck their hats with flowers and ribbons. The town was also the birthplace, in 1729, of Gotthold Ephraim Lessing, a leading writer of the Enlightenment. He is honoured with a small museum on Lessingplatz.

Built on a granite plateau on a bend in the Spree river, the old fortified town of **Bautzen** is the centre of Sorb life. Folklore activities are conducted at the **Hause der Sorben** on Postplatz, and a Sorb theatre (*Deutsch-Sorbisches Theater*) is located on the southern end of town. Take a walk along the ramparts with its sturdy old bastions and towers and visit the **Cathedral of St Peter** to see its fine baroque *Crucifixion* by Balthasar Permoser. Remarkably, the cathedral has been shared by Catholics and Protestants ever since the Reformation. On Hauptmarkt, the **town hall** is baroque, with some handsome patrician houses on either side.

The countryside is also dotted with gracious mansions and hunting-lodges set in their own parks and woodland. One such, just north of Bautzen, is the elegant 18th-century **Schloss Neschwitz**, once the property of the Baron von Vietinghoff, revered in the region as a great ecologist. One of his last descendants is a film producer in Berlin.

Leipzig

Vital industrial and commercial centre for the East German Communist regime, the city was, before World War II, a direct rival to Frankfurt am Main for its publishing houses and trade fairs. It has long been a focus for the cause of German liberty. In 1813, victory here over Napoleon started the liberation of Germany. In 1830 and 1848, Leipzig was a centre of liberal

*K*önigstein is one of many great pillar-like sandstone formations hemming in the whimsically named "Saxon Switzerland".

revolt. In 1989, the town's weekly mass meetings formed the vanguard of East Germany's democratic revolution. After years of crippling industrial pollution and urban neglect, the town's new struggle is for its own resurrection as a centre of culture. Its symphony orchestra at the Neues Gewandhaus remains one of Europe's best. A few monuments remind us that Leipzig is where Johann Sebastian Bach led the St Thomas church choir and Goethe studied at the university.

Modern Leipzig has gone for size. With 26 platforms, the **Hauptbahnhof** claims to be the biggest railway station in Europe. Around it, the most visible buildings are the skyscraper business hotels and the 143m (470ft) university tower.

Relics of the old city have to be hunted down. On the Markt, the **Altes Rathaus** (Old Town Hall, 1556) is a long gabled Renaissance edifice with elegant lantern tower. It lodges a museum of local history. Behind it, on the charming little **Naschmarkt** square, is the handsome 17th-century baroque **Handelsbörse** (Commercial Exchange). Also on the square is a 1903 statue of Goethe as a young student. In nearby Mädler-passage, one of the city's characteristic shopping galleries, is the celebrated old **Auerbachs Keller** (1530), the tavern where Goethe set a famous confrontation of Faust and Mephistopheles. Their statues flank the entrance, and painted in its vaulted rooms are scenes from the master's great drama.

Grimmaische Strasse leads west to the 15th-century Gothic **Thomaskirche**, home of the renowned Thomaner Choir which Bach directed from 1723 to 1756. Motet recitals are held here each weekend. A **Bach monument** stands on the south side, and a modern bronze plaque marks the composer's tomb inside the church.

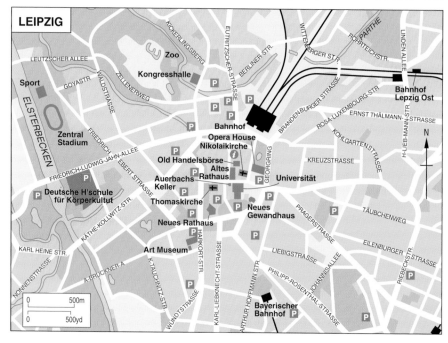

Retrace your steps east towards the giant university and the **Nikolaikirche**, an unassuming Romanesque-Gothic church with a bright neoclassical interior, but famous since the autumn of 1989. It was the crescendo of its Monday meetings, originally convened to fight pollution and the dangers of nuclear war, that led to the downfall of Honecker's Communist government.

In the old law courts building just south of the centre, the **art museum** (*Museum der Bildenden Künste*) has works by Lucas Cranach, Hans Baldung Grien, Rogier van der Weyden, Frans Hals and, from the 19th and 20th centuries, Caspar David Friedrich, Max Liebermann, Lovis Corinth and Edvard Munch.

If you find yourself out at the trade-fair grounds east of the city centre, take a look at the **Völkerschlachtdenkmal**, monument of the Battle of the Nations against Napoleon. It was consecrated on the battle's centenary, 1913, and its ponderous style is in the same tradition as the nationalistic Germania and Deutsches Eck monuments in the Rhineland.

So close to Leipzig that it's hard to tell where one ends and the other begins, **Halle** to the north-west has a deserved reputation for being grimly industrial. The centre has many fine old buildings, spared from destruction in World War II only to suffer from the unrestricted pollution of the decades that followed. The central market square is worth a visit: Handel, born in Halle, played the organ in St Mary's church.

Despite the post-1945 drive to build up East Germany's heavy industry, most land remains agricultural, as here at Gernstedt in Thuringia.

Thuringia

This is the land where medieval minstrels founded the great tradition of the German ballad. Painter Lucas Cranach made his home here and his friend Martin Luther waged his battle for the Reformation. Goethe and Schiller found inspiration for their enlightened ideas and Romantic poetry. The great Thuringian Forest continues to attract romantic ramblers in summer and now skiers in winter.

Weimar

It was the wealth of the town's cultural traditions that prompted Germany's democrats to put Weimar's name on the new republic in 1919. To architect Walter Gropius, it seemed the right place to found his Bauhaus school of architecture and design the same year. The town's enlightened princes amassed a considerable art collection, nurturing in particular the talents of Lucas Cranach. The court also entertained a panoply of Germany's leading poets that included, beside Goethe and Schiller, Christoph Martin Wieland and Johann Gottfried Herder.

To get a feel of things today, start at the august neoclassical temple that is the **Deutsches Nationaltheater** on the west side of the city centre with its double **monument of Goethe and Schiller** (1857). Goethe spent 50 happy years here from 1782 until his death, and was joined for three years by Schiller in 1802. Built in 1709, the **Goethehaus**, Am Frauenplan, is a dignified bourgeois home of the baroque era. The interior, with its Palladian staircase redesigned by Goethe himself, has authentic furnishings. You can see the great man's study with his desk and, most movingly, the bedroom with the armchair in which he died on 22 March

GET YOUR TICKETS HERE

To visit Goethe's house and museum and that of his friend Schiller, you must get a multi-purpose pass from Frauentorstrasse 4. Belying the charm of the places you will visit, the office declares itself responsible for the intimidatingly named *Nationale Forschungs- und Gedenkstätten der klassischen deutschen Literatur* (National Research Sites and Monuments of Classical German Literature).

1832. Look out for Johann Heinrich Tischbein's portrait of Goethe's benefactor, Duke Carl August, who made the poet his finance minister. Among the 18th-century paintings of classical Greek and Roman themes, one depicts Goethe as Orestes. Find time, too, for the beautifully kept garden, and see his personal coach in the stable.

The **Schillerhaus**, Schillerstrasse 12, is organized as a small museum of the writer's life and work. It was here that he wrote his play *Wilhelm Tell*.

In the baroquified Gothic **Stadtkirche St Peter und Paul** (1500), see Lucas Cranach's impressive altar triptych, completed by his son in 1555. The central *Crucifixion* shows the bearded Cranach praying beside the Cross with Luther holding a Bible. A monumental stone relief marks **Cranach's tomb** on the north wall of the chancel—the painter died in 1553. Outside the church, also known as *Herderkirche*, a monument honours the

O̶ne of the most moving experiences at Goethe's house in Weimar is the sight of the Great Man's manuscripts, many of them over 200 years old.

poet Herder, who as Duke Carl August's education minister preached sermons and was buried here.

East of the church, the baroque and neoclassical **Ducal Castle** is now a richly endowed **art museum** (*Staatliche Kunstsammlungen*). The highlight of the collection is a group of 28 Cranachs, including *Martin Luther* in his Wartburg Castle disguise (*see* page 339) with thick beard and full head of hair, and a beautiful portrait of *Sybille von Cleve*. Other masters represented include Tintoretto, Veronese, Philipp Otto Runge, Caspar David Friedrich and Claude Monet. The museum also has a good collection of furniture, artefacts and graphics produced by the Bauhaus workshops in Weimar in the 1920s.

Modern architecture buffs visiting the Walter Gropius buildings in Berlin and Dessau (*see* page 340) should see his first **Bauhaus headquarters** at Geschwister-Scholl-Strasse, just west of Belvederer Allee. He used Henry van de Velde's elegant 1906 building, now an architecture college (*Hochschule für Architektur*), which still has some time-worn pieces of Bauhaus furniture designed by Marcel Breuer. Stroll over to the pretty **Park an der Ilm** where Weimar's 18th- and 20th-century art worlds come together. Nestling against the far slope beyond the Ilm river is **Goethe's Garden House**, where the poet lived for six years from 1776. Up above, on the Am Horn road, is a **Bauhaus model house**, a bright white cube by Georg Muche.

Buchenwald

If the republic of 1918 paid homage to Weimar's culture by drawing up its constitution here, the Nazis showed their contempt for all humanism by building a concentration camp on the town's northwest outskirts. The camp installations have gone, but a **monument** pays tribute to the victims.

Erfurt

The skyline of this old university city bristles with spires, with the cathedral and church of St Severus forming together a striking silhouette on their own hilltop terrace. This is reached by a monumental staircase from Domplatz to the west. The triple-spired **cathedral** is a combination of 12th-century Romanesque, notably in the towers, and 15th-century Gothic. In the interior, notice the stained-glass windows (1370–1420) in the chancel and the fine Gothic oak choir stalls. The bronze Wolfram statue, serving as a candle holder, and stucco *Enthroned Madonna* are both 12th century.

The **Severikirche** (St Severus Church) of 1280–1400, also triple-spired, makes a noble neighbour to the cathedral. Inside, the saint's sarcophagus (1365) portrays him on its lid with his wife and child. Note, too, an alabaster relief of St Michael slaying a dragon.

Back on Domplatz, take a look at its attractive old houses, notably the 18th-century **Green Apothecary** (*Grüne Apotheke*) and the Renaissance **Zur Hohen Lilie**, now a restaurant. There are more fine Renaissance houses on **Fisch-markt**.

The most charming spot in the old town is the **Krämerbrücke**, a bridge over the Gera river lined with art galleries, antique shops and small cafés in half-timbered houses dating from the 17th to 19th centuries.

Renaissance and baroque façades border the bustling Anger, Erfurt's main shopping artery. The **Angermuseum** at

No. 18 has works by Lucas Cranach and Hans Baldung Grien, and a superb collection of Brücke Expressionists, among them Erich Heckel's monumental *Das Leben der Menschen* (The Life of Humanity).

Thuringian Forest

The cool, moist pine forest grows on a mountain ridge rising 800–900m (2,600–2,950ft). The **Rennsteig** hiking trail covers a total of 160km (100 miles) of well-marked paths through the forest

*E*rfurt escaped serious damage during World War II, but suffered from neglect in the decades afterwards. Now its fine old houses are being restored.

GOETHE AT BREAKFAST WITH NAPOLEON

In Erfurt in 1808, a couple of days after his summit with Tsar Alexander, Napoleon found time for a morning meeting with Goethe. The great writer describes Napoleon munching his breakfast while foreign minister Talleyrand stood to one side. He looked up as Goethe came in and said: "*You* are a man".

Goethe remained dumb.

"How old are you?"

"Sixty."

"You keep yourself well," said Napoleon, adding, perhaps by way of explanation, "You write tragedies." Again the writer was at a loss for words.

The emperor went on to criticize Goethe's sentimental novel *The Sorrows of Young Werther*, which he seemed to know inside out. "Why did you do that?" he asked of one passage. "It's not natural." Goethe smiled and said this was the first time he had heard such criticism but, as an artist, he had his reasons.

Then Napoleon turned on his plays, treating them, Goethe observes, like a judge in criminal court, adding at the end of each opinion: "What does Mr Göt have to say about that?"

The interview ended with the great conqueror asking for gossip about the local Duke and Duchess. The author of *Faust* did his best to oblige.

from Hörschel near Eisenach in the west to Blankenstein at the Bavarian border. You can get trail maps from the resort town of **Oberhof**. For more leisurely walks, visit the town's **Rennsteig Garden**, 12 hectares (30 acres) of pretty mountain parkland. Sports facilities include tennis and reservoir lakes for fishing in summer, and good snow on nearby slopes in winter for skiing, bobsleigh and luge runs.

Johann Sebastian Bach (1685-1750)

This giant of late Baroque music was in his own time honoured as harpsichordist, organist and expert on organ-building, but his compositions were regarded as old hat. From the 16th to the 19th centuries, the Bach family turned out scores of musicians—the venerable *Grove Dictionary of Music* lists no less than 78. Five of Johann Sebastian's sons achieved considerable prominence.

In the 1560s, great-great-grandfather Veit Bach, a Thuringian miller, played his cittern (a sort of lute) while grinding the flour at the mill. "A pretty noise they must have made together!" Johann Sebastian wrote later. "However, he did learn to keep time and this was apparently the beginning of music in our family."

The genius of the family was born in Eisenach, Thuringia, March 21, 1685. He had a fine singing voice and joined the boys' choir of St Michael's church, Lüneburg. In 1703 he played violin in the Weimar court orchestra, but soon left to pursue his main passion as organist at St Boniface church in nearby Arnstadt. He walked 300 kilometres (200 mi.) north to Lübeck to hear the great organ-composer Dietrich Buxtehude.

Bach was a merciless critic of other musicians, and his insults of a bassoonist in Arnstadt ended in a street brawl. In 1707, he left in disgust for Mühlhausen where he married his cousin, Maria Barbara. She bore him seven children. Back in Weimar as the duke's *Konzertmeister*, Bach was required to compose one cantata a month and achieved a formidable national reputation.

But it was at Köthen, in the prestigious post of *Kapellmeister* (music director) for the Duke of Anhalt from 1717 to 1723 that he enjoyed the happiest and some of the most creative years of his life—despite the death of Maria Barbara. The duke was himself a musician and encouraged Bach to compose some of his finest chamber and orchestra music: *The Well-Tempered Clavier*, works for the solo violin, the cello suites and the *Brandenburg Concertos* (dedicated to the Margrave of Brandenburg). In 1721, he remarried, choosing this time Anna Magdalena, a trumpeter's daughter and herself a fine soprano. He was as prolific in family life as he was in music: Anna Magdalena bore him 13 more children. But the new duchess, a philistine, resented her husband's preoccupation with Bach, who was obliged to move on again, this time to Leipzig.

His job as choir director for the school of St Thomas, providing singers for four Leipzig

churches, was a step down from *Kapellmeister*. His employers considered him a poor substitute for their first choice, composer Telemann. For his part, Bach was furious with the "cloth-eared" boys he was expected to train. He complained he was not earning enough money because the robust citizenry of Leipzig provided him with less funerals to officiate at than he had been led to expect.

He devoted most of his time to playing, maintaining, repairing and refashioning church organs around the country and progressively abandoning ecclesiastic music for secular composition in the more congenial company of princes and kings. He wrote partitas and cantatas for the Elector Prince of Saxony—later used in his *Christmas Oratorio*—to wangle the job of court composer in 1736. In May 1747, Bach visited his son Emanuel, harpsichordist at Frederick the Great's court in Potsdam. The King gave Bach his own little composition to play around with during a fugue recital. The result became known as *Das musikalische Opfer* (The Musical Offering).

In his 60s, he developed cataracts and underwent two unsuccessful eye operations by the same English charlatan, John Taylor, who blinded George Händel. Bach died on July 28, 1750, leaving Anna Magdalena penniless as his vast progeny squabbled over the inheritance.

Eisenach

Situated on the north-west edge of the Thuringian Forest, the town has preserved two houses that bear testimony to its importance for the culture and civilization of the Western world. **Johann Sebastian Bach's birthplace** (*Bachhaus*), Am Frauenplan 21, stands in a charming tree-shaded square with an imposing statue of the composer (1685–1750). With the aid of manuscripts, prints and musical instruments, the house's small **museum** documents the life of his family. **Martin Luther's house**, Lutherplatz 8, is a fine half-timbered mansion dating back to the 13th century. It has been handsomely restored to document the campaign Luther waged here for the Reformation.

On the market place, the Thuringian counts' baroque town-palace is now a **museum** (*Thüringer Museum*) of medieval sculpture, rococo porcelain and painting by regional artists from the 15th to 19th centuries.

Dramatically perched atop a wooded hill south-west of town, **Wartburg Castle** is accessible by bus, car, foot or, for part of the way, on hired donkey. Begun in 1070 and restored, at Goethe's urging, in the 19th century, the fortress inspired Ludwig II to build his castle follies in the Bavarian Alps and Richard Wagner to write his opera, *Tannhäuser.* Wagner took his theme from a "minstrel war" (*Sängerkrieg*) in 1207 between minnesingers Wolfram von Eschenbach, Heinrich von Ofterdingen and Walther von der Vogelweide. The guided tour starts from a drawbridge at the north end of the fortress. The restored castle is now largely neo-Romanesque and neo-Gothic, but furnishings, tapestries and artwork are authentic pieces from the medieval to baroque eras of the castle's existence.

> ## JUNKER JÖRG'S BAD HABIT
>
> Threatened by papal bull and imperial edict, Martin Luther came to Wartburg disguised as an aristocratic landowner, "Junker Jörg". He discarded his monk's habit, grew his hair to cover his tonsure, and grew a beard. Most of the time, he was cooped up in his castle room, writing tracts and a German translation of the New Testament. Occasionally, he ventured out into Eisenach, accompanied by a squire who tried to teach him aristocratic tics like patting his sword and stroking his beard. One personal habit threatened to uncover his disguise. The great scholar could not resist browsing in the books he came across in town, despite the squire's warning that "landowners do not read books".

Among the main points of interest is the Lutherstube in the west wing where the Reformer took refuge after his excommunication in 1521. The walls are decorated with Lucas Cranach's portraits of Martin and his wife Katharina and a black spot marking the impact of an inkwell that Martin threw at the Devil. Over the centuries the spot has had to be refreshed several times.

Around the southern courtyard is the castle's oldest section, the **Palas** (1190–1220), decorated with mosaics and frescoes from the 19th- and early 20th-century restoration. You will see the Minstrels' Hall (*Sängersaal*) and the apartments of St Elisabeth, 13th-century Hungarian-born countess of Thuringia. The castle also lent its name to East Germany's "up-market" car built in Eisenach in the old BMW factory. But the two-stroke Wartburg, almost medieval in conception (to match the castle), was only bigger, not more efficient, than the lovable little Trabant ("Trabbi") from Zwickau.

Saxony-Anhalt

The region from the Harz mountains over to the Elbe river groups together a part of northern Saxony with the old duchies of Anhalt (named after a family fortress in the Harz). The state includes Wittenberg, where Luther nailed up his 95 Theses, Dessau, second centre of the Bauhaus school, and the cathedral city of Naumburg.

Eastern Harz Mountains

The picturesque medieval town of **Wernigerode** makes a pleasant base from which to explore the mountains. Many of its nicely restored half-timbered houses have intricately carved reliefs. Notice in particular the **Krummelsches Haus**, Breite Strasse 72, and the splendid 15th-century Gothic **town hall**. Regional folklore is well treated at the **Harzmuseum**, Klint-gasse 10. On its hill 350m (1,150ft) above the town, visit the medieval castle fancifully restored in the 19th century and now a **museum** of weapons, armour, ornate harnesses and church sculpture.

For a good first view of the mountains, take a train ride on the **Harzquerbahn** from Wernigerode via the tragi-comically named towns of Elend (misery) and Sorge (sorrow). You will see the **Brocken**, the highest peak in the Harz at 1,142m (3,745ft), where witches danced on their sabbath and the East German Army erected a radar station to detect the evil doings of the West.

In the Harz foothills, **Halberstadt** maintains its medieval appearance around the **cathedral** of St Stephanus. Built from the 13th to the 15th centuries, the church has been restored—war-damage and industrial pollution had taken their toll—as one of the great pure Gothic monuments of Eastern Germany. It preserves a remarkable *Crucifixion* (1220), a finely carved rood screen (1400) and 15th-century stained glass windows in the chancel.

When they were not up on the Brocken, the witches danced around the sheer cliffs of the Bode valley, the charming site of **Quedlinburg**. On a hill above the town's fortified maze of medieval streets are a Renaissance **castle** with rich baroque furnishing and the splendid 12th-century Romanesque **church** of St Servatius. In the nave, notice the capitals finely sculpted with imperial eagles. Germany's King Heinrich I (875–936) and his wife Mathilde are buried in the crypt beneath the Gothic choir. The old town has many handsome 16th-century half-timbered houses, notably in the Hohe Strasse.

Dessau

The former capital of the Anhalt princes was almost totally destroyed in 1945, but it has in Walter Gropius's **Bauhaus building**, Thälmannallee 68, one of the world's most important 20th-century monuments. The great school of architects and artists (*see* page 293) came here in 1925, after an arch-conservative municipality had driven them out of Weimar. The building has a harmony and light that keep it unalterably modern, the uninterrupted three-storey glass screen on its façade being a major, much copied innovation in

Close to the old East–West border, the half-timbered houses of Wernigerode were kept in exceptionally fine shape to attract West German daytrippers.

industrial design. Inside is a permanent exhibition of the school's paintings, artefacts, costumes, theatre décors and architectural models.

Nearby, see three Bauhaus-designed **master houses**, Ebertallee 63–71, where, despite neglect, the pure line and clear functional form have survived. Until 1932, when politics once more forced a move—this time for a brief halt in Berlin before exile—these were the homes of architects Gropius and Mies van der Rohe and painters Lyonel Feininger, Paul Klee, Vasili Kandinsky and Oskar Schlemmer. As a better-preserved example of attractive modern residential architecture, visit Gropius's experimental housing development, the **Bauhaus-Siedlung** (1926–28), in the suburb of Törten.

More traditionally, the elegant white neoclassical **Schloss Georgien**, Puschkin-allee 100, houses a museum (*Staatliche Galerie*) of European painting. Its most notable artists include Cranach, Grien and Dürer; Pieter Brueghel, Rubens and van Goyen; Slevogt and Corot. You can take a stroll in the pretty English garden.

Wörlitz

For a pleasant excursion and picnic in the country, drive 15km (10 miles) east of Dessau to this 18th-century **castle** set in beautiful grounds. Take a gondola on the lake and canals or get lost in the maze. One of the strangest buildings is a fanciful yellow **Gotisches Haus** festooned with turrets on an island in the lake.

Wittenberg

Even if Martin Luther had not nailed his 95 Theses to the door of the court church, the town secured its place in history by electing painter Lucas Cranach as its mayor. The splendid Gothic and Renaissance

town hall where he governed makes a good place to start your tour. Notice the fine gables and grand balcony over the richly decorated porch. On the square is a mighty bronze **Luther statue** (1805) by Johann Gottfried Schadow, the sculptor of the Brandenburg Gate's Quadriga in Berlin, with a wrought-iron canopy by Karl Friedrich Schinkel. Nearby, Luther's fellow humanist Philipp Melanchthon is honoured by a similar monument (1860).

The **Lutherhaus** where Brother Martin lived from 1508 to 1546 is south-east of the city centre at the end of Collegien Strasse. It was part of Augustine monastic buildings. His original study and wood-panelled living room are still intact, complete with benches, dining table and tiled stove. This most important of Protestant museums has a marvellous collection of manuscripts, letters, prints, his university lectern and his pulpit from the town church of St Mary.

Just along the street at No. 60, the **Melanchthonhaus**, in which the great theologian lived for 24 years until his death in 1560, is also installed as a museum. See its garden, in which are the original fountain and stone table, and the scholar's reconstructed herb garden.

The church where Luther preached in Wittenberg was the **Stadtkirche St Marien**, Gothic but with Renaissance belfries added to its octagonal towers. Inside, on the **Reformationsaltar** painted in 1547 by Cranach, father and son, Luther is shown preaching on the predella beneath the central panel of the *Last Supper*.

Cranach's house is at Schloss-Strasse 1, where from 1505 to 1547 he was court painter, mayor and apothecary.

The **Schlosskirche** where Luther started all the trouble in 1517 (*see page 57*) was burned down in 1760 during the

The man who shook 16th-century Europe to its foundations. Martin Luther is honoured in Wittenberg, where he spent most of his life.

Romanesque-Gothic cathedrals. You will see from afar the noble silhouette of its four towers with chancels at either end of the basilica.

In the west chancel are two magnificent groups of Gothic sculpture whose creators, known simply as the masters of Naumburg, were in demand all over Germany, notably in Hildesheim and Mainz. The 12 life-size statues of the cathedral's founders, each highly individualized, constitute a vivid gallery of medieval gentry. Similar energy infuses the sculpted friezes of *Christ's Passion* on the rood screen. They show scenes from real life in the Middle Ages: a Last Supper that is a real meal, Christ's arrest an act of police brutality, and his confrontation with Pontius Pilate a court drama of anger and pathos.

On the town's market square is a handsome late-Gothic gabled **town hall** (1528). Inside, a monumental spiral staircase leads to the stuccoed council chamber. Renaissance **patrician houses** on and around the market square indicate the cathedral town's historic prosperity.

Seven Years' War and rebuilt in its present neo-Gothic form. The wooden door on which Luther posted his 95 Theses has been replaced by a monumental bronze door of 1858. Luther's grave is in the church with Melanchthon's, but with copies of the bronze plaques kept, by the vagaries of 16th-century wars, in Jena's Michaelkirche. The adjoining **castle** is now a museum of natural history.

Naumburg

Reached best from Leipzig or Weimar, the town possesses in its **Dom St Peter und Paul** (1213) one of Europe's great

Mecklenburg

North of Berlin to the Baltic coast lies the sleepy rural lake country of which Bismarck said: "If the world comes to an end, I shall flee to Mecklenburg because everything happens there 100 years later." This is the old *Junker* country of his fathers: vast potato fields and cattle pastures interspersed with groves of poplar, willow and alder. Avenues of chestnuts and limes stretch to the Polish border, planted by Napoleon to protect his troops from the sun on their march to Moscow. A land for camping, hiking, fishing and sailing, and for lazy days at the Baltic beach resorts.

The Lakes

The *Mecklenburgische Seeplatte* is a plateau of scores of lakes and frog-ponds left over from the Ice Age. You might start a tour at **Schwerin** (on a branch of the Berlin–Hamburg Autobahn), surrounded by seven lakes and pretty woodland. A dam divides the town's **Schweriner See** into a *Binnen-* and *Aussensee*. On an island in an inner-city lake joined to the mainland by two bridges is an amusing **castle** rebuilt in the 19th century. Its mixture of neo-Gothic, Renaissance and baroque is vaguely inspired by the Loire Valley's Chambord château. It has a prehistoric museum, an ornate café and a pleasant garden. In the 15th-century Gothic brick **cathedral**, see the fine sandstone *Crucifixion* altar (1440) carved by Lübeck craftsmen. The **art museum** (*Staatliches Museum*), Alter Garten 3, has a collection of Dutch, Flemish and German artists, among them Hals, Rubens, Cranach, Altdorfer and Caspar David Friedrich, but most noteworthy is an unusual group of French 18th-century still lifes by Jean Baptiste Oudry.

Canal cruises are organized to **Plauer See**, which offers good fishing and water sports.

Müritzsee, from a Slavonic word meaning sea, is Eastern Germany's biggest lake, covering 115km² (44 square miles). With its pretty woodland setting, it constitutes a nature reserve and **bird sanctuary** abounding in cranes and osprey. See the natural history museum in **Waren** at the north end of the lake.

Baltic Coast

German unification has made several historic Hanseatic ports—from Wismar to Stralsund—more accessible. It has also encouraged redevelopment of the Baltic seaside resorts to attract holiday-makers seeking a change from the North Sea coast and Frisian Islands. Many among the first rush of Westerners were surprised to find nudist beaches the rule rather than the exception. Some even complained, though West Germans had not previously been noted for their reluctance to strip off.

Wismar

The Hanseatic port city was fortified by the Swedes in the 17th century. Two relics of those days are the **Provianthaus** (storage house) and **Zeughaus** (arsenal), both built in the 1690s. On Marktplatz, dominated by the neo-Gothic town hall, is a lantern-domed **Renaissance fountain**. The step-gabled brick **Alter Schwede** (1380), Marktplatz 20, is the oldest house in town, now a restaurant. You will find some other fine old houses on Lübscher-Strasse.

Bad Doberan

Summer residence for the dukes of Mecklenburg, the spa established in the 19th century still soothes aching limbs at its mud baths. Stretch them later in the **Kamp**, a pretty English park with Chinese pavilions housing a café and art exhibitions. The **Münster**, the town's impressive Cistercian abbey church (1368), combines the simple forms of the Hanseatic hall church with the French Gothic cathedral style. Inside are a fine rood screen *Crucifixion* and lofty canopied ciborium. Notice, too, the 14th-century choir stalls and stained glass.

Take the small-gauge Molli train to the **Kühlungsborn** seaside resort for a bracing stroll along the beach.

Rostock

The former Hanseatic fishing port was the German Democratic Republic's "Gate to the World" and built ships both for the Soviet Union and the West, specializing in ice-breakers and ultra-modern freighters. To see the activity, take a **harbour cruise** from Kabutzenhof quay.

Visit the Gothic brick-built **Pfarrkirche St Marien** with a baroque interior. On the bronze 13th-century baptismal font are scenes from the life of Christ. See, too, the ornate astronomical clock (1472).

West of the Warnow estuary is the resort of **Warnemünde** with its pretty seafront promenade, Alter Strom, lighthouse and Bauhaus-style spa establishment.

Stralsund

The handsomest of Mecklenburg's Baltic ports has an island-like **old town** of Gothic, Renaissance and baroque houses. On the 15th-century **town hall**, notice the distinctive glazed redbrick façade with pierced rose windows and mullions over an arcade that sheltered the old market. Behind it, the 14th-century Gothic **Nikolaikirche** possesses some fine choir stalls and a baroque high altar sculpted by Andreas Schlüter. Among the many old houses, you will see on Mönchstrasse the **Scandinavian houses** from the 17th century, when Stralsund was a Swedish possession.

Beaches and Islands

The peninsula of **Fischland-Darss-Zingst** is a flat tongue of dunes and marshes, tenuously linked to the mainland near Rostock and Stralsund by narrow spits of sand. The whole peninsula constantly changes shape as it is eroded by surf and wind. Writers and painters have long loved the strange light and the isolation of its sandy beaches. Bird-watchers have plenty to see in what is, for the most part, a protected nature reserve. The main resorts are Wustrow, Ahrenshoop and Zingst. West of Fischland proper is the Graal-Müritz beach, 6km (4 miles) long.

Accessible by Highway 96 from Stralsund, the beautiful island of **Rügen** rivals the North Sea's Sylt. The chalk cliffs and pebble beaches were a favourite subject for painter Caspar David Friedrich. Explore the lovely **Jasmund** peninsula where beech woods reach down to the dramatic **Stubbenkammer** coast. Most spectacular of the cliffs is the **Königsstuhl**, 117m (384ft) above the sea. The island's popular resorts include Binz, Sellin and Baabe.

Rügen is Germany's biggest island, but it is linked by causeway to the mainland and can be jammed on holiday weekends. If you are determined to get away from the traffic, head for the island of **Hiddensee**, little more than a strip of sand dunes off Rügen's western end. A ferry goes from Schaprode, and others leave from Stralsund, but they carry passengers and bicycles only—the island is a nature reserve and car-free zone. If you fall for Hiddensee, you will be following in the footsteps of Einstein, Freud, Thomas Mann and generations of bird-watchers.

East of Rügen, the long, thin offshore island of **Usedom** straddles the mouth of the Oder and the Polish border. It's crowded in summer with campers, cyclists, swimmers and sailors (the sheltered water between the island and mainland is good for beginners). Usedom's popularity is not new—though it was more exclusive in 1922 when the writer Maxim Gorky spent the summer at the resort of Heringsdorf working on his autobiography.

WHAT TO DO

Ideas for Days When You Do Not Feel Like Sightseeing

The Germans themselves are an active bunch, and you might feel guilty if you don't actually do something other than travel around looking at their monuments. Sporting facilities are first class, for both summer and winter. Musical and theatrical entertainment are among the world's best, and tradition is still strong enough for folk festivals to be celebrated all year round. Be as busy as you like. Here we suggest just a few ideas for various sporting and cultural activities, and what to look for when you go shopping. For up-to-date details of addresses, prices and ticket-booking, all constantly changing in a volatile world, your best bet is the local tourist office.

Entertainment

Highbrow, middlebrow and lowbrow tastes mix easily on a night out in Germany. The opera-house and the beer hall are not mutually exclusive. After a challenging evening of avant-garde theatre, people may unwind in a disco. However, *Kultur* is still a serious business. The Germans remain the most assiduous concert- and theatre-goers in Europe, and you have to plan ahead if you want good tickets for the "main events", especially opera. Ask your travel agency or the German national tourist office for details of coming programmes, and book in advance where possible. However, good hotels will try to find you seats at the last moment if you are prepared to pay a little extra. The weekly newspaper *Die Zeit,* also on sale outside Germany, has programmes of theatre, concerts and art exhibitions all over the country. The major arts centres have bright, weekly city-magazines similar to London's *Time Out* giving full details and reviews.

Serious beermug collectors buy their mugs only in the tavern or town where they have sampled the brew, scorning to pick them up in souvenir shops.

Music

Germany owes its rich musical heritage, in large part, to the time when the country was divided into scores of duchies and principalities. Competing for the best

347

talents, each royal court offered composers and musicians their own opera-house or concert hall. The states have continued the tradition with handsome subsidies, so that you will never be far from first-class performances with internationally recognized musicians and singers.

The great symphony orchestras are in Berlin, Munich, Bamberg, Leipzig and Dresden. For chamber music, Stuttgart joins these cities in the front rank. The cities where the great composers lived and worked make a special point of staging recitals and festivals (*see* page 38) in their honour—Leipzig, Eisenach and Erfurt for Bach, Hamburg for Brahms and, of course, Bonn for Beethoven.

For opera fans, Bayreuth provides a high temple to Richard Wagner, though without a monopoly on the most imaginative productions. For the rest of the repertoire, Berlin, Munich and Düsseldorf are among the best in the world. Stuttgart is renowned for avant-garde ballet.

Jazz is remarkably popular here, and American stars are often more easily seen in Munich, Berlin, Stuttgart or Frankfurt than back in the United States.

Theatre

Bold, innovative productions of both classical and contemporary drama make theatre here a great experience. Directors do not take a narrow, national view, and so

*J*ust off the Romantic Route north of Dinkelsbühl, Feuchtwangen holds a summer theatre festival. The plays are frequently dramatizations of Grimm's fairy tales.

you can see many British, American, French and Eastern European works in the repertoire. The bard of Stratford, for instance, has long been known to Germans as *unser Shakespeare* (our Shakespeare), performed with a usually refreshing lack of classical solemnity. Your choice is endless: Berlin's Schaubühne, Schiller-Theater and, in the East, the Berliner Ensemble founded by Brecht; the municipal theatres of Düsseldorf, Munich and Stuttgart; and in the heart of the industrial Ruhr—Bochum, Essen and Duisburg.

Recapturing the mordant atmosphere of its heyday in the 1920s, political cabaret has taken on a new lease of life with the eruptive last decade of the century. Seek it out in Berlin, Leipzig and Munich, and unlikely places like the conservative bastion of Passau in Bavaria.

Film

Film has been in a creative lull, but unification is stimulating new talents which emerge at the festivals staged in Berlin (in February) and Munich (in June).

Nightlife

The raciest nightclubs and discos are, of course, in the big cities—on and off the Ku'damm in Berlin, in Hamburg's St Pauli, on the seedy Reeperbahn and aptly named Grosse Freiheit (Great Freedom), around Munich's Hauptbahnhof, and in Frankfurt's Kaiserstrasse and Sachsenhausen districts.

Lively and less tawdry are the nightclubs in the major mountain resorts—Garmisch-Partenkirchen and Berchtesgaden.

Usually more subdued still are the discos in the great spa resorts like Baden-Baden or Wiesbaden, and North Sea and Baltic beach towns—Westerland on Sylt,

Norderney and Travemünde. Many of the restaurants in such resorts still entertain with old-fashioned ballroom dancing.

Gamblers will find the most elegant casinos (baccarat, roulette, blackjack) in Baden-Baden, Bad Homburg and other spas in the Black Forest and Taunus areas.

Sports

In a country where the trade unions have negotiated Europe's first 35-hour working week and long holidays, you can be sure there is plenty of time and place found for sport—summer and winter. And the former East Germany had a mission to excel in sport, so installations are modern and efficient, and there are clubs or national associations galore to give you details of where the best facilities are for your favourite pastime.

Water Sports

In addition to ports along the North Sea and Baltic coasts, notably Kiel and Travemünde, you will find exhilarating possibilities for sailing on the lakes of Bavaria (Ammersee, Starnberger See, Tegernsee and Chiemsee), Berlin's Wannsee and Müggelsee, and Mecklenburg (Müritz-, Plauer- and Schweriner See). You can rent equipment for windsurfing and water-skiing in all the major resorts. To protect swimmers, areas for these activities are carefully marked by flags and buoys.

Canoeing is big on the Neckar and Lahn and rivers in the Black Forest. Try rafting on the fast-flowing Isar in Munich's Englischer Garten.

Even if you are not visiting beach resorts on the lakes or sea coasts, swimming in indoor and outdoor pools is well catered for. Munich makes its Olympic pool available to the public. Spa pools are mineralized for simultaneous therapy and exercise. Speciality of North Sea and Baltic resorts is the *Meerwasser-Brandungsbad* (filtered seawater pools with waves).

Mountains and Forest

The most popular sport in Germany is hiking—not just a casual stroll in tennis shoes, but a serious ramble, with boots and leggings and rucksack and walking stick. From the Black Forest to Berlin's Grunewald or the Thuringian Forest, from the Bavarian Alps to the Harz Mountains, hiking trails are clearly marked. Take your pick among short half-day circuits or longer camping trips. Local tourist offices will help you with detailed maps and indicate the inns along the way if you do not feel like lugging a picnic along. For the more adventurous, they can also advise on renting equipment for mountaineering or hang-gliding. If you prefer flat, open country, try the Eifel or Hunsruck plateaus or Lüneburg Heath—or the mud-flats of the Frisian Islands.

You can also rent a bicycle, most often at the railway station, and take it with you on the train. For horse riding you will find good public stables, for instance, in Grunewald forest or along the Neckar and Lahn Valleys.

First-class gymnasiums are available for work-outs and massages in many big city hotels and particularly in the mountain and spa resorts.

B reezing along on Bavaria's Chiemsee, these fellows have no time for the nearby nonsense of Ludwig's castle.

350

Rivers and Lakes

You must obtain a local licence for fishing. Typically, you will find trout, salmon, eel, carp and perch in the Mosel river. The Bavarian and Mecklenburg lakes are well stocked and Lake Constance is big enough to accommodate everyone without crowding. Hunting also requires a local licence—good game birds are found in the Rhine and Mosel valleys, deer and wild boar in Bavaria.

Everything an angler might need for a good day out. Germany's lakes and rivers can provide some good fishing, but you need a licence.

Golf and Tennis

Champions Bernhard Langer, Boris Becker and Steffi Graf have done wonders in popularizing these sports. You will find more than 250 golf courses in Germany, among the best being 18-holers close to Cologne, Düsseldorf, Frankfurt, Munich and the major spa resorts. The number of municipal tennis courts has mushroomed, and your hotel can often help you with temporary membership at private clubs.

Winter Sports

The Bavarian Alps have the best winter sports facilities. Garmisch-Partenkirchen is one of Europe's leading ski resorts, and Berchtesgaden and Oberstdorf are not far behind. At peak times, especially holiday weekends, you will need reservations. The resorts in the Black Forest, Harz and Eifel are also well equipped and less crowded. Besides challenging ski slopes, there is special emphasis on cross-country skiing through the forests, and ice skating in the major towns, not forgetting Munich's Olympic rink.

Spectator Sports

Bayern Munich, FC Cologne and Eintracht Frankfurt are regularly among the best football (soccer) teams in Europe, and worth a trip out to the stadium.

Horse racing and trotting are big at Munich's Riem, Baden-Baden's Iffezheim and Berlin's Mariendorf. German riders are top rated in the international show-jumping events in Düsseldorf and Cologne.

There are two Grand Prix motor racing circuits—Hockenheim, near Heidelberg, and Nürburgring in the Eifel. At the latter, you can drive yourself outside racing and training periods. As they say in German, *Wrum, Wrum!*

*T*rotting races are just as popular as conventional horse-racing. You can see them regularly at Berlin's Mariendorf and several other tracks.

Shopping

The easy exchange of goods through the European Community, and the Germans' own taste for things exotic and foreign, mean that you can probably find everything here from all over the world. For a quick overview, take the escalator to the top of one of the big department stores such as Kaufhof and walk down through an Aladdin's cave of consumerism. Along with the high standard of living comes a high price tag on most imported goods, so you are better off buying "Made in Germany". Discount shops are few and far between.

Every town has its open-air or covered market: the quality foodstuffs in the bigger ones are a sight to see.

Antiques

Always a high-risk and a high-price business, antique dealing these days is increasingly carried out within a closed circuit of antique dealers. Any moderately priced baroque and rococo furniture or porcelain is probably a copy. You are better advised to concentrate on products of the 19th and early 20th centuries, but genuine Biedermeier, *Jugendstil* or Art Deco may also be very expensive. Even ponderous pieces from bourgeois homes of the pre-1914 Wilhelminian era have moved out of the domain of High Kitsch.

Flea markets have mushroomed all over the country, especially with the influx of goods from Eastern Europe since 1989. Among the best are Berlin's Nollendorfplatz, Munich's "Auer Dult" on Mariahilfplatz, Hamburg's St Pauli or Frankfurt's old slaughterhouse in Sachsenhausen.

Arts and Crafts

Museum shops are a good place to find art posters, lithographs, high-quality reproductions and art books. In museums of classical antiquity like the Glyptothek in Munich or the Egyptian museum in Berlin, you can get excellent copies of Greek vases or ancient sculpture in bronze, plaster or resin. Museum shops also offer a certain guarantee of quality for genuine artisan products—textiles, pottery, pewterware, decorative candles and wood carving. For the widest selection, seek out the workshops of the craftsmen themselves, such as the woodcarvers of Oberammergau or the Black Forest.

Clothes

A few Munich and Düsseldorf designers have made an international reputation in high fashion, and Berlin is again on the up. Even so, most of the labels you will see here—in all the major towns—are French, Italian, Japanese and American.

If you are interested in more traditional clothes, consider the well-tailored garments (coats, jackets and suits) that are made from loden cloth, a Bavarian speciality. Originally developed for hunters, this warm, waterproof wool fabric comes in navy, grey or green for men, but also in brighter colours for women and children.

One of the few regional costumes that does not look ridiculous outside its natural habitat on the village square or carnival procession is the Bavarian *Tracht*: men's smart green-collared grey jackets or women's gaily coloured dirndl dresses with a full gathered skirt and fitted bodice. Unless you are of Bavarian extraction, however, and want to proclaim the fact, keep the slap-happy *Lederhosen* strictly for hyperkinetic kids. These trousers, short or knickerbocker-length, wear forever, and

after a while stand up in a corner all by themselves. Leather and sports wear are good quality, especially for hunting and hiking. Around Hamburg's harbour area, you will find great sailor's gear, waterproof and woollen.

One item in the realm of *haute couture* created in Germany is still available in its original form in its famous green-labelled bottle, Eau de Cologne.

Gourmet Delicacies

The delicatessens make up attractive gift parcels of sausage, hams and pickles. At the pastry shops, goodies that travel best are the *Lebkuchen* (gingerbread) and *Spekulatius* (spiced Christmas cookies). Marzipan comes in all shapes and sizes, including a Hansel-and-Gretel house that you may never want to eat.

Kitchen Equipment

The electrical appliances are superbly designed with the streamlined look of the Bauhaus tradition. You will find an endless array of kitchen knives. One marvellous horror that belongs more properly in our Kitsch section is a nutcracker, particularly popular in Eastern Germany, in the form of a Prussian army sergeant busting the nut between his jaws.

Musical and Precision Instruments

If you are in the market for a musical instrument, you will find the finest harmonicas as well as the leading grand pianos. For listeners, the land of Bach and Beethoven feels duty bound to offer a selection of records second only to that of the United States.

Germany has relinquished its pre-war domination of the camera market to Japan, but artists and spies still go for the Leica and Minox. Best buys are the telescopes and binoculars. Miniature but powerful binoculars are great aids for your sightseeing, not only for long-distance viewing outside, but for inside the cathedrals and palaces to get a close-up of remote details.

Porcelain and Linen

Fine china is a German speciality. The modern designs of Rosenthal are available all over the country, but you will often find the best selection of regional manufacture in or near its place of origin. The most celebrated manufacturers are Meissen (best selection is in Dresden), Nymphenburg (Munich), Frankenthal (near Mannheim), and KPM—*Königliche Porzellan-Manufaktur* (Berlin), many of them reproducing great rococo pieces of their 18th-century heyday.

Bed and table linens here are of the highest old-fashioned quality. The duck- or goosedown quilt or duvet, *Federbett,* is a lifetime investment. In addition to the warm-as-toast winter model, look out for the lightweight for summer. Knowledgeable campers go for the great sleeping-bags.

Souvenirs and Kitsch

The advantage of most "funny" gifts is that they are usually flimsy enough to break before the joke wears off. However, sometimes you will find that the Germans just cannot help making even their most dreadful souvenirs solid enough to last forever, so choose carefully or be prepared to throw them away when people stop laughing.

Some of the best or worst ideas, according to your taste: giant decorated beer mugs—with or without lid—hats with partridge feathers or shaving brushes on the brim, clay pipes with bowl in the form of a lady's bare bottom, a Lorelei doll with bare top and fishy tail. If you cannot resist a cuckoo clock, a speciality of the Black Forest, the biggest selection is in Furtwangen.

In the realm of High Kitsch, with price tag to match, collectors' items wander ambivalently between the comic and hideous: spiked *Pickelhaube* helmets from Kaiser Wilhelm's army or World War II *Wehrmacht* helmets that sometimes turn up, enamelled, as a chamber pot.

A warning: just as the number of church relics of the True Cross could make a dozen crosses, so there are now in circulation enough pieces of the Berlin Wall "certified genuine" to divide the cities of Munich, Hamburg, Frankfurt and Stuttgart, too.

Toys

The great talents the Germans bring to their manufacturing industries find a natural outlet for children—and their parents—in toys of every imaginable kind. Distribution is nationwide but it is a good idea to visit toy museums in major centres like Nuremberg, Munich or Berlin to see the range.

The electric trains are the world's best, with prices to match. Others swear by the model aircraft, boats and spaceships.

A ROSE BY ANY OTHER NAME

Eau de Cologne has gone through a series of different names since it was first concocted in 1709 by Johann Maria Farina. Farina called it "Aqua Mirabilis" (wonder water). "Eau de Cologne" was understandably the preferred name when the French occupied the Rhineland during the Napoleonic Wars. A competitor named his product after his new street number under the French régime—"4711", still going strong. With the assertion of German national identity in the 19th century, some opted for "Kölnisch Wasser"—about as romantic to the German ear as "Cologne Water" would be to the English. Call it what you will, it is still a nice way to finish a shave or freshen up for an important date.

There are construction kits for building your own baroque palace or medieval castle. Berlin is only one of many towns specializing in tin soldiers to re-fight old battles, not even excluding World War II, though here the battles tend to be in the air with Stukas and Messerschmidts against Spitfires and Mustangs.

If this makes German toy shops sound like an exclusively boys' world, the dolls in traditional costume and superb teddy bears and other cuddly creatures more than redress the balance. To spoil the kid-that-has-everything, you can also find exquisite dolls' tea services in copies of Meissen, Frankenthal and Nymphenburger porcelain. The ultimate toy for the truly sophisticated toddler is a little box of Bauhaus building blocks which you can find at major modern art museum shops.

Language

The written language of Germany is known as *Hochdeutsch* or High German, but spoken dialects vary from region to region. English is widely understood and spoken, but don't take it for granted. Most large stores have English-speaking staff.

When entering a shop, it is customary to say *Guten Tag* (Good day) or *Guten Abend* (Good evening) and, of course, *Auf Wiedersehen* (Goodbye) when leaving. To take leave of someone on the telephone you should say *Auf Wiederhören*—literally "until we hear each other again". You'll often hear the less formal *Tschüss* used between friends and acquaintances, meaning "Bye" or "See you soon".

The Berlitz phrase book GERMAN FOR TRAVELLERS covers most of the situations you are likely to encounter on your stay in Germany.

Language Guide

yes/no	**ja/nein**
please/thank you	**bitte/danke**
good morning/ good afternoon	**Guten Tag**
good evening/ goodnight	**Guten Abend/ Gute Nacht**
goodbye	**Auf Wiedersehen**
excuse me	**Verzeihung**
you're welcome	**bitte**
where/when/how	**wo/wann/wie**
how long/how far	**wie lange/wie weit**
yesterday/today/ tomorrow	**gestern/heute/ morgen**
day/week/ month/year	**Tag/Woche/ Monat/Jahr**
left/right	**links/rechts**
up/down	**oben/unten**
good/bad	**gut/schlecht**
hot/cold	**heiss/kalt**
old/new	**alt/neu**

open/closed	**offen/geschlossen**
free/occupied	**frei/besetzt**
early/late	**früh/spät**
easy/difficult	**einfach/schwierig**
Does anyone here speak English?	**Spricht hier jemand Englisch?**
I don't speak (much) German.	**Ich spreche kaum Deutsch.**
Could you repeat that?	**Könnten Sie das bitte wiederholen?**
Could you spell it?	**Könnten Sie es bitte buchsta bieren?**
Can you translate this for me/us?	**Könnten Sie mir/uns das über setzen?**
What does this mean?	**Was bedeutet das?**
I don't understand.	**Ich verstehe nicht.**
Please write it down.	**Bitte schreiben Sie es.**
How much is that?	**Wieviel kostet es?**
I'd like ...	**Ich hätte gern ...**
We'd like ...	**Wir hätten gern ...**
What time is it, please?	**Wieviel Uhr ist es, bitte?**
Where are the toilets, please?	**Wo sind die Toiletten, bitte?**

Customs

I've nothing to declare.	**Ich habe nichts zu verzollen.**
It's for personal use.	**Es ist für meinen persönlichen Gebrauch.**

Money

I'd like to change some pounds/dollars.	**Ich möchte Pfund/ Dollars wechseln.**
Do you accept traveller's cheques?	**Nehmen Sie Reise-checks?**

Can I pay with this credit card?	**Kann ich mit dieser Kreditkarte zahlen?**
What's the exchange rate?	**Wie ist der Wechsel-kurs?**

Getting Around

Where's the bus/ train to ...?	**Wo steht der Bus/ der Zug nach ...?**
What time does it leave?	**Wann fährt er ab?**
Does this bus/train stop at ...?	**Hält dieser Bus/Zug in ...?**
Where's the (main) railway station/ bus stop?	**Wo ist der (Haupt)-Bahnhof/ die Bushaltestelle?**
When's the next bus/train to ...?	**Wann fährt der nächste Bus/Zug nach ...?**
I'd like a ticket to ...	**Ich möchte eine Fahrkarte nach ...**
single (one-way)	**einfach**
return (round-trip)	**hin und zurück**
first/second class	**erste/zweite Klasse**
Will you tell me when to get off?	**Können Sie mir bitte sagen, wann ich aussteigen muss?**
Where can I get a taxi?	**Wo finde ich ein Taxi?**
What's the fare to ...?	**Was kostet es bis ...?**
Are there bicycles for hire at this station?	**Kann man an diesem Bahnhof Fahrräder mieten?**
May I return it to another station?	**Kann ich es an einem anderen Bahnhof zurück geben?**
I'd like a street plan of ...	**Ich möchte einen Stadtplan von ...**
a road map/hiking map of this region	**eine Strassenkarte/ Wanderkarte dieser Gegend**

Medical Matters

Where's the nearest (all-night) pharmacy?	Wo ist die nächste (Dienst-) Apotheke?
I need a doctor/ dentist.	Ich brauche einen Arzt/Zahnarzt.
I have a pain here.	Ich habe hier Schmerzen.
stomach ache	Magenschmerzen
headache	Kopfschmerzen
a fever	Fieber
medical emergency service	Ärztlicher Notdienst
ambulance	Rettungsdienst
hospital	Krankenhaus

Accommodation

I'd like a single/ double room.	Ich hätte gern ein Einzelzimmer/ Doppelzimmer.
with bath/shower	mit Bad/Dusche
What's the rate per night/week?	Wieviel kostet es pro Nacht/Woche?
May we camp here?	Dürfen wir hier zelten?
Is there a campsite nearby?	Gibt es in der Nähe einen Zeltplatz?

At the Hairdressers

I'd like a shampoo and set.	Waschen und Legen, bitte.
haircut	Schneiden
shave	Rasieren
blow-dry (brushing)	mit dem Fön trocknen
colour rinse	eine Farbspülung
Don't cut it too short.	Schneiden Sie es nicht zu kurz.
A little more off (here).	(Hier) etwas kürzer.

Doing the Laundry

Is there a laundry service?	Gibt es einen Wäschedienst?
Where's the nearest laundry/dry-cleaners?	Wo ist die nächste Wäscherei/Reinigung?

Communications

Where's the post office?	Wo ist das Postamt?
A stamp for this letter/postcard, please.	Eine Briefmarke für diesen Brief/ diese Karte, bitte.
express (special delivery)	Eilzustellung
airmail	Luftpost
registered	Eingeschrieben
I want to send a telegram to ...	Ich möchte ein Telegramm nach ... aufgeben.
May I use the telephone?	Kann ich das Telefon benutzen?
Can you get me this number?	Können Sie mich mit dieser Nummer verbinden?
reverse-charge (collect) call	R-Gespräch
personal (person-to-person)	Gespräch mit Voranmeldung
Have you any newspapers in English?	Haben Sie Zeitungen in englischer Sprache?

Driving

international driving licence	Internationaler Führerschein
Car registration papers	Kraftfahrzeugpapiere
Green Card	Grüne Karte
Where's the nearest car park?	Wo ist der nächste Parkplatz?
petrol/gasoline	Benzin

Oil	**Öl**	*Friday*	**Freitag**
Full tank, please.	**Bitte volltanken.**	*Saturday*	**Samstag/Sonnabend**
Check the oil/tyres/ battery, please	**Kontrollieren Sie bitte das Öl/die Reifen/die Batterie.**	*Sunday*	**Sonntag**
		holiday	**Feiertag**

I've had a break-down.	**Ich habe eine Panne.**
There's been an accident.	**Es ist ein Unfall passiert.**

Emergencies

I've lost my wallet/ bag/passport.	**Ich habe meine Brieftasche/meine Tasche/meinen Pass verloren.**
I want to report a theft.	**Ich möchte einen Diebstahl melden.**
My handbag/wallet/ passport has been stolen.	**MeineHandtasche/ Brieftasche/mein Pass ist gestohlen worden.**
I've lost my wallet.	**Ich habe meine Brieftasche verloren.**
Where's the nearest Police Station?	**Wo ist die nächste Polizeiwache?**
Fire	**Feuer**
Help	**Hilfe**
Police	**Polizei**
Stop	**Halt**
Please, can you place an emergency call for me to the ...	**Würden Sie bitte ... für mich anrufen?**
police/fire brigade/ hospital	**die Polizei/die Feuer-wehr/das Krankenhaus**

Days

Monday	**Montag**
Tuesday	**Dienstag**
Wednesday	**Mittwoch**
Thursday	**Dienstag**

Numbers

0	**null**	*18*	**achtzehn**
1	**eins**	*19*	**neunzehn**
2	**zwei**	*20*	**zwanzig**
3	**drei**	*21*	**ein und-zwanzig**
4	**vier**	*30*	**dreissig**
5	**fünf**	*40*	**vierzig**
6	**sechs**	*50*	**fünfzig**
7	**sieben**	*60*	**sechzig**
8	**acht**	*70*	**siebzig**
9	**neun**	*80*	**achtzig**
10	**zehn**	*90*	**neunzig**
11	**elf**	*100*	**hundert**
12	**zwölf**	*101*	**hunderteins**
13	**dreizehn**	*200*	**zweihundert**
14	**vierzehn**	*1,000*	**tausend**
15	**fünfzehn**	*1,100*	**tausendein hundert**
16	**sechzehn**	*10,000*	**zehntausend**
17	**siebzehn**	*1,000,000*	**eine Million**

Eating Out

To help you order ...

Waiter/Waitress!	**Herr Ober/ Fräulein, bitte!**
May I have the menu, please?	**Kann ich bitte die Speisekarte haben?**
Do you have a set menu/local specialities?	**Haben Sie ein Gedeck/hiesige Gerichte?**

What do you recommend?	**würden Sie mir empfehlen?**	*peas*	**Erbsen**
		strawberries	**Erdbeeren**
Do you have vegetarian dishes?	**Haben Sie vegetarische Gerichte?**	*pheasant*	**Fasan**
I'd like a/an/some ...	**Ich hätte gern ...**	*trout*	**Forelle**
bread	**Brot**	*goose*	**Gans**
butter	**Butter**	*mutton*	**Hammelfleisch**
cheese	**Käse**	*hare*	**Hase**
coffee	**Kaffee**	*raspberries*	**Himbeeren**
cream	**Sahne**	*chicken*	**Huhn**
ice-cream	**Eis**	*lobster*	**Hummer**
lemon	**Zitrone**	*veal*	**Kalbfleisch**
milk	**Milch**	*rabbit*	**Kaninchen**
mineral water	**Mineralwasser**	*potatoes*	**Kartoffeln**
mustard	**Senf**	*cabbage*	**Kohl**
pepper	**Pfeffer**	*shrimp*	**Krabben**
potatoes	**Kartoffeln**	*crayfish*	**Krebs**
salad	**Salat**	*cake*	**Kuchen**
salt	**Salz**	*tripe*	**Kutteln**
sugar	**Zucker**	*salmon*	**Lachs**
tea	**Tee**	*lamb*	**Lammfleisch**
wine	**Wein**	*liver*	**Leber**
		mussels	**Muscheln**
Reading the menu		*kidneys*	**Nieren**
eel	**Aal**	*pasta*	**Nudeln**
apple	**Apfel**	*mushrooms*	**Pilze**
orange	**Apfelsine**	*chips (French fries)*	**Pommes frites**
soufflé	**Auflauf**	*peach*	**Pfirsich**
oysters	**Austern**	*rice*	**Reis**
cauliflower	**Blumenkohl**	*venison*	**Reh**
beans	**Bohnen**	*beef*	**Rindfleisch**
button mushrooms	**Champignons**	*brussels sprouts*	**Rosenkohl**
cod	**Dorsch**	*anchovies*	**Sardellen**
duck	**Ente**	*bacon*	**Schinken**

360

snails	**Schnecken**	*turkey*	**Truthahn**
pork	**Schweinefleisch**	*boar*	**Wildschwein**
sole	**Seezunge**	*sausage*	**Wurst**
bacon	**Speck**	*onions*	**Zwiebeln**
turbot	**Steinbutt**		

The Right Place at the Right Price

Hotel accommodation in Western Germany is usually of a high standard. Rooms are equipped with radio, TV and alarm clock, the beds piled high with pillows and fluffy duvets, the plumbing modern and efficient. Breakfast is generally buffet-style, with a satisfying selection of fruit juice, cereals, bread, cheese, cold meat, cakes, fresh fruit and yoghurt. And apart from peak periods in certain cities, such as the Oktoberfest in Munich or the Book Fair in Frankfurt, you will have no problem finding a room to suit your budget. In the states of Eastern Germany, however, the situation is different. There is a shortage of rooms, and though hotel staff are quickly adapting to Western standards, the infrastructure does not yet compare with the rest of the country. If you want to stay in the East, you'd be well advised to book your room several weeks ahead through a travel agent. The German National Tourist Office in your home country can provide up-to-date information on the whole of Germany.

We give below a cross-section of hotels and restaurants, region by region in the same order as the main part of this book. Within each region, cities and towns are listed in alphabetical order. (Note: a Hotel *garni* provides breakfast but usually no other

meals. For more general information on types of accommodation, *see* page 23.)

Key

Hotel	**H**
Restaurant	**R**

Hotels *(for two in double room, with bath, and breakfast)*
Higher-priced:
above 200 DM ▯▯▯
Medium-priced:
130–200 DM ▯▯
Lower-priced:
below 130 DM ▯

Restaurants *(for three-course dinner, per person, excluding drinks)*
Higher-priced:
above 80 DM ▯▯▯
Medium-priced:
40–80 DM ▯▯
Lower-priced:
below 40 DM ▯

Bavaria

Amberg
Altstadt Hotel   HR ▯▯
Batteriegasse 2
92224 Amberg
Tel. (09621) 130 56; fax. 321 63
25 rooms. In the old town. View. Good restaurant (closed July, Friday and Saturday).

Gasthof Goldene Krone   HR   ▯
Waisenhausgasse 2
92224 Amberg
Tel. (09621) 229 94
21 rooms. In the old town.

Augsburg
Hotel Am Rathaus   H   ▯▯
Am Hinteren Perlachberg 1
86150 Augsburg
Tel. (0821) 15 60 72; fax. 51 77 46
32 rooms. Quiet, central, in the old town. Hotel garni.

Hotel u. Restaurant Post   HR   ▯▯
Am Königsplatz
86150 Augsburg
Tel. (0821) 360 44; fax. 336 64
50 rooms. Central. Home cooking.

Lech-Hotel   H   ▯▯
Neuburgerstrasse 31
86167 Augsburg
Tel. (0821) 72 10 64; fax. 71 92 44
39 rooms. In old town. Friendly hotel garni.

Steigenberger Drei Mohren Hotel   HR ▯▯▯
Maximilianstrasse 40
86150 Augsburg
Tel. (0821) 50 360; fax. 15 78 64
107 rooms. Traditional luxury in historic part of town.

Fuggerkeller   R   ▯▯
Maximilianstrasse 38
86150 Augsburg
Tel. (0821) 51 62 60
Traditional and local cuisine. Closed Sunday evening and 3 weeks in August.

Bad Mergentheim

Maritim ParkHotel   HR ▊▊▊
Lothar-Daiker-Strasse 6
97980 Bad Mergentheim
Tel. (07931) 53 90; fax. 53 91 00
116 rooms. Traditional comfort.
Good cuisine.

Victoria   HR ▊▊▊
Poststrasse 2
97980 Bad Mergentheim
Tel. (07931) 59 30; fax. 59 35 00
83 rooms. Centrally situated. Excellent cuisine.

Zum Wilden Mann   HR ▊
Reichengässle 6
97980 Bad Mergentheim
Tel. (07931) 76 38
22 rooms. Friendly pension in old town. Closed Christmas–January.

Bad Reichenhall

Schweizer Stuben im Kirchberg Schlössl   R ▊▊
Thumseestrasse 11
83435 Bad Reichenhall
Tel. (08651) 27 60
Elegant restaurant in a baroque castle. Bavarian specialities. Closed Wednesday and April.

Bad Tölz

Altes Fährhaus   HR ▊▊▊
An der Isarlust 1
83646 Bad Tölz
Tel. (08041) 60 30
Charming, quiet, on outskirts of town. Fine restaurant. 5 rooms. Closed 3 weeks January–February, Monday and Tuesday lunch.

Bamberg

Hotel Brudermühle   HR ▊▊
Schranne 1
96049 Bamberg
Tel. (0951) 540 91; fax. 512 11
16 rooms. Quiet, friendly, in the old town. Game and fish specialities.

Gasthof Wilde Rose   HR ▊
Kesslerstrasse 7
96047 Bamberg
Tel. (0951) 283 17; fax. 220 71
29 rooms. Friendly family-run gasthof with bierkeller.

Hotel National-Ringhotel   HR ▊▊
Luitpoldstrasse 37
96052 Bamberg
Tel. (0951) 241 12
41 rooms. Children welcome. Good cuisine.

Il Bassanese   R ▊▊
Obere Sandstrasse 32
96049 Bamberg
Tel. (0951) 575 51
In the old town. Excellent cuisine. Closed early June, mid-August to mid-September.

Bayreuth

Schlosshotel Thiergarten   HR ▊▊▊
Oberthiergärtnerstr. 30
Wolfsbach
95448 Bayreuth
Tel. (09209) 13 14; fax. 18 29
8 rooms. Holiday hotel in a castle park 6km (4 miles) from Bayreuth. Excellent cuisine.

Waldhotel Stein   HR ▊▊▊
Seulbitzerstrasse 79
Seulbitz
95448 Bayreuth
Tel. (0921) 90 01
59 rooms and suites. Quiet, in the woods. Excellent cuisine.

Zur Lohmühle   HR ▊▊▊
Badstrasse 37
95444 Bayreuth
Tel. (0921) 630 31; fax. 582 86
42 rooms. Family hotel. Excellent cuisine. Closed 2 weeks September.

Berchtesgaden

Hotel Geiger   HR ▊▊▊
Stanggass
83471 Berchtesgaden
Tel. (08652) 50 55; fax. 50 58
49 rooms. Near the forest. Beautiful view.

Hotel Grünberger   HR ▊▊
Hansererweg 1
83471 Berchtesgaden
Tel. (08652) 45 60
65 rooms. Quiet, friendly. Views.

Hotel Vier Jahreszeiten   HR ▊▊▊
Maximilianstr. 20
83471 Berchtesgaden
Tel. (08652) 50 26; fax. 50 29
61 rooms. Central. Lovely view.

Dachau

Hotel-Restaurant Götz   HR ▊▊
Pollnstrasse 6
85221 Dachau
Tel. (08131) 210 61; fax. 263 87
38 rooms. Quiet location. Swimming pool. Sauna. Good restaurant.

Dinkelsbühl

Gasthof zum Koppen   HR ▊
Segringerstrasse 38
91550 Dinkelsbühl
Tel. (09851) 504
17 rooms. In the old town. Excellent restaurant.

Hotel-Restaurant Fränkischer Hof   HR ▊▊
Nördlingerstr. 10
91550 Dinkelsbühl
Tel. (09851) 23 71; fax. 23 32
18 rooms. In the old town. Children welcome.

Donauwuörth

Posthotel Traube (Ringhotel)   HR ▊▊
Kapellstrrasse 14
86609 Donauwörth
Tel. (0906) 60 96; fax. 233 90
43 rooms. Outdoor pool. Closed New Year.

Füssen

Hotel Christine   H ▊▊
Weidachstr. 31
87629 Füssen
Tel. (08362) 72 29
15 rooms. Family-run hotel garni in old town.

Garmisch-Partenkirchen

Dorint Sporthotel   HR ▊▊▊
Mittenwalderstr. 59
82467 Garmisch-Partenkirchen
Tel. (08821) 70 60; fax. 70 66 18
152 rooms. 3 restaurants. Luxurious, in quiet location.

Gabrieles Hotel   H ▊▊
Olympiastrasse 21
82467 Garmisch-Partenkirchen
Tel. (08821) 720 41
21 rooms. Cosy family hotel garni.

Grand Hotel Sonnenbichl   HR ▊▊▊
Burgstrasse 97
82467 Garmisch-Partenkirchen
Tel. (08821) 70 20; fax. 70 21 31
90 rooms. Luxurious. Fine international and Bavarian restaurants.

Hotel Almenrauschund Edelweiss   H ▊
Kreuzstrasse 7
82467 Garmisch-Partenkirchen
Tel. (08821) 25 27
32 rooms. Hotel garni, quiet location, fine view.

Mittenwald

Hotel Jägerhof HR ▯
Partenkirchnerstr. 35
82481 Mittenwald
Tel. (08823) 10 41 44
*50 rooms. Quiet. Good view.
Bierkeller Weinstube.*

Hotel Rieger HR ▯▯▯
Dekan-Karl-Platz 28
82481 Mittenwald
Tel. (08823) 50 71; fax. 56 62
*45 rooms. Near the woods. Indoor
swimming pool. Restaurant closed
Monday.*

Hotel Tonihof HR ▯▯
Brunnenthal 3
82481 Mittenwald
Tel. (08823) 50 31; fax. 39 27
*18 rooms. 4km north of town. In-
door swimming pool. Closed
November to mid-December.*

**Hotel-Pension Aachen am
Franziskaner** HR ▯
Innsbruckerstrasse 2
82481 Mittenwald
Tel. (08823) 17 05;
fax. (089) 857 48 78
*36 rooms. Quiet. Good view. Sauna.
Bowling.*

Munich

Aubergine R ▯▯▯
Maximilianplatz 5
80333 Munich
Tel. (089) 59 81 71
*Celebrated for outstanding cuisine.
Closed 2 weeks August, Sunday and
Monday.*

Boettner R ▯▯
Theatinerstrasse 8
80333 Munich
Tel. (089) 22 12 10
*Small, old world restaurant, ex-
tremely popular. Reservation ad-
vised. Closed Saturday evening,
Sunday, and Monday lunch.*

Casale R ▯▯
Ostpreussenstrasse 42
Denning
81927 Munich
Tel. (089) 93 62 68
*Fine Italian cuisine. Terrace.
Closed Saturday lunch.*

Hotel Am Karlstor H ▯
Neuhauser Strasse 34
80331 Munich
Tel. (089) 59 35 96
*28 rooms. In a pedestrian zone in
the old town. Hotel garni.*

Hotel Am Moosfeld HR ▯▯
Am Moosfeld 39
81829 Munich
Tel. (089) 42 91 90; fax. 42 46 62
*74 rooms. Quiet, family-run hotel.
Restaurant closed Satutday.*

Hotel Daheim H ▯▯
Schillerstrasse 20
80336 Munich
Tel. (089) 59 42 49
*25 rooms. In the city centre. Family-
run hotel garni.*

Hotel Excelsior HR ▯▯▯
Schützenstrasse 11
80335 Munich
Tel. (089) 55 13 70;
fax. 55 13 71 21
*115 rooms. Luxurious, quiet, near
railway station.*

Hotel Grünwald H ▯
Altostrasse 38
81245 Munich
Tel. (089) 863 30 26; fax. 863 23 29
*36 rooms. Family-run hotel garni
near railway station.*

Hotel Marienbad H ▯▯
Barerstrasse 11
80333 Munich
Tel. (089) 59 55 85; fax. 59 82 38
Quiet hotel garni. No credit cards.

Hotel Opera H ▯▯▯
St-Anna-Strasse 10
80538 Munich
Tel. (089) 22 55 33; fax. 22 55 38
*28 rooms. Small, quiet, family-run
hotel garni.*

Hotel u. Gasthaus HR ▯▯
Sollner Hof
Herterichstrasse 63–65
Solln
81477 Munich
Tel. (089) 79 20 90; fax. 790 04 28
*29 rooms. Biergarten. Restaurant
closed Tuesday, Saturday 2 weeks in
August.*

Hotel Vier Jahreszeiten HR ▯▯▯
Kempinski
Maximilianstrasse 17
80539 Munich
Tel. (089) 23 03 90;
fax. 23 03 96 93
*340 rooms. Traditional luxury, all
amenities. Indoor pool. Sauna.*

Hotel Zum Kurfürst HR ▯▯
Kapellenweg 5
Oberschleissheim-Lustheim
81371 Munich
Tel. (089) 315 16 44

*100 rooms. Quiet location in woods
north of the city. Bierkeller.*

Hotel-Pension Theresia H ▯
Luisenstrasse 51
80333 Munich
Tel. (089) 52 12 50
*20 rooms. Hotel garni in city centre.
No pets allowed.*

Hunsinger R ▯▯
Hans-Sachs-Strasse 10
80469 Munich
Tel. (089) 26 68 77
*Small restaurant, excellent fish
dishes. Closed Monday and Saturday lunch, Sunday.*

Park Hilton HR ▯▯▯
Am Tucherpark 7
80538 Munich
Tel. (089) 384 50; fax. 38 45 18 45
*480 rooms. Quiet, luxurious. Indoor
pool. Facilities for children.*

Pension Augsburg H ▯
Schillerstrasse 18
80336 Munich
Tel. (089) 59 76 73
*26 rooms. Family-run. Central, near
railway station.*

Pension Maximilian H ▯
Reitmorstrasse 12
80538 Munich
Tel. (089) 22 24 33
*11 rooms. Quiet, in centre of old
town.*

Preysing-Keller R ▯▯▯
Innere-Wiener-Strasse 6
Haidhausen
81667 Munich
Tel. (089) 48 10 15
*Excellent cuisine in vaulted cellar.
Dinner only. Closed Sunday.*

Sankt Emmerams Mühle R ▯▯
St Emmeram 41
Oberföhring
81925 Munich
Tel. (089) 95 39 71
Lively Biergarten in an old mill.

Tantris R ▯▯▯
Johann-Fichte-Str. 7
Schwabing
80805 Munich
Tel. (089) 36 20 61
*Renowned for creative cuisine.
Closed Monday and Saturday lunch,
Sunday. Reservation essential.*

Nuremberg

Burghotel-Grosses Haus   H   ▯▯▯
Lammsgasse 3
90403 Nuremberg
Tel. (0911) 20 44 14
*46 rooms. Quiet, family-run hotel
garni in the old town. Pool.*

Gasthof Bammes   R   ▯▯▯
Bucher Hauptstrasse 63
Buch
90427 Nuremberg
Tel. (0911) 38 13 03
*Traditional local cuisine. Reserva-
tion advised. Closed Sunday.*

Goldenes Posthorn   R   ▯▯
Glöckleingasse 2
90403 Nuremberg
Tel. (0911) 22 51 53
*Good local cooking. Terrace. Near
St Sebaldus Church. Closed Sunday.*

Hotel Deutscher Kaiser   H   ▯
Königstrasse 55
90402 Nuremberg
Tel. (0911) 20 33 41
*51 rooms. In the old town. Children
welcome.*

Hotel Elch   HR   ▯▯
Irrerstrasse 9
90403 Nuremberg
Tel. (0911) 20 95 44
*In the old town. Children welcome.
Good cooking, dinner only.*

Hotel Hamburg   H   ▯▯
Hasstrasse 3
90431 Nuremberg
Tel. (0911) 32 72 18; fax. 31 25 89
*26 rooms. Quiet location. Children
welcome. Babysitting.*

Hotel Maritim   HR   ▯▯▯
Frauentorgraben 11
90443 Nuremberg
Tel. (0911) 236 30; fax. 236 38 23
*316 rooms. All amenities. Fine
restaurant, closed Sunday and August.*

Kern   R   ▯
Bucher Hauptstrasse 93
Buch
90427 Nuremberg
Tel. (0911) 38 11 93
*Known for fresh carp in winter, as-
paragus in early summer. Closed
Thursday.*

Schwarzer Adler   R   ▯▯▯
Kraftshofer Hauptstrasse 166
Kraftshof
90427 Nuremberg
Tel. (0911) 30 58 58

*Fine local cuisine. Biergarten.
Closed Christmas–New Year.*

Oberammergau

Hotel Alois Lang   HR   ▯▯▯
St-Lukas-Strasse 15
82487 Oberammergau
Tel. (08822) 41 41; fax. 47 23
*43 rooms. All amenities. Garden,
terrace.*

Hotel Wolf   HR   ▯▯
Dorfstrasse 1
82487 Oberammergau
Tel. (08822) 30 71; fax. 10 96
*31 rooms. Family run. Traditional
atmosphere. Garden.*

Oberstaufen

Zum Löwen   HR   ▯▯▯
Kirchplatz 8
87534 Oberstaufen
Tel. (08386) 49 40; fax. 49 42 22
*30 rooms. Indoor swimming pool.
Closed mid-November to mid-
December. Excellent cuisine.
Restaurant closed Wednesday.*

Oberstdorf

Kur u. Sporthotel   HR   ▯▯▯
Exquisit
Prinzenstrasse 17
87561 Oberstdorf
Tel. (08322) 10 34; fax. 10 37
*36 rooms. Good restaurant, dinner
only. Closed Sunday.*

Passau

Heilig-Geist-Stiftsschenke R   ▯▯
Heiliggeistgasse 4
94032 Passau
Tel. (0851) 26 07
*Good local cuisine. 14th-century
inn. Garden. Closed Wednesday and
January.*

Altstadt Hotel–Zum   HR   ▯▯
Laubenwirt
Im Ort 14
94032 Passau
Tel. (0851) 33 70; fax 33 71 00
55 rooms. In the old town. View.

Hotel-Restaurant-Café   HR   ▯
Zum König
Rindermarkt 2
94032 Passau
Tel. (0851) 340 98; fax. 340 97
20 rooms. In the old town.

Passauer Wolf   HR   ▯▯▯
Rindermarkt 6
94032 Passau
Tel. (0851) 340 46; fax. 367 57
*40 rooms. Good cuisine. Restaurant
closed Sunday evening.*

Wilder Mann-   HR   ▯▯
Restaurant Kaiserin Sissi
Rathausplatz
94032 Passau
Tel. (0851) 350 71; fax. 317 12
*60 rooms. Historic building. Indoor
pool. Excellent cuisine.*

Regensburg

Gasthof-Hotel-   HR   ▯▯
Restaurant Held
Irl 11
93055 Regensburg
Tel. (09401) 10 41; fax. 76 82
50 rooms. Good local cuisine.

Hotel am Sportpark   HR   ▯▯▯
Im Gewerberpark D 90
Reinhausen
93059 Regensburg
Tel. (0941) 402 80; fax. 491 72
*96 rooms. Tennis. Bowling. Jazz
cellar. Biergarten.*

Parkhotel Maximilian   H   ▯▯▯
Maximilianstrasse 28
93047 Regensburg
Tel. (0941) 510 42; fax. 529 42
*52 rooms. Central. Magnificent
rococo-style building.*

Zum Krebs   R   ▯▯
Krebsgasse 6
93047 Regensburg
Tel. (0941) 558 03
*Excellent cuisine. Reservation
recommended. Dinner only. Closed
end August to early September, and
Sunday, Monday.*

Rothenburg ob der Tauber

Gasthof Glocke   HR   ▯▯
(Ringhotel)
Am Plönlein 1
91541 Rothenburg ob der Tauber
Tel. (09861) 30 25; fax. 867 11
*28 rooms. Good holiday hotel.
Closed Christmas–New Year.
Restaurant closed Sunday evening.*

Hotel Alter Ritter   HR   ▯▯
Bensenstrasse 1
91541 Rothenburg ob der Tauber
Tel. (098461) 79 47; fax. 58 32
*26 rooms. Central. Good restaurant,
weinstube.*

Hotel Eisenhut   HR ▌▌▌
Herrngasse 3
91541 Rothenburg ob der Tauber
Tel. (09861) 70 50; fax. 705 45
80 rooms. Buildings dating from the
15th and 16th centuries. Good
restaurant. Closed January.

Hotel Tilman   HR ▌▌▌
Riemenschneider
Georgengasse 11
91541 Rothenburg ob der Tauber
Tel. (09861) 20 86; fax. 29 79
65 rooms. In the old town. Wein-
stube.

Scheidegg
Gästehaus Allgäu   HR ▌
Am Brunnenbühl 11
Scheffau
88175 Scheidegg
Tel. (08381) 52 50
17 rooms. Quiet location. View.
Tennis. Good cuisine.

Schwangau
Schlosshotel Lisl-   HR ▌▌▌
Jägerhaus
Neuschwansteinstrasse 1–3
Hohenschwangau
87645 Schwangau
Tel. (08362) 810 06; fax. 811 07
44 rooms. Quiet, near woodland.
Beautiful view.

Tegernsee
Hotel Guggemos   HR ▌▌
Hauptstrasse 23
83684 Tegernsee
Tel. (08022) 39 15
28 rooms. Quiet. Private lakeside
beach. Children welcome.

Seehotel zur Post   HR ▌▌
Seestrasse 3
83684 Tegernsee
Tel. (08022) 39 51
47 rooms. Lakeside. Beautiful view.

Waging am See
Kurhaus Stüberl   R ▌▌▌
Am See 1
83329 Waging am See
Tel. (08681) 400 90
Small restaurant overlooking the
lake. Excellent cuisine, specializing
in freshwater fish. Dinner only.
Closed Monday and Tuesday, and
mid-January to end February.

Wiesenttal
Feiler   HR ▌▌▌
Oberer Markt 4
Muggendorf
91346 Wiesenttal
Tel. (09196) 322; fax. 362
16 rooms. Good local cuisine, spe-
cializing in game. Open weekends
only in winter. Restaurant closed
Monday lunch.

Würzburg
Hofkeller-Weinstuben   R ▌▌
Residenzplatz 1
Weinhäuser
97070 Würzburg
Tel. (0931) 546 70
Biergarten. Closed Sunday evening
and Monday.

Hotel Rebstock   HR ▌▌▌
Neubaustrasse 7
97070 Würzburg
Tel. (0931) 309 30; fax. 309 31 00
80 rooms. Weinstube, regional
cooking, closed Tuesday.

Hotel Schloss Steinburg HR ▌▌▌
Auf dem Steinberg
97080 Würzburg
Tel. (0931) 930 61; fax. 971 21
50 rooms. 7km (4 miles) out of city.
Quiet, small restaurant. Weinstube.
Good view.

Hotel Strauss   HR ▌▌
Juliuspromenade 5
97070 Würzburg
Tel. (0931) 305 70; fax. 305 75 55
80 rooms. In the old town. Closed
early January. Weinstube. Good
cuisine. Restaurant closed Tuesday.

The South-West

Aschaffenburg
Aschaffenburger Hof   HR ▌▌
Frohsinnstrasse 11
63739 Aschaffenburg
Tel. (06021) 214 41; fax. 272 98
65 rooms. Central, near castle and
station. Good restaurant.

Fäth   R ▌▌
Steinbacher Strasse 21
Johannesberg-Steinbach
63741 Aschaffenburg
Tel. (06021) 469 17
8km (5 miles) from Aschaffenburg.
Fine local cuisine. Closed August,
Monday, Friday lunch.

Hotel Gasthof Zum   HR ▌
Ochsen
Karlstrasse 16
63739 Aschaffenburg
Tel. (06021) 231 32; fax. 257 85
35 rooms. Beautiful view of the old
town. Good cuisine. Restaurant
closed Monday.

Hotel Romantik-Post   HR ▌▌
Goldbacher Strasse 19
63739 Aschaffenburg
Tel. (06021) 213 33; fax. 134 83
71 rooms. Central in old town.
Good restaurant.

Landhaus Spessart   H ▌
Dr.-Leissner-Strasse 20
Goldbach, Unterafferbach
63773 Aschaffenburg
Tel. (06021) 521 71
12 rooms. Quiet location 7km (4
miles) from town. Hotel and apart-
ments.

Sonne-Meier   HR ▌▌▌
Hauptstrasse 2
Johannesberg
63743 Aschaffenburg
Tel. (06021) 47 00 77; fax. 41 964
Fine restaurant 8km (5 miles) from
Aschaffenburg. 8 rooms. Closed
Monday.

Baden-Baden
Brenner's Park Hotel   HR ▌▌▌
Schillerstrasse 6
76530 Baden-Baden
Tel. (07221) 90 00; fax. 387 72
100 rooms and suites. Luxurious
spa, beauty and health farm. Swim-
ming pool.

Hotel Restaurant Zum   HR ▌
Altenberg
Schartenbergstrasse 6
Neuweier
76534 Baden-Baden
Tel. (07223) 572 36; fax. 604 60
19 rooms. South of the town. Closed
late November to 24 December
Good cuisine. Restaurant closed
Thursday.

Merkurius   R ▌▌▌
Klosterbergstrasse 2
Varnhalt
76534 Baden-Baden
Tel. (07223) 54 74; fax. 609 96
Good local cuisine. Closed Monday
and Tuesday lunch. 4 rooms avail-
able.

Zum Alde Gott   R   ⫿⫿⫿
Weinstrasse10
Neuweier
76534 Baden-Baden
Tel. (07223) 55 13
Fine restaurant. Terrace. Closed Thursday and Friday lunch and January.

Bad Wimpfen
Gasthaus-Hotel Grüner   HR   ⫿
Baum
Hauptstrasse 84
74206 Bad Wimpfen
Tel. (07063) 294
10 rooms. In the old town. Quiet. Restaurant closed Tuesday.

Hotel Neckarblick   H   ⫿⫿
Erich-Sailer-Strasse 48
74206 Bad Wimpfen
Tel. (07063) 85 48
15 rooms. Hotel garni. Indoor pool. Tennis. Children welcome.

Breisach
Hotel Am Münster-   HR   ⫿⫿
Ringhotel
Munsterbergstrasse 23
79206 Breisach
Tel. (07667) 70 71; fax. 86 03
71 rooms. Indoor swimming pool. Solarium. Weinstube.

Constance
Hotel Baumgartner   H   ⫿⫿
Waldstrasse 1
78465 Constance
Tel. (07533) 57 48; fax. 14 19
14 rooms. Quiet hotel garni. Sailing school, tennis, golf nearby.

Hotel Eden   H   ⫿⫿
Bahnhofstrasse 4
78462 Constance
Tel. (07531) 230 93
18 rooms. Hotel garni in the old town. Terrace.

Mago-Hotel   H   ⫿⫿
Bahnhofplatz 4
78462 Constance
Tel. (07531) 270 01; fax. 270 03
29 rooms. Hotel garni in the old town. Children welcome.

Pension Volapük   HR   ⫿
Im Loh 14
78465 Constance
Tel. (07531) 441 33
19 rooms. Home cooking. Quiet situation in the woods west of city. View.

Seehotel Siber   HR   ⫿⫿⫿
Seestrasse 25
78464 Constance
Tel. (07531) 630 44; fax. 648 13
11 rooms. Elegant. Quiet situation on the outskirts. View.

Steigenberger Inselhotel   HR   ⫿⫿⫿
Auf der Insel 1
78462 Constance
Tel. (07531) 250 11; fax. 264 02
100 rooms. Traditional luxury. Restaurant and weinstube. Children welcome.

Freibug
Hotel Gasthof Schützen   HR   ⫿
Schützenallee 12
79102 Freiburg
Tel. (0761) 720 21; fax. 720 19
17 rooms.Central. Good traditional cooking.

Novotel Freiburg   HR   ⫿⫿⫿
Am Karlsplatz
79098 Freiburg
Tel. (0761) 312 95; fax. 307 67
115 rooms. In the old town. Children welcome.

Park Hotel Post   H   ⫿⫿
Eisenbahnstrasse 35
79098 Freiburg
Tel. (0761) 316 83; fax. 316 80
41 rooms. Hotel garni. In the old town. Children welcome.

Zähringer Burg   R   ⫿⫿⫿
Reutebachgasse 19
Zähringen
79108 Freiburg
Tel. (0761) 540 41
Fine traditional cuisine in 18th-century inn. Closed Sunday and Monday. Reservation advised.

Friedrichshafen
Buchhorner Hof   HR   ⫿⫿⫿
(Ringhotel)
Friedrichstrasse 33
88045 Friedrichshafen
Tel. (07541) 20 50; fax. 326 63
65 rooms. In the old town. View. Children welcome. International cuisine.

Hotel City-Krone   HR   ⫿⫿⫿
Schanzstrasse 7
88045 Friedrichshafen
Tel. (07541) 220 86; fax. 220 80
81 rooms. In the old town. Indoor swimming pool.

Hotel Goldenes Rad   HR   ⫿⫿⫿
Karlstrasse 43
88045 Friedrichshafen
Tel. (0754) 210 81; fax. 210 85
60 rooms. In the old town. International restaurant.

Hotel-Restaurant Krone   HR   ⫿⫿⫿
Untere Mühlbachstrasse 1
Schnetzenhausen
88045 Friedrichshafen
Tel. (07541) 40 80; fax. 436 01
125 rooms. 4km outside the city. Indoor swimming pool.

Hotel-Restaurant Maier   HR   ⫿⫿
Poststrasse 1
Fischbach
88048 Friedrichshafen
Tel. (07541) 49 15; fax. 417 00
48 rooms. Friendly family-run hotel 5km (miles) from town. Closed Christmas to mid-January.

Haigerloch
Gasthof Römer   HR   ⫿
Oberstadtstrasse 41
72401 Haigerloch
Tel. (07474) 10 15
11 rooms. Quiet location, lovely view.

Gastschloss   HR   ⫿⫿⫿
Schlossstrasse 3
72401 Haigerloch
Tel. (07474) 69 30; fax. 693 82
30 rooms. In castle. Restaurant closed Sunday.

Heidelberg
Der Europäische Hof   HR   ⫿⫿⫿
Friedrich-Ebert-Anlage 1
69117 Heidelberg
Tel. (06221) 51 50; fax. 51 55 55
136 rooms. Traditional elegance. Good restaurant.

Holländer Hof   HR   ⫿⫿⫿
Neckarstaden 66
69117 Heidelberg
Tel. (06221) 120 91; fax. 220 85
40 rooms. Charming. Good cuisine. Terrace.

Perkeo   HR   ⫿⫿
Hauptstrasse 75
69117 Heidelberg
Tel. (06221) 222 55 (Restaurant 16 06 13)
25 rooms. Central. Hotel and restaurant in an old inn.

Zum Pfalzgrafen   H
Kettengasse 21
69117 Heidelberg
Tel. (06221) 204 89
24 rooms. Hotel garni in renais-
sance building in the old town.

Hotel Rose   HR
Karlsruher Strasse 93
69126 Heidelberg
Tel. (06221) 37 667; fax. 37 44 85
16 rooms. South of town. Family ho-
tel. Good cuisine.

Hotel Zum Ritter   HR
St Georg (Romantik)
Hauptstrasse 178
69117 Heidelberg
Tel. (06221) 202 03; fax. 126 83
30 rooms. Handsome Renaissance
building in heart of old town. Good
cuisine.

Piccolo Mondo   R
Klingenteichstrasse 6
69117 Heidelberg
Tel. (06221) 129 99
Italian cuisine. Closed Monday.

Simplicissimus   R
Ingrimstrasse 16
69117 Heidelberg
Tel. (06221) 18 33 36
Outstanding cuisine. Elegant atmo-
sphere. Dinner only. Closed Tues-
day, early August.

Zur Herreumühle   R
Hauptstrasse 237
69117 Heidelberg
Tel. (06221) 129 09
Fine local cuisine. Dinner only.
Reservation advised. 14th-century
building.

Heilbronn
City-Hotel   H
Allee 40
74072 Heilbronn
Tel. (07131) 839 58; fax. 16 19 36
18 rooms. Hotel garni. Quiet loca-
tion, good view.

Inselhotel Heilbronn   HR
Friedrich-Ebert-Brücke
74072 Heilbronn
Tel. (07131) 63 00; fax. 62 60 60
120 rooms. Quiet, luxurious, on an
island in the old town. Schwäbisch
cuisine.

Herrenberg
Hotel Hasen   HR
Hasenplatz 6
71083 Herrenberg
Tel. (07032) 20 40; fax. 20 41 00
80 rooms. New hotel in a charming
old town. Good cuisine. 34km (23
miles) from Stuttgart.

Karlsruhe
Hotel Rio   HR
Hans-Sachs-Strasse 2
76133 Karlsruhe
Tel. (0721) 84 50 61; fax. 840 81 00
125 rooms. Quiet. Centrally located.
Closed Christmas and New Year.

Ramada Renaissance   HR
Mendelssohnplatz
76131 Karlsruhe
Tel. (0721) 37 170; fax. 37 71 56
215 rooms. International luxury. 2
restaurants, Weinstube.

Schlosshotel   HR
Bahnhofplatz 2
76137 Karlsruhe
Tel. (0721) 350 40; fax. 350 44 13
96 rooms. Luxurious, in the old town.
2 restaurants. Excellent cuisine.

Hotel Betzler   H
Amalienstrasse 3
76133 Karlsruhe
Tel. (0721) 287 59; fax. 253 63
39 rooms. Family-run hotel garni.
Central.

Lindau
Hotel Bayerischer Hof   HR
Seepromenade
88131 Lindau
Tel. (08382) 50 55; fax. 50 54
104 rooms. On the island, overlook-
ing the harbour. Good restaurant.

adjoining:

Hotel Reutemann mit   HR
Seegarten
Seepromenade
88131 Lindau
Tel. (08382) 50 55; fax. 50 54
64 rooms. Quiet hotel overlooking
the harbour. Indoor pool.

Hotel Toscana   H
Am Aeschacher Ufer 14
Aeschach
88131 Lindau
Tel. (08382) 31 31
18 rooms. Family-run hotel garni
on mainland. Closed January–
February.

Hoyerberg Schlössle   R
Hoyerberstrasse 64
Hoyren
88131 Lindau
Tel. (08382) 252 95
On the mainland. Excellent cuisine.
Terrace. Closed Monday, February.

Insel Hotel   H
Maximilianstrasse 42
88131 Lindau
Tel. (08382) 50 17; fax. 67 56
28 rooms. Hotel garni in centre of
island. Families welcome.

Marbach
Goldener Löwe   R
Niklastorstrasse 39
71672 Marbach
Tel. (07144) 66 63
Dinner and Sunday lunch only.
Closed Monday, and 3 weeks in
summer.

Maulbronn
Gasthof Birkenhof   HR
Bahnhofstrasse 1
75433 Maulbronn
Tel. (07043) 67 63; fax. 77 26
19 rooms. Historic setting. Restau-
rant closed Tuesday.

Münstertal
Hotel Spielweg   HR
(Romantik)
Spielweg 61
Obermünstertal
79244 Münstertal
Tel. (07636) 709 77; fax. 709 66
42 rooms. Friendly atmosphere. Ex-
cellent cuisine. Restaurant closed
Monday, Tuesday.

Neckarsulm
Hotel Restaurant Lamm   HR
Lammgasse 6
74172 Neckarsulm
Tel. (07132) 60 89
22 rooms. Quiet location in the old
town. Restaurant closed Saturday.

Öhringen
Wald-u. Schlosshotel   HR
Friedrichsruhe
Zweiflingen
74613 Öhringen
Tel. (07941) 608 70; fax. 614 68
51 rooms. Luxury retreat 6km (4
miles) from town. Outstanding cui-
sine and wines. Restaurant closed
Monday, Tuesday.

Pforzheim

Hotel Goldene Pforte   HR ▯▯▯
Hohenstaufenstrasse 6
75177 Pforzheim
Tel. (07231) 379 20; fax. 379 21 44
115 rooms. Children welcome. Pool.

Mönch's Schlosshotel   HR ▯▯
Lindenstrasse 2
75175 Pforzheim
Tel. (07231) 160 51
*30 rooms. Quiet. Restaurant closed
Sunday.*

Ravensburg

Hotel Baur   H   ▯
Marienplatz 1
88212 Ravensburg
Tel. (0751) 256 16
*10 rooms. Hotel garni in the old
town.*

Hotel Waldhorn   HR ▯▯▯
(Romantik)
Marienplatz 15
88212 Ravensburg
Tel. (0751) 160 21; fax. 175 33
*35 rooms. Quiet. Outstanding cui-
sine. Restaurant closed Sunday and
Monday.*

Hotel-Restaurant   HR ▯▯
Storchen
Wilhelmstrasse 1
88212 Ravensburg
Tel. (0751) 245 20; fax. 246 48
*20 rooms. Family hotel in the old
town. Bierkeller. Weinstube.*

Reichenau

Hotel Mohren   HR ▯▯
Pirminstrasse 141
78479 Reichenau
Tel. (07534) 485; fax. 13 26
*38 rooms. Weinstube. Good cuisine.
Restaurant closed Tuesday.*

Hotel Seeschau   HR ▯▯▯
(Romantik)
An der Schifflände 8
Mittelzell
78479 Reichenau
Tel. (07534) 257; fax. 72 64
*24 rooms. Fine local cuisine. Closed
January–February.*

Sasbachwalden

Hotel Talmühle   HR ▯▯▯
Talstrasse 36
77887 Sasbachwalden
Tel. (07841) 10 01; fax. 54 04
*30 rooms. 2 restaurants, terrace and
garden. Fine traditional cuisine.*

Sigmaringen

Gasthof Bären   HR ▯
Burgstrasse 2
72488 Sigmaringen
Tel. (07571) 128 62
*20 rooms. Attractive and friendly, in
the old town. Restaurant closed
Tuesday.*

Sindelfingen

Hotel Berlin   HR ▯▯▯
Berliner Platz 1
71065 Sindelfingen
Tel. (07031) 619 70; fax. 619 71 78
*99 rooms. Indoor pool. Good local
cuisine. Restaurant closed Saturday
lunch, Sunday.*

Stuttgart

Alte Post   R ▯▯▯
Friedrichstrasse 43
70174 Stuttgart
Tel. (0711) 29 30 79
*Creative cuisine. Central. Closed
Monday and Saturday lunch. Sun-
day.*

Am Schlossgarten   HR ▯▯▯
Schillerstrasse 23
70173 Stuttgart
Tel. (0711) 202 60; fax. 202 68 88
*125 rooms. Very comfortable. Ele-
gant winter garden. 2 restaurants
and café.*

Hotel Wanner   HR ▯▯
Tübinger Strasse
Böblingen
70178 Stuttgart
Tel. (07031) 22 60 06; fax. 22 33 86
*34 rooms. 19 km from the city. Ex-
cellent traditional Schwäbisch cuisine. Closed Christmas and New
Year.*

Krone   R ▯▯
Brunnenweg 40
72658 Bempflingen
Stuttgart
Tel. (07123) 310 83
*30km (18 miles)south of the city.
Fine modern German cuisine.
Reservation essential. Closed Sun-
day and Monday.*

Martins Stuben im   R ▯▯
Eugelhorn
Neckarstrasse 119
70190 Stuttgart
Tel. (0711) 26 16 31
*Good traditional cuisine. Closed
Saturday and Sunday.*

City-Hotel   H ▯▯
Uhlandstrasse 18
70182 Stuttgart
Tel. (0711) 21 08 10; fax. 236 97 72
*31 rooms. Central. Friendly hotel
garni.*

Tettnang

Landgasthof Ritter   R ▯▯
Ritterstrasse 5
Laimnau
88069 Tettnang
Tel. (07543) 55 30
*Old half-timbered building. Fine
local cuisine. Dinner only. Closed
Monday and 2 weeks in summer.*

Titisee-Neustadt

Schwarzwaldgasthof   HR ▯
Traube
Waldau
79822 Titisee-Neustadt
Tel. (07669) 755; fax 13 50
*30 rooms. Quiet. 10km (6 miles)
from town. Closed March, November. Restaurant closed Tuesday.*

Triberg

Parkhotel Wehrle   HR ▯▯▯
(Romantik)
Gartenstrasse 24
78098 Triberg
Tel. (07722) 860 20; fax 86 02 90
*56 rooms. Quiet. Family hospitality.
Good cooking. Fish specialities.*

Tübingen

Hotel Am Bad   HR ▯▯
Europastrasse
72072 Tübingen
Tel. (07071) 730 71; fax. 753 36
*35 rooms. Family-run. Weinstube.
Swimming pool. Tennis court.*

Hotel Am Schloss   HR ▯▯
Burgsteige 18
72070 Tübingen
Tel. (07071) 210 77; fax. 520 90
*29 rooms. Central, close to the
castle. View.*

Hotel Krone   HR
▯▯▯
Uhlandstrasse 1
72072 Tübingen
Tel. (07071) 310 36; fax. 387 18
*50 rooms. Luxurious. Tastefully
furnished. Good cuisine.*

Hotel Stadt Tübingen HR ▊▊▊
Stuttgarter Strasse 97
72072 Tübingen
Tel.(07071) 310 71; fax. 382 45
*68 rooms. Quiet location. Wein-
stube. Restaurant closed Sunday.*

Landhotel Hirsch HR ▊▊▊
Schönbuchstrasse 28
Bebenhausen
72074 Tübingen
Tel. (07071) 680 27; fax. 60 08 03
*12 rooms. SPicturesque location.
Restaurant closed Tuesday.*

Waldhorn R ▊▊▊
Schönbuchstrasse 49
Bebenhausen
72074 Tübingen
Tel. (07071) 612 70
*Good local cuisine. Friendly atmo-
sphere. Closed Monday, Tuesday,
July.*

Ulm

Florian Stuben R ▊▊▊
Keplerstrasse 26
89073 Ulm
Tel. (0731) 61 02 20
*Outstanding cuisine and wine list.
Closed 3 weeks August, Sunday, and
Monday evening.*

Hotel-Restaurant Neuthor HR ▊▊
Neuer Graben 23
89073 Ulm
Tel. (0731) 151 60; fax. 151 65 13
*90 rooms. Comfortable. Good cui-
sine. Closed Christmas to mid-January.*

Hotel-Restaurant HR ▊
Goldener Bock
Bockgasse 25
89073 Ulm
Tel. (0731) 280 79
*11 rooms. Good traditional cuisine.
Closed Saturday lunch, Sunday.*

Hotel-Restaurant Ulmer HR ▊▊
Spatz
Münsterplatz 27
89073 Ulm
Tel. (0731) 680 81; fax. 602 19 25
*36 rooms. Close to the cathedral.
Schwäbisch specialities.*

Vogtsburg-im-Kaiserstuhl

Schwarzer Adler HR ▊▊▊
Badbergstrasse 23
Oberbergen
79235 Vogtsburg-im-Kaiserstuhl
Tel. (07662) 715

*9 rooms. Fine traditional cuisine
and notable wines. Restaurant
closed Wednesday, Thursday.*

Wangen

Hotel Mohren-Post HR ▊▊
Herrenstrasse 27
88239 Wangen
Tel. (07522) 210 76
*15 rooms. In the old town. Restau-
rant closed Friday.*

Waldgasthof Zum HR ▊▊
Hirschen
Grub 1
Neuravensburg
88239 Wangen
Tel. (07528) 72 22
*6 rooms. Quiet situation in the for-
est, 9km (6 miles) south-west of
Wangen. Tennis.*

Weingarten

Hotel Altdorfer Hof HR ▊▊
Burachstrasse 12
76356 Weingarten
Tel. (0751) 50 090; fax. 50 09 70
*48 rooms. Quiet, south of town.
Closed mid-December to mid-January. Restaurant closed Friday.*

The Centre

Bernkastel-Kues

Hotel Zur Post HR ▊▊
Gestade 17
54470 Bernkastel-Kues
Tel. (06531) 20 22; fax. 29 27
*42 rooms. Close to the railway sta-
tion. Weinstube. Open all year.*

Mosel Hotel HR ▊
Uferallee 3
Wehlen
54470 Bernkastel-Kues
Tel. (06531) 85 27; fax. 15 46
*15 rooms. Quiet, 4km (2 miles) from
town. View. Bierkeller, Weinstube.
Restaurant closed Tuesday.*

Römischer Kaiser HR ▊▊
Markt 29
54470 Bernkastel-Kues
Tel. (06531) 30 38; fax. 76 72
*32 rooms. In the old town. Dancing.
Good cuisine.*

Bonn

Arcade HR ▊▊
Vorgebirgsstr. 33
53119 Bonn
Tel. (0228) 726 60; fax. 726 64 05
*147 rooms. Central. Restaurant
closed Saturday, Sunday, and mid-
July to end August.*

Continental HR ▊▊▊
Am Hauptbahnhof 1
53111 Bonn
Tel. (0228) 63 53 60; fax. 63 11 90
*34 rooms. Centrally located in old
town.*

Günnewig Hotel Bristol HR ▊▊▊
Prinz-Albert-Strasse 2
53113 Bonn
Tel. (0228) 269 80; fax. 269 82 22
*120 rooms. 3 restaurants. Tradi-
tional luxury. Restaurant closes
Sunday, and 4 weeks July–August.*

Halbedel's Gasthaus R ▊▊
Rheinallee 47
Bad Godesberg
53173 Bonn
Tel. (0228) 35 42 53
*Excellent German-French cuisine.
Closed Monday and July.*

Le Petit Poisson R ▊▊
Wilhelmstrasse 23a
53111 Bonn
Tel. (0228) 63 38 83
*Closed Sunday. International and
seafood specialities.*

Cologne (Köln)

Dom-Hotel Cologne HR ▊▊▊
Domkloster 2a
50667 Cologne
Tel. (0221) 202 40;
fax. 202 44 44
*126 rooms. In central zone. Tradi-
tional luxury. Good cuisine.*

Eden Hotel HR ▊▊▊
Am Hof 18
50667 Cologne
Tel. (0221) 258 04 91;
fax. 258 04 95
*33 rooms. Central location near the
cathedral. International restaurant.*

Goldener Pflug R ▊▊▊
Olpener Strasse 421
Merheim
51109 Cologne
Tel. (0221) 89 55 09
*Excellent cuisine. Closed Saturday
evening and Sunday, and 3 weeks in
summer.*

Graugans R ▯▯
Kennedy Ufer 2a
Deutz
50679 Cologne
Tel. (0221) 828 12 34
Fine cuisine. In the Hyatt Regency Koln-Deutz. Closed Saturday lunch and Sunday.

Hotel Buchholz H ▯▯
Kunibertsgasse 5
50668 Cologne
Tel. (0221) 12 18 24; fax. 13 16 65
17 rooms. Hotel garni. Quiet. Children welcome.

Hotel im Wasserturm HR ▯▯▯
Kaygasse 2
50676 Cologne
Tel. (0221) 200 80; fax. 200 88 88
90 rooms. Quiet, elegant. Panoramic restaurant.

Hotel Mülheimer Hof H ▯▯
Mülheimer Strasse 205
Deutz
51063 Cologne
Tel. (0221) 62 40 22; fax. 62 10 09
16 rooms. Hotel garni. Children welcome.

Hotel Savoy H ▯▯
Turiner Strasse 9
50668 Cologne
Tel. (0221) 162 30; fax. 162 32 00
112 rooms. Hotel garni. Central.

Rino Casati R ▯▯▯
Ebertplatz 3
50668 Cologne
Tel. (0221) 72 11 08
Dinner only. Closed Sunday. Fine Italian cuisine and Italian wine list.

Ristorante Pan e Vin R ▯▯
Heumarkt 75
50667 Cologne
Tel. (0221) 24 84 10
Closed Monday. Excellent Italian cuisine.

Soufflé R ▯▯
Hohenstaufenring 53
50674 Cologne
Tel. (0221) 21 20 22
Closed Saturday lunch and Sunday.

Deidesheim
Schwarzer Hahn R ▯▯▯
Am Marktplatz 1
67146 Deidesheim
Tel. (06326) 18 12
Fine cuisine. Reservation advised. Closed Monday, Wednesday and Sunday.

Frankfurt
Hotel Am Zoo HR ▯▯
Alfred-Brehm-Platz 6
60316 Frankfurt
Tel. (069) 49 07 71; fax. 43 98 68
84 rooms. Quiet location. Closed Christmas and New Year. Children welcome.

Hotel Diana H ▯▯
Westendstrasse 83
60325 Frankfurt
Tel. (069) 74 70 07; fax. 74 70 79
27 rooms. Friendly hotel garni.

Hotel Hessischer Hof HR ▯▯▯
Friedrich-Ebert-Anlage 40
60325 Frankfurt
Tel. (069) 754 00; fax.754 09 24
114 rooms. Near station. Traditional comfort.

Hotel Rhein-Main HR ▯▯▯
Heidelberger Strasse 3
60327 Frankfurt
Tel. (064) 25 00 35; fax. 25 25 18
48 rooms. Quiet location. Children welcome.

Humperdinck R ▯▯▯
Grüneburgweg 95
60323 Frankfurt
Tel. (064) 72 21 22
Exceptional cuisine. In villa once home of composer Heinrich Hoffmann. Closed 2 weeks in summer, Saturday lunch, Sunday.

Weinhaus Brückenkeller R ▯▯▯
Schützenstrasse 6
60311 Frankfurt
Tel. (069) 28 42 38
Fine creative cuisine. Reservation advised. Closed Sunday.

Zum Adler R ▯▯
Hauptstrasse 63
Bruchköbel
60437 Frankfurt
Tel. (06181) 759 10
Restored Fachwerkhaus, 20km (12 miles) from city. Traditional cuisine. Reservation essential. Closed Saturday lunch and Monday.

Friedrichsdorf
Sängers Restaurant R ▯▯
Hugenottenstrasse 121
61381 Friedrichsdorf
Tel. (06172) 720 29
Excellent cuisine. 10 rooms. Closed Saturday evening and Sunday.

Geisenheim
Burg Schwarzenstein R ▯▯
Johannisberg
65366 Geisenheim
Tel. (06722) 88 50
Attractive traditional restaurant. Closed Monday.

Koblenz
Hotel Brenner H ▯▯▯
Rizzastrasse 20
56068 Koblenz
Tel. (0261) 320 60; fax. 362 78
25 rooms. Hotel garni. Closed mid-December to early January.

Wacht am Rhein R ▯▯
Rheinzollstrasse 6
56068 Koblenz
Tel. (0261) 153 13
Terrace. Good local cuisine. Closed Saturday lunch in winter.

Zum Schwarzen Bären HR ▯▯
Koblenzer Strasse 35
Moselweiss
56073 Koblenz
Tel. (0261) 460 27 00; fax. 460 27 13
13 rooms. Good cooking. In family since 1810. Closed 3 weeks July–August, restaurant closed Sunday evening and Monday.

Mainz
Europahotel HR ▯▯▯
Kaiserstrasse 7
55116 Mainz
Tel. (06131) 97 50; fax. 97 55 55
96 rooms. Central. Family hotel. Restaurant and brasserie.

Hotel Mainzer Hof H ▯▯▯
Kaiserstrasse 98
55116 Mainz
Tel. (06131) 23 37 71; fax. 22 82 55
99 rooms. Hotel garni overlooking the river.

Zum Löwen R ▯▯▯
Mainzerstrasse 2
Gonsenheim
55124 Mainz
Tel. (06131) 436 05
Excellent cuisine. 5km (3 miles) from city. Reservation advised. Closed Sunday, Monday.

Oestrich-Winkel
Graues Haus R ▯▯▯
Graugasse 10
65375 Oestrich-Winkel
Tel. (06723) 26 19

Excellent cuisine. Modern restaurant in historic house. Reservation essential. Closed Monday and Tuesday.

Speyer

Hotel Goldener Engel HR ▯▯
Mühlturmstrasse 1a
67346 Speyer
Tel. (06232) 132 60; fax. 13 26 95
42 rooms. Quiet. In the old town. Weinstube. Closed Christmas–New Year.

Trier

Hotel Kessler HR ▯▯
Brückenstrasse 23
54290 Trier
Tel. (0651) 767 71; fax. 767 73
21 rooms. In a pedestrian zone in the old town. Restaurant for guests only.

Scandic Crown Hotel HR ▯▯▯
Zurmaiener Strasse 164
54292 Trier
Tel. (0651) 14 30; fax. 143 20 00
212 rooms. 2 restaurants. Modern comfort. By River Mosel.

Wiesbaden

Alte Krone R ▯▯
Sonnenbergerstrasse 82
65193 Wiesbaden
Tel. (06121) 56 39 47
Attractive 17th-century building. Traditional cooking. Closed Sunday.

Hotel Klee am Park HR ▯▯▯
Parkstrasse 4
65189 Wiesbaden
Tel. (0611) 30 50 61; fax. 30 40 48
60 rooms. Quiet, family-run hotel. Garden.

Nassauer Hof HR ▯▯▯
Kaiser-Friedrich-Platz 3
65183 Wiesbaden
Tel. (0611) 13 30; fax. 13 36 32
210 rooms. Central. Traditional luxury. 4 restaurants.

Am Landeshaus H ▯▯
Moritzstrasse 51
65185 Wiesbaden
Tel. (0611) 37 30 41; fax. 37 30 44
20 rooms. Central. Family-run hotel garni. Closed Christmas and New Year.

Worms

Bistro Léger R ▯▯
Siegfriedstrasse 2
67547 Worms
Tel. (06241) 462 77
Informal, local cuisine. Terrace. Closed Sunday.

Hotel Nibelungen H ▯▯
Martinsgasse 16
67547 Worms
Tel. (06241) 69 77; fax. 872 10
46 rooms. Quiet hotel garni. Central, in the old town. Closed Christmas and New Year.

Hotel-Restaurant HR ▯
Stolpereck
Hausmühlstrasse 27
Horchheim
67551 Worms
Tel. (06241) 331 61
6 rooms. Family-run. Restaurant closed Tuesday.

Rôtisserie Dubs R ▯▯
Kirchstrasse 6
Rheindürkheim
67550 Worms
Tel. (06242) 20 23
Noted for seafood. 9km (6 miles) from city. Closed 2 weeks in summer, Tuesday, and Saturday lunch.

Tivoli R ▯▯
Adenauerring 4b
67547 Worms
Tel. (06241) 284 85
Italian cuisine. Terrace. Closed Tuesday and July.

Zell a. d. Mosel

Zum Grünen Kranz HR ▯▯
Balduinstrasse 12
56856 Zell a. d. Mosel
Tel. (06542) 45 49; fax. 43 11
19 rooms. Charming traditional hotel in wine-growing town. River view.

The North-West

Aachen

Aquis-Grana-Cityhotel HR ▯▯▯
Büchel 32
52062 Aachen
Tel. (0241) 44 30; fax. 44 31 37
95 rooms. In the old town. Thermal swimming pool.

Hotel am Marschiertor H ▯▯
Wallstrasse 1-7
52064 Aachen
Tel. (0241) 319 41; fax. 319 43
50 rooms. Hotel garni. Central, in old town.

Amrum

Seeblick Appartement- HR ▯▯▯
Hotel
Strandstrasse
25946 Norddorf
Amrum
Tel. (04682) 888; fax. 2574
Seaside hotel and flats on North Sea island. Closed January to mid-February. Swimming pool, sauna.

Ekke Nekkepenn R ▯
Waaterstigh 17
25946 Nebel
Amrum
Tel. (04682) 22 45
North German and seafood specialities. Closed November–mid-February and Wednesdays, Thursday.

Bargum

Andresen's Gasthof HR ▯▯▯
Friesenstuben
Highway B5
25842 Bargum
Tel. (04672) 10 98
Outstanding seafood and North German cuisine. 5 rooms available. Closed Monday and Tuesday.

Bremen

Grashoff's Bistro R ▯▯
Contrescarpe 80
28195 Bremen
Tel. (0421) 147 40
Local and seafood specialities. Open for lunch and early evening only, Saturday 2 p.m. Closed Sunday.

Hotel Havenhaus HR ▯▯
Am Vegesacker Hafen 12
Bad Vegesack
28757 Bremen
Tel. (0421) 66 40 93; fax. 65 52 12
20 rooms. Quiet, near sailing harbour 22km (14 miles) from city. Good restaurant.

Hotel Mercure-Columbus H ▯▯▯
Bahnhofsplatz 5
28195 Bremen
Tel. (0421) 141 61; fax. 153 69
152 rooms. Central location. Hotel garni. Children welcome.

Hotel Zur Post HR |||
Bahnhofsplatz 11
28195 Bremen
Tel. (0421) 305 90; fax. 305 95 91
195 rooms. Central location. 3
restaurants.

Queens Hotel HR |||
August-Bebel-Allee 4
Neue Vahr
28329 Bremen
Tel. (0421) 238 70; fax. 23 46 17
144 rooms. Modern conference ho-
tel.

Celle
Celler Hof HR ||
Stechbahn 11
29221 Celle
Tel. (05141) 280 61; fax. 346 76
59 rooms. Centrally located in pic-
turesque town. Bierkeller.

Fürstenhof-Endtenfang HR ||
Hannoverschestrasse 55
29221 Celle
Tel. (05141) 20 10; fax. 20 11 20
75 rooms. Excellent cuisine. Swim-
ming pool. Bierkeller.

Hotel Caroline Mathilde H ||
Bremer Weg 37
29223 Celle
Tel. (05141) 320 23; fax. 320 26
28 rooms. Hotel garni. Quiet loca-
tion. Closed Christmas and New
Year.

Dortmund
City-Hotel Dortmund HR ||
Silberstrasse 37–43
44137 Dortmund
Tel. (0231) 14 20 86; fax. 16 27 65
50 rooms. Close to railway station
but quiet. Children welcome.

Hotel Petersmann H ||
Moltkestrasse 2
44135 Dortmund
Tel. (0231) 52 86 01; fax. 52 54 41
9 rooms. Quiet hotel garni, central
location. Family hotel. Restaurant
closed Saturday, Sunday.

Holiday Inn Römischer HR |||
Kaiser
Olpe 2
44135 Dortmund
Tel. (0231) 54 32 00; fax. 57 43 54
126 rooms. Central location. Good
restaurant. Children welcome.

La Table R |||
Hohensyburgstr. 200
Syburg
44265 Dortmund
Tel. (0231) 77 44 44
Fine cuisine. Modern restaurant.
10km (6 miles) south of city. Closed
Monday.

Waldhotel Hülsenhain HR |
Am Ossenbrink 57
Shanze
44227 Dortmund
Tel. (0231) 73 17 67
14 rooms. South of the city, near the
forest. Restaurant closed Monday.

Düsseldorf
Aalschokker R |||
Kaiserswerther Markt 9
Kaiserswerth
40489 Düsseldorf
Tel. (0211) 40 39 48
Reservation advised. Typical re-
gional dishes. Closed Sunday, Mon-
day.

Hotel Bellevue HR |||
Luisenstr. 98
40215 Düsseldorf
Tel. (0211) 37 70 71; fax. 37 70 76
54 rooms. In the old town. Children
welcome.

La Terrazza R |||
Königsallee 30
40212 Düsseldorf
Tel. (0211) 32 85 53
On the 2nd floor of the Kö-Center.
Italian cuisine. Reservation advised.
Closed Sunday.

Lindenhof Hotel H ||
Oststrasse 124
40210 Düsseldorf
Tel. (0211) 36 09 63; fax. 16 27 67
43 rooms. Quiet, family hotel garni.
Children welcome. Indoor swim-
ming pool.

Ramada Renaissance HR |||
Nördlicher Zubringer 6
Mörsenbroich
40470 Düsseldorf
Tel. (0211) 621 60; fax. 621 66 66
245 rooms. International comfort
and cuisine. Swimming pool, sauna.

Victorian R |||
Königstrasse 3a
40212 Düsseldorf
Tel. (0211) 32 02 22
Fine creative German/international
cuisine. Reservation essential.
Closed Sunday.

Essen
Schloss Hugenpoet HR |||
August-Thyssen-Strasse 51
Kettwig
45219 Essen
Tel. (02054) 120 40; fax. 12 04 50
19 rooms. Luxurious restaurant in
late-Renaissance castle 10 km (6
miles) south of city.

Göttingen
Hotel Stadt Hannover HR ||
Goetheallee 21
37073 Göttingen
Tel. (0551) 459 57
30 rooms. Quiet central location in
the old town.

Hamburg
Alsterkrug Hotel HR |||
Alsterkrugchaussee 277
Alsterdorf
22297 Hamburg
Tel. (040) 51 30 30; fax. 51 30 34
03
80 rooms. Children welcome. Inter-
national restaurant.

Atlantic Hotel Kempinski HR |||
An der Alster 72
20099 Hamburg
Tel. (040) 288 80; fax. 24 71 29
256 rooms. Traditional luxury. 2
restaurants. On Aussenalster.

Le Canard R |||
Elbchaussee 139
Altona
22736 Hamburg
Tel. (040) 880 50 57
Outstanding Hamburg/seafood spe-
cialities. Closed Sunday.

Hafen Hamburg HR ||
Seewartenstrasse 9
20459 Hamburg
Tel. (040) 31 11 30; fax. 319 27 36
252 rooms. View. Terrace.

Holiday Inn Crowne Plaza HR
|||
Graumannsweg 10
22087 Hamburg
Tel. (040) 22 80 60; fax. 220 87 04
290 rooms. International comfort.
Indoor swimming pool.

Hotel Mittelweg H ||
Mittelweg 59
Rotherbaum
20149 Hamburg
Tel. (040) 44 30 88; fax. 44 69 53
30 rooms. Central. Quiet hotel
garni. Garden.

Hotel Vier Jahreszeiten   HR ▊▊▊
Neuer Jungfernstieg 9–11
20354 Hamburg
Tel. (040) 349 40; fax. 349 46 02
172 rooms. Elegant. 3 restaurants.
Overlooking Binnenalster.

Hotel-Restaurant   HR ▊▊▊
Lindtner
Heimfelder Strasse 123
21075 Hamburg
Tel. (040) 790 80 81; fax. 790 99 52
16 rooms. In the forest south of the
city. View. Children welcome.

Hotel Rex   H ▊
Kieler Strasse 385
22525 Hamburg
Tel. (040) 54 48 13
32 rooms. Simple hotel garni.

Landhaus Dill   R ▊▊
Elbchaussee 404
Nienstedten
22609 Hamburg
Tel. (040) 82 84 43
French-German cuisine. Weekdays
dinner only; closed Monday.

Landhaus Scherrer   R ▊▊▊
Elbchaussee 130
Ottensen
22763 Hamburg
Tel. (040) 880 13 25
Fine local cuisine in country house
style. Remarkable wine list.

Hamlin

Dorint Hotel Hameln   HR ▊▊▊
164er Ring 3
31785 Hamlin
Tel. (05151) 79 20; fax. 79 21 91
103 rooms. In the old town. Sauna.

Hotel Zur Krone   HR ▊▊▊
Osterstrasse 30
31785 Hamlin
Tel. (05151) 74 11; fax. 74 15
37 rooms. In the old town.

Hotel Zur Börse   HR ▊
Osterstrasse 41a
31785 Hamlin
Tel. (05151) 70 80; fax. 254 85
34 rooms. Friendly traditional
hotel-restaurant. Closed Christmas
and New Year.

Rattenfangerhaus   R ▊▊
Osterstrasse 28
31785 Hamlin
Tel. (05151) 38 88
"Ratcatcher's house"—in Weser
Renaissance building dating from
1603.

Hanover

Alpha-Tirol   H ▊▊▊
Lange Laube 20
30159 Hanover
Tel. (0511) 13 10 66; fax. 34 15 35
15 rooms. Central. Friendly hotel
garni.

Maritim   HR ▊▊▊
Hildesheimer Strasse 34
30169 Hanover
Tel. (0511) 165 31; fax. 88 48 46
293 rooms. Traditional comfort. In-
door swimming pool.

Ratskeller   R ▊▊
Köbelingerstrasse 60
30159 Hanover
Tel. (0511) 36 36 44
Traditional food and atmosphere.
Closed Sunday.

Hildesheim

Forte Hotel   HR ▊▊▊
Am Markt 4
31134 Hildesheim
Tel. (05121) 30 00; fax. 30 04 44
109 rooms. Central. Indoor swim-
ming pool. All amenities.

Gollarts Hotel Deutsches   HR ▊▊
Haus
Bischof-Janssen-Strasse 5
31134 Hildesheim
Tel. (05121) 159 71; fax. 340 64
45 rooms. Restaurant closed Sun-
day.

Hotel Niedersachsen   HR ▊
Lindenkamp 1
31135 Hildesheim
Tel. (05121) 26 11 66
14 rooms. Friendly small hotel.
Home cooking.

Lübeck

Das kleine Restaurant   R ▊▊
An der Untertrave 39
23552 Lübeck
Tel. (0451) 70 59 59
Fine local cuisine. Renaissance
building. Closed Saturday lunch,
Sunday.

Das Schabbelhaus   R ▊▊
Mengstrasse 48
23552 Lübeck
Tel. (0451) 720 11
In old merchant's house. Reserva-
tion recommended. Closed Satur-
day, Sunday.

Kaiserhof   H ▊▊▊
Kronsforder Allee 13
23560 Lübeck
Tel. (0451) 79 10 11; fax. 79 50 83
70 rooms. Hotel garni in restored
patrician house, beautifully fur-
nished.

Lindenhof   H ▊▊▊
Lindenstrasse 1a
23558 Lübeck
Tel. (0451) 840 15; fax. 86 40 23
54 rooms. Central. Quiet hotel
garni.

Sylt

Bistro im Haus   R ▊
Meeresruh
Braderuperweg
25999 Kampen
Sylt
Tel. (04651) 413 83
Terrace. North German/seafood in-
formal restaurant.

Rungholt   HR ▊▊▊
Kurhausstrasse
25999 Kampen
Sylt
Tel. (04651) 44 80; fax. 448 40
68 rooms. Quiet. Holiday island ho-
tel, open mid-March to October.

Walter's Hof   HR ▊▊▊
Kurhausstrasse
25999 Kampen
Sylt
Tel. (04651) 44 90; fax. 455 90
34 rooms. Comfortable resort hotel.

Über 100 Jahre alter   R ▊▊
Gasthof
Alte Dorfstrrasse 5
25992 List
Sylt
Tel. (04652) 72 44
Quaint old inn, specializing in fish
dishes.

Wolfenbüttel

Landhaus Dürkop   H ▊
Alter Weg 45
38302 Wolfenbüttel
Tel. (05331) 70 53; fax. 726 38
30 rooms. Quiet hotel garni north of
town.

Worpswede

Bonner's Hotel garni   H ▊▊
Hinterem Berg 24
27726 Worpswede
Tel. (04792) 12 73; fax. 34 26
8 rooms. View. Near forest. Pool.

Berlin

Alt Luxemburg　　R　　III
Windscheidstrasse 31
Charlottenburg
10627 Berlin
Tel. (030) 323 87 30
Excellent cuisine. Reservation advised. Dinner only. Closed 3 weeks in summer, Sunday and Monday.

Bamberger Reiter　　R　　III
Regensburgerstrasse 7
10777 Berlin
Tel. (030) 218 42 82
Haute cuisine. Reservation recommended. Dinner only. Closed 2 weeks in August, Sunday and Monday.

Berliner Kaffeehaus　　R　　I
Alexanderplatz 2
10178 Berlin
Tel. (030) 212 50 41
Coffee house with dancing at the weekends.

Bristol-Hotel Kempinski　HR III
Kurfürstendamm 27
10719 Berlin
Tel. (030) 88 43 40; fax. 883 60 75
315 rooms. Grand luxury. 3 restaurants. Indoor swimming pool.

Café Arkade　　R　　III
Französischestrasse 25
10117 Berlin
Tel. (030) 208 02 73
Good for after-theatre dinner. Next to Schauspielhaus (theatre).

Berlin Hilton　　HR III
Mohrenstrasse 30
10117 Berlin
Tel. (030) 238 20; fax. 23 82 42 69
340 rooms. Luxurious. Located near the theatre.

Domus　　H　　III
Uhlandstrasse 49
10719 Berlin
Tel. (030) 88 20 41; fax. 882 04 10
73 rooms. Hotel garni. Wilmersdorf area.

Ephraim Palais　　R　　III
Poststrasse 16
10178 Berlin
Tel. (030) 21 71 31 64
Small, elegant restaurant. International menu.

Fioretto　　R　　III
Carmerstrasse 2
Charlottenburg
10623 Berlin
Tel. (030) 312 31 15

Fine Italian cuisine. Closed Sundays. June–August evenings only.

Gastmahl des Meeres　R　III
Spandauerstrasse 4
10178 Berlin
Tel. (030) 212 32 86
Good cuisine. Fish specialities. Closed 3rd Monday in month.

Hotel Astoria　　H　　III
Fasanenstrasse 2
10623 Berlin
Tel. (030) 312 40 67; fax. 312 50 27
29 rooms. Hotel garni close to railway station. Children under 12 stay free of charge.

Hotel Kurfürstendamm　H　III
am Adenauerplatz
Kurfürstendamm 68
10707 Berlin
Tel. (030) 88 28 41; fax. 882 55 28
32 rooms. Hotel garni. Central location. Airport bus.

Hotel Lichtburg　　HR III
Paderborner Strasse 10
10709 Berlin
Tel. (030) 891 80 41; fax. 892 61 06
64 rooms. Central location, Wilmersdorf. Quiet.

Maritim Grand Hotel　　HR III
Friedrichstrasse 158–164
10117 Berlin
Tel. (030) 232 70; fax. 23 27 33 62
350 rooms. 3 restaurants. Luxurious.

Hotel Seehof　　HR III
Lietzenseeufer 11
14057 Berlin
Tel. (030) 32 00 20;
fax. 32 00 22 51
78 rooms. Central location, Charlottenburg. Indoor swimming pool. Garden. Terrace. Outstanding cuisine.

Hotel-Pension Haus　　H　I
Konstanz
Konstanzer Strasse 30
10709 Berlin
Tel. (030) 86 02 68
27 rooms. Simple hotel garni. Wilmersdorf.

Hotel-Pension Wien　　H　I
Brandenburgischestrasse 37
10707 Berlin
Tel. (030) 8 91 84 86
7 rooms. Central location, Wilmersdorf.

Inter-Continental　　HR III
Budapester Strasse 2
10787 Berlin
Tel. (030) 260 20; fax. 260 28 07 60
600 rooms. 2 restaurants. Indoor swimming pool.

Radisson Plaza　　HR III
Karl-Liebknecht-Strasse 5
10178 Berlin
Tel. (030) 238 28; fax. 23 82 75 90
600 rooms. 3 restaurants. Grand modern luxury hotel. Centrally located.

Rockendorf's Restaurant　R　III
Düsterhauptstrasse 1
Waidmannslust
13649 Berlin
Tel. (030) 402 30 99
Elegant, Jugendstil. Reservation essential. Closed 3 weeks in July, Sunday and Monday.

Wernesgrüner Bierstuben　R　II
Karl-Liebknecht-Strasse 11
10178 Berlin
Tel. (030) 282 42 68
Rustic atmosphere. Traditional cooking.

Eastern Germany

Bad Doberan

Hotel Kurhaus　　HR III
August-Bebel-Strasse
18209 Bad Doberan
Tel. (038203) 30 36; fax. 21 26
53 rooms. In old spa and resort town near Rostock. Restaurant.

Brandenburg

Am Stadion　　H　　I
Thüringer Strasse 250
14770 Brandenburg
Tel. (03381) 52 40 05; fax. 55 21 21
13 rooms. Hotel garni.

Cottbus

Branitz　　HR III
Congresszentrum
Heinrich-Zille-Strasse
03042 Cottbus
Tel. (07951) 75 100; fax. 71 31 72
205 rooms. Central conference hotel. Nightclub.

375

Dessau

Dessauer Bierstuben   **R**   ▯
Kavalierstrasse 29A
06844 Dessau
Tel. (0340) 739 09
Traditional fare.

Dresden

Am Zwinger   **R**   ▯▯
Ernst-Thälmann-Strasse 24
01069 Dresden
Tel. (0351) 495 12 81
Central. Traditional cooking.

Astoria   **HR**   ▯▯▯
Strehlener-Platz 1
01219 Dresden
Tel. (0351) 471 51 71;
fax. 471 88 72
*82 rooms. Located in the centre
near the Grosser garden.*

Maritim Bellevue   **HR**   ▯▯▯
Grosse Meissner Strasse 15
01097 Dresden
Tel. (0351) 566 20; fax. 559 97
*328 rooms. First-class, with elegant
architecture. Casino.*

Hotel Gewandhaus   **HR**   ▯▯
Ringstrasse 1
01067 Dresden
Tel. (0351) 495 61 80;
fax. 495 61 20
102 rooms. Modern. Central.

Hotel Königstein   **HR**   ▯▯
Pragerstrasse 9
01069 Dresden
Tel. (0351) 485 63 62;
fax. 495 40 54
*306 rooms. Modern. Sauna. Roof
garden. Near station.*

Hotel Lilienstein   **HR**   ▯▯▯
Pragerstrasse 16
01069 Dresden
Tel. (0351) 485 63 72;
fax. 495 25 06
303 rooms. Modern. Near station.

Mercure Newa   **HR**   ▯▯▯
Petersburger Strasse 34
01069 Dresden
Tel. (0351) 481 40; fax. 495 51 37
*307 rooms. Several restaurants.
Sauna. Opposite the railway station.*

Am Bismarck Turm   **HR**   ▯▯
Münzmeisterstrasse 10
01267 Dresden
Tel. (0351) 493 36 45;
fax. 493 36 48
*93 rooms. Motel-style accommoda-
tion.*

Ratskeller Dresden   **R**   ▯▯
Dr.-Wilhelm-Külz-Ring 19
01109 Dresden
Tel. (0351) 488 29 50
*Town hall wine cellar. Traditional
food.*

Eisenach

Glockenhof   **HR**   ▯▯
Grimmelgasse 4
99817 Eisenach
Tel. (03691) 52 16; fax. 52 17
*23 rooms. Located in historic cen-
tre.*

Ritterstube   **HR**   ▯▯
Schmelzerstrasse 17
99817 Eisenach
Tel. (03691) 774 12
*6 rooms. Restaurant closed Sunday,
Monday lunch.*

Erfurt

Erfurter Hof   **HR**   ▯▯▯
Am Bahnhofsvorplatz 1
99084 Erfurt
Tel. (0361) 53 10; fax. 240 16
174 rooms. Central. Entertainment.

Opus   **R**   ▯▯
Walkmühlstrasse 13
99084 Erfurt
Tel. (0361) 240 47
Closed Sunday, Saturday lunch.

Halle

Rotes Ross   **HR**   ▯
Leipziger Strasse 76
06108 Halle
Tel. (0345) 372 71; fax. 263 31
*44 rooms. Simple hotel, central
location.*

Stadt Halle   **HR**   ▯▯▯
Thalmannplatz 17
06108 Halle
Tel. (0345) 88 80; fax. 259 24
*346 rooms. Modern. Central loca-
tion. Sauna. Disco.*

Leipzig

Deutschland   **HR**   ▯▯▯
Augustusplatz 5
04109 Leipzig
Tel. (0341) 21 460; fax. 28 91 65
283 rooms. Central. 3 restaurants.

Merkur   **HR**   ▯▯▯
Gerberstrasse 15
04105 Leipzig
Tel. (0341) 79 90; fax. 799 12 29
440 rooms. Modern. 4 restaurants.

Hotel Stadt Leipzig   **HR**   ▯▯▯
Richard-Wagner-Strasse 1–5
04109 Leipzig
Tel. (0341) 214 50; fax. 214 56 00
*349 rooms. Modern. Central, near
station. 3 restaurants.*

Auerbachskeller   **R**   ▯▯
Grimmaische Strasse 2
04109 Leipzig
Tel. (0341) 211 60 34
*Central. Historic wine cellar. Tradi-
tional food and atmosphere.*

Meissen

Exklusiv   **HR**   ▯▯
01662 Riemsdorf
bei Meissen
Tel. (03521) 24 56; fax. as for
phone
*Motel-style accommodation. 7km (4
miles) south of Meissen.*

Zur Wartburg   **H**   ▯
Gutenbergstrasse 2
01662 Riesa a.d. Elbe
bei Meissen
Tel. (03525) 258 43
*10 rooms. Simple hotel, 27km (17
miles) north-west of Meissen.*

Neubrandenburg

Vier Tore   **HR**   ▯▯▯
Treptower Strasse 16
17033 Neubrandenburg
Tel. (0395) 51 41; fax. 410 15
*249 rooms. Central, modern. Swim-
ming pool. Disco.*

Borchert garni   **H**   ▯
Engelsring 40
17003 Neubrandenburg
Tel. (0395) 26 07; fax. 44 20 04
*11 rooms. Family run. Friendly,
simple hotel.*

Potsdam

Schloss Cecilienhof   **HR**   ▯▯▯
Neuer Garten
14469 Potsdam
Tel. (0331) 231 41; fax. 224 98
*42 rooms. In part of the historic
Cecilienhof Palace.*

Mercure   **HR**   ▯▯▯
Lange Brücke
14469 Potsdam
Tel. (0331) 46 31; fax. 234 96
*200 rooms. Several restaurants.
Sauna.*

Rostock

Hotel Neptun HR ▮▮▮
Seestrasse 19
Warnemünde
18119 Rostock
Tel. (0381) 54 60; fax. 540 23
350 rooms. Near beach in resort area. Many amenities. Swimming. Bowling.

Hotel Nordland HR ▮▮▮
Steinstrasse 7
18055 Rostock
Tel. (0381) 222 85; fax. 237 06
38 rooms. Centrally located.

Hotel Warnow HR ▮▮
Hermann-Duncker-Platz 4
18055 Rostock
Tel. (0381) 373 81; fax. 347 28
343 rooms. Central. Modern conference hotel.

Promenadenhotel HR ▮
Seestrasse 5
Warnemünde
18119 Rostock
Tel. (0381) 527 82
24 rooms. Near beach in resort area.

Rügen

Am Strand HR ▮▮
Strandpromenade 17
18609 Binz
Rügen
Tel. (038393) 23 87
43 rooms. Beach resort hotel on the island of Rügen.

Villa Aegir HR ▮▮
Mittelstrasse 5
18546 Sassnitz
Rügen
Tel. (038392) 330 02; fax. 330 46
34 rooms. Beach resort guesthouse on island.

Stralsund

Baltic HR ▮▮
Frankendamm 22
18439 Stralsund
Tel. (03831) 29 53 81; fax. 29 53 82
37 rooms. Central.

Usedom

Strandhotel Bansin HR ▮▮
Bergstrasse 30-32
17406 Bansin
Usedom
Tel. (038378) 23 42; fax. 23 43
54 rooms. Beach hotel on Baltic island.

Forsthaus Langen Berg HR ▮
Strandpromenade 36
17406 Bansin
Usedom
Tel. (038378) 321 11; fax. 91 02
29 rooms. Beach hotel on Baltic island. Sauna.

Wald und See HR ▮▮▮
R-Breitscheid-Strasse 8
17406 Heringsdorf
Usedom
Tel. (038378) 511; fax. as for phone
39 rooms. Resort retreat on Baltic island.

Weimar

Weimar Hilton HR ▮▮▮
Belvederer Allee 25
99425 Weimar
Tel. (03643) 72 20; fax. 72 27 41
295 rooms. 3 restaurants. Swimming pool. Sauna.

Elephant HR ▮▮
Markt 19
99423 Weimar
Tel. (03643) 614 71; fax. 653 10
102 rooms. Historic hotel. 3 restaurants. In the old town.

Zum Weissen Schwan R ▮▮
Frauentorstrasse 23
99423 Weimar
Tel. (03643) 617 15
Traditional food in restored historic house.

Wismar

Altes Brauhaus H ▮▮
Lubsche Strasse 95
23966 Wismar
Tel. (03841) 32 23; fax. as for phone
16 rooms. Small hotel garni.

Alter Schwede R ▮▮
Am Markt 16
23966 Wismar
Tel. (03841) 35 52
Traditional food in charming old house.

Wittenberg

Goldener Adler HR ▮▮
Markt 7
06886 Wittenberg
Tel. (03491) 20 53; fax. 20 54
40 rooms. Simple hotel in historic part of town.

Index